SERVING INTERNAL AND EXTERNAL CUSTOMERS

ANNE SWARTZLANDER, PH.D.

Business and Computer Technology Department
Pellissippi State Technical Community College

PEARSON

Prentice
Hall

Upper Saddle River, New Jersey
Columbus, Ohio

Library of Congress Cataloging-in-Publication Data

Swartzlander, Anne.
  Serving internal and external customers / Anne Swartzlander.
      p. cm.
Includes bibliographical references and index.
  ISBN 0-13-028341-X
  1.   Customer services. I. Title.
  HF5415.5 .S93 2005
  658.8'12—dc21

2003011007

Publisher: Stephen Helba
Executive Editor: Elizabeth Sugg
Editorial Assistant: Cyrenne Bolt de Freitas
Production Liaison: Brian Hyland
Production Editor: Pat Anglin, Carlisle Publishers Services
Director of Manufacturing and Production: Bruce Johnson
Managing Editor: Mary Carnis
Marketing Manager: Leigh Ann Sims
Manufacturing Buyer: Ilene Sanford
Design Director: Cheryl Asherman
Cover Designer: Kevin Kall
Interior Design: Carlisle Communications, Ltd.
Composition: Carlisle Communications, Ltd.
Printing and Binding: Courier Westford

HF
5415.5
.S93
2004

Prentice-Hall International (UK) Limited, *London*
Prentice-Hall of Australia Pty. Limited, *Sydney*
Prentice-Hall Canada, Inc., *Toronto*
Prentice-Hall Hispanoamericana, S.A., *Mexico*

Prentice-Hall of India Private Limited, *New Delhi*
Prentice-Hall of Japan, Inc., *Tokyo*
Prentice-Hall Singapore Pte. Ltd.
Editora Prentice-Hall do Brasil, Ltda., *Rio de Janeiro*

10 9 8 7 6
ISBN: 0-13-028341-X

CONTENTS

4

PEOPLE   56

5

EXCEPTIONAL PERFORMANCE   77

6

NONVERBAL COMMUNICATION   100

7

VERBAL COMMUNICATION   124

8

LISTENING   142

9

TELEPHONE COMMUNICATION   161

10

ELECTRONIC COMMUNICATION 189

11

PROBLEM SOLVING 214

12

EXCEPTIONAL CUSTOMER SERVICE   233

13

CUSTOMER PROBLEM RESOLUTION AND RECOVERY   262

PREFACE

This textbook is intended for an undergraduate customer service course. The textbook explains customer service and its importance in the context of organizations and explains methods of individual behavior and interpersonal communication to improve customer service skills. Exceptional customer service leads to customer loyalty and retention and, ultimately, to organization success. Customer service can be found in every business and organization. Everyone in an organization provides service to external or internal customers during their work day. Customer service happens whenever, wherever, and however customers interact with the organization.

Whether you are just starting out in your career or have years of experience, you will recognize better or alternative ways to say and do things that will provide exceptional customer service. You may have heard that customer service is common sense. You may have heard that customer service is plain, ordinary good manners. It is both. It is also learning and practicing specialized customer service skills so they become as natural as breathing. On an individual level, better customer service skills lead to less stressful, more productive, and more satisfying work lives.

The textbook is based on a model of customer service in which customers are the focus and the strategy, systems and people of organizations and businesses interact to provide what internal and external customers need and expect. The first part of the book sets the stage for learning the customer service skills in the rest of the text. Chapter 1 explains an encompassing view of customer service and the importance of exceptional customer service in the twenty-first century business environment. Chapter 2 discusses the design and implementation of customer-oriented strategy and systems. Customer expectations and the value and creation of customer loyalty are covered in Chapter 3. Chapter 4 explains the concept that employee satisfaction equals customer satisfaction and outlines the factors that contribute to employee satisfaction. In Chapter 5, the textbook looks at individual attitudes and styles as they apply to performance and teamwork. Chapters 6 through 10 provide guidelines and recommendations to improve listening effectiveness, nonverbal and verbal communication skills, and telephone and electronic communication skills. Chapter 11 presents information on solving problems, enhancing creativity, making decisions, and resolving conflicts, all of which are essential in a customer service provider's job. Chapter 12 covers techniques for providing service to specific categories of challenging customers, including angry, wrong, demanding, dishonest, and abusive customers. It also addresses diversity and the special needs of multicultural customers and customers with disabilities. In Chapter 13, we illustrate how to resolve customer problems and keep customers when our best efforts fail.

The chapters include Experience Discussion and Skill Development exercises so students can share their wide-ranging experience, broaden their perspective, and supplement their skills. Each chapter has a project, exercise, or case at the end to practice the recommendations and discover different and better ways to solve customer problems.

One of the goals in writing this textbook was to provide evidence that exceptional customer service does make a difference to the bottom line and that the prescribed behavior accomplishes its intention. Consequently, each chapter contains information on research studies and expert knowledge with accompanying source citations.

While writing this text, I found a list of "what students should learn in college." These are primarily "soft" skills that usually are not taught in college. However, they are all directly related to providing exceptional customer service. This list is as follows:

listening	working as a team
effective communication	making effective decisions
understanding people	how to capture opportunity to change
value-first method of dealing with others	taking responsibility and ownership of a job

SUPPLEMENTS

For course support materials, please visit www.prenhall.com/business_studies.

ACKNOWLEDGMENTS

The catalyst for writing this textbook was teaching customer service during the past ten years. I have learned much from my students—in-class, out-of-class, and from the web course. They have contributed thought-provoking questions and creative solutions for customer service problems and dilemmas.

Many thanks go out to the experts that provided valuable content suggestions, including Dr. Phil Dover, Babson College, Babson Park; Randy Porter, Heald College; Dr. David Andreas, Kansas State University; John O'Brien, Wenatchec Valley College; and Joseph D. Chapman, Ball State University.

I am indebted to all my one-time frontline employees, bosses, and colleagues who demonstrated what exceptional customer service is and what it is not. I was inspired to teach customer service and write this book when I was a retail store manager, supervising ten frontline employees who excelled at their customer service jobs even though they often struggled to satisfy the sometimes rude and downright impossible customers.

Not to be forgotten is the exceptional customer service of the entire library staff at Pellissippi State. They were all incredibly helpful and professional. Thanks as well to the six anonymous reviewers who provided useful comments and suggestions. Not the least, I want to thank Larry for his unwavering support and wry humor during the writing of this book. I am also grateful to Joey for her faithful assistance.

Last of all, I am grateful to all the exceptional service providers I have encountered over the years. You have taught me the most. Thanks for the stories.

I welcome questions and comments to aswartzlander@pstcc.edu.

Dr. Anne Swartzlander

CUSTOMER SERVICE

OBJECTIVES

1. Define customer service.
2. Describe customers' perceptions of services in the United States.
3. Explain why customer service is important in today's business environment.
4. Explain the relationship of customer service to marketing, operations, and human resources.
5. Outline the customer service model.

DEFINITION OF CUSTOMER SERVICE

Exceptional customer service is consistently meeting and exceeding customers' needs and expectations. Customer service is a philosophy, not a job or a department. When we think of customer service, many of us picture a customer service desk or a telephone representative. Many organizations have viewed customer service as after-sales service, customer support, and complaint handling. Dourado from eCustomerServiceWorld.com argues that many companies have traditionally misdefined customer service, using a departmental approach. He defines customer service as "the customer's complete experience of doing business."[1] *Customer service* is the behaviors and attitudes of a company and its personnel toward customers during all interactions and communication with them.

Experience Discussion 1.1

1. Give examples of situations that you have experienced as a customer that illustrate the following types of customer service:
   a. Customer service that was completely unacceptable
   b. Customer service that was below your expectations

      c. Customer service that met your expectations
      d. Customer service that exceeded your expectations
2. What products and industries do you associate with customer service?
3. Where do you find customer service?
4. Who provides customer service?
5. Do you think customer service has improved, stayed the same, or gotten worse in the past 10 years?

Since customer service is a customer's complete experience of doing business, then all companies and organizations provide some type of customer service—from service companies, to manufacturers, to retailers, to nonprofits, to government agencies. Customer service is found at every point of contact between customers and employees. In order for frontline personnel to meet customer needs and expectations, they need support from the rest of the company employees—from their coworkers and supervisors, other departments, and company executives. All employees then become customer service providers for either external or internal customers. In addition, customer service is found wherever and however customers intersect with providers. The interaction may be in person, on the telephone, by mail, via the Internet, or through machines and equipment, such as an ATM.

CUSTOMERS' PERCEPTIONS OF THE QUALITY OF SERVICES

Customer satisfaction in the United States leaves much to be desired. The *American Customer Satisfaction Index* (ACSI) measures satisfaction with the quality of goods and services as experienced by customers. Based on a scale of zero to 100, it is lower now than in 1994 when it was developed. In 1994, the national index was 74.2. In the third quarter of 2002 it was 73.1 (see Figure 1.1). It is lower for services than it is for goods. Americans believe that some services have improved, namely parcel delivery and ex-

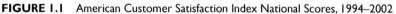

FIGURE 1.1 American Customer Satisfaction Index National Scores, 1994–2002

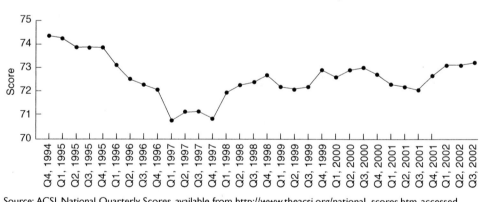

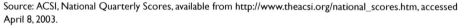

Source: ACSI, National Quarterly Scores, available from http://www.theacsi.org/national_scores.htm, accessed April 8, 2003.

press mail, but satisfaction with airlines, hospitals, telephone service, banks, department stores, and fast-food chains has decreased. Ratings seem to be lower for companies that have more contact with customers, such as airlines and hotels. Customers tend to rate niche companies—companies that focus on smaller specific target markets—higher than companies with large market shares, perhaps because niche companies are more in touch with their customers' needs. Researchers have found a positive and significant relationship between a company's individual ACSI score and its financial performance, including profit, return on investment, and stock performance. Fornell believes that poor service distorts our picture of the economy. If service quality decreases, the price of a service does not buy the same service that it used to.

The American Customer Satisfaction Index was created in 1994 by Claes Fornell at the University of Michigan Business School. It is cosponsored by the American Society for Quality and the international consulting firm CFI Group.

The ACSI survey gathers information on 190 companies representing 35 industries in 7 major economic sectors plus federal and local government agencies. The ACSI represents 30 percent of U.S. gross domestic product in sales to American household consumers. It measures approximately 5000 branded products and services that are representative of all goods and services. Some of the service companies are Nordstrom, Sears, Wal-Mart, McDonald's, Kroger, Exxon, Marriott, Wells Fargo, State Farm Insurance, Delta Air Lines, UPS, Walt Disney, Knight Ridder, and Sprint.

The index is a weighted average from an econometric model of consumers' responses to 17 questions rated on a scale of 1 to 10. The questions address and link customer expectations, perceived quality, perceived value, overall satisfaction, complaints, and customer loyalty (see Figure 1.2). The index is based on random-digit-dialing telephone samples, with more than 70,000 consumers interviewed annually. The randomly selected respondents are recent purchasers of a specific brand or model of the goods and services. At the 90 percent confidence level, the margin of error is a plus or minus 0.2 percentage point for the national index, a 1.0 percentage point for manufacturing industries, and 1.7 percentage points for service industries.[2]

FIGURE 1.2 The American Customer Satisfaction Index (ACSI) Model

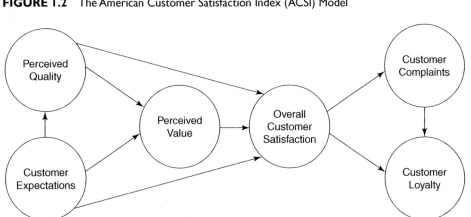

Source: Claes Fornell, Michael D. Johnson, Eugene W. Anderson, Jaesung Cha, and Barbara Everitt Bryant, "The American Customer Satisfaction Index: Nature, Purpose, and Findings," *Journal of Marketing* 60, no. 4 (October 1996): 8.

Other research shows that customers believe that customer service is better at some companies but still sporadic. Leonard Berry, author of *Discovering the Soul of Service,* says, "I give service in America a C minus." Americans carry experiences with one company to others, assuming that if Federal Express can provide exceptional service, supermarkets ought to be able to as well. Customers know that great service is possible.[3]

IMPORTANCE OF CUSTOMER SERVICE

Customer service is important in today's business and marketing environment due to sociocultural, demographic, technological, and economic factors, which are outlined below.

Sociocultural and Demographic Factors

In general, Americans are smarter customers than they used to be. Their consumer sophistication has increased due to more education and experience. They have higher expectations than they used to for customer service and product quality. Their expectations have become demands. The Internet has led to less company and brand loyalty due to changing buying habits and methods, including more choices, more convenience, more information, and more access to data than before for comparison shopping. Customers are becoming more likely to express their dissatisfaction and seek resolution for problems. They want complaints resolved quickly. They believe there is too much stereotyping based on gender, age, ethnicity, and appearance.

Several societal conditions have contributed to a focus on the quality of life. Americans detect a general decline in civility and want a more humane quality of life. Concern for moral values is at an all-time high. Both stress in everyday life and job stress have increased. Consumers are searching for simplification, control, and balance in their lives. They seek mental, physical, and spiritual well-being. Customers face too many choices, too much conflicting information, and too little time. Shopping is no longer an enjoyable activity. They are less patient about being put on hold. Service and convenience are high priorities. This all translates to a need for courteous, helpful, respectful, and knowledgeable customer service providers.

Marketers and demographers use birth year to identify segments of the population. In 1999, the 55-plus demographic group, the Mature Generation, controlled 70 percent of the total U.S. wealth and represented 50 percent of all discretionary income. As an example of this group's numbers in the market, the group transacts more than 5 million auto loans each year and represents 40 million credit card users. Consumers who are relatively affluent and have discretionary income want innovative, stress-free entertainment, travel, and leisure time experiences. They are willing to pay for high-quality household and personal services to have more leisure time. They expect exceptional customer service.

The Baby Boomers, the largest generation in American history, born between 1946 and 1964, are in the process of turning 50 plus. The Leading Boomers are moving into a new life stage. Their budgets are stretched as they send their children to college, save for retirement, and take care of aging parents. Family and home are their primary interests. Conspicuous consumption and status seeking are no longer the top goals. They are more interested in quality and reliability. Boomers are not a homogeneous group. The Trailing Boomers, born in the early 1960s, are in their 40s and in some ways are more similar to Generation X.[4]

Generation X consumers, born between 1965 and 1985, make up 16 percent of the population. They grew up as latchkey kids in a difficult time with the highest divorce rates, AIDS, corporate downsizing, and ecological threats. They are independent, savvy, and realistic. They are more knowledgeable about household products than Boomers were at their age because they participated in household chores at a younger age. Products and services that keep them in touch and in control, such as cell phones, pagers, answering machines, e-mail, and fax, are considered necessities for this group. Xers dislike advertising that is hype, insincere, and hypocritical. Products must be perceived as useful, fulfilling a genuine need. They are more diverse and accepting of ethnic and sexual diversity.

When Boomer families began to have children, the birthrate climbed again through 1994, creating an "Echo-Boom," or Generation Y. This generation, now 9 to 25 years old, makes up 26 percent of the population, and has substantial buying power and influence. The members of Generation Y have grown up in a time of great economic optimism. They are the most educated and the most sophisticated and informed consumers in the history of the United States. They know how to get information and make informed buying decisions. They insist on being treated with respect. Customer service is expected. They will not buy if they are patronized. They trust their friends' opinions, and so word of mouth is a significant source of consumer information. They take technology for granted and stay connected through the Internet and cell phones. Their standard of convenience is "effortless," such as "grab-and-go" food. Teamwork and getting along with others, particularly members of different racial and ethnic groups, are considered important skills for success.[5]

Technological Factors

Product complexity and proliferation, for example, the escalating cell, local, and long distance telephone choices, have made products and services even more difficult to choose, so buyers need more information, which salespeople often do not volunteer or know. The technological complexity of products has increased beyond the ability of consumers and even some service people to maintain and repair them easily and correctly.

Automated telecommunications, retail scanners, and other technology have allowed companies to be more productive with fewer employees. Savings could be passed on to customers who were willing to settle for less personal service and faster shopping. However, in some cases, technology has been misapplied. It was supposed to provide better customer service—and it has—but technology has also created more customer difficulties, such as when customers end up in an automated telephone loop or cannot reach a live person. The solution is now part of the problem. It's been reported that employees, who are being monitored by computer to measure productivity and performance, may hurry callers or even fake a disconnection so their average call duration will not be too long.[6]

In addition, technology has diminished the human touch. Due to the proliferation of technology in every aspect of their lives, customers want more interpersonal contact. Many customers use an ATM for bank transactions, but when they go to a bank teller, they expect the recognition, friendliness, and respect that they don't get from a machine. When checking out of a retail store, customers want acknowledgment and appreciation for their business. Scott Gross, who wrote *Outrageous! Unforgettable*

Service . . . Guilt-Free Selling, says that as companies replace people with technology, the remaining employees with one-on-one time with customers will have an even greater impact on customers' impressions and evaluations.[7]

Economic Factors

An economic shift has led to an increase in service jobs and a decline in manufacturing and agriculture jobs in the United States. The growth of service industries and the globalization of the economy and increasing competition have resulted in greater scrutiny of services. Other economic reasons suggested for the decrease in service satisfaction include cost cutting, deregulation, and labor issues.

The high inflation in the 1970s and early 1980s forced companies to keep prices down by cutting costs. They slashed employee hours, wages, and training. Consumers were willing to give up service for lower prices. Customer service received lip service, but management did not really believe that better customer service would increase sales. In the 1980s and 1990s, the strategy of downsizing, reengineering, and retrenchment of many companies also led to cost reduction to maintain profits. Satisfaction with goods was higher because manufacturers can replace workers with machines, while service companies cannot. Dissatisfaction increases when there are fewer employees to serve more customers.

Another cause of declining service quality is the effect of deregulation on several service industries, such as telecommunications and airlines. Deregulation led to major industry shake-ups, sometimes causing breakdowns in service quality. Deregulation increased competition, which led to reducing costs and streamlining services.

The post–Baby Boom shortage of young workers created a scarcity of candidates for minimum-wage service jobs. The labor shortage forced companies to hire less qualified workers, again decreasing service. In addition, young entry-level workers view minimum-wage service jobs as beneath them and as dead-end jobs with no chance for advancement. Standardizing services to cut costs has made jobs boring and has led to lack of employee motivation as well. Employee turnover in these entry-level frontline jobs was and continues to be high. When turnover is high, customer service experience and training decrease. The low unemployment rate in the late 1990s also lowered the quality of customer service due to the skill levels of the available labor for frontline jobs. Customer service levels eroded.

Improvement in services has also been slowed down by the lack of emphasis on services marketing strategy in some companies and by the relative difficulty of measuring service quality. Fornell believes that there has been a considerable amount of talk about increasing investment to improve service quality but not much actual effort.[8] In the 1980s, the marketing concept, which emphasizes a customer focus, notwithstanding, many companies tended to be inwardly focused rather than outwardly focused on customers. In 1987, Kenneth Bernhardt of Georgia State University maintained that corporate executives had insulated themselves from their customers. Companies had insufficient awareness of the rising expectations of customers. They seemed to be unaware of how much customers are influenced by past experiences, helpful salespeople, and responsive after-sales service. Bernhardt claimed that all executives could see was the short-term, quarterly sales numbers and the bottom line. Management believed that better service cost too much. They treated customer service as a cost rather than as an investment. They failed to define customer satisfaction in terms that link it to financial results.[9]

One service example, detailed in *Time* magazine in 1987, was a customer who took a foul-smelling piece of fish back to the supermarket and received a refund only after answering brusque questions and filling out forms. No one apologized or seemed to care that the dinner had been spoiled.[10] Ironically, a variation of the fish story occurred in the author's household a month ago. The fish was not spoiled, but the fish that was supposedly cod was not cod. The supermarket employee just handed over the refund without a word. Another example from the 1980s was a customer who had to take an entire day off from work because the delivery people refused to predict what time they would arrive. Delivery prediction is not much better these days.

However, considerable evidence suggested that it costs much more to get new customers than to keep current ones. There was clearly recognition on the part of many companies throughout the 1990s that customer service needed to be improved. Marketers began reallocating their marketing budget toward retention of customers rather than acquisition. Mass media advertising costs increased, and so marketers began to focus on keeping current customers rather than acquiring customers. Top-level management realized they must support and appreciate the customer service function. Many corporate executives had not recognized that in service businesses the most important employee is the one who actually delivers the service. Service jobs were considered unimportant. If training was done at all, it concentrated on technical skills rather than people skills. Executives began developing new and innovative employee selection, training, and motivation systems. They realized the value in empowering frontline service employees and resolving complaints quickly.

In the past decade, service companies have recognized a need for better customer service as a competitive edge. Services have been added to tangible products to differentiate them from competitive products. The public or government sector also recognized the need for better customer service. Since consumers vote and pay taxes, they believe they have a right to expect more of government agencies. Citizens need information and have urgent questions and legitimate complaints.

Twenty-First-Century Customers

Futurists predict that customers will become even smarter, more informed, more skeptical, more demanding, and more powerful in the twenty-first century. Access to information in real time on the Internet means customers will be able to compare any product. At a click, they can defect to another company. At a click, they can tell thousands of other customers about a good or a bad experience. To learn what their goals will be in the future, we will need to go beyond traditional customer research and tap into customer values and unexpressed needs. Oliver, author of *The Shape of Things to Come,* believes we must empower and integrate customers into our processes. We need to make them partners, the source of product innovation. In addition, customer service personnel are in a unique position to contribute to knowledge about customers.[11]

One overriding concern will be time. Service businesses must save customers time and make customers' lives easier, more convenient, less stressful, and less complicated. Customers will value information and purchase options wherever and whenever they want them. Amazon.com is moving in this direction with its access to product information, ease of purchasing, and prompt delivery. Customers want assistance managing and simplifying their lives. As the world becomes more complex, customers will value services such as direct home delivery of necessities and customized communication to track family and household activities.[12]

According to Patricia Seybold in *The Customer Revolution,* customers will be in control. The total customer experience is what will matter. Consumers and business customers want to do business with companies that truly care about them as people and as businesses. Businesses will need to be adaptable and be able to change rapidly.

* Customers want real-time product information about everything, including disclosure about product problems. They want information formerly provided only to specialists, such as medical research, genetic engineering, and raw weather data, so they will be informed and can make their own decisions easily. They want open equal access to the same information that agents, such as licensed investment brokers, have.
* Customers want their choice of distribution channels so they can buy anywhere, anytime, any way they want. They want a seamless experience. In other words, they do not want to hear that they have to call a different telephone number to get technical support for a product. They want to be able to see and purchase goods in a store that they have researched on the Internet. They want companies to value their time constraints.
* Customers want convenient access and complete information about their transactions from anywhere, anytime. Customers want process and logistics transparency so they can find out the status of any process or transaction. They want consistent end-to-end execution of product and service delivery.
* Customers want pricing transparency. They expect up-to-the minute pricing information on a global basis so they can compare prices or choose their own prices.
* Customers want even more control over their personal information to protect it, keep it private, and move it wherever they want.[13]

Skill Development 1.1

1. Discuss how your generation views the quality of customer service.
2. Can you think of any other changes or factors that affect customers' expectations and attitudes toward customer service?

RELATIONSHIP OF CUSTOMER SERVICE TO MARKETING, OPERATIONS, AND HUMAN RESOURCES

Marketing

Marketing is the process of planning and executing the conception, pricing, promotion, and distribution of goods and services to create exchanges that satisfy individual and organizational goals. The marketing philosophy of the latter part of the twentieth century has been the marketing concept, which is the idea that the social and economic justification for an organization's existence is the satisfaction of customer wants and needs while meeting organization objectives, in particular, profit. The marketing functions are commonly known as the *marketing mix,* the *"4 Ps"*—providing the right *product,* in the right *place,* at the right *price,* and with the right *promotion.* A *product* is defined by marketers as anything that can be offered for purchase, consumption, or acquisition. Products can be goods (tangible objects), services, persons, places, events, ideas/causes, or organizations. A *service,* a specific type of product, is considered an action or performance.[14]

Skill Development 1.2

Name a product and describe it in terms of the 4 Ps: product, place, price, and promotion. Can you think of anything that this mix is missing in terms of customer service?

Marketing services is different from marketing goods. One way to look at goods and services is to place them on a continuum, going from a pure good to a pure service (see Figure 1.3). A pure good is a tangible product, a commodity without any services attached. Examples would be salt or wheat. A pure service is a performance that includes few to no tangible aspects. Examples are surgery and insurance. In between are goods sold with services, such as an automobile and its warranty or a copy machine and its installation and maintenance contract. In the middle on the intangibility side of the continuum are service businesses that have goods as an essential element, such as a restaurant. Business-to-business products are often accompanied by services, and services are accompanied by products, blurring the distinction between the two.

Characteristics of Services

Since customer service is an essential part of service delivery, we will explain how services marketing differs from goods marketing. From a marketing perspective, services are considered different from goods due to four unique characteristics. The effect of these service characteristics is that services are more difficult for consumers to buy. In addition, in some ways, services are also more difficult to market.

1. *Intangibility.* Services have no physical properties. They are intangible. They cannot be seen, smelled, heard, tasted, or felt. Customers purchasing a service receive nothing tangible; the value of the service depends on their personal experience of the service performance. The perceived quality of a service is largely a

---

FIGURE 1.3   Goods-Services Continuum

Tangible Pure good				Intangible Pure service
Consumer				
Salt	Automobile	Restaurant	Car repair	Surgery
Shoes			Plumbing repair	Education
Business to Business				
Wheat	Tools	Copy machine		Legal services
Backhoe			Delivery service	Office maintenance

subjective matter. Customers' expectations of the service are integral to their satisfaction with the outcome.

2. *Inseparability.* Many services are sold and then simultaneously produced and consumed. Goods are produced, sold, and then consumed. A service cannot be easily demonstrated nor a sample examined ahead of time. Production of the service cannot be separated from the service providers, and so the quality of the service depends on the quality of the employees. Quality assurance must happen before and during production, rather than after production. Customers must trust a service company to deliver on its promise. A service is often delivered wherever a customer is, by people who are beyond the direct control of management. If improperly performed, some services cannot be recalled. If the service cannot be repeated, an apology or compensation is the only means of recourse for customer dissatisfaction. Because production and consumption occur simultaneously in many cases, there are often multiple customers at the same time.

3. *Variability.* Services are nonstandardized and variable, different every time the service is performed. Delivery of many services requires human interaction. Services often require buyer involvement or customer participation. Examples are getting a haircut, taking a car in for repair, and having federal income taxes done. If customers provide incorrect information, quality is affected. Each time a service is performed, the service provider may be a different person or in a different mood, and so quality changes. The customer may be different in some way, for example, in a hurry or under stress, and so quality perceptions change. Other customers affect the service received, say, when they are noisy in a restaurant, are in a hurry and cut in front of another customer in a checkout line, or take their time making a purchase decision while another customer waits.

4. *Perishability.* Services cannot be stored, warehoused, or inventoried. This causes supply and demand mismatches and, thus, difficulties for service providers and customers. Customer service is affected by customer waiting times, for example, in retail checkouts, restaurants, banks, and a telephone queue. Capacity limits, such as on an airplane or in a car wash, may result in loss of customers.

Experience Discussion 1.2

Choose a service and identify and describe it in terms of its four characteristics. What does each characteristic mean for customer service?

Evaluating the quality of services is more difficult than evaluating the quality of goods. A *search* quality is a characteristic than can easily be assessed before purchase. Search focuses on tangibility. A shirt or blouse is a good with numerous search characteristics. A customer can see its color, feel the fabric, determine its size, try it on to see how it fits and feels, see how it looks on, learn fabric content and care, compare its compatibility with other clothing, and ask someone else how it looks. An *experience* quality is a characteristic that can be determined only after use, such as the quality of a restaurant or movie. Customers do not know the quality before the purchase. A *credence* quality is a characteristic that is difficult to judge even after purchase because customers do not have the necessary knowledge or experience. An example is medical services. A will is the ultimate credence good because the purchaser never is able to determine the quality of the legal services. Services are inherently more risky to purchase.

The Ps of Marketing

In the past decade, the marketing philosophy has shifted from the marketing concept to *relationship marketing,* focusing on the retention of and long-term relationships with customers. Some professionals believe that this shift is long overdue and that marketing may be behind the curve in adapting to the shift to the service economy. The field of marketing has concentrated on marketing tangible products or goods for most of its existence. Product possession has been the objective. Since services are different from goods and require processes and people to deliver them, more than one marketing practitioner has urged the marketing field to incorporate more "Ps." Needham in *Marketing for Higher Awards* added three more "Ps"—people, provision of customer service, and process management.[15] All three are essential in services marketing. Lovelock and Wright use eight Ps in their services marketing and management textbook, adding physical evidence, productivity and quality, process, and people to the 4 Ps.[16]

Gronroos, a European marketing expert, believes that the 4 Ps are obsolete because by definition they force a separation between product, price, place, and promotion and a lack of integration. It is what he calls "toolbox" thinking. He also believes that the 4 Ps are not designed for a customer-oriented approach, because they focus on the means, the Ps, rather than the end, the consumer. He concludes that merely adding Ps isn't the answer for many businesses. All functions must be integrated throughout the company to achieve a customer-oriented relationship marketing approach.[17]

Operations and Human Resources

Consumer and business services are operations- and people-driven. The purchase of many tangible products occurs in a retail setting, which is considered a service business as well. Therefore, operations and people are the keys to success. Operations develops and manages the systems, processes, procedures, and policies enabling customers to purchase products and receive after-sales assistance. The customer service function has often been part of the operations area. The quality of the customers' purchasing process depends on the quality of customer service that is provided with a service or good. Customer service personnel are considered the front line in terms of winning customers' loyalty. It's the employees with knowledge of customers who make marketing and communication succeed.[18] Southwest Airlines is an example of this truth. The CEO, Kelleher, believes in Southwest's service culture and employees. Southwest has had 25 years of continuous profit by consistently offering what customers see as value—recognition as individuals, reliability, and low fares.[19]

Customer Relationship Management

Marketing, operations, human resources, and customer service have traditionally been in separate business departments. Relationship marketing and customer relationship management (CRM) are changing that. Customer relationship management is a business strategy aimed at all the aspects of marketing and service that pertain to customers. Software-based systems manage the information a business gathers about its customers, including history and experiences, purchases, returns, preferences, demographics, and complaints. The goal is to improve the customer experience by empowering employees and the business through knowledge of customers. The business activities to identify, select, acquire, develop, and retain loyal and profitable customers have previously been carried out separately in marketing and operations. Today, companies are combining these functions to differentiate their businesses.

Contact centers, formerly known as call centers, allow customers to contact the company by whatever methods they desire and are used for sales and customer service. The customer contact center will be at the center of this integration and represent the company to the customer. Workflow will involve the entire company. The contact center in the early 2000s will be even more essential to the bottom line than it has been in the past. It will be at the very core of a customer-focused enterprise, the point where systems, people, and technology combine to acquire, develop, and retain loyal and profitable customers.[20] The customer service provided will be one of the keys to retaining customers.

CUSTOMER SERVICE MODEL

This section describes a model that is used to organize the information in the textbook (see Figure 1.4). Customers are the focus of customer service. The other parts of the model are the customer service strategy, systems, and people or human resources. This text takes the view that all business functions and people serve customers. Each component of the model affects and interacts with the other components. In this chapter, we will outline the model. Details will be addressed in Chapters 2 to 4.

FIGURE 1.4   Customer Service Model

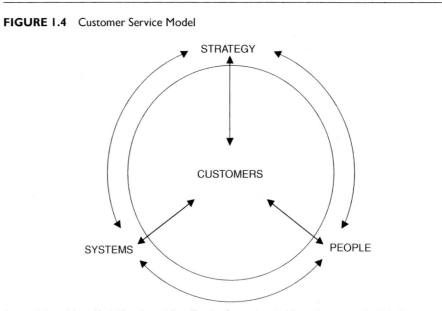

Source: Adapted from Karl Albrecht and Ron Zemke, *Service America! Doing Business in the New Economy* (Homewood, IL: Dow Jones-Irwin, 1985).

Customers

Customers are in the middle. They are the focus. To understand exceptional customer service and the value of interpersonal communication with customers, we first must recognize that customers are the reason we have a job. Without customers, there is no job. We say customers are the focus rather than customers' experiences so that we remember that each customer is an individual. We are offering customers an experience and a relationship. Those go to the heart of the requirement for exceptional customer service performance and communication skills.

Strategy

Exceptional customer service is built from and by the philosophy of the company's leaders. The company's mission, values, and vision must be based on customer service as a priority. The company founders and executives must be committed to the customers' experience and relationship with the business. The company designs its products and delivery to fulfill customers' needs and expectations in terms of both the quality of the products and the quality of customer service. If a product is a good, services accompany the product. If a product is a service, customer service is an integral part of the product. On the other hand, exceptional customer service is not a cure-all. The company needs quality products in the first place and needs to execute well in other areas.

Systems

Operations is defined as the set of activities that creates goods and services through the transformation of inputs into outputs.[21] In this text, we use the term *systems* to represent all the physical facilities, equipment, processes, procedures, and policies that serve customers. Systems are planned and managed with the customer in mind. All systems affect the quality of customer service. The environment, including the equipment and the physical appearance of the company, contributes to customer service.

People

All actions, behavior, and skills of company personnel influence customer service. Employees' attitudes, work ethic, knowledge, communication skills, teamwork skills, and management skills make a difference in the customer experience. All employees have responsibility for customer service. Frontline people, anyone who interacts with external customers who are purchasing the product, are the most important employees in the delivery of exceptional customer service. Management and all other personnel support the front line. Employees must be recruited, trained, motivated, evaluated, and rewarded for service.

Textbook Mind Map

Figure 1.5 is a mind map of the organization of the textbook, showing chapter topics and how they are related. Chapters 2 to 4 discuss the components of the model: strategy, systems, customers, and people. Chapters 5 and 11 provide information about improving individual performance and problem-solving skills. Chapters 6 to 10 are the interpersonal communication skills chapters. Chapter 12 focuses on providing customer service to special types of customers. Chapter 13 explains problem resolution and recovery.

FIGURE 1.5   Textbook Mind Map for Customer Loyalty

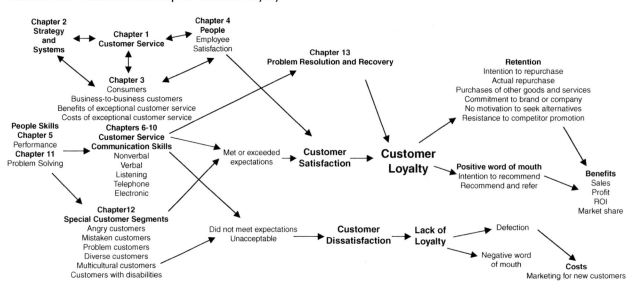

TERMS

customer service

American Customer Satisfaction Index

marketing

marketing mix

4 Ps

product

place

price

promotion

service

intangibility

inseparability

variability

perishability

search, experience, and credence
      characteristics

relationship marketing

operations

systems

DISCUSSION QUESTIONS

1. What is customer service?
2. What are customers' perceptions of service quality at the beginning of the twenty-first century? Why?
3. Why are businesses increasing their emphasis on customer service?
4. Describe twenty-first-century customers.
5. List and explain the four characteristics of services that make them different from tangible products.
6. Why are the 4 Ps considered insufficient for promoting exceptional customer service.

7. What is the relationship between customer service, marketing, operations, and human resources?
8. Outline the customer service model.

EXERCISE—BE YOUR OWN CUSTOMER[22]

To see how good your company's customer service is, try some of the following suggestions. Pick a few and be careful not to take up your company's time unnecessarily.

1. Call 30 minutes before work officially begins. Did you get a helpful recording?
2. Call during the day. How friendly was the receptionist? How helpful was the receptionist?
3. Call during lunch. Were you able to accomplish what you wanted?
4. Call after hours. Were you able to reach a human? How easy was it?
5. Ask for someone and see if you are automatically transferred to voice mail.
6. Call and ask for yourself when you're out of the office.
7. Ask for the president during working hours. See if you can get through. How easy was it? How accessible was the president's office to a customer? Did you get the question, "What's this in reference to?"
8. Place an order during working hours. How easy was it? How pleasant was it?
   a. Order something that is out of stock.
   b. Try to order something that the company doesn't carry.
   c. Ask who else sells the same type of products or services.
   d. Try to get a lower price.
9. Try to place an after- or before-hours order. Were you able to do it, or did you have to have someone call you back?
10. Try to place an after- or before-hours service call. Did you get help?
11. Call with a complaint. Have a billing problem. Have a delivery problem. Have a quality problem. Was the problem handled in a memorable way?
12. Press "0" and see what happens. Press the "automated" numbers. How easy was it to find your way? How long did it take?

NOTES

1. Phil Dourado, "Why Web Service Is So Bad," eCustomerServiceWorld, available from http://www.eCustomerServiceWorld.com/earticlesstore_articles.asp?type=article&id.=531, accessed June 10, 2001.
2. Summarized from http://www.theacsi.org, accessed May 14, 2002; Claes Fornell, Michael D. Johnson, Eugene W. Anderson, Jaesung Cha, and Barbara Everitt Bryant, "The American Customer Satisfaction Index: Nature, Purpose, and Findings," *Journal of Marketing* 60, no. 4 (October 1996): 7–19; Eugene W. Anderson and Claes Fornell, "Foundations of the American Customer Satisfaction Index," *Total Quality Management* 11, no. 7 (September 2000): 869; and Jaclyn Fierman, "Americans Can't Get No Satisfaction," *Fortune* 132, no. 12 (December 11, 1995): 186–192.
3. Katie Hafner, "Is the Customer Ever Right?" *The New York Times,* July 20, 2000, G1; and James E. Fisher and Dennis E. Garrett, "Moving to the Next Level: How Organizations

Are Addressing the New Consumer Affairs Challenges," *Customer Relationship Management,* June 1998, 14–19.

4. Michael Ramundo, "Customer Service: The Right Trend for the '90s," *Marketing Prospectus,* n.d.; Cathy Hunt, "Emerging Global Consumer Trends," *Customer Relationship Management,* September 1997, 26–29; and Alison Wellner, "Generational Divide," *American Demographics* 22, no. 10 (October 2000): 54.

5. Karen Ritchie, "Marketing to Generation X," *American Demographics* 17, no. 4 (April 1995): 34–40; Lisa Goff, "Don't Miss the Bus!" *American Demographics* 21, no. 8 (August 1999): 49; and Alison Wellner, "Get Ready for Generation Next," *Training* 36, no. 2 (February 1999): 42–47.

6. Hafner, "Is the Customer Ever Right?"

7. Louisa Wah, "The Almighty CUSTOMER: The Customers of Tomorrow Will Reign with Relentless Power, and They're Already a Latent Force. Is Your Company Prepared for a New Generation of Customer That Will Be Demanding beyond Imagination?" *Management Review,* February 1999, 16.

8. Daniel Pedersen, "Dissing Customers, Why the Service Is Missing from America's Service Economy," *Newsweek,* June 23, 1997, 56–57.

9. Thomas Oliver, "Studies: Both Workers, Management Are at Fault," *The Atlanta Journal/The Atlanta Constitution,* Sunday, March 1, 1987, n.p.

10. Stephen Koepp, "Pul-eeze! Will Somebody Help Me; Frustrated American Consumers Wonder Where The Service Went?" *Time* 29 (February 2, 1987): 49–55.

11. Wah, "The Almighty CUSTOMER."

12. Larry Hochman, "What Service Must Become," *Customer Service Management* 28 (November/December 1999): 27.

13. Patricia B. Seybold, *The Customer Revolution: How to Thrive When Customers Are in Control* (New York: Crown Business, 2001).

14. Charles W. Lamb, Jr., Joseph F. Hair, Jr., and Carl McDaniel, *Essentials of Marketing,* 2d ed. (Cincinnati: South-Western College Publishing, 2001), 6–7.

15. M. O. Fashanu, "Triad Makes for Better Ps," Letters to the Editor, *Marketing News,* June 18, 2001, 8.

16. Christopher Lovelock and Lauren Wright, *Principles of Service Marketing and Management,* 2d ed. (Upper Saddle River, NJ: Prentice Hall, 2002), 13.

17. Christian Gronroos, "From Marketing Mix to Relationship Marketing—Towards a Paradigm Shift in Marketing," *Management Decision,* 35, no. 3–4 (March–April 1997): 322–340.

18. Don E. Schultz, "'It's the Employees, Stupid!'" *Marketing News,* September 28, 1998, 6.

19. Ken Irons, "Why Marketers Lag Behind in the Shift to Service," *Marketing,* July 31, 1997, 14.

20. Patricia J. Mitchell, "Aligning Customer Call Centers for 2001," *Telemarketing & Call Center Solutions,* April 1998, 64–69.

21. Jay Heizer and Barry Render, *Principles of Operations Management,* 3d ed. (Upper Saddle River, NJ: Prentice Hall, 1999): 4.

22. Adapted from Jeffrey Gitomer, *Customer Satisfaction Is Worthless, Customer Loyalty Is Priceless: How to Make Customers Love You, Keep Them Coming Back and Tell Everyone They Know* (Marietta, GA: Bard Press, 1998).

CUSTOMER SERVICE STRATEGY AND SYSTEMS

OBJECTIVES

1. Describe the characteristics of an exceptional customer service strategy.
2. Explain the concept of customer experience.
3. Explain service fairness.
4. Explain how systems affect customer service.
5. Describe the characteristics of exceptional customer service systems.
6. Discuss how a company's systems can be improved.

CUSTOMER SERVICE MODEL

This chapter addresses the customer service strategy and systems components of the model outlined in Chapter 1 (see Figure 2.1). Companies must begin with a concept of the value and experience they are offering customers. This is based on a customer-oriented vision and philosophy of the company. Chapters 3 and 4 focus on the customer and people parts of the model.

CUSTOMER SERVICE STRATEGY

A strategy that has satisfied customers in the past may not satisfy customer expectations and demands at present or in the future. Companies need to develop a strategy that leads to customer loyalty—retention rates, increased business—share of wallet, and insusceptibility to competitors' promotion—price tolerance. The strategy must incorporate exceptional customer service.

FIGURE 2.1   Customer Service Model

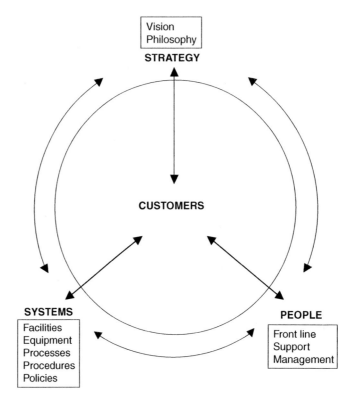

Source: Adapted from Karl Albrecht and Ron Zemke, *Service America! Doing Business in the New Economy* (Homewood, IL: Dow Jones-Irwin, 1985).

CHARACTERISTICS OF AN EXCEPTIONAL CUSTOMER SERVICE STRATEGY

In 1985, in *Service America!,* Albrecht and Zemke described a service *strategy* as "a distinctive formula for delivering service; such a strategy is keyed to a well-chosen benefit premise that is valuable to customers and that establishes an effective competitive position." It is based on the company's vision, values, and beliefs: "This is what we are, this is what we do, and this is what we believe in."[1] A customer-oriented strategy reflects the character and spirit of the business. The strategy must differentiate a company's products from those of its competitors in a meaningful way in the eyes of the customer. The core product may be the same, but the added value is the difference from company to company and is a key customer decision-making factor.

The strategy must convey a concept that employees can understand, relate to, and put into action. It provides a common purpose for the organization, management, support employees, and frontline employees. It lets employees know what is important to the company, what the priorities are, and what they need to accomplish. It must have a motivating factor sufficiently powerful to enlist commitment from employees. The strategy must be possible to do. It cannot have too many peripheral features that will make it too complex and ultimately too costly to do. It should not be used or promoted until the organization is ready. A company should not over-promise and underdeliver.

The strategy should be continually evaluated in light of changes in the marketplace. It will be in transition depending on customer expectations and sociocultural, economic, demographic, technological, political, ecological, and competitive changes. Development of a company vision, philosophy, and strategy for customer service is an ongoing long-term learning process.[2]

CUSTOMER EXPERIENCE STRATEGY

One expert has said that companies are suffering from *"management myopia,"* believing that they are in a product and/or service business, rather than taking the broader view that the value they create is a *total customer experience*. Management myopia is similar to marketing myopia, a term coined by Levitt in the 1980s, which is the tendency for companies to focus narrowly on their business, as the railroad companies did, failing to see that they were in the transportation business and eventually losing business. Businesses must create customer experiences to differentiate their business and create loyalty, much like Disney has done. Studies indicate that consumers are not influenced by tangible characteristics of products and services as much as by subconscious sensory and emotional elements from the total experience. Unique customer experiences contribute to reducing competition. A holistic customer experience cannot be easily copied.[3]

Holistic customer experiences include exceptional interpersonal customer service. Customers do business with companies and people they like. A customer experience strategy is based on shared values and the ability to understand what each customer feels is and is not important. Employees need to be able to do what is best for customers. The emotional connection with customers must be genuine. It is difficult to imitate a strategy in which employees provide sincere acknowledgment and fulfillment of customer needs and expectations.[4]

Developing a Customer Experience Strategy

Differentiating a company's products from those of its competitors is necessary for success. Many companies focus on their products for ways to be different. Instead, examining their customers' entire experience with their product can yield innovative ideas for even the most commonplace product. A company has the opportunity to differentiate itself at every point where it comes in contact with its customers' consumption chain—from the moment they realize they need the product to the time when they no longer want it and decide to dispose of it or throughout an entire service transaction. To develop a strategy, a company should create *customer scenarios* for specific target markets and map what they do from beginning to end, identifying all the steps through which customers pass, from being aware of a product to discontinuing its use.

Customers go through a decision process when purchasing a product or service: recognition of need, search, evaluation of alternatives, purchase, and post-purchase evaluation (see Figure 2.2). The company should ask who, what, when, where, how, and why at each stage. Consider the entire customer experience. Think about the challenges the customers face, rather than focus narrowly on the products the company sells. How do customers become aware of a need for the product? How do they find it? How do they decide among alternatives? What do customers need help with when they use the product or receive a service? Do they understand the

FIGURE 2.2 Customer Decision-Making Process

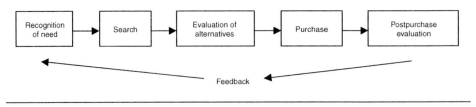

process for a service? What happens when customers get the product home or to their office? Where is the product stored? What about returns and exchanges? What if a service is unsatisfactory? Handling things well when customers are dissatisfied can be as important as meeting the need that motivated initial purchase. How often do they need a service? How is the product repaired or serviced? How is it disposed of? One example of understanding the decision process is making customers aware of their need for the product in a way that is unique and subtle. Oral-B developed toothbrush dye that fades when the brush needs to be replaced.[5]

Seybold discusses further the concept of scenarios of customer experiences. She explains that a company can find ways to reach into its customers' lives, helping customers use products more effectively and saving them time. A company can become more indispensable to customers. Scenarios prompt companies to look beyond the points at which customers come into contact with companies to identify the needs of the customers when using a product. Scenarios should be mapped for all target segments and as many variations as possible. Determine the activities and information needed for each step. This will lead to common needs or a specific need for a large segment that a company can use to create a strategy. Buzzsaw.com saw a way to help construction businesses integrate all their needs, which include setting the project scope, schedule, and budget; getting financial backing; recruiting the team; developing the design; producing plans and specifications; managing the bidding and negotiations; managing the construction process; and managing the facility. Buzzsaw developed a website with all the needed resources, services, and products for communication, management, and collaboration. When Buzzsaw realized the enormous variety of scenarios in construction, it organized the information so owners, architects, engineers, general contractors, construction managers, and facility managers could design their own scenario and use the parts they needed.[6]

Jeffrey Bezos, founder of Amazon.com, wants Amazon to be the "earth's most customer-centric company." The company is "obsessed" with the customer experience, concentrating on making it seamless to purchase from the website. Bezos believes a company must be superior in all four of the things customers want: selection, ease of use, prices, and service. Being customer-centric means listening to customers and figuring out what they want and how to give it to them, inventing and innovating on behalf of customers, and personalizing, putting each customer at the center of his or her own universe.[7]

The Container Store, headquartered in Dallas, is another good example. It sells organization containers and storage for every possible household item. Its core strategy is to improve customers' lives by giving them more space and time. It has retail stores, catalogs, and an online store. The Container Store has made the search process less complicated and more convenient. It's one thing for customers to need closet storage and go to a store or online and buy the pieces they need. The Container Store thought it through and realized that customers need help laying out their closet and storage design. The company sells products combined with value-added service by helping customers design closets or other storage from beginning through do-it-yourself installation. It provides templates, measurements, and one-on-one assistance. Its service strategy enables customers to contact the company for information and assistance by any means and anytime they want—by telephone, e-mail, and the website.

Skill Development 2.1

Map the purchase of gasoline. Ask who, what, when, where, why, and how for different target segments and situations. How can a company selling gasoline help customers? Is there a way to differentiate this product?

Leonard Berry outlined five tactics for retailers that focus on the total customer experience and provide value. The tactics are interrelated. If any one of them is absent, the overall customer experience is diminished.

* First, solve customer problems; sell customers solutions like the Container Store does. The Container Store selects versatile quality merchandise and organizes its stores with customer access in mind. It hires carefully, trains thoroughly, and treats its employees very well so they are willing and able to provide solutions for customer problems. The proof that it works is in the company's average double-digit annual sales growth.
* Second, save customers' time. Give them access, search, possession, and transaction convenience. Offer convenient locations and operating hours. Be available by telephone, e-mail, and the Internet. Make it easy to find and select products with high inventory levels and fast delivery. Design systems for completing transactions and rectifying problems quickly and easily. ShopKo is a competitor of Wal-Mart in the Midwest and Northwest. ShopKo makes it easy by being in stock 98 percent of the time, opening a checkout whenever two customers are waiting in any line, and linking the services of its bricks and clicks stores. Berry reminds us that too few open checkouts can save short-term payroll dollars but lose customers in the long run. Some retailers and service providers insist on delivering their product or service at their convenience rather than the customers'. Being available at home when the company wants to arrive is very costly to customers in time and dollars.
* Third, connect with customers' emotions. Provide an experience that is sincere and creates trust. Create an atmosphere that connects with the target market and fits the customer's lifestyle and needs. An example is Barnes & Noble, which creates environments in which customers want to spend time.
* Fourth, treat customers with respect. We have all heard of situations in which store employees were having a personal conversation and ignored customers or, worse, an auto repair company that deceived customers. Respect means acknowledgment, consideration, courtesy, and fairness. It means clean, neat, organized physical spaces that value customers' time. It means straightforward pricing, fair return policies, and legitimate advertising.
* Fifth, set the fairest, not the lowest, prices. Customers have become skeptical of manipulative pricing strategies and promotions. Use everyday fair

pricing based on the value of the customer experience. Sell at regular but competitive prices and hold genuine sales promotions. Fair pricing will win customers' trust and pay off in the long run.[8]

Another example of a service vision and philosophy that drives a company, its systems, and its people is L.L. Bean. The company has always followed Berry's retailing advice. When L.L. founded the company, he said, "I do not consider the sale a success until the goods are worn out and the customer still satisfied." Anecdotal evidence shows that L.L. Bean stands behind its products. No matter the reason for dissatisfaction, L.L. Bean will make it right.

Consider the philosophy of a company whose strategy is simply, "Just say yes." Employees are empowered to spend up to $250, and more if necessary, to fix a problem. No one is allowed to say no to a customer even if the company did not make a mistake. What matters is that a customer thought it did. If employees cannot find a way to say yes, they are to pass the situation to a supervisor, although this is discouraged. The only two people in the company that can say no are the owner and the general manager, and they never do. Employees, in fact, sign a statement to this effect. The last few lines of the statement are, "Will an employee ever get in trouble for doing too much to help a customer? No. Will an employee ever get in trouble for not doing enough to help a customer? Absolutely."[9]

Even though a fire department is not a service for which customers always have a choice, a Pennsylvania fire department has developed a customer service strategy. The Lancaster Township Fire Department exists to serve its customers. The members of the department emphasize compassion, helpfulness, honesty, and respect. They know that a fire is the worst day of their customers' lives, so they understand their fear and show compassion. They will do anything necessary to make it easier. They will call family and friends to help, they tell the truth about injuries, and they understand when people are angry.[10]

McMaster-Carr, an industrial distributor, is an example of a business to business company that has a strategy for meeting customer needs and more. This is an e-mail sent by a friend of the author:

"Hello, Customer Service: Yesterday I received a shipment of small but unusual tools that I had ordered within the previous 24 hours. Outstanding! This was not the first occurrence of such performance. I am an engineer, and I have ordered from you for both business and personal use. You are a benchmark company with respect to your catalog, your product descriptions, your inventory, your customer service, and your fast order fulfillment. In my experience, no one else has even come close. Please continue to follow your strategy as quoted from your website: '. . . serve our customers by stocking an extremely broad product line, then quickly deliver those products where they are needed in just about a day.' Now, if it were just somehow easier to get a new copy of your yellow catalog (hint, hint)." He got his catalog.

Another way to provide an exceptional customer experience is to offer a guarantee. Due to the nature of services, it is more risky to offer a service guarantee than a guarantee or warranty on a tangible product. Customer expectations and perceptions of service quality are subjective. Quality control is more difficult since services are produced and consumed at the same time. The quality of the service varies depending on the circumstances, provider, and customer. The service performance can be different each time if a service provider does not follow standards. Since customers themselves and other customers affect the quality of service, a situation may be out of the company's control.

However, in some cases, an explicit service guarantee may be the only way to differentiate a company's service from the competition and provide a trustworthy customer experience. A guarantee cannot be just a marketing strategy. It must be based on a customer-oriented company strategy and the value of the customer experience. The company must build its organization, systems, and people skills around it. A guarantee forces a company to examine every conceivable source of customer dissatisfaction and fix it. Federal Express's "absolutely, positively overnight" guarantee promised that a customer's service would be free if FedEx did not live up to its promise. Then, FedEx made sure it was possible to do so.[11] Hampton Inns' money-back service guarantee, a full refund if a guest is dissatisfied for any reason, cost the company $1.1 million during the first full year, but it also created $11 million in new revenue and repeat business. Hampton Inns found that service quality issues were fixed sooner and faster than they had been and that employee morale was higher and turnover was lower.[12]

In these various strategy models and examples, several characteristics stand out. The strategy must focus on the total customer experience with the company and its products or services. It must focus on the customers' goals and entire use of the product or service from beginning to end. It must solve customers' problems, making their lives easier and saving them time. The strategy must put customers first with exceptional customer service offering excellence, respect, knowledge, helpfulness, fairness, reliability, assurance, empathy, responsiveness, teamwork, innovation, integrity, and social responsibility.

SERVICE FAIRNESS

In developing an exceptional customer service strategy, a company should consider the issue of service fairness. Fairness means being genuine and trustworthy. Fairness means not wasting customers' time. It means acknowledging and fixing mistakes quickly. L.L. Bean trusted the integrity of his customers. Hampton Inns believes in resolving any dissatisfaction. In the particular case of services as products, they are performances and are difficult to evaluate before purchase. Customers cannot drive them around the block and kick their tires. In many cases, the customers must buy the service in order to experience it and then evaluate it. Even then, they may not be able to judge the quality of legal or medical services. The purchase of services is inherently risky. Customers must trust a company will deliver and conduct itself honorably. Trust offsets the risk and uncertainty.

Because of the trust factor, a strategy directed toward an exceptional customer service experience must incorporate the idea of service fairness. Seiders and Berry define *service fairness* as "the level of justice in a service company's behavior as perceived by a customer." Fairness is part of what determines customer confidence and loyalty. The responses of customers who believe they have been treated unfairly are immediate and lasting. Customers who believe a company's actions are unfair are more likely to switch to a competitor. They are more likely to retaliate with unfavorable word of mouth. On the other hand, customers will also react strongly when they believe that a company has been more than fair, and they will become more loyal. Companies that offer an explanation and compensation for a problem are perceived to be fairer.

Perceived vulnerability is a factor. Unfairness will exist when customers feel vulnerable and at a disadvantage, such as when they lack information, expertise, freedom to choose, or recourse. Federal and state consumer protection laws, licensing, and industry self-regulation mitigate these problems to some extent, but companies still engage in unethical and illegal practices. Customers are particularly sensitive to unfairness when a service must be bought on faith and is difficult to judge due to technical complexity. They worry when a service is performed in their absence and self-protection is difficult. The more severe the outcome, the more intense the reaction.

Poor service by itself, such as rudeness, is not considered unfair. Unfair practices involving illegal and unethical behavior include the following with examples:

* Lack of accountability
  * *Negligent service operations*—price scanner overcharges
  * *Wasting customers' time*—long checkout lines
  * *Hiding behind unreasonable policies*—10-day waiting period for checks to clear
  * *Denying responsibility*—blaming a customer for misunderstanding a policy
  * *Exploitation of a monopoly*—delayed response to customers' billing concerns
  * *Nonenforcement of regulations*—facility safety hazards
* Exploitation
  * *Deceptive, misleading, unclear, or missing information*—fine print
  * *Misrepresentation*—inappropriately promoting a financial investment
  * *Hidden agenda*—trading customers up to a product with a higher commission
  * *Invasion of privacy*—selling confidential customer information
* Discrimination
  * *Selective manipulation*—providing inferior service to poor or unprofitable customers
  * *Targeted bias*—discrimination against a particular racial or religious group

Here is an example to illustrate unfairness arising out of unethical practices. Meg thought her car might have a gas leak because the mileage per gallon was much lower than usual. She believed it was unlikely but obviously not something to ignore. She went to an auto repair and tire company from which she had purchased tires a couple of times. She explained the problem to the owner and asked to have the car checked for a gas leak due to the low miles per gallon. After a long time, the owner came out to the waiting room and told her that there was no gas leak but that they were checking the spark plugs. She told him she was sure the plugs were fine because they had been replaced recently. Then he told her that the mechanic had already removed the plugs. He informed her that she would owe $20 to have them put back in, even though they did not need to be checked. She was rather ignorant of auto repair procedures and did not want a confrontation, and so she paid the $20. However, since she had specifically asked the manager to check for a gas leak, she believed the company had taken advantage of her lack of knowledge and gender and been very unfair. She and her husband have not been back to this auto repair store since. This is a case of unambiguous unfairness. This is the type of unfair action that will cause an immediate, angry response—defection, along with retaliation from a customer, by unfavorable word of mouth.

Other triggers for perceived unfairness are controllability, intention, and recurrence. Was the situation within the company's control? Has it happened before, and should the problem have been fixed? Was the company aware of the potential for negative effects but still did nothing? For example, customers think that long lines at a supermarket and out-of-stock items are unfair because they believe those are controllable problems. If an event that is usually perceived as just plain poor service happens frequently, customers may feel that's unfair because the company should have corrected the problem. Customers may perceive a return policy that is more restrictive than competitors' policies as unfair. They might view new bank fees for once-free services as unfair.

If a supermarket has an express checkout limited to 10 items, the customer in front of another customer has a full grocery cart, and the clerk allows the customer to go through the line, this is a matter of the degree of unfairness. A customer's reaction will be frustration rather than anger. If customers understand that it is very difficult for the clerk to ask the customer to go to another line, customers may not think it is unfair. If it happens often, it is more likely to be considered unfair. Retaliation may not be switching to a competitor, but the perceived unfairness may be expressed to the clerk or to store management.

A company can prevent perceptions of unfairness by examining its policies. Policies that are seen as illogical, inflexible, and disrespectful are targets for perceived unfairness. All customer service personnel must be trained about the importance of perceived fairness, situations likely to trigger it, potential customer responses, and ways to prevent the perception.

If customers have to jump through hoops to resolve an unfair situation, their negative response escalates. For example, if a supermarket scanner overcharges, many stores will give customers the item free. If customers have to ask and the employee grudgingly complies, customers will think this is more unfair than the overcharge in the first place. Employees should offer explanations and compensation. Some companies believe that explanations and compensation are undesirable messages that reveal service inadequacies and acknowledge guilt. Research shows that this is not true. Blaming customers, the industry, or employees and denying responsibility increase feelings of unfairness. Telling customers that their expectations or perceptions are unreasonable will be perceived as blaming, and it shows a lack of company accountability.[13]

Experience Discussion 2.1

Give examples of service unfairness that you have experienced.

Profitable versus Unprofitable Customers

It has been reported within the past few years that companies favor their profitable customers over their unprofitable ones. This is perceived as unfair by many customers. An example is the rumored practice of keeping unprofitable customers on hold longer and giving them less attention than profitable customers. Harrison makes some convincing arguments against this approach. He says that believing that marketing to unprofitable customers will only produce customers that are even more unprofitable is absurd, pointing out that many customers start out as unprofitable customers. A single 20-year-old is probably not profitable to a bank but someday will be. Companies can't afford to ignore any customer who has the potential to grow into a profitable customer. Instead, companies should figure out what to offer to make customers profitable. For example, banks could motivate customers to consolidate more of their finances and stay at the bank for a lifetime. Harrison also says that the assumptions behind the calculation of unprofitable customers are fallible and that even some bank executives lack confidence in them.

A company could turn away unprofitable customers only to lose their profitable relatives and friends and create negative word of mouth. An example illustrates this point. A bank sent an 80-year-old woman a letter explaining its new policy of a minimum monthly balance in checking accounts to avoid a service charge of $25. The woman's son had two accounts with over $100,000 at the bank, he paid most of her bills and purposely kept the balance low, and the family had a 50-year relationship with the bank. We can imagine the son's reaction and the woman's negative word of mouth about the bank's "total disregard for customers." A database could have flagged this situation to prevent it, but the woman was still an unprofitable customer from the bank's point of view. Companies are also wasting their marketing acquisition investment and potentially creating negative publicity. Furthermore, if a company is selling unprofitable relationships, that is, selling at a loss, perhaps it has a pricing problem, not an unprofitable customer situation. In addition, a company could alienate employees who believe the favoritism is unfair.[14]

On the other hand, there is evidence that unprofitable customers are a drain on a company, considering that about 80 percent of revenue and profit is generated by 20 percent of customers. The question to consider is the reason why some customers are unprofitable. Bank customers may be unprofitable because they are savers, have only a no-fee checking account with a minimum balance, and use the ATM almost exclusively. Target segments do not all have the same needs and expectations. If a company aligns its service offerings accordingly, each segment and the company should benefit. High-value customers who contribute to sales and profit receive value-added services, while checking account–only customers are encouraged to use Internet banking to keep the costs of serving customers low. This seems fair.[15]

DEFINITION OF SYSTEMS

This section discusses how a company's systems affect customers. The systems themselves affect the quality of service that customers receive. Systems also create barriers for customer service providers in delivering exceptional interpersonal customer service experiences.

Operations management is the set of activities that creates goods and services through the transformation of inputs into outputs. The transformation or production function is evident in producing goods. The transformation is less obvious for services. In a service company, operations manages *systems*, which include all the physical facilities, equipment, processes, procedures, and policies that produce the service. The systems deliver the service.

Services are operations-driven. The systems actualize the service priorities as set out in the service strategy. The facilities and equipment are the buildings, technology, machines, and other materials necessary to deliver a service. *Processes* are the methods and sequences of events that produce the service. *Procedures* are step-by-step instructions that detail how services are performed. *Policies* are guidelines or rules that ensure consistency in customer transactions in line with the company's philosophy and strategy. They are decision rules indicating how a company will handle specific situations. Policies must be specific, factual, and understandable.[16] The processes, facilities, equipment, procedures, and policies are combined to deliver a total customer experience. Specific examples of systems include:

* *Restaurant*—procedures of the servers and cooks
* *Automobile dealer*—financing procedures
* *Dentist's office*—appointment procedures and policies
* *Department store*—store layout
* *Gas station*—gas pumps
* *Pest control company*—dissatisfaction policy
* *Hotel*—checkout procedures

* *Manufacturer*—ordering and billing procedures
* *Wholesaler*—inventory system
* *Supermarket*—scanner and cash register
* *Specialty store*—security system
* *Shoe store*—servicescape and atmospherics

Skill Development 2.2

Refer to the map of gasoline purchase that you created for Skill Development 2.1. Examine the systems to determine what works well and what does not work so well.

CHARACTERISTICS OF EXCEPTIONAL CUSTOMER SERVICE SYSTEMS

Exceptional customer service systems that provide a total customer experience are customer-oriented, effective, flexible, and cost effective.

Customer-Oriented

Systems should be designed with customers in mind. The systems must satisfy customers' needs and expectations. For example, think about the first thing that happens in an emergency room. Patients must register. A hospital emergency room admission system is often focused on payment rather than pain. Admitting personnel first ask for name, address, and insurance. Never mind that a mother wants to tell the nurse about her daughter's broken arm and be assured they will get help. To address the patients' needs, one nurse decided she would turn the form around and ask for the problem first. Once the emotional need was relieved, she would go back to getting necessary details.

A more benign example is the "milk's-in-the-back-of-the-store" system. For customers who want convenience, the layout in supermarkets is not a customer-oriented practice. Store layout is intended to lead customers through the entire store to encourage additional buying. This is true even though shoppers who spend the most money in supermarkets rate timesaving higher than customers who spend less.

Even simple procedures can be frustrating. How many times have we stood in front of the credit card swipe machine in a retail store trying to figure out how to use it? Which way does the card go on this one—left, right, down, or up? Do we have to punch debit or credit, and where is it? Do we need to punch "yes" if the amount is correct? The machines are different from one retailer to the next. Salespeople sometimes seem to be impatient when we don't press the right button at the right time. Has a salesclerk ever said, "You have to press 'yes,' " or reached out and pressed a button for you?

Policies that seem perfectly reasonable from a company's viewpoint can often annoy and frustrate customers. It is reasonable to protect the seller's interests, but many policies seem to be based on a distrust of customers, such as return and adjustment procedures involving time-consuming processes and multiple forms and signatures. Catalog companies have learned that the ease and fairness of their return policies and procedures promote confidence and additional sales. More flexible return policies encourage customers to experiment with new and unfamiliar products. In truth, restrictive policies actually cost a company more time and money internally than they save. Such policies also open the door to competition. A return policy, such as the following: "You must have a receipt to return a product after thirty days. The product must be in its original packaging with all tags and labels intact. The product must be returned to the original store in which it was purchased. All return adjustments will be in the form of a store credit" is not exceptional service. On the other hand, "If you are not satisfied for any reason, ever, return the product and we will replace the product or refund your money" is exceptional customer service.

Another example of how a customer orientation could provide an exceptional value is in airline travel. Keep in mind that travel itself is stressful. We have to fight the traffic going to the airport and then we have to find a parking place. We give our luggage to a stranger. Then we stand in line to give a ticket to another stranger, who pays more attention to the computer than to us. Someone decides where we will sit. Next we are ordered to go to a gate, if we can find it. It's way down at the end of Concourse D. Meanwhile, we are electronically searched. The equipment beeps and everyone is looking at us. We empty our pockets. We arrive at the gate and sit and wait, trying to listen for the boarding call. We wait some more. We hope the flight isn't canceled. We think about safety. We stand in line to board and give our paper boarding pass to another stranger. When we get on the plane, the flight attendant orders us to put our seat in the upright position, tells us to use a restraining device, and informs us about safety procedures. We could be white-knuckle flyers to boot. Granted the procedures are necessary but don't we deserve some high touch somewhere along the way? This need is part of what has made Southwest Airlines successful. The company uses humor and fun for the personal aspect.[17]

Many online businesses provide no customer service telephone number, no telephone number at all, no e-mail address, and no street address on their website. Or if they do provide this information, they bury it so that it takes too long to find, or customers have to fill in personal information on a form to reach the company by e-mail. Companies say that it costs too much to staff telephones and respond to e-mails. Another example of poor service is one in which online customers are stuck on a screen and cannot find their way back to where they were. Programmers have not thought about how customers will use the system. Customer Experience Management (CEM) solutions seem to offer one answer to these website problems. CEM solutions include software that can monitor user transactions for playback and map navigation paths. Companies can also employ test users who report their actual experience online.[18]

A system may not be considered customer-oriented when companies increase productivity by using customer participation. For some customers, an everyday example is pumping our own gas. Consider the recent food safety issues with serve-yourself salad bars. Some companies' procedures seem intent on increasing customer responsibility and abdicating the company's obligation. Have you ever encountered a dry cleaner that asks you to sign a waiver absolving the company of responsibility when it dry-cleans a wool coat? Isn't dry cleaning the service it is offering?

Customers receive mixed and non-customer-oriented messages from companies. What does it say to customers when there are only two out of ten checkout lines open, several people are waiting in each one, and other employees in the store seem to be doing everything else but taking care of customers. How do customers feel when they are directed to move from workstation to workstation to be served? Do they feel processed? What do customers think when a company offers a new customer a free gift and the current loyal customers get nothing? Companies should eliminate or change any procedures that send underlying negative messages, no matter how insignificant those messages may seem.[19]

Companies should not overpromise and underdeliver. The integrated marketing communication of the company—the advertising, personal selling, sales promotion, and public relations—should reflect the strategy of the company. The systems of the company should carry out the strategy of the company and match the marketing communication. This confirms the notion that marketing, operations, and human resources should be integrated. If the marketing message is that the company will deliver fast, friendly service, then operations needs to make sure the service is fast and friendly. It is not necessarily an employee problem if the service is lacking. It may be a systems problem. If marketing overstates delivery when it's not possible for operations to deliver, there will also be a mismatch. Compare the frontline operations budget and employee training budget with the marketing communications budget, or compare the marketing communications budget with the "word-of-mouth budget." This may convince companies to integrate these functions.

Effective

Systems should be effective, "do the right things right." The customer experience must be delivered consistently. An effective system is Disneyland; the cleanliness and beauty of the grounds is part of Disney's service strategy, and operating systems are designed to accomplish this effectively and unobtrusively. An ineffective system is one in which the salesperson does not know where a product is in the store or cannot answer product questions. Home Depot employees are assigned aisles and learn product locations. They either know or learn how to use the products for which they are responsible. An ineffective system is apparent when customers call a company with a simple question and are transferred to several people and still do not get an answer. Clearly, the company never thought about the question.

An example of a customer-oriented system poorly executed is a discounter's one-time slogan: "If there are more than three people in a checkout line, we will open up another one." A system may exist, but the employees are not trained how it works or how to use it. A recent Harris study of 5797 online respondents in early 2001 showed that 35 percent of supermarket shoppers said that there were not enough checkouts open and there were not enough employees in specialty departments. This study measured both the frequency of problems and their importance to customers to produce an impact score. The higher the score, the more the company gained if it fixed the problem. Lack of checkout staff received a score of 17, twice the next highest score of 9 for being well stocked. Four of the top six reasons for dissatisfaction were due to inadequate staffing and inefficient or unfriendly service. About one-third of the shoppers said the frequent shopper program did not meet their needs. The program's score was zero.[20]

Systems should be planned and managed so they work. Sometimes poor-quality service is blamed on employees when in reality the problem lies with poorly designed systems. If our food at a restaurant does not arrive promptly, should we blame the server, the cook, or the system? Dissatisfaction with service is often blamed on the people delivering the service, but Leonard Berry asserts that the real problem is "complicated, illogical, redundant, and out-of-date procedures."[21] Historically, service systems have not been seen as something that needs to be designed and managed. Many service systems have just evolved. One attitude is "if it ain't broke, don't fix it." The company just has not figured out that the system was broken as far as customers were concerned.

Flexible

Systems should be flexible. Systems should be able to respond to change and exceptions. A service by its very nature varies from employee to employee, customer to customer, and time to time. The discounter who refused to credit a legitimate receipt-accompanied return because the customer had cut up the credit card is a case in point.

There is some current evidence that a few retailers are being less flexible rather than more flexible about returns. Return policies have become leaner and meaner in recent years. Reasons given for the change include tough competition, profit squeeze, and excess inventory. Retailers say they need to protect themselves from less than honest customers, like those who wear or use merchandise and then return it. However, inflexible return policies fail to separate the mostly "good guys" from the "bad." More retailers have shorter return periods, give store credit only, make no exceptions for no receipt, or have a "no returns" policy. For example, a heel broke the first time a customer wore a new pair of shoes. When she tried to return them, she was turned down by the New York store where she bought them. Even L.L. Bean has become more restrictive, asking customers to explain why they are dissatisfied to discourage customers who take advantage of their previous no-questions-asked policy. Lands' End is still sticking to its "Guaranteed period" policy and will take back anything anytime, even if it's worn or dirty.[22]

Systems should also be flexible enough to juggle demand and supply. Since services cannot be stored, the potential for demand to exceed supply at any given time is very real. Hotels cross-train housekeepers and desk clerks so they can switch jobs if demand for a function increases. Companies try to smooth demand by using reservations and differential pricing and by promoting off-peak times, such as early bird specials at restaurants.

Cost Effective

Systems must be cost effective. The added costs of a system cannot exceed the benefits, at least long term. A company that does not make a profit will not stay in business. One of the reasons systems have not been fixed is the emphasis on short-term profit over long-term quality. Consider a proposed standard to respond to and resolve 95 percent of requests for information while customers are on the phone, with no more than a 30-second hold. The standard is intended to provide the company with a competitive advantage and encourage customer loyalty. The standard would reduce costly callbacks and customer dissatisfaction. The current level is 60 percent. The company has to decide if it needs additional technology and training to meet the standard. Then the company must calculate whether the standard will pay for itself by reducing other costs and increasing loyalty and repurchase. Another way to measure costs versus benefits is to compare the costs of system reengineering with the profit lost by service failures. The value of lost customers can be calculated by their annual and lifetime value. This is explained in more detail in Chapter 3.[23]

Experience Discussion 2.2

Choose a system at your organization and determine whether it meets the four recommended characteristics.

Servicescapes

Servicescapes is a newly coined expression for the actual service sites, whether physical or cyberspace. It relates to the tangible side of a service—the facilities and furnishings. It consists of the store or office and everything that goes into it. It includes the cognitive, material, cultural, and experiential dynamics of place. Servicescapes are about returning a sense of place to the marketing of services and selling of goods. The image and trade dress of retail stores is not a new concept. An example is themed consumer space in restaurants and malls. Servicescape theory encompasses the use of architecture, decor, materials, layout, signage, lighting, atmospherics such as music and aromas, and dressing rooms, to represent a store image and provide an overall customer experience. As Berry suggests, respect for customers means clean, neat, organized physical spaces that value customers' time. A servicescape must also take into consideration the physical and informational privacy needs of customers. Another question being explored is the role of the store environment as a source of information for consumer decision making. How do stores and businesses assist in information search? What features of a store site assist customers in their evaluation and choice of alternatives. Another area of exploration is customer-oriented websites and how they provide information and customer experiences.[24]

SYSTEMS IMPROVEMENT

One way to improve systems is to blueprint company systems, listing all activities, processes, sequences, and material and people resources. A *blueprint* is a visual representation of the sequence of activities required for service delivery that shows the front-stage elements, which are visible or apparent to customers, and the backstage elements and the links between them.[25] Figure 2.3 illustrates a basic front-stage blueprint of a credit card customer at a supermarket. A blueprint can also be helpful as a map for a customer scenario as discussed previously in the customer experience section of the chapter. Frontline employee and customer input is crucial. Redesign systems to be more customer-oriented and effective. This process will help

FIGURE 2.3   Front-Stage Blueprint—Overview of Process of Shopping at a Discount Store

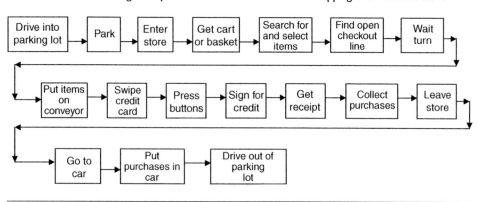

the company make the systems more responsive and reliable for customers, isolate places where service is weak or prone to failure, and make decisions about staff needs, allocation, and development clearer. It will also show where automation might save money, it will point up where personalized human contact is necessary, and it will separate activities that require participation from customers from those that do not. The company can play "what-if" games to enhance the total customer experience.

One company found numerous complications, errors, and bottlenecks when it mapped its systems. Some customers had several files due merely to misspellings or variations of their name. The company eliminated the duplicates. Problem orders were put aside to process after the easy orders. Since the original department did not correct errors, it never knew why the errors were happening. The company began focusing on the problem orders to increase awareness of mistakes. Errors were returned to the employees who made them, and the employees began being more careful with their work. Once the employees accomplished this, they flowcharted their processes. They determined that they were duplicating efforts, performing unnecessary work, and increasing errors, and they discovered that many steps could be combined or eliminated. The result of their analysis and their changes was that they increased productivity, saving 20 hours of work a week, and improved service to customers.[26]

TERMS

strategy
management myopia
total customer experience
customer scenario
service fairness
systems

processes
procedures
policies
servicescapes
blueprint

DISCUSSION QUESTIONS

1. What are the characteristics of a customer-oriented strategy?
2. What are five tactics for retailers for providing a total customer experience?
3. Find and describe a company that understands the total customer experience.
4. Describe an unfair customer service experience. Describe a fair customer service experience.
5. Define systems.
6. What are the four characteristics that systems should have to provide exceptional customer service? Give a concrete example of each one.
7. How does the concept of a servicescape relate to customer service?
8. How can a company make sure its systems provide exceptional customer experiences?

EXERCISE—BLUEPRINTING AND ANALYZING A SYSTEM

Pick a reasonably simple system that is not working as well as it should. Look at it from the point of view of customer orientation, effectiveness, flexibility, and cost-effectiveness.

1. Blueprint the system to figure out all the processes and steps involved. Analyze it and answer the following:
   a. Is it customer-oriented?
   b. Is it effective?
   c. Is it flexible?
   d. Is it cost effective?
   e. Was it planned?
   f. Is it managed?
   g. Are there customer complaints?
   h. Do you think customers quit purchasing from your company because of it?
2. State the major problem with the system.
3. Develop several alternatives to solve the problem.
4. Analyze the solutions in terms of advantages and disadvantages.
5. Choose one of the solutions and justify why you chose it.
6. Develop an implementation plan.

NOTES

1. Karl Albrecht and Ron Zemke, *Service America! Doing Business in the New Economy* (Homewood, IL: Dow Jones-Irwin, 1985), 64.
2. Albrecht and Zemke, *Service America!*
3. Lewis P. Carbone, "Total Customer Experience Drives Value," *Management Review* 87, no. 7 (July–August 1998): 62.
4. David Freemantle, "Do Your Customers Really Like You?" *Customer Service Management,* March/April 1999, 57–60.
5. Ian C. MacMillan and Rita Gunther McGrath, "Discovering New Points of Differentiation," *Harvard Business Review* 75, no. 4 (July–August 1997): 133–142.
6. Patricia B. Seybold, "Get Inside the Lives of Your Customers," *Harvard Business Review* 79, no. 5 (May 2001): 81–89.
7. Christopher Price, "Obsessed with Customer Service and Experience: Case Study: Amazon," *The Financial Times,* February 2, 2000, 15.
8. Leonard L. Berry, "The Old Pillars of New Retailing," *Harvard Business Review* 79, no. 4 (April 2001): 131–137.
9. Human Resources Net, December 11, 1997, available from http://www.HRNET @cornell.edu [no longer exists].
10. Jeffrey Gitomer, "Put Out the Fire and Protect the Customer," *Philadelphia Business Journal* 20, no. 7 (March 30, 2001): 20.
11. Charles A. Jaffe, "Guaranteed Results," *Nation's Business,* February 1990, 62–65.
12. Ron Zemke, "Preventative Recovery," *Customer Service Management,* November/December 1999, 40–41.

13. Kathleen Seiders and Leonard L. Berry, "Service Fairness: What It Is and Why It Matters," *The Academy of Management Executive* 12, no. 2 (May 1998): 8–21.

14. Ronald S. Swift, *Accelerating Customer Relationships. Using CRM and Relationship Technologies* (Upper Saddle River, NJ: Prentice Hall PTR, 2000), 8.

15. Ralph Harrison, "The Unprofitable Customer Argument," originally published on TheBankingChannel.com, June 3–10, 2001, available from http://www.crm-forum.com/library/art/art-105/art-105.html, accessed July 3, 2001.

16. Jay Heizer and Barry Render, *Principles of Operations Management,* 3d ed. (Upper Saddle River, NJ: Prentice Hall, 1999), 4.

17. Jeffrey Gitomer, *Customer Satisfaction Is Worthless, Customer Loyalty Is Priceless: How to Make Customers Love You, Keep Them Coming Back and Tell Everyone They Know* (Marietta, GA: Bard Press, 1998).

18. Michele Pepe, "It's All about the Customer—An Offshoot of CRM, Customer Experience Management Solutions Keep Customers Happy—and Coming Back," *Computer Reseller News,* March 12, 2001, 111.

19. Sandra Moore, "Customers Must Trust CS Message," *Marketing News,* May 7, 2001, 14.

20. "Long Grocery Lines Turn Off 35% of Shoppers," *PR Newswire,* April 25, 2001.

21. Leonard L. Berry, "Improving America's Service," *Marketing Management* 1, no. 3 (1992): 31.

22. Monique P. Yazigi, "You Buy It, You Keep It, More Stores Are Saying," *The New York Times,* May 30, 1999, Sec. 9, 1.

23. Berry, "Improving America's Service," 29; and Albrecht and Zemke, *Service America!*

24. John F. Sherry, Jr., ed., *ServiceScapes: The Concept of Place in Contemporary Marketing* (Chicago: American Marketing Association, 1998).

25. Christopher Lovelock and Lauren Wright, *Principles of Service Marketing and Management,* 2d ed. (Upper Saddle River, NJ: Prentice Hall, 2002), 13.

26. Bureau of Business Practice, Inc., *Excellence Achieved. Customer Service Blueprints for Action from 50 Leading Companies* (Waterford, CT: Bureau of Business Practice, Inc., 1990), 25–27.

CUSTOMERS

CHAPTER

3

OBJECTIVES

1. Define and categorize external and internal customers.
2. Define customer loyalty.
3. Discuss customer needs and expectations.
4. Describe customer expectations and loyalty research.
5. Explain the benefits of exceptional customer service.
6. Outline the costs of exceptional customer service.

EXTERNAL AND INTERNAL CUSTOMERS

Customers are the focus of company strategy, systems, and people. In order to understand customers, we need to identify them and determine how to keep them loyal. This chapter focuses on defining and describing customers, analyzing customer loyalty, determining customer needs and expectations, and assessing the benefits and costs of exceptional customer service.

Definition of Customers

Customers include *external customers,* to whom companies sell products and services, and internal customers, employees of the company. Companies sell to consumers, businesses, or both. Thus, there are two types of external customers, *consumers* or the ultimate end users, who are individuals and households, and business-to-business (B2B) customers (see Figure 3.1).

Consumers

The end users are the decision makers for company-to-consumer transactions. In a household, there may be more than one decision maker and one or more influencers.

FIGURE 3.1   Customers

External Customers

Consumers
Ultimate end users
Individuals
Households

Business-to-Business Customers
Producers—Manufacturers, service businesses
Resellers—Wholesalers, retailers
Governments—Federal, state, local
Institutions—Schools, hospitals, nonprofits

Buying center
Decision maker
Influencer
User
Purchaser
Gatekeeper

Types of Customers
Current—Longtime, recent, new, frequent, occasional
Defectors –
Intentionally pushed away
Bought away
Moved away
Pulled away
Unintentionally pushed away
Potential – new to market, competitors' customers

Internal Customers
Frontline employees
Department/support employees
Management

For example, grocery shoppers will be influenced by their children, spouse, or other household members. Each spouse may make decisions for certain products, or the spouses may make the decisions jointly.

Customers can be current, former, or potential. Current customers can be longtime customers or new customers, and each type will have different perceptions of the company and different expectations. Longtime customers may be more forgiving of a customer service mistake because they know the problem is not typical. On the other hand, they may be more likely to complain. If a customer service provider is busy and not helpful to a new customer, that customer may well not return. Current customers might also be frequent or occasional customers, depending on the product and the customers' needs. Longtime and frequent loyal customers are likely to be more profitable.

A company has former customers—those who have defected to a competitor, no longer buy the product due to dissatisfaction, or no longer need the product or service. For example, a supermarket will have former customers who are now shopping at a competitor's store. A dry cleaner will have former customers who have been unhappy with its service and now use a do-it-yourself product or try to avoid purchasing clothing that needs to be dry-cleaned. A company should also view its competitors' customers as potential customers. Companies will also have other potential customers, those who eventually may have need for the company's products, such as a household with a new baby.

Most companies divide their customers into market segments. A market segment is a group of people with specific characteristics to whom a company aims a specific marketing mix. Market segmentation variables include demographic (age, income), geographic (region of United States, country), psychographic (lifestyle, attitudes), and benefit (for example, nutrition, taste, price, low-calorie benefits in snack food) segmentation. Each segment may have different expectations for customer service. For example, research shows that there are substantial differences in expectations between men and women, between younger and older customers, and among people with different ethnic backgrounds.[1]

Business-to-Business Customers

The *business-to-business customer* market includes four categories of customers: producers (manufacturers and service providers), resellers (retailers, wholesalers), governments (federal, state, local), and institutions (for example, hospitals, schools, churches). One example of a business-to-business customer relationship would be an ALCOA sheet aluminum manufacturing factory and a soft drink can manufacturer; another would be Hewlett-Packard and a college. Business customers buy products to produce products for consumers for personal consumption. The products include major equipment (for example, expensive machines, office buildings, factories), accessory equipment (power tools, office equipment), raw materials (wheat, lumber), component parts (automobile tires, air bags), processed materials (chemicals, plastics), supplies (maintenance, repair, operating), and business services (janitorial, legal). These products and services help produce the product, become part of the product, or help run the business.[2]

Identifying business-to-business customers is more complex than identifying consumers because usually there is more than one person in an organization who becomes involved in purchasing decisions. The group of people is often called the *buying center*. The buying center can include the purchasing agent or department, product users, gatekeepers (who regulate the flow of information), influencers, and deciders. In smaller companies, the customer could be just one person with all the roles, such as an office manager. In other companies, there may be as many as five or more customers. Sometimes, the company's customer list is based on the salespeople's contact person, who may well be the purchasing agent, but not the user or decider. Companies need to know about the satisfaction and loyalty levels of all customers in the company and their relative influence on the purchasing decision. They need to know if the user is satisfied with the product and customer service. They need to know if the purchasing agent, gatekeeper, and decider are satisfied with their contact with the company.

Business-to-business marketing is very different from consumer marketing because more people and procedures are involved in the process, the buying process is more organized, and relationships are longer term. In addition, there are more joint efforts and alliances between buyers and sellers, and the products and services are more technically complex and custom-designed.

In many cases, business-to-business companies need to know about the customers of their customers in order to add value and provide a complete customer experience. For instance, a manufacturer that sells ceramic tile to retailers needs to know the needs and expectations of the ultimate user, the consumer. Manufacturers sell to retailers or sell to wholesalers who sell to retailers, and so the manufacturers need information about the entire supply chain.

Internal Customers

Internal customers include every employee in the company. *Frontline employees* are defined as the individuals who have contact with customers and are directly providing service to customers. Other employees in the firm support their efforts. The customer relationship goes both ways, from frontline employees to support or staff and from staff to frontline employees. For example, a service representative in a customer contact center is a customer of the information technology department if the representative needs assistance with software or equipment. A distribution center's employees are customers of the retail store employees when they need information about inventory. Exceptional customer service cannot be delivered to external customers unless all employees provide support to each other. External customers will be dissatisfied if computer systems are down or inventory is short.

Experience Discussion 3.1

1. Describe your organization's external customers.
2. Who are your primary internal customers?
3. Whose internal customer are you?

CUSTOMER LOYALTY

In today's business environment, companies need to measure and analyze customer expectations, satisfaction, and loyalty. The information can be used to develop customer experiences, understand the company's competition, identify and prioritize opportunities for system and product improvements, determine employee training needs, and provide a way to recognize and reward individual employees and teams.

Identifying Loyal Customers

There is a strong correlation between high customer loyalty and retention rates and sustainable high profits and long-term profitability.[3] Research has found that customer satisfaction can lead to customer loyalty. However, a satisfied customer is not necessarily a loyal customer. Satisfaction is a necessary condition but not a sufficient one. Xerox and American Express have found that only customers who score at the highest levels of satisfaction are loyal purchasers and providers of positive word of mouth.[4] We also know that dissatisfaction drives the lack of loyalty more than satisfaction leads to loyalty. That suggests that problem resolution and recovery are an important aspect of customer service.[5]

Automobile retail sales are an example of high satisfaction rates but low customer loyalty. Automobile buyer satisfaction rates are in the 90 percent range. The repurchase rate is much lower, below 50 percent, which suggests that high satisfaction does not necessarily lead to high loyalty and repurchase. It should be noted that one reason satisfaction rates are so high is that dealerships sometimes systematically encourage high satisfaction rates on new-purchase surveys.[6] Research has also found that 60 to 80 percent of customers who say they are satisfied and very satisfied still defect. Believing that this indicates that satisfaction is not being measured accurately, many companies attempt to improve their satisfaction measurement.

According to experts, a better idea is to measure *customer loyalty*. There is controversy in the marketing field about what customer loyalty is. Three aspects have been used to measure loyalty: overall satisfaction, intent to recommend, and intent to repurchase. What companies really need to measure is how many customers are still purchasing from the company and how many have defected. Companies need to know:

* What percentage of customers they keep each year
* What the customers' primary expectations are
* What percentage of customers they lose each year
* The top three reasons their customers leave[7]

Lexus measures repurchase loyalty on auto purchases and follow-up service. The company tracks which customers come back and which do not. Then it uses satisfaction research to understand customer decisions.[8]

The Customer Loyalty Institute defines customer loyalty as repeat purchases, increased purchases across the product line, referral of others, and immunity from the pull of competition. The institute says, "Meet customer expectations and you may create an attitude—customer satisfaction. Exceed expectations where it counts most to the customer and you may create a behavior—customer loyalty."[9]

Gitomer says satisfied customers may tell someone about you if asked, may refer others if asked, and may buy if convenient. Very satisfied customers tell a few people about you, refer a few people, and sometimes return. Loyal customers are those who tell everyone about you, refer everyone proactively, and always return to buy.[10]

Customer loyalty is a product of both customer attitudes and behavior. The bottom line is how many customers repurchase how often. Customers are behaviorally loyal for many reasons beyond their attitudes about a company. They are loyal due to convenience, accessibility, lack of any other choices, price, high search and evaluation costs, and high switching barriers, such as a long standing relationship with a salesperson or the cost and hassle of changing banks. Customers' attitudes can be loyal, but their purchase behavior may reflect one of the other factors.[11] Brandt describes the attitudes of loyal customers as:

1. An intention to buy again or buy additional products from the same company
2. A willingness to recommend the company
3. A strong preference for or a commitment to a brand or company
4. Little or no motivation to seek alternative brands or companies
5. Disinterest in or general resistance to enticements from competitors

He describes the behavior of loyal customers as:

1. Actual repeat purchases
2. Purchase of more and/or different products and services from the same company
3. Positive word-of-mouth communication and other referral behavior[12]

Experience Discussion 3.2

1. What companies are you loyal to? Why?
2. What companies are you satisfied with but not necessarily loyal to? Why?

CUSTOMER NEEDS AND EXPECTATIONS

Customer Perspective

Companies need to determine what their customers need and expect. The best way to find out is to ask customers. Many factors affect customer satisfaction and loyalty. Companies can determine what customers expect and whether the company is exceeding, meeting, or not meeting expectations over time. While product quality is an important research topic, this section focuses primarily on service quality and characteristics related to customer service.

Customers want to be valued by the companies with which they do business. Customers respond more strongly to the way they are treated than anything else. A study sponsored by the American Society for Quality Control found that less than 10 percent defected for reasons unrelated to the business, such as moving or no longer needing the product; less than 10 percent preferred a competitor's product; and about 15 percent left because they were dissatisfied with the product. More than 65 percent defected because of poor customer service.[13]

A retailing research study found that positive personalization—positive social interaction between service providers and their customers—positively influenced customers' evaluation of overall service quality and repurchase. Personalization is characterized as warm and personal at the positive end of the spectrum and cold and impersonal at the negative end. Employees who engage in friendly conversation with customers, get to know customers, show warmth toward customers, and are courteous can enhance customers' shopping and service experience.[14] Customer service providers often say that it takes too much time to develop relationships. However, research has found that 98 percent of customer interactions were actually faster and more efficient if the provider took the time to establish a relationship and rapport with a customer.[15]

A team of researchers found five primary factors that contribute to positive attitudes toward service quality. They are reliability, assurance, responsiveness, empathy, and tangibles. Reliability is the ability to perform the promised service dependably and accurately. Assurance is the knowledge and courtesy of employees and their ability to inspire trust and confidence. Responsiveness is willingness to help customers and provide prompt service. Empathy is caring, individualized attention that the firm provides its customers. Tangibles are the appearance of physical facilities, equipment, personnel, and communication materials.[16] A recent study of business-to-business marketing found that reliability and responsiveness were important evaluation criteria. Businesses want companies to perform as promised and solve problems promptly. Personnel competence was also an important consideration.[17]

Jeffrey Gitomer in *Customer Satisfaction Is Worthless* describes what customers want in everyday language:

- *Value*—To customers, this is offering a fair price and providing support throughout product ownership.
- *Fairness*—This is treating customers fairly during transactions and in the event of a problem. Recall the concept of fairness as it was addressed in Chapter 2.
- *Control*—Companies should put customers' needs first. An example is a physician's office that calls to tell patients that the doctor is running about an hour behind due to an emergency. Patients can adjust their schedules so they do not have to wait as long at the doctor's office.
- *Communication and information*—This means letting customers know what they need to know when they need to know it. These days, more than ever, customers need information and education about products, policies, and procedures. Many products have become extremely complicated, and procedures and policies vary widely.
- *Options and alternatives*—For example, customers expect if one company can offer several alternative ways to contact it, all companies should be able to do that.
- *Attitude*—Customers want positive, eager, and willing employees prepared to meet customer needs.[18]

Sometimes companies believe that they know what customers want. Research has found that this is not always true. Take, for example, a focus group for an automobile dealer. The moderator's discussion guide had been carefully worked out in advance addressing numerous customer issues concerning car buying and service. The first topic that was mentioned by the eight focus group participants was nowhere on the discussion guide. What do you think it was? It was the way salespeople and service people treated women. Not only was it the first topic of conversation from the women, but the men also chimed in, giving examples of things that had happened to their wives, mothers, and daughters. After the focus group, the sales manager was in denial. The owner of the dealership said that he was aware of the problem and that he had hired a female salesperson once but "it didn't work out," as if that were the only solution. This is also an example of company executives who think customer expectations are unreasonable, unworkable, or too costly. Do physicians understand that we don't want to wait an hour past our appointment time? Do companies understand our frustration when we are placed on hold forever?

Skill Development 3.1

Make a list of customer service characteristics that you would incorporate into a customer survey, mystery shopping, or comment card.

Relative Importance of Expectations

Companies need to find out what is most important to customers. Companies will find that everything is important to customers unless they examine relative importance. In other words, they need to know, out of ten factors, which one is most important, second most important, etc., all the way down to the least important. Companies also need to make sure the variables considered important actually have an impact on the customers' behavior by measuring how they affect loyalty—for example, repeat purchases.

A problem may not happen very often but still be a problem that will cause customers to defect, such as a lost hotel registration. On the other hand, it may happen often but not be as important to customers, such as slow room service.[19]

Sometimes what the company considers important may not be what is most important to customers. For instance, a service company faced the need to cut costs due to economic conditions. The company had already made cuts, but now it needed to cut staff by a substantial amount. Upon asking its customers, the firm was surprised to discover that customers preferred to deal with the company by telephone, rather than in person. The company was able to reduce personnel in branch offices with no loss in customer satisfaction.[20]

An excellent way to examine performance compared with importance is to plot service quality characteristics on a chart such as Figure 3.2. The matrix provides priorities for improvement. For example, Peterson's Lumber has measured the importance and performance of its lumber and supplies delivery service. If performance is high and importance to customers is high, the characteristic, on-time delivery, is a strength that a company can use as a competitive advantage. If performance is low and importance is high, the company has a weakness, in this case, the perceived helpfulness of salespeople, that should be improved. If performance is high and importance is low, the characteristic, product quality, is "nice to have" but is not seen as different from that of competitors so it's not as high in importance. It will not keep or create customers. However, if product quality decreases, it could contribute to customer loss. If performance is low on a characteristic that is of low importance to customers, the characteristic, courtesy of delivery people, is not a priority for the company. Apparently, courtesy is not a major issue for the builders and construction workers receiving the supplies. However, the company should continue

FIGURE 3.2   Service Performance and Importance for Peterson's Lumber

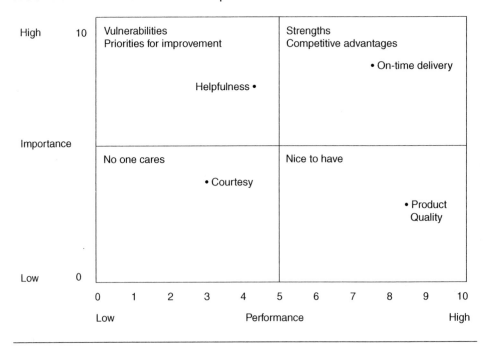

measuring all characteristics because they may become more or less important to customers over time and because performance could improve or deteriorate.

Competition Perspective

A company should compare its satisfaction and loyalty levels with those of the competition. One way to measure competition is to do blind surveys in which the respondents do not know the company conducting the survey. The performance-importance matrix can also be used to compare performance relative to competition. A company can conduct a blind survey and plot other companies' performance scores along with its own scores. For example, as Figure 3.3 shows, the competitor has a higher score on salespeople helpfulness, which means that it definitely should be a priority for improvement. On-time delivery is still a strength for Peterson's Lumber.

Benchmarking is another way to compare a company's systems with the best. Information is gathered from the firm that is best in a particular function, such as L.L. Bean in customer service or Federal Express in timely delivery. Instead of having an arbitrary goal to be 10 percent better internally, the goal becomes to be as good as the best and get ahead of competitors.

Employee Perspective

In addition to directly asking customers about satisfaction, companies should ask their frontline employees—all employees who have direct contact with customers—about customer satisfaction. Train employees to pay attention and to ask customers

FIGURE 3.3   Competitor Comparison for Performance and Importance

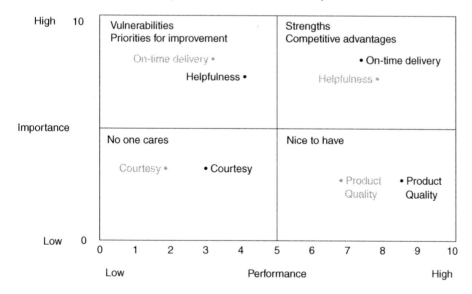

Black Bold – Peterson's Lumber
Gray – Competition

for their opinions. Employees see what causes customer dissatisfaction. They know when customers are dissatisfied with a new policy. They hear about service failures directly from customers. A study of 14 companies representing a range of industries found that employees were good estimators of overall customer satisfaction.[21]

Employees have ideas about the real causes of problems. One study of the hospitality industry found that employees attributed the cause of dissatisfaction to system failures and company rules rather than to themselves. They believed that they could not recover from a service failure or accommodate customer needs due to poorly designed systems or procedures, lack of system knowledge and its constraints, bureaucratic procedures, lack of authority to take action, and inability to provide a logical explanation to customers.[22]

In addition to traditional surveys, two good general questions to ask employees are what is the biggest problem they face and if they could make one decision to improve customer service quality, what would it be? Another creative way to approach the question is to suggest to employees that they have a magic wand and can make one or two improvements.[23]

CUSTOMER EXPECTATIONS AND LOYALTY RESEARCH

Research Methods

There are many research methods for gathering customer input. They include focus groups and telephone, mail, and Internet surveys. Many companies use comment cards distributed in stores to learn about customer needs, expectations, satisfaction, and loyalty. Another method that has been available for many years and is currently popular is mystery shopping. This involves researchers posing as customers who evaluate customer service by observing in stores or businesses. The project at the end of this chapter will give students experience in this method. Other methods are customer advisory panels and complaint analysis.

Marketing needs to be concerned with every customer interaction with the company. Marketing needs to listen to the customer. Think about the comment card, which is often small, boring, and hidden. Sometimes the cards are so little used and seemingly unimportant, they become soiled, coffee-stained, or lost. Compare those with the company's latest television commercial or magazine advertisement. It makes one wonder how much the company really values customers' opinions. Customer feedback should be as carefully designed as a television commercial or a point-of-purchase display.[24]

Actionability of Research

The data and information gathered from customers and employees should be actionable. *Actionability* means being able to directly use the results of research to develop and compare with standards. When research is designed, ask questions about factors that can be measured and changed. "Friendly" cannot be measured. Ask customers who object to long holds, how long is too long. The following are some examples of standardized procedures. Answer the phone within three rings. Return all calls and e-mails within 24 hours. Follow the proper telephone greeting. Put customers on hold correctly. Companies may find that they have no performance standard to measure. They may find that their standard does not match customer expectations. They may discover that employees are not meeting the standard. Standards make everyone aware of a goal and can be used to measure how each employee and the company are doing.

For example, consider the standard to resolve 95 percent of complaints on the first call. First, a company needs to know if the standard meets or exceeds customer expectations. If it does, does that lead to customer loyalty? If it does, then the company needs to know how often the standard is met. This will involve defining a complaint and finding a way to track complaint calls. Next, if the standard is not being met, find out why. Determine whether it is an operations or service representative problem. Find out whether meeting the standard is possible and what it will cost to meet the standard.

Research Process

Companies should measure expectations and performance of service quality characteristics and customer satisfaction and loyalty continuously. A one-time "snapshot" view or even annual surveys do not provide sufficient information. Staying up to date on customer expectations and determining priorities require continuous learning. Customers have changing needs. Their expectations are progressive, changing and increasing over time. A monthly measurement of a sample of customers is ideal. Quarterly or semiannually is a minimum. Companies need to use ongoing research processes to stay in touch and provide trend data to know whether they are improving. Then companies should continuously monitor measurement systems and evaluate them to make sure they are still useful.

Implementation of Research Findings

The results of customer and employee feedback should be used to improve operations and customer service. There are never enough funds and time to solve all problems. That is why companies should determine what is most important to customers so they can establish priorities. They can redesign systems. If the results of company surveys require changes in operations, companies can blueprint the steps of the system, determine where they can use a value-added strategy, and incorporate that into their standards. For example, when checking in a hotel guest, a value-added standard would be to use the guest's name as soon as the employee knows it. The company can set customer service standards for providers. Tie new priorities and standards to performance reviews and recognition and reward systems. In addition, authors Chip Bell and Ron Zemke stress in *Service Wisdom* that companies should use the feedback to emphasize strengths and replicate beneficial practices rather than to highlight only problems and mistakes.[25] A company should post customer feedback where employees will see it. Post positive results and celebrate them.

BENEFITS OF EXCEPTIONAL CUSTOMER SERVICE

One of the primary *benefits of providing exceptional customer service* is *customer retention*—keeping customers. This costs less than getting new customers, and marketing to loyal customers costs less. A second benefit is favorable word-of-mouth information and referrals, bringing in new customers. A third benefit is increasing loyalty through effective complaint resolution. Research shows that companies that have the highest customer service quality ratings achieved more than twice the market share, return on investment, and return on sales as companies that had inferior service.

Customer Retention

Traditionally marketing has focused on acquisition marketing. The strategy of marketing's 4Ps—product, price, place, and promotion—has been to acquire new customers through product design, price enticements, distribution changes, and creative promotion. With too many sellers selling me-too products, market share growth must come from stealing customers from competitors. While the company is acquiring customers, dissatisfied customers are defecting, going elsewhere, and generating negative word of mouth. The loss of customers results in lost revenue and more marketing dollars to replace the lost customers. Most companies really do not know how many customers they lose every year or what it costs them. There is evidence that companies lose 10 to 30 percent of their customers every year.[26]

Recently marketing has refocused toward what is known as relationship or *retention marketing*—keeping customers. It costs less to keep current customers than it does to get new customers. The estimate that is usually used is five times as much. There are too many variables to accurately measure this. Measuring and comparing marketing dollars and dollars spent on keeping customers is difficult at best. It varies widely by industry and company. However, most experts say that however much more it costs, it does cost more to get a customer than to keep a customer.

A 1997 study of 3200 shoppers found that one in ten customers will switch retailers after just one bad experience, such as refusal to accept a return or a scanner price error.[27] A nationwide survey of 1000 customers in 2001 found that 22 percent would walk out of a store without making a purchase if they experience bad customer service. About 20 percent would stop shopping at the store. One-quarter said that they had told friends and urged them not to shop there.[28]

A broad study of industries found that a 5-percentage-point shift in customer retention resulted in 25 to 100 percent profit shifts. In other words, if retention goes up 5 percent, profit increases from 25 to 100 percent. Sales revenues and market share grow due to repeat sales and referrals. Then costs decrease because the expense of replacing customers declines. Employee turnover decreases due to higher job satisfaction, which in turn increases customer retention through better customer service. Employee productivity also improves, and human resource costs decrease. So costs go down, revenues go up, and profits increase. The profits in turn allow increases in employee compensation. Profits are also used to increase offerings and services to increase customer value. Customer and employee retention go up again, continuing the cycle.[29]

The cycle can go the other way. Loss of customers decreases sales and increases costs. Employees are laid off and employee satisfaction decreases, which in turn lowers customer satisfaction. Prices may be lowered to gain new customers; however the new customers may be price shoppers, not likely to ever be loyal. Customer retention decreases even more, and marketing costs must go up to acquire new customers.

Sometimes companies are aware they have lost a customer; often, though, this is not the case. The customers just disappear. Some companies actually eliminate customers from their database and then have no way to contact them. Some catalog companies do this if a customer has not ordered for a while. Perhaps the customer decided that the prices were getting too high, the delivery costs had increased too much, or the product quality had deteriorated. Perhaps the customer defected to a competitor but finds it is no better. A company needs to know this. How many times could companies get a customer back if they fixed or changed one of these things? Defection is a sign that something is wrong. Find out what needs to be fixed. One of the best ways to determine what causes the churn, customer turnover, is to ask defecting customers why they are leaving. One company found that about half of them took the time to tell them.[30]

Companies need to segment customers based on their reason for *defection*. Five distinct defector categories have been identified (see Figure 3.1).

* *Intentionally pushed away*—A company may intentionally encourage customers to leave if they are problem customers. Problem customers use excessive resources and hurt employee morale. Southwest Airlines CEO Herb Kelleher says that they write to problem customers and say, "Fly somebody else. Don't abuse our people." Companies may also lower service to problem customers to limit the costs of serving them and to encourage unprofitable customers to defect. This presumes that the cost of making the customer profitable is too high.

* *Bought away*—If price is the only issue, some customers are bought away. They are prone to switching back and forth, and so offering lower prices is not a long-term solution to loyal customers.

* *Moved away*—Some customers move away, literally, or they no longer need the service, such as when children no longer need day care or when a company goes out of business. Some loss of customers is unavoidable. Many experts claim that "uncontrollable losses," such as customers moving away or changing buying needs, amounts to less than one-third of all customer losses. The other two-thirds involve the quality of the service.

* *Pulled away*—Customers are pulled away by a better value from a competitor. This can occur even if the price is higher or the product is less convenient if customers think the value is higher.

* *Unintentionally pushed away*—Customers who are unintentionally pushed away are those that are dissatisfied with the product quality, delivery, or service. Brand loyalty research has shown that loyalty is fleeting. Companies may lose customers if they improperly handle their complaints. A single occurrence can cause complainers to defect. Customers may not like changes the company has made and defect. Another reason customers defect is that they feel like they are being taken for granted, such as when they go into a retail store and are ignored.

Which of these customers are worth trying to get back? The ones who are unintentionally pushed away and the ones who have been pulled away by a better value.[31] Research shows that customers will pay more for value and satisfaction. A recent survey showed that customers would spend up to 10 percent more for the same product with better service.[32]

Studies have found that at least one-quarter of problems are caused by customers themselves. For instance, a service failure is caused by customers not paying attention to company policies. A product "fails" because customers did not read installation directions. However, what if a company denies any responsibility for customer confusion, saying essentially, "Why don't those stupid customers read the directions?" Whose responsibility is it when the customer cannot find the "any" key on the computer keyboard? If customers call to ask "dumb" questions and either have to wait on hold forever or are intimidated or belittled by technical support, they may defect. To them, lack of good information and assistance is product and service failure.[33]

One of the biggest losses to a company from inadequate customer service is the loss of revenue. The loss of 1 customer a day amounts to 365 customers a year. If each customer spends $5 a day at a company, or $1825 per year, that costs the company $666,125 a year, plus the cost of replacing the customers plus the cost of negative word-of-mouth information. According to Blanding, a chain of supermarkets with 70 stores estimates that it loses on average 2 customers a week at each location, which is 140 customers per week, or 7280 customers each year. If the individual customers spend on average $2600 per year, in a year the company has lost almost $19 million.[34]

Another consideration is the lifetime value of customers. Consider individual, family, and household purchases of a product and complementary products over a lifetime, whether the company sells cars, food, dental services, or custom software. A Cadillac dealer calculated that a lifetime customer would spend $332,000 at one of his ten dealerships.

Word-of-Mouth Information

Research has repeatedly shown that *word-of-mouth information* is an important factor in consumers' purchasing decisions. Dissatisfied customers tell about twice as many people as satisfied customers. Technical Research Assistance Programs (TARP) reported that dissatisfied complainers told a median of 9 to 10 people about their experience versus satisfied complainers who told 4 to 5 people. A General Electric study found that 61 percent said the opinions of friends were useful, whereas only 29 percent said advertising was helpful. A Louis Harris study showed that 72 percent used word of mouth most often, whereas only 33 percent used advertising most often. In a Whirlpool study, 38 percent relied on friends and relatives and only 6 percent on advertising.

In his classic summary of the impact of word of mouth, Arndt reported that mass media dominate in the product awareness stage, but informal sources—that is, word of mouth—are of major importance in the product evaluation stage. He also found that negative word of mouth had a stronger effect on purchasing decisions than did positive word of mouth. Customers are more likely to use word-of-mouth information for riskier products, higher-priced products, and a costly problem resolution.[35]

Average consumers receive a minimum of 200 marketing communications a day or 1400 per week. They act on only about one of the 1400. In contrast, consumers act on approximately one out of three word of mouth messages.[36]

The Internet has given unhappy customers a way to spread their word-of-mouth gripes even further. There are numerous websites where customers can complain about their latest awful experience. Intel, Nike, Mrs. Fields Cookies, and Hilfiger have all been blasted. Some companies are monitoring these sites to use the complaint feedback to improve. Others are trying to stop the sites by accusing sites of trademark infringement.[37]

Complaint Resolution and Loyalty

Most research has found that *complaint resolution* yields customer loyalty. A classic study conducted by TARP for the U.S. Office of Consumer Affairs found a direct relationship between customers who complain and their intent to repurchase. For products costing $1 to $5, 70 percent would buy again if the company resolved their complaint. For customers whose complaint was resolved on the spot, 95 percent would buy again. Even among those whose complaints were not satisfactorily re-

FIGURE 3.4   Percent of Dissatisfied Customers Who Will Repurchase

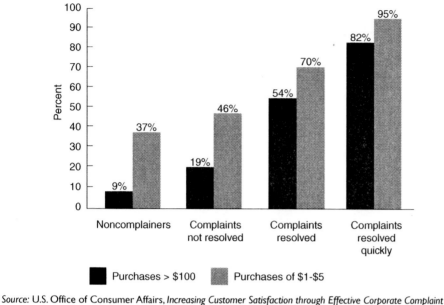

Source: U.S. Office of Consumer Affairs, *Increasing Customer Satisfaction through Effective Corporate Complaint Handling,* 1986, 5.

solved, 46 percent would buy again. Only 37 percent who did not complain would buy again. For products over $100, 54 percent would buy again if the company re-solved their complaint, and 82 percent would buy again if it is resolved quickly. Only 9 percent of noncomplainers would buy again (see Figure 3.4).

TARP found similar results in studies of large ticket durable goods, automotive services, and financial services. This positive relationship may not occur if the company handles the complaints poorly by taking too long to act or creating unrealisti-cally high customer expectations about the potential resolution.[38] Research has also found that the most negative reactions to poor recovery from complaints are from customers previously loyal. They expect problems to be taken care of effectively, and when they are not, these customers are the most vocal critics.[39]

TARP developed a model for measuring the return on company dollars in-vested in complaint resolution. The return on investment was as high as 400 percent for retailers, 170 percent for banking, and 100 percent for automotive services. Re-solving complaints clearly adds to the bottom line. The money spent on resolving complaints paid off in terms of increased sales, additional sales from positive word of mouth, and reduced third-party and liability claims, to name a few.[40]

Unfortunately, most customers do not complain. Studies in the 1980s found that about 70 percent of consumers with product and service problems did not com-plain. A study sponsored by the U.S. Office of Consumer Affairs (USOCA) and con-ducted by TARP in 1986 found that 60 percent did not complain about their dissatisfaction with a large-ticket durable good, 50 percent did not complain about a problem with a medium-ticket durable good, 37 percent did not complain about a large-ticket service, and 45 percent did not complain when dissatisfied about a small-ticket service.[41] There is no evidence that this situation has improved. In fact, some customer service consultants believe that our tolerance for defects in goods, services, suppliers, and leaders has risen.[42] Burke Customer Satisfaction Associates surveyed 1200 department store shoppers and found that loyal shoppers were more inclined to complain. The rest assumed that poor products and bad service were par for the course.[43]

If customers do not complain, companies lose the opportunity to find out why the customers defect. While increasing complaints sounds counterintuitive, that is exactly what companies should do if they want to retain customers. We will cover this topic in more detail in Chapter 13. With the advent of customer relationship management, contact centers, previously known as call centers, have evolved into Internet-connected centers to provide multiple ways for customers to contact a company for complaints or other purposes. The average call distribution for the toll-free numbers is 59 percent for inquiries, 24 percent complaints, and 20 percent orders and promotions.[44]

In 1998, the Center for Client Retention conducted a consumer loyalty study of 6000 telephone (800 number) customers of members of the Society of Consumer Affairs Professionals in Business. There were 23 companies involved, including Coca-Cola, Domino's Pizza, Procter & Gamble, Mattel, Frito-Lay, Columbia Gas of Ohio, and Comcast Cellular Communications. Three-quarters of the customers were either "delighted" or "very satisfied" with the way consumer affairs had addressed their concern or answered their question. The research showed that 90 percent of the customers who were "delighted" with their experience with the company's consumer affairs department said they were "very likely" to repurchase the product or service, while only 37 percent of those who were "very dissatisfied" would buy again. Courtesy, professionalism, amount of time spent, encouragement to call again, and expression of appreciation for business were found to be the most important characteristics of their contact. The 88 percent who ranked the "ability to demonstrate concern and interest" and "show enthusiasm" the highest were "very likely" to repurchase. The researchers also found that 73 percent were more willing to recommend a company's product after a good experience.[45]

Skill Development 3.2

1. Have you ever defected from a company? What happened to make you defect?
2. Does your company know how many customers defect each year? How could it find out?
3. Do you seek word-of-mouth advice from your family, friends, and associates?
4. How often do you discuss good and bad customer experiences?
5. How often do you complain to a company? What caused you to complain?

COSTS OF EXCEPTIONAL CUSTOMER SERVICE

Providing exceptional customer service costs money. A company must still make a profit to stay in business. If a company's expenses are higher than revenues, the company cannot succeed. What does exceptional customer service cost? It partly depends on what the company is already spending on customer service. The following assumes that the company is spending a typical amount of money on customer service objectives. The *costs of exceptional customer service* will be over and above that.

Strategy Costs

Assuming a company is offering good but not exceptional service, the company will spend money to develop or update its customer service strategy. The company will need to measure and analyze customer expectations, satisfaction, and loyalty. It will need to determine its customer defection rate and the reasons for defection. This will involve external customer and frontline employee research. It may analyze its customers by target market. The company will also examine internal customer service to benefit external customer service. Competitor strategy will need to be assessed. The company will then need to determine a differentiated strategy for providing exceptional customer service. It will also need to communicate the strategy to company personnel and customers. Last, the process of customer feedback, analysis, and changes will involve ongoing costs.

Systems Costs

If the company determines that systems need changing, this will cost money. All the technology that serves customers may need to be updated or improved. For example, there may be telecommunications, Internet, inventory control, and/or transaction technology needs. The company may need more efficient and accurate equipment. A company may need to redesign operating systems to be more customer-oriented, effective, and flexible. For example, the company might find it needs a more customer-oriented store layout or higher inventory levels.

In order to resolve complaints fairly and quickly, a complaint management system and its implementation will cost money. This could include compensation for dissatisfaction, such as free products, coupons, and other incentives for the customer to repurchase. New systems and policies may require new or improved customer information and education.

People Costs

In Chapter 4, we will discuss employee satisfaction and its impact on customer satisfaction. Some examples of "people" costs for exceptional customer service are the following:

* Funds spent on hiring qualified employees
* Higher wages to retain employees
* Employee benefits
* Customer service training
* Management and supervisor training
* Employee motivation and rewards for exceptional customer service performance
* Acceptable working conditions
* Time for meeting for communication and participative decision making
* Additional payroll to cover checkouts, the sales floor, telephones, and/or Internet communication
* Nonmonetary cost of employee emotional effort and labor

TERMS

customer	actionability
external customers	benefits of exceptional customer
consumer	service
business-to-business customer	customer retention
buying center	defection
internal customer	word-of-mouth information
frontline employees	complaint resolution
customer loyalty	costs of exceptional customer service

DISCUSSION QUESTIONS

1. Describe the customers at an employer or other business with which you are familiar.
2. What are internal customers?
3. What is customer loyalty?
4. How can companies determine customer expectations?
5. Why do companies need to know the importance of service quality characteristics?
6. Why is customer retention important?
7. What is the difference between acquisition marketing and retention marketing?
8. Explain the five defector categories.
9. What are the benefits of resolving customer complaints?
10. What are the benefits of exceptional customer service?
11. What are the costs of exceptional customer service?

PROJECT—MYSTERY SHOPPING

This project focuses on the interpersonal aspects of the customer service of a business. The method for gathering information is "mystery shopping." The project can be conducted individually or by a student team. The project is intended to provide you with experience in recognizing, describing, and evaluating exceptional to unacceptable customer service in real-world situations.

The process and requirements for the mystery shopping project are the following:

1. Choose the business. It should not be one at which one of the team members or a close relative or friend is employed or was recently employed. Retail is easiest, but a business service is also acceptable. If necessary due to team members' residence location, you can go to different stores in a chain, but it is better if you choose one specific location. As you know, management styles differ and will affect the evaluation. Have your choice approved by the instructor.
2. Design a questionnaire that each team member can use to evaluate customer service at the business. There should be 10 interpersonal-type questions, focusing on factors such as courtesy and helpfulness and on communication skills such

as listening and nonverbal behavior. The questions should be closed-ended questions with more than two response categories. For example, use rating responses such as "poor/fair/good/very good/excellent" or "unacceptable/below expectations/meets expectations/exceeds expectations," rather than "yes/no." Leave space on your questionnaire form to make comments about ratings.

You should provide a place at the top of your questionnaire to enter the day, date, and time of day and any other specific parameters of your visit (location, number of shoppers, approximate number of customers in the store, number of employees visible, whether the manager is on site).

You may use one open-ended question at the end. You can formulate a question about product or policy knowledge or use other scenarios that will aid your ability to evaluate, such as role-playing a complaint.

Your team will probably want to conduct a "practice" trip to help you decide what to ask. Another way to improve your questionnaire is to discuss your project with management and ask for permission to interview a few customers and frontline employees. Part of the evaluation of your project will be focused on the comprehensiveness and logic of your questions and evaluation.

3. The next step is for each team member to conduct at least three mystery shopping visits to the business and fill out the questionnaire immediately after leaving the store. The employees of the store should not know that you are doing mystery shopping. You do not need to make a purchase (unless it is a restaurant). You should spend enough time in the store to be able to answer all the questions completely. You may conduct your visit alone or with others. You may do the mystery shopping at any time of the day or week.

4. Tabulate the answers from all questionnaires and calculate frequency and percent distributions. For example, of 20 ratings for the courtesy of the salesperson, the frequency is 5 "unacceptable," 6 "below expectations," 9 "met expectations," and 0 "exceeded expectations." The percent distribution would be 25 percent "unacceptable," 30 percent "below expectations," 45 percent "met expectations," and 0 percent "exceeded expectations."

5. Write a report about your project.
   a. Begin with an introduction to explain what business it is, where it is, precisely what you did when, etc.
   b. Describe the results of your mystery shopping. Illustrate the results from the 10 questions using tables and graphs (for example, Excel). Some of your graphs should be made into visual aids (preferably PowerPoint or transparencies) for your presentation.
   c. Briefly describe the findings from your "role play" or "critical incident."
   d. Make recommendations on how the business could improve its interpersonal customer service. You may want to do a visual aid of these in "bullet" form for your presentation. Keep in mind that your evaluation will not entail a large enough "sample" to be representative; it is intended only to give you practice and insight. It is to be understood that your report does not necessarily indicate what type of customer service the business generally provides.
   e. Cite any sources of information, such as a manager or employee interview and a company website.
   f. Put a blank copy of your questionnaire in the appendix. "Raw data" (the completed questionnaires) are not required.

6. Present your report to the class with visual aids.

NOTES

1. Patricia Braus, "What Is Good Service?" *American Demographics* 12, no. 7 (July 1990): 36–39.
2. Charles W. Lamb, Jr., Joseph F. Hair, Jr., and Carl McDaniel, *Essentials of Marketing,* 2d ed. (Cincinnati: South-Western College Publishing, 2001).
3. Frederick F. Reichheld, Robert G. Markey, Jr., and Christopher Hopton, "The Loyalty Effect—The Relationship between Loyalty and Profits," *European Business Journal* 12, no. 3 (Autumn 2000): 134.
4. Stephen S. Tax and Stephen W. Brown, "Recovering and Learning from Service Failure," *Customer Relationship Management,* March 1999, 22–27.
5. Maura Burke Weiner, "Using Customer Feedback Data to Prioritize Quality Improvement Actions," speech at the Society of Consumer Affairs Professionals Spring Conference, April 1993.
6. Reichheld, Markey, and Hopton, "The Loyalty Effect," 134.
7. Kathleen Sindell, *Loyalty Marketing for the Internet Age: How to Identify, Attract, Serve, and Retain Customers in an E-Commerce Environment* (Detroit: Dearborn Trade, 2000), 77.
8. Reichheld, Markey, and Hopton, "The Loyalty Effect," 134.
9. The Customer Loyalty Institute, presentation at the Society of Consumer Affairs Professionals Spring Conference, April 1993.
10. Jeffrey Gitomer, *Customer Satisfaction Is Worthless, Customer Loyalty Is Priceless: How to Make Customers Love You, Keep Them Coming Back and Tell Everyone They Know* (Marietta, GA: Bard Press, 1998); and Karen Leland and Keith Bailey, *Customer Service for Dummies,* 2d ed. (New York: IDG Books Worldwide, 1999).
11. William D. Neal, "Debate Still Going Strong," Letters to the Editor, *Marketing News,* April 9, 2001, 6; and Michael A. Jones, David L. Mothersbaugh, and Sharon E. Beatty, "Switching Barriers and Repurchase Intentions in Services," *Journal of Retailing* 76, no. 2 (summer 2000): 259.
12. D. Randall Brandt, "Attitude Does Matter. A Response to June 5, 2000 *Marketing News* article by William Neal," [White Paper Series online], 2000, Burke, available from http://www.burke.com/whitepapers/whitepapersdocs/volume_2_2000_issue_6.doc, accessed September 22, 2001.
13. Clay Carr, *Front-Line Customer Service* (New York: John Wiley & Sons, 1990).
14. Banwari Mittal and Walfried M. Lassar, "The Role of Personalization in Service Encounters," *Journal of Retailing* 72, no. 1 (Spring 1996): 95–110.
15. Leland and Bailey, *Customer Service for Dummies.*
16. A. Parasuraman, Leonard L. Berry, and Valarie A. Zeithaml, "Guidelines for Conducting Service Quality Research," *Marketing Research,* December 1990, 34–44; and Jack W. Cushman and Linda M. Cushman, "Service Recovery: Implementation Strategies for Operations," *Customer Relationship Management,* September 1998, 22–25.
17. Geoffrey L. Gordon, Roger J. Calantone, and C. Anthony di Benedetto, "Business-to-Business Service Marketing: How Does It Differ from Business-to-Business Product Marketing?" *Journal of Business & Industrial Marketing* 8, no. 1 (1993): 45–57.
18. Gitomer, *Customer Satisfaction Is Worthless.*
19. D. Randall Brandt, "Business Trends: Focusing on Problems to Improve Service and Quality," *Mobius,* Spring 1990, 23–31.
20. Robert R. Shullman, "Economic Conditions Mean You Have to Cut Something—But What, and Where? Customers Can Help Provide the Answers," promotion from Willard and Shullman, Inc., November 1990.
21. The Forum Corporation, *Customer Focus Research, Executive Briefing,* April 1988, 6.
22. Mary Jo Bitner, Bernard H. Booms, and Lois A. Mohr, "Critical Service Encounters: The Employee's Viewpoint," *Journal of Marketing,* October 1994; and Leonard L. Berry, "Improving America's Service," *Marketing Management* 1, no. 3 (1992) 29–38.

23. Parasuraman, Berry, and Zeithaml, "Guidelines for Conducting Service Quality Research," 34–44; and Jim Sterne, *Customer Service on the Internet,* 2d ed. (New York: John Wiley & Sons, 2000).

24. Laura A. Liswood, "Service Customers: Before They Run the Other Way," *Bank Marketing,* November 1987, 24.

25. Chip R. Bell and Ron Zemke, *Service Wisdom* (n.p.: Lakewood Books, 1989).

26. Douglas Pruden and Terry Vavra, "Don't Let Lost Customers Short Circuit Your Retention Efforts," *Customer Relationship Management,* March 1996, 33–35; and Reichheld, Markey, and Hopton, "The Loyalty Effect," 134.

27. "Marketing Briefs," *Marketing News,* October 26, 1998.

28. "Poor Service a Thorn for Retailers," *MMR* 18, no. 6 (April 16, 2001): 18.

29. Reichheld, Markey, and Hopton, "The Loyalty Effect," 134.

30. Pruden and Vavra, "Don't Let Lost Customers," 33–35.

31. Michael Lowenstein, "From Retention to Reincarnation," *Customer Loyalty Today* 8, no. 1 (December 2000): 8.

32. Leland and Bailey, *Customer Service for Dummies.*

33. Pruden and Vavra, "Don't Let Lost Customers," 33–35.

34. Warren Blanding, *Customer Service Operation: The Complete Guide* (New York: AMACOM, 1991).

35. Cynthia J. Grimm, "Understanding & Reaching the Consumer: A Summary of Recent Research," *Mobius,* Fall 1987, 18–25.

36. George Silverman, "Heard It from a Friend," *Quirk's Marketing Research Review,* February 2002, 34–37.

37. Jennifer Tanaka, "Foiling the Rogues," *Newsweek,* October 27, 1997, 80.

38. Grimm, "Understanding & Reaching the Consumer," 18–25; and U.S. Office of Consumer Affairs (USOCA), *Increasing Customer Satisfaction through Effective Corporate Complaint Handling,* 1986.

39. Tax and Brown, "Recovering and Learning from Service Failure," 22–27.

40. USOCA, *Increasing Customer Satisfaction.*

41. USOCA, *Increasing Customer Satisfaction.*

42. Randall Rothenberg, "Despite Technology's Advance, Our Tolerance for Defects Rises," *Advertising Age* 72 (April 16, 2001): 18.

43. Sterne, *Customer Service on the Internet.*

44. Society of Consumer Affairs Professionals, "More Companies Are Using Toll-Free Numbers/Internet to Build Customer Loyalty" [news release online], available from http://www.socap.org/Publications/800study.html, accessed July 3, 2001.

45. Society of Consumer Affairs Professionals (SOCAP), "Consumer Loyalty in 1998," *Customer Relationship Management,* December 1998, 20–21; and SOCAP, "New Report Finds How Companies Treat Consumers Is a Major Driver of Brand Loyalty and Impacts Future Sales" [news release online], available from http://www.socap.org/Publications/loyalty.html, accessed July 3, 2001.

CHAPTER

4 PEOPLE

OBJECTIVES

1. Explain the people component of customer service.
2. Describe internal customer service.
3. Describe frontline employees' role in customer service.
4. Explain why employee satisfaction equals customer satisfaction.
5. Describe the factors that contribute to employee satisfaction.
6. Discuss the next-generation workforce.

THE PEOPLE COMPONENT

People are responsible for customer service. To provide exceptional customer service and to create and maintain loyal relationships with customers, a customer-first philosophy must exist among all people in an organization. Every employee of an organization ultimately serves customers. This chapter focuses on how an organization creates a human resources environment that enhances a customer-oriented approach. It is not intended to be a comprehensive human resources manual but to point out specific ideas and techniques recommended by customer service experts. It admittedly emphasizes exceptional conditions to promote exceptional customer service.

In this textbook, a *frontline employee* is any employee that has direct contact with external customers, providing external customer service. Frontline employees are involved at every point that customers interact with the company. They deliver service, provide information, and solve problems. Internal employees support frontline employee efforts. In addition, frontline employees and internal employees provide service to each other. This is referred to as *internal customer service* in the text. Some employees will have both frontline and internal responsibilities. For example, a retail manager has management functions and also often interacts with external customers. A business-to-business account representative provides service to customers and to others in the company.

Business practices that positively influence customers' perception of overall service quality include seeing exceptional service as an important value and living up to it, aligning the larger organization to serve customers, building capability to serve customers, and seeking innovative ways to serve customers better. Other factors are helping employees learn how to serve customers better and setting customer-focused performance goals and standards. Frontline employees need the knowledge, skills, resources, and authority to take care of customers and provide exceptional service.

INTERNAL CUSTOMER SERVICE

One way to make sure external customers are well taken care of is to provide exceptional service to customers within the company, the internal customers. Internally, we are each other's customers, and our ultimate goal is to serve our external customers and make our company successful. For example, a coworker asks for a copy of a report because he is trying to track down a customer's problem. A second coworker provides it and helps the internal customer and the external customer. The next day, the second coworker is working on a project to improve a system that customers use. She goes to the first coworker and asks his advice. Again, he supports internal and external customers by providing his input.

Every job in the company is part of the chain that provides customers with service. Departments should not be isolated from each other; each employee needs to understand what everyone does and how it fits into satisfying the customer. An employee is part of the chain if he is packing or unpacking merchandise. An employee is part of it if she maintains the building. A manager is part of the chain. Managers should stay in close contact with what's happening on the front line. If employees are having customer problems due to a misguided policy, the manager's job is to solve the problem for the employees and the external customers.

Skill Development 4.1

1. Give the job title of an internal customer and explain how you could provide customer service to the coworker.
2. Explain how an internal employee could provide you with customer service.

FRONTLINE EMPLOYEES' ROLE

Management is not in charge of service; frontline people are. Because frontline employees are the ones who deliver service directly to customers, power for customer service needs to shift from management to the front line. Jan Carlzon, of the Scandinavian airline SAS, has said, "Your job as managers is no longer to do business; it's to provide your frontline people with the skills and resources to do business for you."[1] Traditionally, frontline people have seemed to be the least important. Many of them are certainly the lowest paid. At one time, customer service was a function that handled customer inquiries and problems, such as returns and complaints. Management sometimes viewed customer service as an expense. However, companies exist to support service to customers. Southwest Airlines believes that employees are

FIGURE 4.1   Cause of Customer Problems

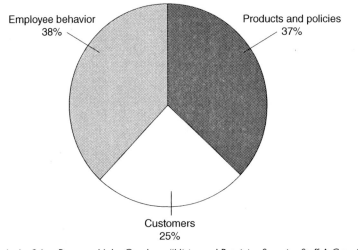

Employee behavior
38%

Products and policies
37%

Customers
25%

Source: Monica Jenks, Selma Baum, and John Goodman, "Hiring and Retaining Superior Staff: A Growing Challenge for the 1990s," *Mobius*, Spring 1990, 18–21.

more important than customers. The company knows that happy employees result in happy customers.

Management needs to recognize that employees are not always the cause of customer dissatisfaction. In 1990, retailers estimated that 37 percent of customer dissatisfaction was actually caused by company products and policies and 25 percent by the customers themselves (as discussed in Chapter 3), for a total of 62 percent. The rest, only 38 percent, was the result of employee behavior (see Figure 4.1).[2]

Frontline employees serve as an early warning system for problems. They see even more than customers see, day to day, from a different angle. They know when management has hired poorly qualified people or trained too little or too late. They see operations breaking down before customers do and often shield customers from problems. One study showed that employee ratings of service quality were significantly lower than customer ratings, perhaps because employees knew more about the weaknesses of their service than customers did.[3]

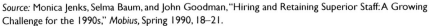

Experience Discussion 4.1

As a frontline customer service provider, what problems with other coworkers or systems have you noticed?

EMPLOYEE SATISFACTION EQUALS CUSTOMER SATISFACTION

The equation expressed in the heading above and illustrated in Figure 4.2 succinctly sums up an essential principle. Numerous research studies, including research at Ryder Truck, NCR, and Allstate, have demonstrated a direct relationship between

FIGURE 4.2   Employee Satisfaction

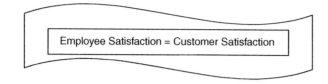

Employee Satisfaction = Customer Satisfaction

"Employee satisfaction is the ability to consistently meet/exceed employees' needs, wants and expectations throughout the life cycle of the employee relationship, resulting in motivation, loyalty to their employer, increased productivity and, therefore, excellent service to customers."

Source: John Goodman and Marlene Yanovsky, "Treating Employees as Customers: Estimating the Bottom Line Impact of Employee Dissatisfaction and Setting Rational Priorities," *Customer Relationship Management,* September 1997, 22.

employee satisfaction and customer satisfaction and customer intention to repurchase. Research has found that when employees have a positive view of a company's human resource policies, customers have a positive view of the quality of service they receive. The same "spillover effect" suggests that if a company treats employees fairly, they will treat customers fairly. If employees are satisfied, customers are satisfied.

Employee satisfaction increases *employee loyalty.* A strong relationship has been found between employee perceptions of human resource management fairness and employee acceptance of and satisfaction with human resource decisions. Employees judge the fairness of a company by human resource decisions in hiring, performance appraisals, and reward systems. Fairness also contributes to employee commitment to the company. Employees demonstrate their commitment by being more willing to make extra effort for customers. In addition, employee motivation decreases if a company treats customers unfairly, for example, a company not responding to complaints or charging inflated prices. It has also been found that high employee turnover is associated with low employee ratings of the quality of service an organization provides. The result is that if employees do not believe a company is providing high-quality service, they are more likely to leave.[4] The bottom line is that if employees are satisfied and loyal, employee absenteeism, lack of productivity, and turnover decrease, and productivity and performance improve.[5] Because employee turnover is costly and employee retention is becoming essential, lack of employee loyalty is a critical issue.

Technical Assistance Research Programs (TARP), a customer service research and consulting firm, has found that employees' perceived ability to do their jobs efficiently and serve their customers has the greatest effect on loyalty. When employees lacked the tools, training, and authority to solve customer problems and requests for assistance, they were less motivated and productive. In addition, research has shown that employees are more likely to be satisfied and committed to an organization when their most important issues and concerns are addressed. We also know that issues and concerns vary from company to company and industry to industry. Therefore, companies need to determine what the key issues and concerns are. To determine how employee satisfaction affects loyalty, companies need to assess employees' attitudes about internal problems. TARP has found that not handling employee concerns when they were expressed had serious effects on employee loyalty. An employee satisfaction survey showed that the majority of employees did not complain about problems. What was more problematic was that, of those employees that did complain, only about half got an acceptable answer and only one-fifth were completely satisfied with the answer. About half of the employees would not recommend the company, and one-quarter were not motivated.[6]

Experience Discussion 4.2

Have you ever complained about a problem at work? Did you get an acceptable answer? Were you completely satisfied with the answer?

FACTORS CONTRIBUTING TO EMPLOYEE SATISFACTION

A company needs simple procedures and clear personnel policies, which are administered fairly and consistently by all management for all employees. The following is a list of the factors that contribute to employee satisfaction:

- respect
- thorough, honest, responsive communication
- sound hiring practices
- fair, attractive compensation
- supportive work environment
- comprehensive, ongoing training
- exceptional supervision and management
- participatory decision making
- empowerment
- realistic performance standards
- regular, just performance evaluations
- meaningful recognition and rewards
- opportunities for advancement and personal growth
- motivation for retention

Job Title

Frontline customer service personnel have a wide range of job titles since service is provided at every point an external customer comes in contact with the company. There are salespeople, receptionists, restaurant hosts and servers, cashiers, managers, contact center representatives, and many more. One title that human resources personnel should consider changing is customer service representative. The title has become closely associated with clerical work. We know a representative does far more than clerical work. Possibilities for a job title are customer representative, customer consultant, account specialist, technical specialist, product specialist, client service representative, service specialist, and customer agent.

Internal Communication

When companies communicate their philosophy and goals, employees feel more valuable to the company and are more motivated and loyal.

1. The philosophy of the organization and the message of customer satisfaction and loyalty should appear where employees will see and hear it. Examine em-

ployee newsletters, bulletin boards, meetings, and memos to assess the level of exposure. Repetition is important, but only if the message is heard and considered credible. Do employees understand the customer value and loyalty message? Is it covered only during orientation? Is it in the employee handbook? Is it part of the job description and performance review? Do employees use it in their daily routine?

2. The results of customer satisfaction and loyalty measures need to be shared with all employees. Do employees hear all results, both good and bad? Are employees recognized for good efforts?

3. Communication should have top-down, bottom-up, and horizontal channels. Are there systems for obtaining employee input? Do employees participate? Employees who feel underused and ignored become unproductive and start looking for jobs elsewhere. Open a communication avenue for high-potential employees to offer their ideas, and make sure everyone hears good and bad news as soon as possible and at the same time.

> If management says, "Here is what is happening in our organization, in terms of products, sales, profits, and competition," employees think, "I am capable of helping you because I know what's going on."

4. Companies must focus on hearing and handling employee concerns. Employees need clear, truthful, and timely answers to their questions and concerns. If messages from top management show a willingness to solve employee problems, employees will be willing to solve customer problems.

> If management asks employees, "What are your problems, and how can I solve them?" this translates to an employee saying to a customer, "What can I do to help you?"

> "Each of us is the company, so we all share accountability for what happens around here" translates to "I am empowered to help you and take pride in my ability to do so."

> "We stand behind each other's decisions and support each other" translates to "You can count on me and my company to deliver on our promises.".[7]

It is impossible to build a customer service–minded culture when executives regularly sacrifice customer and employee interests for short-term profit. Leonard Berry has said, "Sustaining employee pride is impossible in a company that systematically misleads customers in promotions, engages in phony pricing schemes, or refuses to redress legitimate, post-sale customer grievances. . . . Employees will ask themselves, 'Why give my all for a company that lacks integrity?' "[8]

Experience Discussion 4.3

How would you rate the internal communication at your company?

Hiring

Appropriately qualified people are needed for exceptional customer service. Flattening the organization, eliminating middle management layers, and increasing the number of workers for which managers are responsible are actions that have led to more delegation and the need for higher-quality staff. More employees are required for the extended hours that customers have demanded for convenient service. Increasing use of the telephone has increased standards for verbal communication skills. More use of e-mail requires employees with writing skills. Demographic shifts decreased the number of young people in the workforce, and so candidates have been harder to find. When the economy is strong and the unemployment rate is low as it was in the 1990s, it is even harder to find good employees.

Reid Systems, a developer of applicant screening tools, along with several large supermarket chains, recently analyzed applicant responses to preemployment customer service assessment questions. The findings were disconcerting. Almost half of the job applicants believed that customers should be told when they were wrong and that customers had to follow rules if employees were going to help them. Thirteen percent said if customers do not ask for help, then they don't need it. Ten percent would not help a customer if it weren't their job. Six percent admitted to repeatedly arguing with customers and coworkers in recent jobs.[9] Careful hiring and customer service training are clearly needed.

Job descriptions need to stress employee contribution to customer satisfaction and job enhancement features such as empowerment and opportunities for advancement to attract good staff. No job should be considered menial; all jobs are important to customer satisfaction and loyalty, including the employees who provide maintenance and cleaning, fax documents, or stock shelves. All contribute to the customer's perception of service.

Important work ethic characteristics are reliability, responsibility, adaptability, self-esteem, and maturity. Customer service employees should enjoy interacting with and helping people and have the ability to listen and respond with empathy. They should have problem-solving skills and be able to stay calm and polite under fire. In some types of jobs, they need to be articulate and have good voice quality. In some, they need to be computer literate and be able to quickly navigate through menus and screens. They should be accurate, but not necessarily fast, typists. Some companies are adding a requirement for some college to get more qualified applicants and raise the level of perceived professionalism of customer contact jobs.[10]

Experts say that job performance will increase the better the fit between the job and the characteristics of an employee. Saville & Holdsworth Ltd. has developed a model of competencies that are common to all customer service roles (see Table 4.1). With participation from employees, a company can determine the competencies needed in a job, list them in order of priority, and attach an importance weight to each one. Then the job candidates' and employees' characteristics are compared with the competencies needed. This process makes it more likely the fit will be good for new employees. The fit might not be perfect for existing employees. The process points out training needs for these employees or may suggest a restructure of job demands. Because the competencies are objective and measurable and employees participate in the process, they are more able to gain from training or adjust to a new role.[11]

Companies use a variety of screening methods. They have found that more than one interview works best to differentiate job candidates. Some companies use team interviews composed of several candidates to see how applicants interact. Others interview using a team of company personnel, sometimes frontline employees, to gauge interpersonal and communication skills. Allowing candidates to preview the job, providing them with a real experience if possible, helps them see what they would be doing. Good candidates will present their qualifications to match the job.

Companies use *situational interviews* to determine how applicants handle various situations. One example is asking potential employees to talk about how they handled a particularly stressful or difficult situation or how a situation was handled for them as a customer. Another is the use of a simulated telephone conversation with

TABLE 4.1   Model of Customer Service Competencies

People
    Relating to customers
    Convincing
    Communicating orally
    Communicating in writing
    Team working

Information handling
    Fact finding
    Problem solving
    Business awareness
    Specialist knowledge

Dependability
    Quality orientation
    Organization
    Reliability

Energy
    Customer focus
    Resilience
    Results driven
    Initiative

Source: Karen Janman, "The Key to Superior Customer Service," *Customer Service Management,* July–August 1999, 55–57.

a staff member acting as a customer. Pen-and-pencil tests seem to do no more than weed out unlikely candidates rather than finding those most likely to be successful.

When hiring for a telephone position, experts suggest that the first interview be done by telephone. If candidates do not sound good on the phone, they will not sound good to customers. Verbal and nonverbal communication skills are also important. A role-played taped conversation can determine factors such as rate of speech, articulation, and use of language. Another requirement for telephone customer representatives is to take accurate and relevant notes about a caller's needs.[12]

Experience Discussion 4.4

What was the process the last time you were hired? How would you rate the effectiveness of the process?

Compensation

Compensation should be, at a minimum, externally competitive and internally equitable. Many frontline customer service jobs, especially those in retail, are entry-level jobs at the low end of the pay scale. It is difficult at best to train employees adequately and keep them. Incentive pay may be part of the answer. In addition to paying for sales and profit, compensation should also be linked to customer satisfaction, retention, and loyalty. If companies pay only for quantity and productivity, employees have no incentive to produce quality work. To retain top people, companies may need to pay more than the going rate to attract good people and keep them from leaving once they are trained.

Fair benefits, such as insurance and retirement options, are also a consideration. Employees want to be able to balance their work and their personal life. Be flexible about working hours so employees have time for outside responsibilities. They will be less stressed and reward companies by being more productive. Flextime can also reduce tardiness and absenteeism.

Work Environment and Conditions

Employees need good working conditions. Customer service jobs are stressful. Pleasant environments make a difference. Work and break areas should be clean, orderly, safe, and comfortable. That sounds simplistic and trite, but the reality is that those conditions do not always exist. One company provides a true break room, which has absolutely nothing related to the job anywhere in the room, so that employees can completely remove themselves from the stress of their jobs.

An office work area should have enough separation to provide some privacy but still promote community among service representatives and teams. Some personalization of work areas to recognize individuality and diversity in working styles is preferred by most employees. Employees should have the proper equipment and tools. Ergonomics, noise abatement, and proper lighting all help relieve stress. The lowest-paid workers should be treated the same as everyone else.

One problem in contact center jobs that leads to stress and burnout is a continual stream of telephone calls with not enough breaks in between to finish paperwork. Therefore, service representatives are constantly being interrupted in the middle of what they are doing and never quite get all their other work done. One solution is to allow service representatives to sign off the telephone until they are done with the paperwork. This can cause a slowdown in telephone response but can help productivity in the long run and reduce turnover from stress. Another way to deal with it is to allow 30- to 60-minute staggered time periods for service representatives to do their research and paperwork.[13]

Training

Marketing gets customers in the door, but customer service training keeps them coming back. Customers may be influenced to try a business due to promotion, but they may not return if they are not treated well. John Tschohl, founder of the Service Quality Institute, recommends investing 10 percent of the annual advertising budget to train employees for a minimum of 40 hours each year. Employees who are trained feel more valuable, are more motivated, and are more productive.[14]

In retail, restaurant, and other consumer service companies, virtually all employees are frontline employees. In some companies, training is largely concentrated on day-to-day job skills. Employees are taught the procedures of their job and the policies of the company. They are taught how to operate any equipment or technology that they use, such as a cash register, computer, software, telephone, and office equipment. They learn about the products. If there is any customer service training at all, it may be as limited as watching a video or reading a manual. In companies in which customer service is the job, such as customer contact centers, more emphasis is placed on customer service training. To provide exceptional internal service, everyone in an organization should have opportunities for customer service training. The more skills and knowledge employees have, the better job they will do, the easier it will be, and the more valuable they will be to the company.

Training can improve customer service in business-to-business companies and other organizations, such as health care, insurance, education, and financial institutions. A research study at a hospital in Virginia found that customer service training for all emergency room personnel decreased patient complaints and increased patient compliments. Complaints about rudeness, insensitivity, and lack of compassion decreased the most. The patient satisfaction survey showed that the training also improved the rating of the skill of the physician and the skill of the nurse, overall satisfaction, and likelihood of returning. A few of the topics of the 8-hour training session were customer service principles, stress recognition and management, communication, negotiation skills, and empowerment.[15]

What do frontline customer service providers and other employees want and need to know to provide exceptional customer service? First, they need basic communication skills, which include listening, nonverbal and verbal communication, telephone, and e-mail skills, depending on the type of job. The communication training should be focused specifically on application to customers. Customers are demanding, and so employees also need problem-solving, conflict resolution, and teamwork skills. Employees who are expected to be empathetic need to know about customer behavior so that it is easier to put themselves in the customers' shoes. They need to understand customers' attitudes and expectations.

All employees need to know:

* Why and how their jobs are important to customers and the organization
* What is going on in the organization so they feel knowledgeable and capable of helping customers
* Whom to ask and where to go for answers to customer questions
* Where their job fits into the total picture and how they affect other employees' jobs
* How a mistake will affect customers, other employees, and the organization
* How often, when, and specifically how their performance of their responsibilities will be measured and evaluated quantitatively and qualitatively
* How to improve their performance and increase their contribution to the organization and how to develop themselves in their jobs

Managers and supervisors need to update their own training to know exactly what frontline customer service personnel are taught so they can monitor and coach behavior and performance. Any employees who manage new hires also need training in coaching skills.

Companies can use videotapes, audiotapes, books, CD-ROMs, web-based self-study, or people for training. Training should be conducted from well-developed, structured materials so that it is clear, logical, and consistent. Employees that train should have expertise in how people learn most efficiently and should know how to manage various learning styles and training methods. Each skill may require a different learning format. Interpersonal skill training may require more hands-on learning, whereas technical training can rely more on computer-based training.[16] Each type of job, company, and industry will have different needs.

The intangibility of customer service skills makes it difficult to teach through words alone, and so employees need to see exceptional customer service when an expert performs it. Part of training can be conducted on the job through mentors and role model programs. New employees need to be able to practice doing the job in realistic circumstances but in a situation in which mistakes are treated as helpful learning opportunities.

Training should be done not only during orientation but also continuously or periodically. Jobs become routine, and so employees need refresher training. Things change, and so employees need update training. They may need corrective training to reinforce skills.

Experience Discussion 4.5

What kind of training did you receive the last time you started a new job? Was it adequate?

Supervision and Management

Exceptional supervisors and managers are necessary to have exceptional employees. This is not a new idea. In 1984, Richard Normann wrote, "Various studies have shown that it is almost impossible to develop—and even more to maintain—a particular kind of climate and relationship between frontline personnel and customers unless the same climate and basic values prevail in the relationship between frontline personnel and their supervisors."[17]

What characteristics do exceptional supervisors have? They are available, fair, consistent, considerate, and honest. They are good listeners. They set a good example. They support, inform, teach, coach, correct, trust, respect, appreciate, recognize, and reward employees. They promote teamwork. They use tact and diplomacy. They do not overreact. They fight for what their employees need. They share responsibility if anything goes wrong. If they make a promise, they keep it. They reward performance. Remember, we said exceptional supervisors for exceptional employees to provide exceptional customer service.

In classes, college students have described the following behaviors and characteristics of what they see as "bad bosses." Having been promoted from sales work or frontline customer service, some bosses do not have managerial and people skills. Some do not have expertise in the field, and so they do not understand the frontline job. The bosses make an appearance, tell everyone what to do, and then disappear. They do not listen. They ignore employee problems and needs. They criticize employees in front of other employees and customers. They have favorite employees.

A supervisor who is concerned about employees and their questions and problems sets an example for employees to be concerned about customers and coworkers. If a supervisor stands behind employee decisions and supports employees, employees know that customers can count on the company. Performance should be measured so management has accurate and specific information about each employee. Management should manage proactively rather than reactively, anticipating the potential for employee dissatisfaction.

Participation

Participation in decision making enhances employees' knowledge of the company and their perception of control over their environment. Customer service personnel should be asked to identify service breakdowns and identify root causes of customer dissatisfaction, increasing the perceived value of their jobs to both themselves and the company. Frontline personnel know what's going wrong and why customers are dissatisfied. Their participation in prevention activities, investigating how to

change systems or prevent problems, enhances job satisfaction and reinforces training. One participation method is to form problem-solving teams to address specific
problems and provide innovative solutions. The teams can also include customers
to provide input and help staff understand expectations.[18]

Empowerment

Empowerment means that frontline employees are given the appropriate authority to
act on behalf of the customer. According to many service experts, when employees
are empowered, customers receive the best service. Research has shown that empowerment in a bank setting leads to less ambiguity about job responsibilities and
less conflict with supervisors. Empowerment also leads to higher adaptability, more
confidence, and higher job satisfaction. In addition, some experts believe that lack
of authority is a major contributor to frustration and burnout when employees are
not able to help customers.[19]

Most customer problems and requests are reasonably easy to handle. Empowerment may not be needed and may even be detrimental when the service is standardized due to regulations, such as student financial aid services or quality control
issues. Empowerment enters the picture when a customer is the victim of a real or
perceived mistake by the company or when a customer situation doesn't fit routine
company practices, policies, and procedures. Then, service providers need to be able
to find quick and mutually agreeable solutions to customer problems. Delay in resolution and unresolved problems create the potential to lose loyal customers. Empowerment is most recommended when a service is based on a relationship rather
than simply a transaction. Empowerment is also more appropriate in heterogeneous
service markets with more diverse customers and fewer hard-and-fast rules.

In order for empowerment to succeed, companies need to communicate a
customer-oriented mission, hire people who are capable of being totally empowered, and praise empowerment successes. They need to set clear standards for empowerment and train employees accordingly. Employees need to know their
problem solution options. Part of their training should include employee discussions of their reactions and solutions to potential scenarios. In addition, frontline
employees' decisions will be better if the employees have information on customers'
histories. Companies also need to be aware that a successful empowerment process
needs time to evolve.

While empowerment increases customer satisfaction and decreases supervisory costs, it can be risky in terms of costs. For example, it's possible for employees
to be overly generous in refunds and compensation for customer problems. Companies have found that employees learn rapidly from a mistake. In most circumstances, companies, such as Xerox and Blue Cross Blue Shield, have found that
empowerment has little or no long-term effect on costs or profit. In fact, some companies have found that personnel do too little for customers rather than too much.
There is also evidence that employees can recognize customers who are trying to
take advantage or commit fraud, even on the telephone.[20]

Empowerment Model.   One way to approach concerns about costs is to consider
the seriousness of the negative consequences of a wrong decision to the company
and assess the capability of the service personnel to handle empowerment. Figure
4.3 shows a matrix, developed by Gutierrez and Dambly, for determining empowerment conditions. A very serious consequence is that the result of a decision could be

FIGURE 4.3   Empowerment Model

Employee
Capability

	Nonserious	Serious	Very Serious
High	Totally empowered	Postapproval	Guidelines
Moderate	Postapproval	Guidelines	Preapproval
Inexperienced	Guidelines	Preapproval	Not empowered

Seriousness of Consequence to Company

Source: Adapted from Juan Gutierrez and Tom Dambly, "Build Customer Loyalty through Employee Empowerment," *Mobius,* Summer 1990, 27.

very damaging to a company due to high costs, high revenue loss, or excessive legal liability. On the other hand, a decision may cost a company very little and not have serious consequences. The second step is to determine the potential of each employee. A very capable employee is committed to company philosophy, has confidence, makes sound decisions, is willing to take calculated risks, and is willing to change behavior based on constructive criticism. Employees who are viewed as not capable of empowerment may be new and still learning or may not have the right level of confidence in their decision-making abilities.

There are five categories of empowerment: totally empowered, postapproval, preapproval, guidelines, and not empowered. In postapproval, employees report what they did and are coached on mistakes. Preapproval involves employees recommending a solution and a supervisor helping make the decision. In the guidelines condition, parameters are set for time, costs, and effort, limiting exposure for the company. If the situation is beyond the guidelines, the employee is not empowered and refers it to a higher level. As the grid shows, a very capable employee is totally empowered for nonserious consequence decisions and has guidelines for very serious consequence decisions. An employee who is not ready for empowerment can use guidelines for nonserious consequence decisions and is not empowered for very serious consequence decisions. Empowerment is a process that evolves as consequences are determined and personnel gain experience. One problem with this approach is that employees may resent their empowerment capability classification and want more authority. Others may welcome a lack of empowerment because they lack confidence in their decisions. Both of these situations benefit from experience and time on the job.[21]

Skill Development 4.2

Using the empowerment model in Figure 4.3, think of potential situations at a company in each of these categories: very serious, serious, and nonserious consequences. Determine what solutions would be acceptable to customers and the company. How would each of the three types of employees need to handle the situations?

Performance Standards

Companies need to establish quality standards that define how their services and products will be delivered. These are the amount and quality of work or output the employees are expected to produce within a given time frame. They are measures of productivity and are used to maintain cost control and to verify performance for incentives and rewards. Companies should be cautious in setting these standards such that productivity standards are complemented by equally strong customer service quality standards. Sometimes a productivity standard and a quality standard are incompatible, such as responsively solving a customer problem but also meeting a quota of so many calls completed in an hour. The standards must be based on customer expectations for friendly, attentive, patient interpersonal communication and satisfactory problem resolution. Standards should be designed with customers and employees in mind. Frustration is directly proportional to the degree that production is the primary emphasis.

Skill Development 4.3

1. What could be the problem for an employee in quadrant A? B? C? D?
2. What remedy would you suggest for an employee in each quadrant?
3. Using Figure 4.4, think of a coworker or employee who is not performing well. Place the coworker on the matrix in terms of his or her knowledge and attitude. Explain why. Figure out the best solution for the employee.
4. Where are most of the performance problems in your company?

Performance Evaluations

Evaluate staff on a regular basis using clear standards and measures. One aspect of an evaluation is factoring in causes of poor performance. It may not be the employee's fault. A company will not have dedicated employees if it fires without cause. Figure 4.4 shows a matrix that examines two employee measures, training and attitude. An employee who is not performing well may need more training or may not be motivated or a combination. If the employee has a good attitude, but not enough knowledge and skills (quadrant A), training is the remedy. If the employee is well trained but not motivated (quadrant D), the answer may be to determine what will motivate. An employee who is well trained and has a good attitude but is not

FIGURE 4.4   Training versus Attitude Matrix

Quadrant A—The employee does not have adequate training, but has a good attitude.
Quadrant B—The employee has adequate training and a good attitude.
Quadrant C—The employee does not have adequate training and does not have a good attitude.
Quadrant D—The employee has adequate training but not a good attitude toward the job.

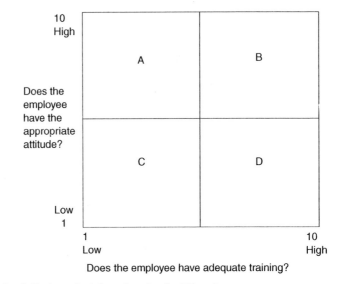

Source: Games People Play (out of print), attributed to Fred Margolis.

performing may be in the wrong job (quadrant B). Since customer service is not a job that is suitable for everyone, employees may perform better if they are moved to a job more in tune with their abilities and goals. An employee with neither adequate training nor a good attitude (quadrant C) may benefit from training, but this may be a hiring mistake. Sometimes it will be necessary to terminate those whose attitudes and behaviors are having a negative effect on other employees. There are also other factors that affect employee performance, such as stress and burnout, a hostile work environment, and poor supervision. Companies need to analyze the situation. Employee loyalty will not happen without company loyalty to employees.[22]

Recognition and Rewards

Employees leave companies because they do not feel appreciated. Recognition of their contributions increases pride and self-esteem and, therefore, productivity and exceptional customer service efforts. Employees need to be rewarded for individual performance, team performance, and company performance. If management believes that service work is work that nobody good really wants to do and that employees cannot be motivated, that means that the manager or company has turned the work into the type of job that nobody wants to do. Companies like Walt Disney and Embassy Suites keep employees motivated and turnover way below average for their industries by job rotation, cross-training, learn-and-earn incentives, and other techniques.

Informal Rewards.   Studies have shown that informal recognition is a stronger motivational tool than formal rewards. Employees know that someone has noticed their efforts and has taken the time to seek them out and say something. One example is a simple on-the-spot thank you or praise for a job well done. The praise should be timely so the connection between the reward and situation is emphasized. It should be done on the employee's own turf rather than in a supervisor's office. Managers should do it when they have employees' full attention, not when employees are rushing down the hallway or are in the middle of paperwork.

Informal rewards can be simple. A thank-you note from a manager or a senior-level executive will be appreciated and saved. Put up customer letters of praise and compliment. Have a pizza party. Bring coffee and doughnuts for breakfast. Take the employees to lunch. Send flowers or a potted plant. Let an employee come to work an hour late with pay. Give a gift certificate. Give money on the spot. Use humor. Make it fun. Give out silly certificates of achievement. Recognize teamwork. Don't forget the support staff, especially those that are not visible to everyone, like the computer technician that solves every problem that comes her way.

Formal Rewards.   Give serious money tied to customer satisfaction and retention. Send the employee to an outside training program. Give an employee a day off. Host a team for a fancy dinner. Give out travel awards.[23]

Reward Variety.   One size does not fit all. Vary awards to suit the person. Each generation and different types of employees will respond to different motivation and reward systems. For example, although it cautions not to stereotype, the Society of Consumer Affairs Professionals suggests some ways to motivate Generation X workers. First, train them for their next job. They understand that they will not stay at one company their entire career. The way to keep them is to help them learn and be more marketable later on. Second, Gen Xers are independent and like freedom to figure things out on their own. Give them a project with clear goals and let them do it. Third, they like constant feedback. Formal annual reviews are not enough. Provide them with timely, informal feedback about their job performance. Fourth, offer them as much information as possible; they are very adept at combining data and technology to solve problems.[24]

Advancement

To attract and retain staff, the opportunity for promotion is critical. In one study in retailing, 58 percent of the employees in the customer service department had over 5 years in the same job. The employees did not believe that advancement was possible and were no longer motivated to do a good job. Many companies are positioning customer service as part of an employee's "tour of duty." Being on the front line in customer service gives employees more insight into customers and the company. Some employees may not be eligible for promotion. Cross-training provides backup and gives employees faith that they can make lateral moves in an organization.[25]

Retention

Employee turnover can cost a company as much as 20 percent over and above an annual salary.[26] Each time an employee leaves, it costs a company to hire and train a replacement. A recent study examined employee turnover in relation to customer satisfaction in six industries. The industries were personal computing, banking, retail, telecommunications, investment management, and property and casualty insurance. More than 60 percent of the 3000 customers were not satisfied with the service they received. Over half, 57 percent, thought that poor employee training was a cause of the service failures. They believed that employee turnover and retention were affecting the quality of service.[27]

Three of the most common periods of time during which employees may leave are when they are first hired, when they are concerned about promotion, and when they become bored. In addition to the employee satisfaction factors, there are specific actions a company can take during these times.

In the first case, when a new employee is hired, he or she may be overwhelmed with unfamiliarity and unexpected job circumstances. Experts suggest pairing the new recruit with an experienced employee who can guide the new employee through the transition.

In the second case, an employee may be ready for a promotion, but there are no slots available. The employee is very vulnerable to a competitor who will offer him or her the next step on the ladder. A company could find the employee a challenging special project until there is a slot available.

In the third case, productive employees do not tolerate boredom. Competitors start to look very attractive. Find out what the employee's interests or special job satisfiers are and tailor the job to make it more challenging and rewarding.[28]

NEXT-GENERATION WORKFORCE

To be successful, a twenty-first-century company needs agility to cope with continuing technological and social change. Organization goals will be achieved only through the efforts of the workforce. The *next-generation workforce* will need skills to thrive in a changing world. Employees will need to continually adapt to change and be responsive to changing and increasing customer needs and demands. Agility means that employees will have to be able to change and execute faster than ever. Roles and responsibilities will change more often. A company will need to understand and overcome people's resistance to change.

Because responsibility for satisfying customers is being pushed to the front line, employees need empowerment, teamwork, and consensus decision-making skills even more than they have in the past. They need to be much more responsive and faster in fulfilling customer needs and expectations. They will not be able to wait for management to make decisions. Since a company will need to invent new processes and products demanded by customers, it will need to rely on the creativity of its entire workforce more than ever. Employees will need to be able to use different thinking styles, analyze problems, and apply critical thinking processes. They will need to understand what the barriers are to creative thinking and how to overcome them. These skills are not new, but they take on even greater importance.

Ultimately, everyone serves customers so that responsiveness will prevail throughout the whole company. Employees will need to know how to identify their external customers and their needs. They will need to know who their internal customers are, what their needs are, and how to meet them. A company must shift from departmental or functional thinking to process thinking. Departmental thinking causes people to consider only the impact on themselves and their department.

They do not think about the effect of their decisions on other departments. If they do not interact with external customers, they forget about them as well. If one department changes a system to lower costs, that may raise costs to another department or adversely affect customer service. Process thinking recognizes how the entire company works together to serve customers.

Finally, people will need to be more proactive in career and life management. Since change is a given, they will need to know how to set goals, develop plans to meet their goals, manage time, stay organized, and maximize their productivity. Employees will need to know how to set what one consultant calls SMART goals (specific, measurable, achievable, realistic, and timely). Again, these are not new skills, just more important given the independence of work in the twenty-first century. Management will need to plan how their workforce will acquire all these skills. Many of these issues are discussed in later chapters in the text.[29]

TERMS

frontline employees	situational interviews
internal customer service	empowerment
employee satisfaction	employee turnover
employee loyalty	next-generation workforce

DISCUSSION QUESTIONS

1. Define frontline customer service provider.
2. How is internal customer service related to external customer service?
3. Explain why employee satisfaction equals customer satisfaction.
4. What can a company do to have satisfied employees?
5. What are some examples of a good supervisor? What are some examples of a bad supervisor?
6. What training is needed to provide exceptional customer service?
7. Consider the training at your company. What additional training is needed?
8. Define empowerment. How does a company use empowerment successfully?
9. Give an example of a situation in which a productivity standard and a customer service standard are incompatible.
10. Explain the skills needed by the next-generation workforce.

CASE—THE ROOT CAUSE OF THE PROBLEM

Mike and Jodi Brown were building a house on 5 acres in Wood County. When they were getting ready to have their gas line installed, they marked a route through the field in front of their house so gas company would know where to dig the trench. Their aim was to make it the shortest route but not dig a trench through the roots of any large trees. The house was 600 feet from the road. Figure 4.5 shows a diagram of the route and house and tree placement.

FIGURE 4.5   House Site

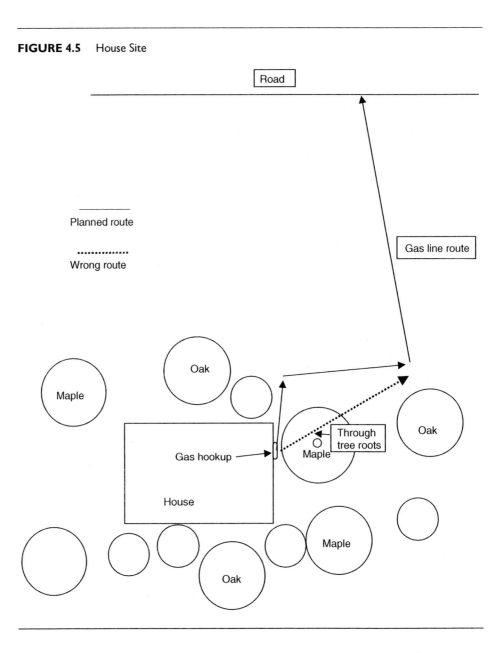

The maple tree next to the house was about 30 feet tall, and the house had been planned around the large trees. The Browns were concerned that cutting through the maple tree roots would damage the tree and cause it to die. They carefully planned the route to keep the trench away from the maple tree roots and clearly marked the location with 4-foot stakes wrapped at the top with orange tape and the word "GAS" written on the stakes.

Mike Brown met with the house construction supervisor, Dave, and the gas company crew supervisor, Dan, to make sure they understood the route for the trench and the reasons for its location. The gas company said it would be doing the work within the next week. Mike checked with Dave to make sure that he would be on site.

About a week later, Mike went to the house site late on a Wednesday afternoon. He discovered that the gas company had dug a trench 4 feet from the maple tree right through the tree roots, ignoring the stakes and marked route. (See the dotted line on Figure 4.5.) Mike was told that when the gas company showed up to do the job, Dave, the construction supervisor, was at lunch, and Dan, the gas crew supervisor, was not with the crew because he was at the dentist. The crew went ahead with the job.

Mike complained to the gas company. It said the only thing it could do was pay for damages or repair. The maple tree would not die immediately, but it could within 5 years. There will be no way to prove that the tree died because of the trench. Furthermore, a 30-foot tree cannot be replaced.

1. What happened here? What are the "people" problems?
2. What should the gas company do?
3. What should Mike do?
4. How could this problem be avoided in the future?

NOTES

1. Phil Dourado, "Why Web Service Is So Bad," eCustomerServiceWorld, available from http://www.eCustomerServiceWorld.com/e-articles_articles.asp?type-article&id=531, accessed June 10, 2001.
2. Monica Jenks, Selma Baum, and John Goodman, "Hiring and Retaining Superior Staff: A Growing Challenge for the 1990s," *Mobius,* Spring 1990, 18–21.
3. Leonard L. Berry, "Improving America's Service," *Marketing Management* 1, no. 3 (1992): 29–38.
4. David E. Bowen, Stephen W. Gilliland, and Robert Folger, "HRM and Service Fairness: How Being Fair with Employees Spills Over to Customers," *Organizational Dynamics,* Winter 1999, 7–34.
5. D. Randall Brandt, Jaci Jarrett Masztal, and William H. Newbolt, "An Outside-In Approach to Defining Targets for Measures of Employee Satisfaction and Commitment," *White Paper Series* 2, no. 7, available from http://www.burke.com, accessed October 2001.
6. John Goodman and Marlene Yanovsky, "Treating Employees as Customers: Estimating the Bottom Line Impact of Employee Dissatisfaction and Setting Rational Priorities," *Customer Relationship Management,* September 1997, 22–25.
7. Sybil F. Stershic, "The Flip Side of Customer Satisfaction Research (You Know How Your Customers Feel, But Have You Talked to Your Employees Lately?)" *Marketing Research,* December 1990, 45–50; and Michael Lowenstein, "Securing the Service with a Smile," *Customer Loyalty Today* 7, no. 9 (October 2000): 6.
8. Berry, "Improving America's Service," 36.
9. Brenda Paik Sunoo, "Results-Oriented Customer Service Training," *Workforce* 80, no. 5 (May 2001): 84.
10. Jenks, Baum, and Goodman, "Hiring and Retaining Superior Staff"; and Steve Jarvis, "Call Centers Raise Bar on Hiring Criteria," *Marketing News,* September 11, 2000, 4.
11. Karen Janman, "The Key to Superior Customer Service," *Customer Service Management,* July–August 1999, 55–57.
12. Marnie Feasel, "Training Can Produce Better Reps," *Call Center Solutions,* October 1998, 138–143; Jenks, Baum, and Goodman, "Hiring and Retaining Superior Staff," 19; and Ron Zemke, ". . . World-Class Customer Service," *Boardroom Reports* 21, no. 24 (December 15, 1992): 5–7.
13. Stershic, "Flip Side of Customer Satisfaction Research" and Berry, "Improving America's Service."

14. John Tschohl, "How Do You Keep Employees?" available from http://www.customer-service.com/articles/employ.html, accessed November 25, 1998.

15. Thom A. Mayer, Robert J. Cates, Mary Jane Mastorovich, and Deborah L. Royalty, "Emergency Department Patient Satisfaction: Customer Service Training Improves Patient Satisfaction and Ratings of Physician and Nurse Skill," *Journal of Healthcare Management* 43, no. 5 (September 1998): 427.

16. Jenks, Baum, and Goodman, "Hiring and Retaining Superior Staff," and Feasel, "Training Can Produce Better Reps."

17. Richard Normann, *Service Strategy and Management* (n.p.: 1984), 47.

18. Jenks, Baum, and Goodman, "Hiring and Retaining Superior Staff," 19; and Lowenstein, "Securing the Service with a Smile."

19. Jean-Charles Chebat and Paul Kollias, "The Impact of Empowerment on Customer Contact Employees' Role in Service Organizations," *Journal of Service Research* 3, no. 1 (August 2000): 66–81.

20. Jenks, Baum, and Goodman, "Hiring and Retaining Superior Staff."

21. Juan Gutierrez and Tom Dambly, "Build Customer Loyalty through Employee Empowerment," *Mobius*, Summer 1990, 25–28.

22. Attributed to Fred Margolis, *Games People Play* (out of print).

23. Zemke, ". . . World-Class Customer Service;" Tschohl, "How Do You Keep Employees?" and Clay Carr, *Front-Line Customer Service* (New York: John Wiley & Sons, 1990).

24. Society of Consumer Affairs Professionals, "Four Ways to Manage Generation X," available from http://www.socap.org/Publications/Quicktakes/4wmanagex.html, accessed on July 3, 2001.

25. Jenks, Baum, and Goodman, "Hiring and Retaining Superior Staff," 21.

26. Jenks, Baum, and Goodman, "Hiring and Retaining Superior Staff," 18.

27. Jeffrey Marshall, "Employee Retention Linked to Better Customer Service," *Financial Executive* 17, no. 2 (March 2001): 11.

28. Lowenstein, "Securing the Service with a Smile."

29. Doug Howardell, "Creating a Next Generation Workforce," available from http://www.theacagroup.com/nextgen.htm, accessed June 10, 2001.

EXCEPTIONAL PERFORMANCE

OBJECTIVES

1. Illustrate positive and negative attitudes and mind-sets.
2. Define and describe the characteristics of emotional intelligence.
3. Describe self-talk.
4. Describe personal style systems: the responsiveness/assertiveness style system and the Myers-Briggs Type Indicator.
5. Discuss the benefits, necessary conditions, processes, and challenges of teamwork.
6. Outline personal change adaptation, goal-setting, and time management techniques.

ELEMENTS OF EXCEPTIONAL PERFORMANCE

Providing exceptional service to customers begins with exceptional individual effort and performance. Understanding our attitudes, personal styles, and behavior improves our ability to perform our jobs, work on teams, and manage our lives. This chapter discusses our positive and negative attitudes, our emotional intelligence, and self-talk and examines how they affect our customer service delivery. It addresses two types of personal styles to help us understand how we and others think and act. The chapter also includes a section on teamwork to suggest ways to improve our performance. Finally, we look at change, goal setting, and time management so we can use our understanding about ourselves to improve our customer service behavior.

POSITIVE AND NEGATIVE ATTITUDES AND MIND-SETS

Our attitudes and mind-sets influence our actions and reactions. What are the characteristics and behaviors of employees who are exceptional customer service providers?

* They have a positive, can-do attitude. They focus on the positive aspects of a situation and expect positive outcomes.
* They are adaptable and see shades of gray. They can see both sides of an issue. They figure out how two people can both be right.
* They do what they say they will do.
* They assume good intentions.
* They empathize with people even if they don't agree with them.
* They genuinely try not to make mistakes.
* If they make a mistake, they don't make excuses.
* They are on the job every day on time.
* They don't miss deadlines.
* They do not play politics.
* They don't complain. They solve problems.
* They are part of the solution, not part of the problem.
* They are great team members.
* They set a great example.
* They take pride in what they do.[1]

Conversely, think about the employees at a company where you have worked. Was one of your coworkers a whiner? Did one of your fellow employees bring personal problems to work? How did the behavior of these workers affect customers? Here are some examples of difficult people and negative attitudes:

Apathetic April—Who cares? Why bother?

Arrogant Art—He can one-up anyone's story or success.

Blameless Bill—He always has an excuse. It must be someone else's fault.

Bottleneck Bob—He is always late with everything.

Bureaucratic Bert—Everything must be done by the book.

Clueless Clyde—He doesn't know anything and doesn't want to know anything.

Malicious Marcy—She's two-faced. Look out for the knife in your back.

Motor Mouth Mona—She never stops talking.

Narrow-Minded Nathan—We've always done it this way.

Negative Nell—See that black cloud? She never has a good word to say about anything.

Obsequious Olive—She's a brownnoser, a flatterer, and a complete phony.

Pity Polly—Her life is a mess—and she will tell you all about it.

Snobbish Sam—Only certain people are worth his effort.

We do not want to be any of these people. Certainly, they are stereotypes, but these behaviors will get in the way of doing our best job for customers. They can be "toxic" in that they spoil the environment for everyone else. If we have coworkers who match these examples, the best thing to do is avoid them. We will also encounter customers who demonstrate some of these behaviors. This is human nature. Exceptional customer service is about accepting the world as it is, warts and all.

Experience Discussion 5.1

Tom Peters has some unique and thought-provoking suggestions for achieving success:

1. Build it now. Just do something. Now. Change is too fast to wait until it's perfect.
2. Embrace failure. Learn from mistakes. Peters says that we seem to have a need to be protected from all risks. Moving forward cannot be done without mistakes.
3. Keep smiling. "You'll never do anything interesting right the first, or 31ˢᵗ, time."
4. Cherish curiosity. Ben Bradlee, legendary *Washington Post* editor, describes it as "compulsive spontaneity" and "advanced immaturity."
5. Steal the world blind. Cherry-pick ideas from anywhere.
6. Dare to be outrageous. This can often fail. However, Peters says that those who dare are "responsible for virtually all the world's progress."
7. Support mindless optimism, an unrealistic belief in the possibility of success. It drives accomplishment.
8. Never look back. Take life as it comes and go on.
9. Honor paradox. Wildly successful people are perfectionists and have a high tolerance for disorder. Think about it.
10. Tell the truth.

Peters says, "A personal rut is danger No. 1 in today's topsy-turvy climate!"[2] Give examples and discuss these ideas.

EMOTIONAL INTELLIGENCE

In explaining emotional intelligence, we should first note, in a simplistic sense, that we have two minds. One is the rational mind, the thinking part. The other is the emotional side, the feeling part. They operate interdependently, ordinarily in balance. Sometimes our rational mind ignores or vetoes our emotional side. Sometimes our emotions take over. Without getting into the evolution and scientific workings of the brain, we can see that we are both thinking and feeling people. Intelligence tests have historically measured the thinking or cognitive side, the IQ. This takes into consideration verbal and mathematical-logical intelligence. Scientists have theorized that there are actually multiple intelligences, for example, kinesthetic (Michael Jordan), musical (Mozart), spatial (Frank Lloyd Wright), and interpersonal (Martin Luther King, Jr.). This section addresses emotional intelligence, akin to interpersonal intelligence, because it strongly affects how we react to customers.

Emotional intelligence means how people handle their emotions or feelings. For some, healthy emotional intelligence is inborn. Others must pay more attention to their emotions and learn how to manage them. Emotional intelligence can improve over time with awareness and practice. People who have a healthy level of emotional intelligence have five important characteristics:

1. *They know their own emotions.*   They are aware of their true feelings as they happen. Being aware of their feelings lets them choose an appropriate response rather than just reacting. They know what their early stress warning signals are. They recognize how their body reacts to stress and notice when the fight or flight reflex kicks in. Thus, they have more time to prevent themselves from acting automatically and choosing the wrong words or actions. Emotional intelligence keeps them from overreacting. A few seconds can damage a customer relationship.

2. *They manage their emotions.*   Once they recognize their feelings, they can handle them. They are more able to shake off anxiety or irritability and recover. They can bounce back from difficult situations quickly. They can focus on the next customer without dwelling on the last one.

3. *They can motivate themselves.*   Emotions can interfere with mental clarity and cause the "we can't think straight" response, common in test anxiety. Self-motivation involves the ability to deny emotional impulses and put off gratification to pursue a goal. We motivate ourselves to persist and use optimism to succeed. Customer service personnel put aside their emotions to pay attention to customers to help them reach their goals.

4. *They recognize the emotions of others.*   They are able to notice nonverbal communication and understand what people need and want. They are empathetic and can see things from a customer's perspective. This may be one of the most essential characteristics for customer service.

5. *They know how to handle interpersonal relationships.*   They use their insight about people's feelings and concerns to develop rapport. They are natural leaders, knowing how to organize groups and persuade people to work toward a common goal. They are talented at negotiation and conflict resolution.[3]

Emotional intelligence is a benefit in a working environment because we are more attuned to coworkers and customers, we can handle uncomfortable situations and conflict, and we can motivate ourselves to reach our goals. The question is how can we increase our emotional intelligence? We become more aware of our feelings. We resist inappropriate emotions. We practice rebounding from upsetting situations. We learn to pay more attention to our customers' feelings.

SELF-TALK

Self-talk is the voice inside that we can hear telling ourselves things about ourselves and others. Self-talk can create self-fulfilling prophecies. If we see ourselves failing, it may happen. Negativity generates negativity. An affirmation is an assertion that something is true. Negative affirmations are statements like "I can't" and "I never. . . " They are negative labeling of who and what we are and what we can and cannot do. Negative self-talk creates substantial stress. Negative self-talk causes worry. Worry can be described as obsessing about potential events over which we have no control. Of the things we worry about, 40 percent will never happen. And 58 percent will turn out better than we think. Only 2 percent are actually worth worrying about. Worry is stressful exactly because we have no control.

The following are examples of the misconceptions of negative self-talk:

* *All-or-nothing thinking.*   We see things in black-and-white categories. If our performance falls short of perfect, we see ourselves as a total failure. "I messed up that order. I'm going to get fired."

* *Overgeneralization.*   We see a single negative event or emotion as a pattern of defeat. Instead of describing our error, we attach a negative label to ourselves. "I'm a loser."

* *Disqualifying the positive.*   We reject positive experiences by insisting they "don't count" for some reason or other. It is saying, "I was just lucky" when someone congratulates us about our success. In this way, we can maintain a

negative belief that is contradicted by our everyday experiences. Minimization is minimizing our own desirable qualities and, by contrast, someone else's imperfections.

* *Emotional reasoning.* We assume our negative emotions necessarily reflect the way things really are. "I feel it; therefore it must be true."

* *Mental filter.* We pick out a single negative detail and dwell on it exclusively so that our vision of reality becomes darkened, like the drop of ink that discolors the entire beaker of water. "It's raining again. It's going to be a lousy day."

* *Jumping to conclusions.* We make a negative interpretation even though there are no definite facts that convincingly support our conclusion. Mind reading is arbitrarily concluding that someone is reacting negatively to us and not bothering to check it out. Personalization is seeing ourselves as the cause of some negative external event for which in fact we were not primarily responsible. This may be how we react to an angry customer, taking it personally. A fortune-teller error is anticipating that things will turn out badly and feeling convinced that our prediction is an already-established fact.

* *Should statements.* We try to motivate ourselves with "shoulds" and "shouldn'ts," as if we had to be punished before we could be expected to do anything. "Musts" and "oughts" are also offenders. The emotional consequence is guilt. When we direct should statements toward others, we feel anger, frustration, and resentment.

* *Labeling.* Labeling is attaching a negative label to people based on an action or their appearance, "That guy is a total jerk." Mislabeling involves describing an event or person with language that is emotionally loaded and highly biased.[4]

Positive thinking, seeing ourselves winning, helps people succeed. Self-talk also influences how we label and treat other people. People with emotional intelligence recognize how their emotions create negative and positive self-talk and know how to change the negative. We can use positive affirmations to handle worry and anxiety. We can say statements such as "I can do well on this math exam" or "I can handle this customer situation" to ourselves. We can write them on a Post-it note for our desk. We can write them in our day planner.

PERSONAL STYLE TENDENCIES

Everyone has ways of behaving and reacting based on personality traits. In this section, we call it styles. We will cover two style systems. One, the responsive/assertive scale (origin unclear), is used by many consultants. The other is the Myers-Briggs Type Indicator.

The objective of personal style tools, such as the responsive/assertive scale and Myers-Briggs Type Indicator, is to help people understand themselves and others. Each style has its strengths and weaknesses, which will be outlined below. The tools determine preferences, not skills. They do not add up to a complete understanding of a person. They can be misused to label and pigeonhole people. They can also be used wrongly to judge one type as better than another. One style or type is not better than any other. People will not always act in accord with their style. It will depend on the circumstances, the relationship, their stress level, their motivation, and countless other factors.[5]

Responsiveness versus Assertiveness Style System

This personal style system is based on responsiveness and assertiveness. *Responsiveness* is the inclination of people to outwardly show their feelings and develop relationships. High-responsiveness people are open, friendly, informal, emotional, changeable, and relationship-oriented. Low-responsiveness people are reserved, businesslike, formal, rational, independent, disciplined, and task-oriented. *Assertiveness* is the amount of control that people attempt to exercise over other people and over situations. High-assertive people are competitive, fast-acting, risk taking, direct, and take-charge people. Low-assertive people are cooperative, slower acting, risk avoiding, and more easygoing.

People have a tendency toward one of four dominant style types: amiable, expressive, analytical, or driver (see Figure 5.1). Some people have a secondary inclination toward a second type. Amiables are less assertive and more responsive. Expressives are more assertive and more responsive. Analyticals are less assertive and less responsive. Drivers are more assertive and less responsive. People with high responsiveness are more trusting, and people with low responsiveness are more cautious.

Below we will describe some of the characteristics of each style and suggest some ideas about providing customer service to each type. Keep in mind that no one is a perfect example of a style. The descriptions are the extremes in each case. People's behavior is the result of numerous influences. The descriptions are tendencies only, and the suggestions cannot always be used literally.

FIGURE 5.1 Responsiveness/Assertiveness Style

Responsiveness \ Assertiveness	Low	High
Low	**Analytical** Less assertive Less responsive Technician Cautious	**Driver** More assertive Less responsive Controller Cautious
High	**Amiable** Less assertive More responsive Supporter Trusting	**Expressive** More assertive More responsive Promoter Trusting

Amiables.   Another term for an amiable is *supporter*. Amiables are supportive, co-operative, friendly, and patient. They are excellent listeners. They like personal relationships. Most people feel comfortable with amiables. Amiables dislike risk. They are unassertive and dislike conflict so much that they might tell people what they think others want to hear rather than what they are actually thinking. They don't always get what they want because they don't speak up. They will often have jobs in the helping professions. If they are supervisors, they are good coaches. They make excellent customer service providers.

Customers and coworkers will find amiables to be friendly, attentive, and helpful. Since they are relationship-oriented, amiables may find it much easier to be empathetic with customers. On the other hand, because they do not like conflict, they may have a tendency to escape from difficult customer situations. When they are empowered, they will need to be careful about being too agreeable. Coworkers may try to take advantage of amiables because amiables will be cooperative and unassertive. They will need to learn how to be tougher.

As customers, amiables want sincere, friendly attention. Since they are not as assertive, they may not ask for help when they need it. If they have a problem, they may not bring it to a company's attention. If they do, they will not be aggressive about it. They won't know what they want for a resolution.

Expressives.   An alternative term is *promoters*. Expressives are outgoing, animated, humorous, intuitive, and persuasive. They thrive on involvement with others and prefer to deal with people informally. They like to be on a first-name basis with people. They are able to motivate others. They often work at a fast pace. They may communicate their feelings intensely and lash out if criticized. Salespeople are often expressives.

As providers, expressives are among the friendliest employees. They want customers to be happy, but they may tend to be too talkative. They may not remember all the details of their job, but they work fast.

As customers, expressives will be very friendly to customer service personnel. Calling them by their first name will be preferred. If expressives have a problem, they are likely to tell a long story. Be prepared to listen, listen, and listen some more. It will be easy to tell when expressives are angry. Analyticals will be frustrated by expressives' volatility and disorganization. Drivers will be compatible in terms of pace but will want to get business done. Amiables will like expressives but may have the urge to flee if an expressive is upset.

Analyticals.   Analyticals are *technicians*. They are usually systematic and like details and facts. They evaluate situations objectively. They are good at working independently and are good problem solvers. They prefer an organized environment. They are quiet and reserved. They try to make decisions free of personal and emotional considerations. Their actions and decisions are cautious and slow. They do not like change. They can overanalyze and avoid making decisions. They avoid expressing feelings and exhibit less body language. They may have financial or science-related jobs.

Although they pay close attention to customers and details, analytical providers will seem the least friendly to customers. They will probably be calm in difficult situations, but they may push customers to be logical about their problems.

Customers who are analyticals will be less inclined to engage in small talk. When they ask questions, they expect very specific answers. If they have a problem, they will be very detailed in explaining it. They will often know how they want it solved. They want to know when it will be solved. Customer service providers who are a different style may need to downplay it to make analyticals more comfortable. For example, an exuberant expressive might annoy some analyticals. Those with different styles should be prepared to be specific and explain. Expressives and drivers may need to slow down and be patient. Amiables will be most compatible as long as they understand analyticals' reserve.

Drivers.   Drivers can also be called *controllers*. Drivers are task-oriented, results-oriented, and bottom-line-oriented. They like to take control of people and situations. They are intense, efficient, decisive, and independent. They exhibit very direct body language. They make quick decisions. They like competition and are risk takers. They are workaholics and achievers. They may not communicate a warm, caring attitude and often seem insensitive to the feelings of others. They can be considered "dominating" and "cold." Many CEOs are drivers.

Driving customer service providers may have a tendency to rush customers, especially if they are analyticals. They aren't the warmest employees, but they will get things done.

Customer service providers may find drivers fairly aggressive. Drivers are time-driven. Transactions will be quick. They expect customer service providers to be fast, and so providers should stick to business. If drivers have a problem, they will be direct and clear in their requests. They may argue for what they want. They want to be right. If we can agree with their facts, we should say so. Amiables will need to guard against being pushovers. Analyticals will need to think faster. Expressives may seem disorganized to drivers.

Many people are a combination style with a strong preference for one style and a moderate preference for another. Someone who is mostly an analytical, but whose secondary preference is driver, would be called a driving analytical. With higher assertiveness, the driving analytical may be more decisive and be more of an achiever and risk taker.[6]

Experience Discussion 5.2

Consider a small advertising agency with 10 employees. The CEO is a driver with a touch of expressive. There are three account executives. One is a driver, another is an expressive driver, and the third is an analytical driver. The VP, administration, is an analytical amiable. The two graphic designers are both expressives. The director of production is an amiable. The director of research is a driving analytical. The receptionist is an expressive amiable.

1. Do their styles seem to fit their jobs?
2. Describe how they might interact as internal customers.
3. What should the three account executives be aware of as they interact with their clients?

Myers-Briggs Type Indicator

The *Myers-Briggs Type Indicator* is another personality style assessment tool. It helps people understand themselves, their natural strengths, and their potential areas for growth. It also helps people understand other people and helps build teamwork skills. While we will not necessarily know what our coworkers' and customers' types are, it will help us understand how they may be different. The inventory measures eight mental functions: extraversion, introversion, sensing, intuition, thinking, feeling, judging, and perceiving.

The inventory is based on Jung's work in which he identified two main mental activities and two ways people focus their energy. One of the two mental activities was perceiving, having to do with taking in information. The other mental activity was judging, meaning organizing information and coming to conclusions. He said that people perceive by either sensing or intuition and judge by thinking or feeling. He also observed two ways people focus their energy: extraversion and introversion. Extraversion means to be energized by the world of people, experiences, and activity. Introversion means being energized by ideas, internal thoughts, and emotions.

Briggs and Myers developed his theory to create 16 types. They believe that people have natural preferences for these functions and develop habits and patterns of behavior based on them. The inventory identifies where our preferences lie on a continuum for each dichotomy (see Figure 5.2), for instance, whether we are on the sensing end or intuitive end of that continuum or somewhere in the middle. For example, a score may indicate that we show preferences for the type ISFP, which means we use introversion, sensing, feeling, and perceiving. The preferences interact, and the combination provides an underlying personality pattern. Based on their style, people develop behaviors, skills, and attitudes, but we are also influenced by our environment, all of our experiences, and our choices.

The preferences indicate how we prefer to focus our attention and energy, how we prefer to take in information, how we orient ourselves to the external world, and how we prefer to organize information and make decisions. There is no right or wrong way to do these activities. The words for the style dimensions—*extravert, introvert, sensing, intuitive, thinking, feeling, judging,* and *perceiving*—are used in a different way from what we may be used to. Extravert does not necessarily mean talkative or gregarious, introvert does not mean shy or inhibited, feeling does not mean emotional, judging does not mean judgmental, and perceiving does not mean perceptive.

FIGURE 5.2 Myers-Briggs Type Indicator Dimensions

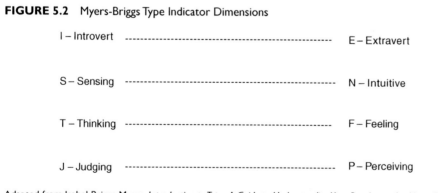

Adapted from Isabel Briggs Myers, *Introduction to Type: A Guide to Understanding Your Results on the Myers-Briggs Type Indicator*, 6th ed., revised by Linda K. Kirby and Katharine D. Myers (Palo Alto, CA: Consulting Psychologists Press, 1998).

Introvert-Extravert Dichotomy—This preference involves our source of energy. A metaphor is how we charge our energy batteries. *Introverts* focus on their internal world of ideas and experiences. They prefer to communicate in writing, are private and reserved, and work out problems by reflecting on them. They direct their energy inward and receive energy from reflecting on their thoughts, memories, and feelings. They tend to think things through before speaking. They are quick to listen and slow to speak. *Extraverts* focus on the external world of people and activity. They prefer to communicate by talking, are sociable and expressive, and learn best by doing or discussing. They receive energy from interacting with people and taking action. They like to try things out. They tend to speak first, reflect later. They are quick to speak and slow to listen. About 75 percent of Americans are extraverts and 25 percent introverts. Analyticals and amiables tend to be introverts, and drivers and expressives are more likely to be extraverts.

Sensing-Intuitive Dichotomy—This preference indicates the way we acquire information, by observation or by introspection. *Sensors* are factual and concrete. They observe and remember specifics, trust experience, and understand ideas and theories through practical applications. They like to take in information that is real and tangible. They are attuned to practical realities. They are literal; when they want to know the time, they want to know it is 4:10 p.m. *Intuiters* are imaginative and creative. They are oriented to future possibilities, focus on patterns and meanings in data, move quickly to conclusions, and trust inspiration. They see the big picture and focus on relationships and connections between facts. They are especially attuned to seeing new possibilities. About 70 percent of the U.S. population are sensors.

Thinking-Feeling Dichotomy—One way to describe this preference is whether we pay more attention to thoughts or emotions. *Thinkers* are analytical and skeptical. They solve problems with logic. They are reasonable and fair and want everyone treated equally. They mentally remove themselves from a situation to look at the pros and cons objectively. *Feelers* are empathetic and compassionate and strive for harmony. They are fair and want people treated as individuals. They assess the impact of decisions on people. They like to consider what is important to them and to others involved.

About two-thirds of males prefer thinking decisions, and about two-thirds of females prefer feeling decisions. An analytical is a thinker. An amiable is a feeler. This preference does not indicate the difference between someone who is cold-hearted and insensitive and someone who is warm-hearted and sensitive. Feelers are more comfortable revealing their emotions. Thinkers have the same emotions, but they prefer to hide them.

Judging-Perceiving Dichotomy—We can describe this preference as the way we approach time and our environment. *Judgers* are judicious about time. They are organized, methodical, and systematic and make short- and long-term plans. They like to live in a planned, orderly manner. They like to have things settled. They try to avoid last-minute stresses. They seek closure, and getting things done energizes them. *Perceivers* are perceptive of options. They are flexible, spontaneous, casual, and adaptable. Detailed plans feel confining to them. They like things open to change. They resist closure to obtain more data. They are resourceful in adapting to the demands of the moment. They feel energized by last-minute pressures.[7]

Having explained the preferences, we, once again, need to emphasize that they are not absolutes. Human beings are very complex and cannot be described in four easy words. Just because someone is on the introversion side of the scale and likes to work alone does not mean that the person is not capable of functioning very well on a team. Throughout our lives, we have learned to adapt to different ways of thinking and being. If we are very accustomed to operating in one manner, it will take more energy and attention to alter our behavior, but it can be done.

This style system can be used more for understanding ourselves than customers. It would be difficult to tell what style a customer is. If a situation is not going well with a customer, we may recognize that our style and a customer's are different. This is a case in which we try to match the customer's style a little closer, talking details, not talking, paying more attention to time, or empathizing more with emotions.

Skill Development 5.1

1. Describe how each preference might affect your customer service performance.
2. Describe how each preference might affect your customers' behavior.

TEAMWORK

Being able to work well on a team is a prerequisite for jobs in the current business environment. In a knowledge-based environment, leveraging intellectual capital is a path to corporate success. Teamwork is also a component of providing service to internal customers. When successful, teamwork can help companies accomplish more, with more commitment and harmony. Working on a team also strengthens individual skills so that employees are even better at working with customers. This section will discuss the benefits, necessary conditions, processes, and challenges of teamwork. It is not meant to be a complete handbook for successful teamwork but to introduce basic concepts.

Numerous studies in many disciplines have found that cooperative teamwork, rather than competition and independence, can help people communicate, empathize, support others, discuss issues constructively, solve problems, achieve at higher levels, and feel confident and valued as persons. Studies that have directly tested the contribution of teamwork to customer service find similar benefits.

Teams need goals, resources, and rewards. Without a clear set of goals, there is nothing to drive and organize the work. Without sufficient resources, achieving goals is frustrating and may not be possible. Without rewards, motivation falters. According to team experts, three psychological conditions are essential to a team's effectiveness as well:

1. Mutual trust among members
2. A sense of group identity—that is, a feeling among members that they belong to a unique and worthwhile group
3. A sense of group efficacy—that is, the belief that the team can perform well and that the team members are more effective working together than working alone.[8]

These conditions are hard to achieve. Without these, teams can function, but they will not be as effective as they could be. Later in this section, we will discuss how teams can reach trust, group identity, and group efficacy by examining the emotional intelligence of teams.

Stages of Team Growth

Next, we discuss the *stages of team growth*. As a team, the members do not naturally begin working well together. They go through predictable stages.

Forming.   The first stage is forming. There is considerable confusion about roles and goals. Team members are figuring out what their role will be and who will be the leader (if that's not already determined). The team members withhold their full participation until they know whom to trust. Team members try to determine acceptable group behavior and ways to deal with group problems. The team members try to define the task, figure out how they will get it done, and determine what information they need. They often discuss irrelevant issues while they figure out what is relevant. They complain and focus on barriers. Team members' emotions are anxiety, insecurity, lack of trust, defensiveness, and anger. Individuals are in the process of transitioning to member status. They do not get much done, but this is perfectly normal.

Team leaders or facilitators should acknowledge and empathize with members' feelings of confusion, ambivalence, and even annoyance. Facilitators can reassure everyone that frustrations and barriers are common. They help the team cope with new ways of approaching both the doing and the managing aspects of work. They help define work expectations and the boundaries of authority and responsibility. Facilitators can encourage the team to tackle the doable parts of the project first.

Storming.   In storming, the most difficult stage, team members are resistant to the task, argue about what they should do, and establish unrealistic goals. Members may be defensive and competitive. Some want to gain influence to be leaders or recognized experts or to get the team to adopt their priorities and methods. Some want to use the group to increase their visibility and power. Team members start choosing sides and develop a pecking order. They pull apart instead of uniting. The team members decide they trust some of the other team members, they don't trust others, and they are not sure about a few. The task-oriented don't care about group dynamics. There is a lot of disunity, jealousy, and tension. Communication may be direct and aggressive.

They wonder if the problem has been defined correctly. They feel time pressure. Conflicts arise among those who want to get it done quickly, those who want to proceed more deliberately, and those who want to procrastinate. There are conflicts between those who have decided how a job should be done and those of a more experimental nature. Some want more autocratic direction; others want a more democratic, open atmosphere. Leaders or facilitators need to let the team know that the conflict and tension are normal. The members of the team need to understand that they must learn to handle stress early on. They are still not making much headway, but they are taking more time to listen to each other and are beginning to understand each other.

Norming.   The third stage is norming. Team members begin to accept the team, their membership in it, their roles, the team norms, their other team members, and the team's common goal. They become more cooperative and cohesive to work toward the goal. They develop routines for handling problems, new situations, and crises. They have been self-serving; now they are serving the group. The team members accept that their diversity and their different skills, talents, and personal styles are needed to get the entire job done. They learn that without differences, there is little creativity. They begin to realize that if they help each other, they can accomplish the project. The task-oriented begin to understand that paying attention to group dynamics will help get things done. The team starts making progress.

Performing.   In this stage, the team has settled its relationships and begun to understand each other's strengths and weaknesses. Even reticent members become involved and often become more proactive. There may still be some ups and downs as things change, such as if a member leaves or a leader changes. The members may challenge whether or not they really need a leader. They begin performing, solving problems, making decisions, and working through group issues. They start getting a lot of work done.

The intensity and the duration of the different stages vary from team to team. Some teams reach the performing stage quickly; others never do. Understanding that the stages, in particular storming, are going to happen and are normal may reduce some of the frustration and help a team get to the performing stage.[9]

Team Emotional Intelligence

A team is made up of the sum total of the talents and strengths of the team members. A team will be more successful when there is social harmony, the result of the emotional intelligence of the combined team. To be effective, a team must be aware of the feelings of its members and its group emotions. Emotions, in this case, are a whole range of feelings, from impatience to frustration to apathy to pride.

Two ways to promote awareness of team members' feelings are interpersonal understanding and perspective taking. Interpersonal understanding is listening, acknowledging, understanding, and empathizing with each team member's feelings. These skills can be transferred to dealing with customers. Perspective taking is considering decisions and issues from each team member's perspective, making sure no one is left out and all objections and questions are dealt with to reach a consensus rather than majority rule. It is often the case that three out of four team members are in favor of a decision, and the fourth team member disagrees. Many teams will proceed based on a majority vote, and the fourth person feels powerless and may be less likely to cooperate. The team must ask for input and deal with the fourth team member's objections and reluctance to reach consensus.

A team must regulate emotions by forming norms for confrontation and consideration. Problems need to be resolved, or they will make the team ineffective. Teams should acknowledge that a conflict exists and make it a team issue. For example, if a team member does something outside team behavior norms, say that the team member continually misses meetings, the team must confront the team member. If the team does not, trust will disappear. The confrontation must make two things clear: that the team member is not following team norms and that the member's contribution is vital to the team's success.

The team must also deal with overall team emotions, such as team malaise, panic, and discouragement. The team must be aware that an emotion exists. Then the team can regulate the emotion by several means. One example is for team members to speak up when they feel the team is not being productive. Another is to allow the team 5 minutes to whine and moan about a setback. Then the members have to stop and go back to work. A team can also build and celebrate team spirit. A good example is a team of four students in an online web course. They had spent half a semester communicating by e-mail on case assignments, never face-to-face. They decided to meet for lunch over semester break, resulting in a much more cohesive, cooperative team.[10]

Common Team Problems

Successful teams understand that communication cannot be taken for granted. Team members should be aware of how their communication affects the other team members and the usefulness of the discussion. Adapting communication behavior to fit the norms of a team is no different from adapting when we are talking to our boss, our children, or our mother-in-law. It's good practice for adapting to our customers. Listening and nonverbal and verbal communication will be covered in later chapters and will help in adapting communication.

One of the requirements for successful team functioning is effective listening. A common problem is that team members interrupt speakers before they have finished their comments. People often are thinking of their response before speakers have made their main point. A norm should be established for taking turns that is regulated by a facilitator or the team leader. Using the idea of perspective taking, all team members should be heard to get the best ideas, reach consensus, and successfully reach goals.

Other behaviors that diminish team effectiveness are making inappropriate and rude comments to each other and not listening effectively, including attribution, discounts, yes-butting, naysaying, and plops.

* *Attribution* is ascribing a motive to someone about the person's behavior. The team member is assuming he or she understands the person's reaction and may be wrong. For example, "Nick, you never want to do anything new" or "Sandy, you are such a worrywart."
* *Discounts* are statements that put down other team members and make their comments and opinions seem useless. For instance, a team member will interrupt and take over the conversation or make a derisive comment like "Mark, you are so predictable. You always have to bring up that disaster."
* *Yes-butting* (a term that derives from the words *yes but*) is a technique that recognizes what someone says but then quickly puts down the idea. It may be used under the mistaken idea that it softens the blow. However, the speaker hears it as discounting. For example, "I think what Tom suggested is an innovative idea, the kind that he's known for. But I think there's one slight flaw that would be easy to overlook and makes it unworkable in this circumstance."
* *Naysaying* is always throwing out an opposite and often negative view to crush any ideas. The statements kill discussion and will cause team members to stop participating. Examples are:
  * "We tried something like that a few years ago. Boy, did it cost us."
  * "That'll cost too much. Management won't go for it."
  * "We tried that. It didn't work."
  * "It will take too long."
  * "We've always done it this way."
  * "Too innovative for this company."

  Everyone breathes a sign of relief, abandons the discussion, and perhaps loses a feasible idea. The team leader should make it clear that demeaning, derogatory, or cynical comments do not provide solutions and will hamper open-minded discussion. If someone makes this kind of comment, another team member can point out how the current situation is different or how the idea can be adapted.
* *Plops* are comments made that are completely ignored by everyone. Speakers of the comments sit there feeling foolish and wondering why no one

heard or cared what they said. Some people, frequently those higher up the ladder, develop the habit of cutting people off when they are halfway through. A dominator will do this. The team leader can insist that everyone get a chance to speak by recognizing speakers in order and preventing interruptions. True collaboration and learning require effective listening.

Team member problems include a dominator and a nonparticipator. A dominating participant is often a driver or controller. The team member uses up a disproportionate amount of "air time," talking too much and taking over the discussion. Team members don't question the dominator's confident assertions, even if they are opinions masquerading as facts. The dominator pressures for action and forces decisions. The dominator will say that the team is wasting time and that the members have to vote or take action. This ends everyone else's contributions. The team cannot build a sense of team accomplishment or momentum.

Reluctant participants are those who never speak or get involved. There can be many different reasons. Each of us has a different threshold of need to be part of a group and a different level of comfort speaking in a group. The participant may have been discounted on previous teams and fear more rejection. Teams need to determine the reasons for nonparticipation and motivate the team member to participate.

Free riders do not do any work and are never prepared. They often defend and support another team member who then defends them. The best way to cure this is to reward them for what they do do. Punishment usually doesn't work.

Process problems are floundering and sidetracking. *Floundering* is wondering what the team should do next. The team is overwhelmed by the task. The goals are not clear. The members start in one direction, stop, and go off in another direction. They resist moving to the next step. They have directionless discussions and cannot make decisions. Members don't want to say they don't agree with the group's conclusions. The work is not based on consensus.

Sidetracking happens when team members go off on tangents and digress from the topic at hand. The team has a wide-ranging, unfocused discussion, straying from the subject. Sometimes this is innocent, but sometimes it is avoiding the real tasks. Sometimes a team member with a short attention span will do this. Sidetracking needs to be quelled early or the team will become ineffective. One solution is to use a written agenda with time estimates. Another is to write topics or items on a flipchart to keep people on track.[11]

Skill Development 5.2

Pick one of the common team problems. Explain the problem and discuss how it could be resolved.

Team-Building Roles

Each team member takes on various roles on a team and can help the team correct some of the problems noted above. The following are examples of the *team roles*.

A facilitator/gatekeeper helps a team eliminate internal and external obstacles so that it can achieve meeting and overall team goals. A facilitator makes it easier for the team to do its work. In a meeting, the job involves keeping the team discussion on track and making sure that all team members have an opportunity for input. The facilitator/gatekeeper can direct a sidetracked conversation back on track. All team members are secondary facilitators who share responsibility for productivity. They monitor themselves to minimize disruptive behavior and intervene to prevent other problems. A process observer helps the team look at how it is functioning.

Supporters encourage and support another's point of view even if they disagree with it, thus encouraging contribution. For example, supporters should keep their ears tuned for plops. An amiable is good at this job.

The confronter will directly confront the undesirable behavior of another team member who is yes-butting or discounting someone else.

The mediator helps with disputes by interpreting the different sides, checking the interpretation, and clarifying differences and areas of agreement, trying to move the team discussion along. An amiable-analytical would be able to do this.

When a team begins to flounder and get confused about details and ideas and starts to wonder if it is accomplishing anything, a summarizer, who perhaps is the minutes taker, can summarize what has been said.

Guidelines for Productive Team Meetings

During the first meeting, the team members should get to know each other, share contact information, work out decision-making issues, decide who will do what, and establish norms for attendance, promptness, and participation. Establish a norm that every team member gives the meeting full attention (does not take cell calls, leave early, discuss personal topics, etc.).

1. Use agendas. Agendas should include topics, type of topic (discussion, decision, information), presenters, and time line. They should be sent in advance of the meeting.
2. Have a facilitator who keeps meetings focused and moving.
3. Have a summarizer take minutes. Include key subjects and main points raised, decisions made, who will do what by when, and items to discuss later or at a future meeting.
4. Draft an agenda for the next meeting.
5. With the guidance of the process observer, evaluate the meeting to determine how to improve next time.[12]

Myers-Briggs Type Indicator and Teams

Below are some rather exaggerated descriptions of how the different types might function in a team.

Extraverts. Extraverts think aloud, refining their ideas as they talk. Extraverts find it very difficult to listen to other people's point of view. They would much rather talk their way into or out of a conflict. They should remember that silence from an introvert does not mean agreement. Since extraverts will dominate conversations, a gatekeeper needs to track whether all team members have equal say.

Introverts. They are busy thinking about the situation and are reluctant to express their point of view. Reluctant team members may be introverts. They need to be drawn out by other team members. They need to say what they think, maybe more than once, to make sure everyone else knows what they want. They need to learn that extraverts are thinking aloud.

Sensors.   They approach problem solving and conflict from the point of view of facts. In meetings, they will follow the agenda. They want solutions that are straightforward and feasible. They need to see how a goal or decision affects everything else. They tend to dismiss off-the-wall ideas and limit creativity.

Intuitives.   They can see how the issue is related to everything else because they look at the big picture. They tend to bypass the agenda. They know how to work through a problem but don't know how to implement the solution. In fact, some of their ideas can be unfeasible, so they need to listen to the thinkers and sensors about reality.

Thinkers.   They approach things logically and tend to forget how people will be affected. They avoid conflict that deals with interpersonal issues because they are uncomfortable around emotion. They need to think about emotions and feelings as data to weigh in decision making. They like to have the pros and cons of each alternative listed. Thinkers believe in win-lose. They think that's the only possible outcome.

Feelers.   They like to express emotion, and the give-and-take of discussion may hurt their feelings. They need to not take things personally. Feelers want to reach consensus. They have to learn that some decisions aren't going to be harmonious for everyone.

Judgers.   They want control. They see black and white. They expect others to follow through, and they count on it. They know what the decision should be immediately. They need to let all options be considered.

Perceivers.   Perceivers tend to be able to see both sides of an issue and will argue for either one. They can play devil's advocate and are good at coming up with alternative solutions. They like adapting to last-minute changes. They present their ideas as tentative and modifiable. They do not pay attention to time constraints and may not be helpful in actually reaching a decision.[13]

PERSONAL MANAGEMENT TECHNIQUES

Learning new customer service skills, such as the communication skills in Chapters 6 to 10, involves changing our behavior. Whether we are adjusting a negative outlook, increasing our emotional intelligence capability, enhancing our style strengths, working on our style weaknesses, or learning teamwork, change is required. This section looks at change and how we can adapt to it. Then we focus on goal setting and time management, two individual life management skills.

Adaptation to Change

In Chapter 4, we explained that change requires organizations to constantly adapt, and we reviewed the skills needed by the next-generation workforce. Although it seems as if rapid change has always existed, futurists predict that change will accelerate. Competition on a national and international basis is fierce. Technological developments cause new ways of doing things. Change is difficult for many people to handle. This section discusses why that is so and provides some ideas for making it easier for both companies and individuals.

As discussed in Chapter 4, one of the requirements of a twenty-first-century company is to be agile. To be agile we must change. It is natural to resist change. We like our habits. We are comfortable. Change is uncomfortable. We do not like uncertainty. Change does away with the way we have always done things and replaces it with methods with which no one has much experience. New means more work.

A strong advantage is needed for people to change direction. People don't understand what change will bring or how it will benefit the organization and themselves. Employees may not see any benefits to offset the risks. They cannot see change as being in their self-interest. Employees fear loss of control, power, and prestige. They may feel their jobs are in jeopardy. We will be afraid of change if it threatens our sense of belonging and our belief in our ability to perform. If a change affects how we interact with our coworkers and makes some of our skills obsolete, we will fear the change. A short-term mentality, a focus on the quarterly bottom line, and preference for instant gratification make change even harder. If we lack foresight, which is the ability to project into the future, we cannot visualize what tomorrow will bring. Employees can also suffer from information overload, as they are flooded with new ideas, plans, and requirements. A new program can seem like a "management fad of the month." Employees have seen change that has not worked. In some companies, employees wonder if the company will see a new program through.

On the other hand, change is challenging and exciting. It brings out the best in some people. People enjoy learning and mastering new things. We like variety in our everyday lives. Consider the four styles: driver, analytical, expressive, and amiable. Which one would thrive on change? Which one would be most likely to resist? How would each style react? Our guess is that competitive drivers would be among the first to accept change. Analyticals would think about it for a while. Amiables, being agreeable, might go along, but it would be hard to tell what they are thinking. Expressives would probably be the most vocal about what is happening. Clearly, since people are a combination of characteristics, it is hard to determine.

Organizational Change

To incorporate change into an organization, it is vital to communicate with employees. We fear change that we perceive threatens us. The change may be new technology, such as we have experienced with the Internet. It may be a reorganization of the company with changes in departments and bosses. It may be a new customer service initiative with a renewed emphasis on providing exceptional service. The following are some suggestions for making transitions easier:

1. Clearly and continuously define and communicate the purpose, importance, and direction of any change. Communicate organizational commitment. Make the process and results clear.
2. Communicate the benefits and advantages to all internal and frontline employees. Answer the employees' question: "What's in it for me?" Communicate the program's impact on the employees' job, responsibilities, status, and security.
3. Communicate why past practices and priorities are no longer appropriate, and spell out new ones. Provide examples of successful implementations. Show employees where a similar program has improved a situation.

4. Slow down and listen to the "customer," in this case, employees. Involve as many as possible in planning, problem solving, and decision making. This will lead to more insight, ownership, and commitment on the part of the employees.

5. Provide the resources and training that people need to adapt to something new.

6. Look at resistance and failure as an opportunity to learn. Resistance is natural and often valid. Management should not expect easy solutions or have unrealistic expectations. Take time to explore reasons for resistance. Employees may have ideas that will improve the plan. Be willing to alter the implementation plans based on input.

7. Communicate expectations and accept mistakes. Let commitment grow. Change takes time and energy.[14]

Goal Setting

Determining our goals helps us improve our performance, manage time, and manage stress. To be effective, *goals* should:

1. Be in writing
2. Belong to an individual or a team
3. Be specific and measurable
4. Be attainable and realistic
5. Be time-specific

Experts tell us that writing anything down helps us visualize it better and remember it. For a goal to be measurable, it should state how much, how many, and by when. The notion of a goal being realistic means that if we saved $2500 a year for 35 years, we could have $1 million. An unrealistic goal is working 12 hours a day, 7 days a week. That is not sustainable behavior. The goals should also have checkpoints and a deadline.

Time Management

There are many ways to manage time better—and not managing time creates unnecessary stress. We can focus on the short term—the next hour, day, or week. We can also practice long-term planning to reach our goals. Both short-term and long-term planning will help us balance our work, family, leisure, and spiritual lives.

Many people resist time management systems, but they find after they use a system for a while that they can't live without it. Buy a system. Make your own. Use what works for you. Some people like a calendar notebook. Others use a regular loose-leaf notebook. Personal digital assistants have become popular. Some people track only appointments. Others have detailed daily "to-do" lists.

One way to prioritize time is to use the importance-urgency matrix (see Figure 5.3). Important and urgent tasks are crises, deadline-driven projects, and pressing problems. Not important and urgent tasks are interruptions; unimportant phone calls, meetings, and e-mails; and unnecessary reports. Important but not urgent are planning, crisis prevention, preparation, empowerment, and relationship building. Not important and not urgent are time wasters, worthless phone calls, busywork, irrelevant e-mails, and many pleasant activities. Many people operate in

FIGURE 5.3　Importance and Urgency Priority System

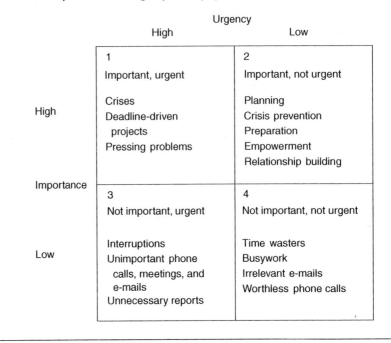

quadrants 1 and 3, spending all their time on the urgent, whether it is important or not important. It is often difficult to get much else done. However, people find if they spend more time in quadrant 2, planning and preparing, there are fewer tasks in quadrants 1 and 3. They can reduce crises and prevent problems from happening so they are no longer in the urgent category.

TERMS

emotional intelligence
self-talk
responsiveness
assertiveness
amiables
expressives
analyticals
drivers
Myers-Briggs Type Indicator
introverts
extraverts
sensors
intuiters
thinkers

feelers
judgers
perceivers
stages of team growth
attribution
discounts
yes-butting
naysaying
plops
floundering
sidetracking
team roles
goal

DISCUSSION QUESTIONS

1. Describe a coworker with a negative attitude. Describe a coworker with a positive attitude. How does each coworker treat customers?
2. What is emotional intelligence? What are the five characteristics of emotionally intelligent people?
3. Give an example of negative self-talk that you have heard in the workplace.
4. Describe the responsiveness/assertiveness style system.
5. Describe the four dimensions of the Myers-Briggs Type Indicator.
6. Describe the stages of team growth and apply them to a team.
7. Identify team roles and each role's responsibility.
8. Why do we sometimes avoid change?
9. Write a goal statement.
10. Plan the next week according to the importance-urgency matrix.

PROJECT—CUSTOMER SERVICE COMMUNICATION SKILLS

This is an individual project designed to help you improve your customer service communication skills. Unless new customer service skills are incorporated into everyday lives, people do not benefit as much from learning about customer service. The project is designed the way it is because this system works quite well for accomplishing goals.

Project Steps

1. *Skill to improve*—Identify three specific interpersonal job communication skills that you want to improve.

    If you are not currently employed, use another "service" situation, such as a volunteer activity or teamwork in a class. It is not advisable to use your communication with your family because the relationship is unlike that between a customer and a customer service provider.

    The skill can be something simple, such as putting a customer on hold on the phone, or something complex, such as improving the way you react to an angry customer on the telephone. Skills like "improving telephone communication" or "listening better" are too broad.

    Determine what will benefit you the most. Think about what you can actually accomplish during the project time period.

    Examples of interpersonal communication skills and situations are the following:
    * Listening
    * Nonverbal communication
    * Verbal communication
    * Telephone communication
    * Electronic (e-mail) communication
    * Communicating in difficult customer situations
    * Communicating with diverse customers
    * Resolving complaints

For each of the three skills, determine what you have been doing and then, based on what you learn in the course, what you want to do instead.

2. *Goal*—Determine your goal. What you want to do instead is your goal. State your goal in a specific and measurable way, something like, "I am going to put my customer on hold the correct way 100 percent of the time by [date]." Refer to the goal-setting steps in the chapter.

3. *Action plan*—Develop an action plan to help you change your behavior. The plan should be detailed. It should be how, not what, you plan to change. It should include specific steps and reminders.

    It should *not* be merely a mental reminder to yourself throughout the day. Mental reminders usually do not change ingrained habits. As an example of a plan, suppose you want to change how you put a customer on hold. The plan would be to place a reminder Post-it note on the telephone(s) and keep a list of the correct procedures near your telephone.

    In the case of reacting to an angry customer, you could make a list of the steps you will follow and keep it handy to reread at various times as a reminder and to reread after an encounter to see how well you did. You could also write a reminder to yourself on your daily planner. Another good way is to write out exactly what it is you want to say in a given circumstance.

4. *Monitoring method*—Design a method by which to monitor yourself and to determine whether you have improved the behavior or not. To monitor yourself, one simple way is to design a form to tally the times you have and have not met your specific goal. Another idea is to have a coworker or supervisor monitor you.

5. *Implement the plan*—Work on skill 1 first, then move on to skill 2 and then to skill 3. Spend about 3 weeks on each one so that you can assess your success for the final report.

6. *Assessment of success*—Determine your progress at changing your behavior. Some goals will take much longer to accomplish than others, and so you may have ongoing plans. You can also think about how you could change your goal, plan, or monitoring method if you are not as successful as you want to be. A good way to help yourself succeed is to figure out a way to reward your success.

    Be thorough. Think it out. Figure out a way that will work for you in your situation. Remember the goal must be measurable. If you have trouble figuring out a way to monitor yourself, it's probably because your goal is not measurable.

7. *Written report*—Write a report with a title page including the following for each of the three skills:

    1. Description—Describe your job and the type of company, or describe the service activity.
    2. Skill
    3. Goal
    4. Action Plan
    5. Monitoring Method
    6. Assessment of Success

NOTES

1. Karen Leland and Keith Bailey, *Customer Service for Dummies,* 2d ed. (New York: IDG Books Worldwide, 1999).

2. Tom Peters, "Emphasize the Right Stuff," *Customer Service Management,* July/August 1999, 40–41.

3. Daniel Goleman, *Emotional Intelligence* (New York: Bantam Books, 1995); and Nancy Pettigrew, "Emotional IQ: Aptitude for Success in Consumer Affairs," *Customer Relationship Management,* December 1999, 14–16.

4. David D. Burns, *Feeling Good: The New Mood Therapy* (New York: William Morrow, 1980), 31–41.

5. Scott Arbuthnot, "Personality Type Tools: Be Aware of How You Use Them," *SalesDoctors Magazine,* September 15, 1997, available from http://www.salesdoctors.com/diagnosis/3type.htm, accessed February 10, 2000.

6. Sandy Smith, Seminar for Ackermann Public Relations and Marketing, n.d.

7. Otto Kroeger and Janet M. Thuesen, *Type Talk: The 16 Personality Types That Determine How We Live, Love, and Work* (New York: Dell Publishing, 1988); and Isabel Briggs Myers, *Introduction to Type: A Guide to Understanding Your Results on the Myers-Briggs Type Indicator,* 6th ed., revised by Linda K. Kirby and Katharine D. Myers (Palo Alto, CA: Consulting Psychologists Press, 1998).

8. Vanessa Urch Druskat and Steven B. Wolff, "Building the Emotional Intelligence of Groups," *Harvard Business Review,* March 2001, 81–90.

9. Peter R. Scholtes, *The Team Handbook: How to Use Teams to Improve Quality* (Madison, WI: Joiner Associates, 1988); Richard S. Wellins, William C. Byham, and Jeanne M. Wilson, *Empowered Teams* (San Francisco: Jossey-Bass Publishers, 1991); and Thomas L. Quick, *Successful Team Building* (New York: AMACOM, 1992).

10. Druskat and Wolff, "Building the Emotional Intelligence of Groups," 81–90; and Goleman, *Emotional Intelligence.*

11. Francie Baltazar-Schwartz and Marc Schwartz (with Jon Caswell), "The Four Cornerstones of Team Building, Part II: Communication," *Mobius,* December 1994, 19–22; Scholtes, *The Team Handbook;* and Quick, *Successful Team Building.*

12. Scholtes, *The Team Handbook.*

13. Kroeger and Thuesen, *Type Talk.*

14. Leonard L. Berry, "Improving America's Service," *Marketing Management* 1, no. 3 (1992), 29–38; Mark Frohman, "Lower-Level Management: The Internal Customers of Change," *Industry Week,* November 5, 1990, 28–34; and Douglas Howardell, "Overcoming People's Fear of Change," available from http://theacagroup.com/overcome.htm, accessed June 10, 2001.

CHAPTER 6

NONVERBAL COMMUNICATION

OBJECTIVES

1. Discuss the importance of nonverbal communication in customer service situations.
2. Define nonverbal communication and the six channels of delivery.
3. Explain the functions of nonverbal communication.
4. Define and describe body, voice, space, touch, artifactual, and time communication.
5. Discuss the effect of nonverbal communication on customer service communication.

IMPORTANCE OF NONVERBAL COMMUNICATION

This chapter focuses on nonverbal communication. First, we will explain the importance of nonverbal communication in the customer service context. Then, we will define what nonverbal communication is and the functions it serves. This will be followed by a discussion of six channels used to deliver nonverbal communication and the way cues are used and interpreted.

Importance

Nonverbal communication plays a significant role in customers' perceptions of customer service providers. Courtesy, attentiveness, helpfulness, and friendliness are reflected by a provider's body language and voice.[1] According to a recent study of service situations, customer dissatisfaction can result from the inappropriate nonverbal communication of customer service personnel.[2]

Most of the meaning of face-to-face communication is transmitted by nonverbal communication rather than words. Research has shown that about two-thirds of a message or more comes from nonverbal communication and one-third from the actual words. If the information is factual or technical, the proportion is higher for words and lower for nonverbal.[3]

Nonverbal communication is particularly important because nonverbal messages are more believable than verbal communication. Our nonverbal communication may contradict our words and send mixed messages. A *mixed message* is a single communication that contains two meanings. One part, usually the verbal, is positive. The other part, usually the nonverbal, is negative. If words say one thing and nonverbal cues say something else, people believe the nonverbal. For instance, this often happens in supermarket checkout lines. The salesclerk greets us but never makes eye contact. He says thank you while turning away to scan the next customer's groceries. Positive words but negative nonverbal behavior. Unfortunately, customers always believe the negative message in this exchange because they know it is unconscious behavior.

Sending and understanding nonverbal communication is a difficult, but critical, communication skill to learn. Showing appropriate nonverbal cues is hard because even though some are intentional, for the most part we display the cues unconsciously. While it is impossible not to communicate nonverbal messages, it is hard to evaluate and understand nonverbal language because it cannot be interpreted with 100 percent accuracy—contrary to some popular books' suggestion that we can "read a person like a book." Verbal and written communication have been studied extensively, but we have not studied positive and negative nonverbal communication nor developed our sensitivity to reading cues as much. Meanings depend on the situation, the relationship between the sender and the receiver, and culture. We will point out differences as we discuss the various types of nonverbal messages. In addition, focusing on a single cue, like eye contact, can be misleading. Nonverbal communication is best looked at as a group of messages that serve a function. We can be more accurate if we pay attention to the overall nonverbal message.[4]

DEFINITION AND FUNCTIONS OF NONVERBAL COMMUNICATION

Definition

Nonverbal communication is defined as everything except words. It is conveyed through six channels: kinesics, vocalics, proxemics, haptics, artifactual, and chronemics (see Figure 6.1). Kinesics, or body language, includes messages sent through eyes, faces, and body movements, posture, and gestures. Vocalics, sometimes called paralanguage, consists of cues delivered by voice volume, speaking rate, voice quality, pitch, regularity, vocalizations, articulation, and accents. Proxemics is our use of space, and haptics is our use of touch to communicate. Artifactual communication includes appearance and adornment, olfactics, and environment. Olfactic cues are those associated with smell. Our environment sends messages via our surroundings, based on factors like decor, color, and arrangement. Communication through time, or chronemics, is based on how we use and perceive time.

FIGURE 6.1   Nonverbal Communication Channels and Functions

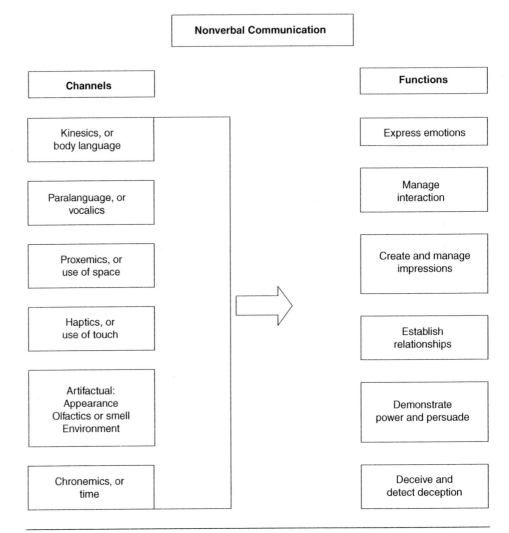

Functions

According to a nonverbal textbook, messages sent through the channels work together to express emotions, manage interaction, create and manage impressions, establish relationships, demonstrate power and persuade, and deceive and detect
deception (see Figure 6.1). Thinking about these functions should convince us that
nonverbal communication will have a substantial effect on our customers.

1. *Express emotions.*   Basic emotions, delivered mostly through facial expressions, like happiness, anger, and sadness, are fairly universal across cultures. When more than one emotion is expressed, interpretation is more
   complex. We may freely show our emotions at times or control them to
   hide how we feel. A frown will send an unacceptable message to a customer.
2. *Manage interaction.*   Nonverbal communication is used to manage the
   give-and-take of interaction or conversations with others. Eye contact
   shows we are listening and encourages customers to continue talking.

3. *Create and manage impressions.*   Nonverbal cues allow people to make judgments about us. We can create and manage those impressions. Our appearance, for example, the way we dress, can convey professionalism. We make judgments about others from their nonverbal cues.

4. *Establish relationships.*   We send messages to people to show how we feel about them and to establish relationships. We use relational messages to welcome or rebuff approach and conversation. A smile demonstrates friendliness to our customers, encouraging a relationship. Avoiding eye contact tells people to stay away.

5. *Demonstrate power and persuade.*   We use messages to demonstrate our degree of power over others and to persuade and influence people. Powerful people exert control by using time and territory—by setting meeting times and places.

6. *Deceive and detect deception.*   People control nonverbal behavior to purposely deceive. Other cues can expose deception. People can hide deception with high eye contact and a smile, but their voice may show anxiety.[5]

For specific examples of nonverbal communication, positive and negative, see Table 6.1.

There are numerous claims about differences between men's and women's nonverbal communication. Some have favorable meaning for men and negative meaning for women and vice versa. Some are true; others are not. Experts advise us to become more aware of nonverbal communication, so that we can more consciously use body language that projects the correct impression. Androgynous people adjust to others by using masculine or feminine nonverbal communication styles, depending on the needs of the situation. If responsiveness and assertiveness are required, adaptation is appropriate. Androgynous people can assess situations, relate to more different kinds of people, and respond more appropriately. They can show warmth, empathy, sincerity, helpfulness, assertiveness, submissiveness, risk taking, and competitiveness at different times in different circumstances.[6]

Skill Development 6.1

Using Figure 6.1, name a nonverbal cue for each of the functions and explain how it could be used or interpreted.

BODY LANGUAGE

Body language, or *kinesics,* is communicated with our eyes, face, and body. Cues are delivered by eye movement, facial expressions, body and head movement, posture, and gestures.

Eye Behavior

Eyes communicate. Eyes have been identified as the "divine eye," the "evil eye," and the "windows of the soul" in Egyptian, Mexican, Greek, American, and other cultures. We use expressions like "shifty-eyed," "bug-eyed," "see eye to eye," "eyesore," "eye-opener," and "gave me the eye."

TABLE 6.1   Positive and Negative Nonverbal Communication

Positive

Initiating and maintaining appropriate eye contact	Open-body position, body and head facing person, leaning forward
Smiling	
Affirmative head nods	Relaxed posture
Moderate amounts of gesturing and animation	Postural mirroring, exhibiting similar or congruent posture
Firm but not expansive gestures	Close interpersonal distances
Relaxed gestures	Nonverbal and verbal messages consistent
Illustrator gestures and vocal inflection used to emphasize key words and phrases	

Negative

Rolling your eyes	Nervous gestures such as hand-wringing and lip licking
Narrowing your eyes	Shrugging your shoulders
Squinting your eyes	Tapping your foot
Eye contact of short duration, averting eyes, visual inattentiveness	Relative absence of gestures
	Indirect body orientations
Evasive eye contact	Closed-body posture, body rigidity, body tension
Unpleasant facial expression	Slouching, hunching shoulders
Frowning	Walking with your head down
Scowling	Moving slowly
Out-of-context smiling	Frequent throat clearing
Raising your eyebrows	Sighing that suggests annoyance or impatience, especially to an annoyed customer
Covering your mouth with your hand	
Smoking	Sounding impatient, annoyed, condescending
Eating	Crowding customers
Chewing gum	Touching inappropriately

Eye behavior includes eye gaze, eye contact, and eye movement. Eye gaze means our eyes are focused directly on the other person's eyes. Usually we think of *eye contact* as two people looking each other in the eye. We call this mutual eye contact. Staring is eye gaze that persists no matter what the other person's eyes do. When we make initial eye contact, we signal that we are willing to interact. Positive emotions, like interest, increase gaze. Negative emotions, such as anxiety, decrease gaze.

Eye contact is an important aspect of nonverbal customer service behavior. Eyes signal whether people are willing to interact, are paying attention, and are interested. Studies show that direct eye gaze is seen as a sign of credibility, competence, and trustworthiness. High eye contact has also been linked with friendliness, courtesy, empathy, sincerity, and self-confidence. Low eye contact is associated with being defensive, evasive, submissive, and inattentive.

Research has shown that if people think the other person will show emotion on his or her face, they will make less eye contact to maintain the person's privacy. This natural tendency is unfortunate if we are dealing with a dissatisfied customer. Customers want to know that we are interested, and so appropriate eye contact is important.

A person's eye gaze can be measured by frequency, duration, and proportion of time.

- Frequency is the number of times that we look at the person's eyes.
- Duration is the number of seconds that we look at the person's eyes. In every culture, there are conventions for the appropriate duration of eye contact. Among Americans, about 3 seconds is the average duration of eye contact, and the average length of mutual eye contact is just over 1 second.[7] Research shows that the longer we maintain eye contact, the more self-esteem we are perceived to have. South Americans and Arabs believe that strong eye contact, to the point that Americans would call it staring, shows interest and sincerity. In other cultures, such as some Asian and Hispanic cultures, long-duration eye contact is considered rude or disrespectful. In some Latin and Native American cultures, children are taught to avoid direct eye contact with adults.
- Proportion of time measures how much time we spend looking at or away from the person. Experts suggest that maintaining eye contact about 60 percent of the time is moderate and appropriate. Women seem to look at a speaker more than men and engage in mutual eye contact more than men. The *visual dominance ratio* is the percentage of time looking at the person's eyes while talking relative to the percentage of time looking while listening. The higher the ratio, in the range of 55 percent looking while speaking versus 45 percent looking while listening, the more we are seen as being substantially more powerful, being higher in status, having more expertise power, and having more desire for interpersonal control. Women's ratios are usually lower than men's, looking while talking less than looking while listening, no more than 40 percent versus 60 percent.

Eye movement is explained by the movement of our gaze and pupil size. *Gaze omission* is unintentional and means we have not noticed the person or we have our eyes focused on someone or something else. *Gaze aversion,* is deliberately moving our eyes away from the other person's eyes. Gaze aversion occurs during eye contact when we look down or to the side. Purposely not looking at another person is *gaze avoidance.* An example is a salesperson who pretends she doesn't see a customer and never makes eye contact. Pupillometric studies, measuring pupil reaction, show that pupils enlarge as interest increases and get smaller as interest decreases. Pupils also increase for positive emotions and decrease for negative emotions.

People who avert their eyes are perceived as less trustworthy, less competent, and less credible. In turn, averted eyes lower our persuasive effectiveness. In addition, a downward glance is perceived as a sign of weakness and submission. During a job interview, gaze aversion, moving our eyes away from the interviewer's eyes, and limited-duration eye contact reduce one's chances of being hired. Low eye contact and aversion will also affect customers' perceptions.

In order to provide exceptional customer service, credibility is an essential asset. Credibility enhances communication in providing information, selling, solving customer problems, and carrying out other service activities. Credibility is made up of competence (knowledge and expertise), trustworthiness (honesty and sincerity), and dynamism (energy and confidence in communicating). Studies have found that one nonverbal behavior that contributes to credibility in terms of both competence and trustworthiness is maintaining eye contact while communicating. Eye movements that lower credibility are averting eye contact, looking down at notes for extended periods, and blinking excessively.[8]

People who look away when greeting someone and make limited eye contact may be shy. However, in American society, most interpretations of gaze aversion, low eye contact, and a low visual dominance ratio are negative. Gaze aversion is seen as deceptive behavior. Limited eye contact is seen as disinterest. For instance, have you ever been speaking with a person who looks over your shoulder and around the room, not making eye contact? A natural interpretation of this behavior is to wonder with whom the person would rather be talking. Since the interpretation of low eye contact and averted eyes is usually negative, it is best to try to change the negative eye behaviors.

We should be aware that much of the information communicated by our eyes happens out of our level of awareness and is, therefore, beyond our ability to consciously control, like pupil dilation. What we can make an effort to control is increasing our visual dominance ratio; that is, increasing our eye contact while talking. We can also make eye contact when greeting someone, rather than looking away, and can prevent other gaze aversion.[9]

Facial Expressions

The primary function of facial expressions is to communicate emotion. The six general classes of emotion expressed by the face are happiness, surprise, fear, anger, sadness, and disgust. The facial expressions that show these emotions seem to be universal across cultures. Emotional blends, which are more than one emotion, are more difficult to interpret. For example, disappointment is a combination of sadness and surprise.

A smile conveys the emotion of happiness. It is virtually a universally understood gesture of friendship. Smiling is usually a universal component of greeting. Social involvement is also a cause of smiling. Smiling in social circumstances does not have to be accompanied by happiness. In fact, smiling occurs in uncomfortable social situations as a way to establish and maintain friendly interaction. Smiles can be expressions of empathy, reassurance, apology, or conciliation.[10]

Smiling people are perceived as more sincere, competent, and sociable than unsmiling people. Due to the friendliness function of smiling, service providers should begin and end service encounters with a smile. Many people vividly remember the end of an interaction. If a smile is accompanied by eye contact, the perception of warmth, friendliness, and sincerity is even higher.[11]

Research indicates that women's faces are more expressive than men's since men have been socialized to show less emotion. Women, Caucasian women at least, smile more than men. Nonsmiling women are perceived as less relaxed and less happy. This is not true when men do not smile. It is more difficult to read the meaning behind a woman's smile than a man's smile. Women may be smiling because they are happy or because the social situation requires it. They may smile to cover other feelings. For men, a smile usually means they feel positive.

Facial expression management techniques include:

* Simulation, or pretending to have an emotion
* Inhibition, or hiding a feeling
* Masking, or substituting one emotion for another
* Intensifying, or exaggerating a feeling
* De-intensifying, or underplaying an emotion

Customer service representatives often need to manage their emotions with customers. Simulation is acting like we feel an emotion when we do not. This is very common for customer service providers. It is part of the acting job we do, for example, smiling when we may not be happy. Inhibition is pretending not to have an emotion. Even though the rude behavior of a customer may annoy us, we must hide our annoyance. Masking is showing an emotion that is different from the one we have. Intensifying a feeling is pretending to have stronger feelings than we actually have. We might exaggerate our admiration when a customer shows us pictures of her new baby granddaughter. De-intensifying means to restrain an emotion to show milder feelings than we actually have.

When customers are angry or upset, the best facial expression to use is a relaxed expression showing interest. The absence of positive facial expressions is perceived as a lack of warmth and friendliness. A face must show interest and attention to increase credibility. It's noteworthy that our facial expression not only influences the impressions of other people but also influences our own positive and negative feelings. That means smiling can make us feel more positive.[12]

Body Movements

We communicate through our body movement, posture, and gestures. The way we walk can communicate our attitude, indicating whether we are uncertain or confident. Body movements that show we are interested and care about the customer include facing the customer, nodding, and leaning forward slightly. An open posture, meaning facing a person squarely, arms at sides, legs slightly apart and relaxed, can show interest, liking, and respect. Body movements that will make customers think we are impatient or indifferent to them are turning away, stepping backward, leaning back, looking at our watch, and pushing away from our desk. Crossed arms or legs may show defensiveness. Lack of any gestures, as when we put our hands behind our back, can give the impression that we are defensive and uncomfortable with the customer.

Nodding our heads is a very common body movement that can mean several things. We use nods to show that we are listening and want the speaker to continue talking. Nodding very rapidly can mean the listener agrees. It can also mean the listener wants to speak or end the conversation. Noting other body language will provide the answer. If the listener leans forward and opens his or her mouth slightly, we can tell the listener wants to talk.

Historically, gesture communication predates verbal communication. Researchers have identified five categories of gestures: emblems, illustrators, affect displays, regulators, and adapters (see Figure 6.2). We often think of gestures as hand gestures, but the categories include body and head gestures as well. *Emblems* are cues with a direct verbal translation, such as a hand wave for good-bye and sign language for those who are hearing impaired. These cues are intentional and universally understood within a group or culture. However, emblems are very different across cultures.

Illustrators are also used intentionally to increase clarity or emphasize verbal messages, such as pointing when giving directions or demonstrating size and shape. They differ from emblems in that some cannot be represented by a word or phrase and they do not occur without conversation.

Affect displays are less intentional than the previous two categories, and they display emotion. They are likely to provide information that the communicator will not disclose voluntarily. The emotion displayed is associated more with facial expressions than with body cues. The face will often display the emotion and the body the

FIGURE 6.2   American Gestures

intensity of emotion. A stiff posture may show anxiety. Lack of body movements makes it more difficult to interpret the emotion.

Regulators monitor, maintain, or control the beginning, length, and termination of conversations, for example, regulating whose turn it is to talk. They include turn yielding, turn maintaining, turn requesting, and turn denying. Turn yielding cues to indicate the other person should speak are nodding in someone's direction and making direct eye contact. Turn maintaining cues, so that a person can continue talking, include vocalizing an "er" pause and audibly inhaling a breath. Turn requesting cues are leaning forward and beginning to gesture. Turn denying by avoiding eye contact or shrugging our shoulders communicates that we do not want to speak. We need to be sensitive to each other's movements in this regard. Regulators are also used extensively in greetings and farewells. Here, experts suggest that restraint in movement is the best approach. A smile or a head gesture is appropriate. Sweeping gestures are not.

Adapters satisfy some need. They are the most involuntary movements and offer the most information about the individual. They exert nervous energy and help people feel more comfortable. The movements are idiosyncratic and are directed toward either ourself or an object, for example, biting one's nails, tapping a pencil, chewing gum, scratching one's head, or swinging a foot. Some adapters are distracting and are considered impolite. Repetitive, unnatural, and exaggerated gestures of any kind are also distracting.[13]

Open postures with arms in a relaxed pose show confidence. A stiff posture is perceived as nervousness. Moving a leg or foot repeatedly, tapping one's fingers, and playing with objects show lack of confidence and lower credibility. Movements and gestures should be natural and spontaneous and should be performed without nervousness. A firm handshake is essential to credibility.[14]

Skill Development 6.2

How do you interpret each of these nonverbal behaviors in a face-to-face discussion?

Leaning toward you

Sighing

Fidgeting

Tilting head

Yawning

Smiling frequently

Looking at the ceiling

Jingling keys

Raising eyebrows

VOICE CUES

Another expression for voice cues is *paralanguage*. The sound characteristics that distinguish one person's voice cues from those of another are volume, rate, quality, pitch and pitch range, regularity, vocalizations, articulation, accent, and silence. The

FIGURE 6.3   Paralanguage and Functions

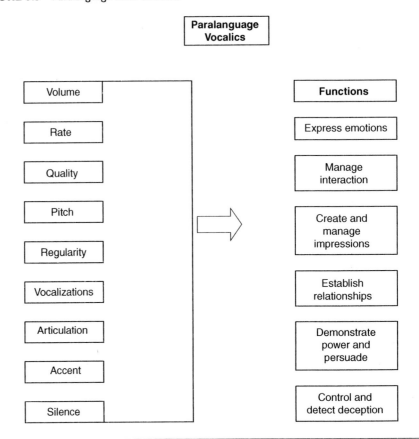

cues reflect our gender, age, emotion, interest, health, and energy level. Gender can be guessed with almost complete success from a voice. Voice cues serve similar functions to body language (see Figure 6.3). Our voices are "leakier" than our faces in revealing our emotions.[15]

Volume

Volume, or loudness, is the most basic characteristic. Loudness is measured in decibels. If a voice cannot be heard, no meaning can be conveyed. A whisper at 10 decibels is as detrimental to conversation as volumes that are too loud.

Rate

Rate of speech is the number of sounds emitted during a given unit of time. People vary widely in what they prefer as listeners. Moderate speech is 130 to 160 words per minute, 100 to 120 words per minute is considered too slow, and over 160 words per minute is considered too fast. Slower speech is considered less credible than faster speech. Faster speech, up to 50 percent faster, is more persuasive. As the rate of speech increases, people are perceived to be more intelligent, objective, and intense. It is interesting to note that when the rate is increased by 50 percent, comprehension drops by only about 5 percent.[16]

Quality and Pitch

Voice quality is the way a person's voice sounds. Everyone has a unique voiceprint, much like having unique fingerprints. Voice quality is a combination of volume and pitch. Resonance is the fullness of sound in the facial cavity. A resonant voice has a deep, rich sound. Pitch is the musical note that the voice produces. *Pitch* range, sometimes referred to as inflection, is the musical interval between the high and low pitches that we use in speaking. Emotional communication is associated with higher pitch. Excitement and volatile anger are associated with higher pitch. Sadness, surprise, and quiet anger are associated with low pitch. Lower-pitched voices are considered more credible and powerful.

Smiling, which is partly psychological and partly physiological, changes voice inflection. Smiling causes the soft palate at the back of our mouth to rise and makes the sound more fluid. Our breathing also changes our inflection. When we are upset, our breathing becomes shallower and quicker, making our vocal cords tighten and our voice sound strained. Taking longer, slower, deeper breaths will create a calmer tone of voice.

Monotone speech has a narrow pitch range. There is a tendency after we have answered the telephone a hundred times in a day for our pitch to become monotone or singsong, making us sound like a disinterested, bored robot. Dr. Morton Cooper, author of *Change Your Voice*, says that if we present information in a monotone voice, people remember only 7 percent of what we say. If our pitch range is more appropriate, 38 percent is remembered. Too much inflection or pitch range can be as bad as too little. For example, consider voiceovers on some television commercials.[17]

Experience Discussion 6.1

If we vary our pitch and emphasize different words in the same sentence, the meaning completely changes. Repeat this phrase with an emphasis on each word in turn. What does each one imply?

I never said you broke the glass.

I **never** said you broke the glass.

I never **said** you broke the glass.

I never said **you** broke the glass.

I never said you **broke** the glass.

I never said you broke the **glass.**

Improving Voice Quality

An attractive voice is one in which the pitch is neither too high nor too low and has moderate levels of resonance, articulation, and loudness. An unattractive voice is breathy, husky, nasal, flat, or throaty. Researchers have determined that impressions of people with attractive voices are more favorable than those with unattractive voices. An attractive voice can be very powerful in creating positive impressions.[18]

FIGURE 6.4 Mask

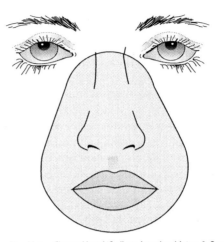

Source: Morton Cooper, *Change Your Voice, Change Your Life* (Los Angeles: Voice & Speech Company of America, 1984).

Cooper, who has trained numerous entertainers, is considered an expert on improving voice quality. He has developed a method for hearing and understanding what our natural voice sounds like and learning to use that voice rather than a habitual, unnatural voice. The quality of our voice can be improved by projecting through the "mask." The mask is the bridge and sides of the nose down to and around the lips, as shown in Figure 6.4. By producing sound through the mask rather than through the lower throat or the nose alone, the voice opens up, becomes flexible, shows more expression and warmth, and has more range and carrying power.

Cooper claims that there could be two pitch levels in a voice, an optimal, or natural, level and a habitual, or routine, one. If they are different, the voice is being misused and the pitch is too high or too low. Divide the throat into thirds: lower throat, middle throat, and upper throat. Good voices have balanced upper- and middle-throat resonance through the mask, with natural lower-throat resonance. Breath support for speech should be centered at the diaphragm.

The first step in improving your voice is finding your optimal (or natural) pitch. Say "umm-hmmm" with the lips closed using rising inflection as though you are spontaneously and sincerely agreeing with someone. The sound should be your right voice. If you are doing it correctly, you should feel a slight tingling or vibration around the nose and lips. This indicates correct tone focus. If your pitch is too low, you will feel too much vibration in your lower throat and very little, if any at all, in the mask.

If you are not sure you have found your natural voice, try a second Cooper test. Stand and place one hand on your chest and the other hand on your stomach. Breathe in with your stomach moving out, keep your lips closed, make humming sounds, and press in with one hand under the sternum in a quick staccato fashion. The sounds will escape through the nose, but you will feel a buzz around the mask: your mouth and nose. The resonance you feel from the mask gives your natural voice a clear and efficient sound. This is the voice you were born to use. Now say "umm-hmmm" in that same voice. If you are holding yourself too stiffly, try raising your hand above your head, as high as you can. Now say "right"; say it again, only louder. Say "hello." Now say "umm-hmmm." This should be your natural voice.[19]

Skill Development 6.3

Vocal Quality Test Paragraph–Tape yourself reading or speaking a paragraph of 150 words. Time it. Listen to the tape and rate yourself on the voice cues below. Have someone else listen to the tape and rate you. Compare the results to see what voice cues you might want to change.

Volume
* Too soft
* Too loud
* Just right

Rate
* Slow–110–120 words per minute, over 80 seconds for 150 words
* Fast–over 160 words per minute, under 50 seconds
* Moderate–130–150 words per minute, 60 seconds

Quality
* Too high, whiny
* Too low, gravelly
* Nasal
* Natural voice, clear

Pitch
* No variation; sounded monotonous
* Too much variation; sounded phony
* Good, varied; sounded natural

Regularity
* Numerous unnatural pauses
* Rhythmical

Vocalizations
* Too many
* Few to none

Articulation
* Overenunciated; sounded mechanical
* Mumbled, slurred words, or dropped endings
* Enunciated well; each word was clear

Accent
* Intense
* Moderate

Regularity

Regularity is whether our speech is rhythmical. People who vocalize many pauses, either silent hesitations or filled with "uhs," "ers," and "you knows," are considered less credible. Long pauses are associated with anxiety. Hesitant pauses lower perceived competence, but purposeful pauses raise it. Fluent speakers, with no long pauses, hesitations, and repetitions, are considered more credible.

Vocalizations

Vocalizations are sounds that are not words, such as "uh-huh" and "um." They also include crying, yawning, moaning, and belching, all of which are unacceptable in customer service environments.

Articulation

Articulation is the process of making transitions between individual sounds and words to be understood. Americans all use some imprecise, substandard articulation among friends and family. In general, men use more nonstandard forms than women. Women use them less often in public. Some less formal forms of articulation are deliberately chosen in some situations. This would be the case when customer service providers are matching the style of their customers.

Accent

Accent affects credibility and persuasiveness. In general, people who speak with a general American accent or dialect are thought to be more competent than those who do not. This is why television and radio broadcasters strive for a neutral accent. The more intense the accent, the more it lowers credibility.

Silence

Silence is not strictly a vocal cue, but it does affect communication in a variety of ways. Silence has numerous positive and negative meanings. Silence can connect or separate people. For example, silence may mean we are not listening. Silence can heal or wound. Silence can reveal or hide information. Silence can show agreement or disagreement, as when we do not like what we are hearing. Silence may indicate thought or the lack of thought. Silence, especially after a question, may indicate thinking, or it could reveal uncertainty.

Voice Cue Meaning and Use

Emotions have some identifiable voice features. A happy voice is higher pitched, with gentle upward pitch variation, regular rhythm, and pure tones. Anger is apparent by a raised pitch in rage, a lower pitch in cold anger, raised intensity, harsh voice quality, and faster speech rate.

Voice cues also allow people to form impressions about us. A moderately loud volume and moderately paced voice is perceived as more confident and credible than a softer volume and slower-paced voice. Pitch variation is a positive characteristic, enhancing perceptions of competence and sociability. A weak voice, a very slow rate of speech, a monotonous pitch, poor pronunciation, long pauses, and filler words contribute to negative credibility. A confident, strong voice that is fast enough to keep the receiver interested but not so fast as to be unintelligible enhances credibility.

Men's voices naturally sound deeper, louder, and more rotund due to shorter, thicker vocal folds, larger chests, and larger larynxes and pharynxes. Female voices sound higher, smaller, and more strident due to physiological features opposite of men's. In addition, part of the difference in sound is due to adaptation to beliefs about appropriate gender sounds. Because a lower pitch is perceived to be stronger and less emotional, women's pitch has actually lowered slightly over the last several decades.

People who use a conversational style, which includes lower pitch, slower rate, lower to moderate volume, and less inflection, are considered trustworthy, kind, warm, friendly, and pleasant. A public speaking style, which is higher pitch, faster rate, higher vocal intensity, and more inflection, is associated with intensity, competence, and dominance. A public speaking voice will increase perceptions of competence but reduce perceptions of friendliness. Because of this, people who need to use a public speaking voice should also include nonverbal nodding, eye contact, and smiling to convey warmth and friendliness.[20]

According to Karen Ritchie, the author of "Marketing to Generation X," Gen Xers, especially those on the coasts and the highly educated, have a unique speech pattern called the "rising inflection." This means raising the voice at the end of a statement, which makes the sentence sound like a question. Their speech is also peppered with modifiers like "perhaps," "sort of," "you know," "totally," and "like." An example is "He's just, sort of, like, you know, clueless?" She says that they speak this way to be more accommodating and acknowledge that the listener may have a different point of view based on their sensitivity to diversity. To Boomers, this sounds hesitant and uncertain, and they leap to offer advice. However, Xers are just being polite.[21] If you are an Xer or a Boomer who has encountered this speech pattern, be aware of the potential for misunderstanding in a customer service role.

Some communication experts suggest we pace our rate of speech to our customer's. *Pacing* is a way of matching a customer's rate of speech, leading to the creation of rapport with the customer. In the United States, this is especially true if a fast-talking New Yorker is speaking with a slower-talking Texan. Service providers will create misperceptions if they start wanting customers to slow down or speed up. It is better for customer service personnel to pace their customers rather than thinking we can hurry them up or slow them down. Pacing also applies to intensity, or the strength of emotion projected. Level of intensity rises if customers are upset or angry. Service providers should increase their intensity, but not match emotion, to show concern.[22]

Deception

People behave differently when they are trying to deceive than when they are telling the truth. They use cues to hide the fact that they are lying. Customer service providers sometimes need to be able to tell whether a customer is being honest. Deception is difficult to detect. Gaze avoidance is not a reliable cue since deceivers learn to look people directly in the eye. Facial expressions are easier to control than voices. Deceivers smile, but sometimes the smile may look rather false. Experts say that it is easiest to control the face and upper body. It is not as easy to control the voice and lower body. Generally, people who are lying speak less fluently than those telling the truth. Voices may be shaky, giving away their anxiety. Their speech is filled with hesitations and grammar errors. They have often planned what to say, and so their speech sounds rehearsed. Voice pitch may be higher. Arms and legs fidget.[23]

Skill Development 6.4

Using a tape recorder, experiment with voice cues. Try different volumes and rates of speech. Practice expressing emotions on the telephone, such as alert, frustrated, confident, panicked, calm, happy, sad, angry, sleepy, bored, confused, ill, and apathetic. Practice different voice qualities, such as harsh, shrill, muffled, nasal, squeaky, and childish.

USE OF SPACE

Proxemics is the study of how individuals use space to communicate. People balance their use of space to affiliate or connect with people and to protect privacy. To successfully communicate, we must be able to recognize and adjust to social norms. Two classifications of proxemics, distance and privacy, are applicable to customer service situations.

Distance concerns the distances people use to separate themselves from others in order to satisfy their needs. There are four types: intimate, personal, social, and public, with cultural norms established (see Figure 6.5). Intimate distance is up to 18 inches, generally reserved for loved ones. Personal space, 1.5 to 4 feet, refers to our personal space "bubble," in which we are not touched unless an arm is extended. It is reserved for close friends. Handshakes take place in this area, but when completed, people generally back off. The social distance norm is 4 to 12 feet. It is the area where most business is conducted. The public distance norm is 12 feet or more. This is where we want to keep strangers.

People lay claim to public space by placing personal property to mark it, such as a jacket on the back of a chair in a cafeteria. Students often claim the same chair in a classroom throughout a course. If someone else takes their seat, they feel that their space has been invaded.

These norms vary by age, gender, degree of acquaintance, status, situation, U.S. region of residence, country, and culture. Children stand closer to one another than do adults. Two women will sit closer to each other than two men will. Women tolerate closer approaches than men. Men tend to have larger personal space bubbles than women do. People of equal status stand closer than those of unequal status. Asians tend to stand further apart than Europeans and North Americans. Latin

FIGURE 6.5   Proxemics Norms

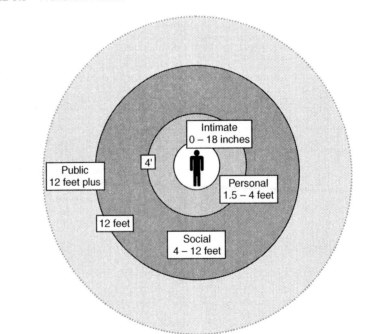

Americans, southern Europeans, and Middle Easterners stand much closer together than Europeans and North Americans.[24]

Experience Discussion 6.2

Try standing closer to a stranger than you usually would. Describe what happened.

Customer service providers and, in fact, all employees need to understand these zones. Intruding on others' space is at best unsettling, at worst threatening. If customers move away from us, we may be encroaching on their space. Use social space with customers. If a customer is standing too close for comfort, be discreet about moving away so that it is not too obvious. Turn sideways for a moment, step sideways, and then turn back. Space distance can be too far and inhibit conversation—say, if we are sitting behind a large desk and the customer is sitting in a chair that is any distance from the front of the desk. Inside a company, employees' personal space should be respected. Using someone else's telephone, setting something on someone else's desk, and opening someone else's drawer are all invasions.

Privacy is the selective control of access to one's self or to one's group and includes physical, social, psychological, and information privacy. The violation of privacy norms and expectations can lead to negative impressions and conflict in customer service situations. Information privacy is of great concern to consumers. They want to know how companies are using their personal information, particularly financial and medical. Many consumers do not want their information sold to other businesses. In addition, identity theft, in which someone steals a person's name, Social Security number, and other personal information to commit fraud, has been increasing.[25]

TOUCH

Touch communication is also called *haptics*. The two types of touch that are relevant to customer service are functional-professional touch and social-polite touch. Functional touch is touch that is used to accomplish a service, for example, touch used by a dentist or a hair stylist. An example of social touch is a handshake, which we discuss in Chapter 7.[26]

The appropriateness of social touching differs markedly by culture, between men and women, and, as we have seen in recent years, over time. Rules about touch, about who can touch whom, are very strong. In the United States, touch is currently considered unacceptable in many public and business situations. Touching is much more common in Italy, France, and Latin America. In the Middle East, opposite sexes never touch each other in public although same sexes do. In Japan, touching in public is impolite.

ARTIFACTUAL COMMUNICATION

Artifactual communication is the exchange of messages by means of clothing, cosmetics, color, and objects or other material things. We can determine age, gender, status, lifestyle, occupation, socioeconomic class, group memberships, and nationality by artifactual communication. Women's clothing became more comfortable and practical when they began working outside the home. In the 1990s, baseball caps became a reflection of age, lifestyle, and group membership. One of the main functions of nonverbal artifactual communication is impression creation and management, controlling how others perceive us.

Appearance and Adornment

Our physical appearance provides information about us and affects communication. We read people's character, personality, status, and other qualities from their age, gender, height, weight, body build, attractiveness, and many other features. Americans have positive associations toward physical attractiveness. We unconsciously stereotype based on people's age, gender, weight, and a host of other characteristics.

People are also judged by grooming, dress, and adornment. Customer service personnel's clothing, shoes, hair, makeup, and fingernails should be clean, neat, and appropriate. Clothing has been found to be a strong determinant of at least four image dimensions: credibility, likability, interpersonal attractiveness, and dominance. Many companies require uniforms for functional reasons, identification purposes, and image enhancement. In professional services, a suit projects competence and credibility. One research study found that college students perceived a formally dressed professor as knowledgeable, organized, and prepared. The same professor more informally dressed was seen as fair, flexible, friendly, and enthusiastic.

We also judge customers by their appearance. In a customer service environment, we need to see every customer as an individual who wants and deserves to be treated with courtesy and respect no matter what the person's appearance seems to say. Do you treat your customers who are wearing suits better than those who dress in jeans? Do you treat teenagers differently from older people?[27]

Olfactics

Olfactic cues, which are associated with our sense of smell, applies to grooming and wearing perfume or cologne. Heavy perfume or cologne is often considered inappropriate in a business setting. Some people are allergic. For others, fragrances are unpleasant and can be overpowering. A recent study has shown that perfume may lower women's perceived competence. The study examined four situations—no perfume, light use, moderate use, and high use. Positive perceptions of competence were highest in the no-perfume case and decreased the more perfume the women used.[28]

Environment

People also derive impressions about us from environmental cues, such as the decor and colors of our office and the style or expense of furniture. Our image is also affected by having a messy versus an organized workplace. A messy office creates a negative impression. We have all heard, "My office is a mess, but I know where everything is." Perhaps it's an unfair perception, but some people still wonder if we know what we are doing.

Experience Discussion 6.3

1. Watch participants in a meeting or classroom, and note examples of nonverbal communication. What do the cues tell you about the people?
2. Describe an example of artifactual communication in the classroom or other meeting place.
3. Examine the environment of someone's office or a place of business. What does it tell you about the person or business?

TIME

Chronemics concerns the use of time—how it is organized, how people react to it, and what messages it communicates. Time can be categorized as formal, informal, or psychological time. Formal time, such as an hour or a semester, is arbitrary, established for convenience and culturally understood. People define informal time, terms such as "right away" and "soon," differently. This can create misunderstanding; for example, "as soon as possible" does not mean the same thing to everyone. A customer may interpret it as within the hour when the customer service representative meant by the end of the day.[29]

Pacing, which was discussed in voice cues, also applies to people's perception of time. Matching our pace with customers' expectations of timing can help. Notice body language and respond appropriately. If customers are in a hurry, speed up. If we are in a hurry and customers are leisurely, rushing them may be annoying or intimidating. It sends the message that they do not have our full attention.

If we are uncertain what a customer's nonverbal communication means, the best approach is to tactfully check. Mention the behavior in question and provide alternative possibilities. Perhaps a coworker keeps glancing at his watch. We could say we have noticed him looking at his watch and ask if he has something on his mind or he has an appointment. It may be a nervous adapter, or perhaps it's not a good time to talk. If the latter, he may appreciate it if we quickly end the conversation or make plans to finish it at another time.

Monochronic and Polychronic Time

Definitions and perceptions of time vary from culture to culture. Clock accuracy actually varies in different parts of the world. One aspect of time consists of monochronic and polychronic time. *Monochronic time* means doing only one thing at a time. It is perceived as almost tangible. People talk about it almost like it is money, being "spent," "lost," and "wasted." It causes people to not want to be interrupted and separates people into those deserving time and those not. Monochronic time is typical of American business. It is a learned concept. Even though it seems natural and logical, the opposite sense of time exists in other cultures. *Polychronic time* means doing many things at once. It is more typical of Mediterranean, Arab, and South American countries. There is involvement with people. Completing transactions between people is more important than sticking to schedules. Polychronic people spend considerable time with customers or clients and build lifetime relationships. The link creates a mutual desire to be helpful. Two people with opposite time views will find each other's world very different and difficult (see Table 6.2).

TABLE 6.2   Monochronic and Polychronic Time

Monochronic	Polychronic
Do one thing at a time	Do many things at once
Concentrate on the job	Are highly distractible, easily interrupted
Take time commitments, like deadlines and schedules, seriously	Consider time commitments an objective to be achieved, if possible
Are committed to the job	Are committed to people and relationships
Follow plans closely	Change plans often and easily
Are concerned about not disturbing others, follow rules of privacy and consideration	Are more concerned with relationships than with privacy
Show respect for private property, seldom borrow and lend	Borrow and lend things often and easily
Emphasize promptness	Base promptness on the type of relationship
Favor short-term relationships	Favor lifetime relationships

Source: Edward T. Hall and Mildred Reed Hall, "Monochronic and Polychronic Time," in Laura K. Guerrero, Joseph A. DeVito, and Michael L. Hecht, eds., *The Nonverbal Communication Reader,* 2d ed. (Prospect Heights, IL: Waveland Press, 1999), 239.

This difference in time perspective will certainly affect global customer service and international customers.[30]

Waiting

Time is important to customer satisfaction. Because it is lost time, waiting has a negative effect on customer service evaluation. Researchers have found at least eight factors that influence time estimates.

1. Unoccupied time feels longer than occupied time. If customers' attention is occupied in a beneficial way, a wait will seem shorter.
2. Preprocess waits feel longer than in-process waits. Waiting before receiving service seems longer than once service begins.
3. Anxiety makes waits seem longer. If customers believe that they lack control over a situation, a wait will seem longer.
4. Unexpected waits are longer than known, finite waits. Customers expect to wait until their appointment time in a medical office. After that, not knowing how long the wait will be makes it seem longer.
5. Unexplained waits are longer than explained waits. If customers are not kept informed, they feel powerless. Waiting will cause them to become irritable and rude.
6. Unfair waits are longer than equitable waits. Even if a wait is short, customers can be irritated if there seems to be no reason for the wait or the first-in, first-out rule is violated.
7. The more valuable the service, the longer customers will wait.
8. Solo waits feel longer than group waits. In other words, waiting alone makes a wait seem longer than if a group of customers waits.[31]

Responsiveness, which is important to customers' evaluation of service, has an element of time. It is the idea that someone is alert, is aware of the importance of time, reacts to a situation quickly, and responds attentively. Service providers can show responsiveness through eye contact and attentive body movements. In a monochronic time mode, customers may seem like interruptions to our other tasks. Have you ever waited while a salesperson finishes writing something before she greets you? If our conversation with a coworker or if an obviously personal telephone call takes precedence over customers, our customers will be annoyed. We need to adjust priorities and give customers our full attention. Customers come before everything. If customers approach us while we are working on something, put it aside. Immediately acknowledge customers and let them know that they come first.

Being late causes others to wait. It can imply that our time is more important than anyone else's, that we are indispensable, and that we are busier than anyone else, which can seem unfair at best and rude at worst. Some people seem to wear their consistent lateness as a badge of honor. People can joke about someone always being late, but eventually customers may take their business elsewhere. Punctuality is still important. It's common courtesy. Since explained waits do not seem as long as unexplained waits, if we are going to be late due to events beyond our control, we should let people know.

TERMS

mixed message	volume
nonverbal communication	rate of speech
body language	voice quality
kinesics	pitch
eye contact	vocalizations
visual dominance ratio	articulation
gaze omission	pacing
gaze aversion	proxemics
gaze avoidance	haptics
emblems	artifactual communication
illustrators	olfactics
affect displays	chronemics
regulators	monochronic time
adapters	polychronic time
paralanguage	

DISCUSSION QUESTIONS

1. Why is nonverbal communication important in customer service situations?
2. List and define the six delivery channels of nonverbal communication.
3. Describe the functions of nonverbal communication.
4. Explain positive and negative eye movements.
5. What are the five classifications of gestures? Give an example of each.
6. What are the characteristics of appropriate customer service paralanguage?
7. What space zone should you use with customers?
8. How does our artifactual communication influence customers' impressions?

9. As a customer service provider, how could you shorten perceived customer waiting time?
10. How would you describe the nonverbal communication of:
    * An exceptional customer service representative handling a customer's problem?
    * A physician with a "good bedside manner"?
    * A credible customer service provider?
    * A deceptive person?

CASE—I CONTACT

Rick Anderson, a professor at Greene State University, received a telephone call from Mr. Steele, a local businessman, requesting a reference for a recent graduate. In the course of the conversation, Mr. Steele said that he was very impressed with the young woman he had interviewed.

However, he also said that he had interviewed several other graduates and was not impressed with them. Rick asked him why that was. Mr. Steele commented that he particularly noticed a lack of eye contact and confident manner.

We form our first impression of people the minute we see them, before any verbal exchange takes place. During an encounter, we exhibit nonverbal behaviors that influence people's impressions.

1. What are some examples of the other times in business when first impressions are very important?
2. What are characteristics that describe the first impression that you want to make?
3. What nonverbal communication will project these characteristics?
4. How can you create and manage impressions in a job interview?

NOTES

1. D. S. Sundaram and Cynthia Webster, "The Role of Nonverbal Communication in Service Encounters," *Journal of Services Marketing* 14, no. 5 (2000): 378–391.
2. Mary Jo Bitner, Bernard H. Booms, and M. S. Tetreault, "The Service Encounter: Diagnosing Favorable and Unfavorable Incidents," *Journal of Marketing* 54 (January): 71–84.
3. Dale G. Leathers, *Successful Nonverbal Communication, Principles and Applications,* 3d ed. (Needham Heights, ME: Allyn and Bacon, 1997).
4. Michael L. Hecht, Joseph A. DeVito, and Laura K. Guerrero, "Perspectives on Nonverbal Communication. Codes, Functions, and Contexts," in Laura K. Guerrero, Joseph A. DeVito, and Michael L. Hecht, eds., *The Nonverbal Communication Reader,* 2d ed. (Prospect Heights, IL: Waveland Press, 1999), 3–18.
5. Hecht, DeVito, and Guerrero, "Perspectives on Nonverbal Communication."
6. Kay E. Payne, *Different but Equal. Communication between the Sexes* (Westport, CT: Praeger Publishers, 2001), 131–142.
7. Leathers, *Successful Nonverbal Communication.*
8. James P. T. Fatt, "It's Not What You Say, It's How You Say It," *Communication World* 16, no. 6 (June–July 1999): 37–41; and Sundaram and Webster, "The Role of Nonverbal Communication."

9. Leathers, *Successful Nonverbal Communication;* and Gerald W. Grumet, "Eye Contact, The Core of Interpersonal Relatedness," in Guerrero, DeVito, and Hecht, *The Nonverbal Communication Reader,* 62–73.

10. Robert E. Kraut and Robert E. Johnston, "Social and Emotional Messages of Smiling," in Guerrero, DeVito, and Hecht, *The Nonverbal Communication Reader,* 74–78.

11. Leathers, *Successful Nonverbal Communication.*

12. Payne, *Different but Equal;* and Peter A. Anderson and Laura K. Guerrero, "Expressing and Managing Emotion with Nonverbal Communication," in Guerrero, DeVito, and Hecht, *The Nonverbal Communication Reader,* 275–283.

13. Paul Ekman and Wallace V. Friesen, "Hand Movements," in Guerrero, DeVito, and Hecht, *The Nonverbal Communication Reader,* 48–52; and Leathers, *Successful Nonverbal Communication.*

14. Fatt, "It's Not What You Say, It's How You Say It"; and Sundaram and Webster, "The Role of Nonverbal Communication."

15. Michael Argyle, "Nonverbal Vocalizations," in Guerrero, DeVito, and Hecht, *The Nonverbal Communication Reader,* 135–148.

16. DeVito, *Messages: Building Interpersonal Communication Skills* (New York: HarperCollins College Publishers, 1996).

17. Carol L. Sill, "Why Did We Lose That Customer?" *Tile & Decorative Surfaces,* March 1995, 30–34, 66.

18. Beth Semic, "Vocal Attractiveness, What Sounds Beautiful Is Good," in Guerrero, DeVito, and Hecht, *The Nonverbal Communication Reader,* 149–155.

19. Morton Cooper, *Change Your Voice, Change Your Life* (Los Angeles: Voice & Speech Company of America, 1984).

20. Fatt, "It's Not What You Say, It's How You Say It"; Sundaram and Webster, "The Role of Nonverbal Communication"; and Leathers, *Successful Nonverbal Communication.*

21. Karen Ritchie, "Marketing to Generation X," *American Demographics* 17, no. 4 (April 1995): 34–40.

22. Leathers, *Successful Nonverbal Communication;* and Sundaram and Webster, "The Role of Nonverbal Communication."

23. D. Eric Anderson, Matthew E. Ansfield, and Bella M. DePaulo, "Love's Best Habit. Deception in the Context of Relationships," in Pierre Philippot, Robert S. Feldman, and Erik J. Coats, eds., *The Social Context of Nonverbal Behavior* (Cambridge, United Kingdom: Cambridge University Press, 1999), 375.

24. Larry Smeltzer, John Waltman, and Donald Leonard, "Proxemics and Haptics in Managerial Communication," in Guerrero, DeVito, and Hecht, *The Nonverbal Communication Reader,* 184–191; and Leathers, *Successful Nonverbal Communication.*

25. Leathers, *Successful Nonverbal Communication.*

26. Smeltzer, Waltman, and Leonard, "Proxemics and Haptics in Managerial Communication."

27. Leathers, *Successful Nonverbal Communication.*

28. R. Kelly Aune, "The Effects of Perfume Use on Perceptions of Attractiveness and Competence," in Guerrero, DeVito, and Hecht, *The Nonverbal Communication Reader,* 126–132.

29. Leathers, *Successful Nonverbal Communication.*

30. Edward T. Hall and Mildred Reed Hall, "Monochronic and Polychronic Time," in Guerrero, DeVito, and Hecht, *The Nonverbal Communication Reader,* 237–240.

31. Deborah K. Unzicker, "The Psychology of Being Put on Hold: An Exploratory Study of Service Quality," *Psychology & Marketing* 16, no. 4 (July 1999): 327–350.

VERBAL COMMUNICATION

OBJECTIVES

1. Explain why verbal communication is important.
2. Identify and illustrate acceptable verbal communication.
3. Classify and illustrate unacceptable verbal communication.
4. Discuss difficult customer conversations.
5. Describe customer-oriented principles and guidelines for written documents and other print communication.
6. Outline best practices for business etiquette.
7. Discuss civility in the workplace.

IMPORTANCE OF VERBAL COMMUNICATION

Numerous research studies corroborate the importance of verbal communication in the workplace. A business communications study found that, in addition to listening and following instructions, the most important verbal communication skills were conversational skills, skill in giving feedback, the ability to communicate with the public, meeting skills, presentation skills, and skill in handling customer complaints.[1] Through their verbal communication, customer service providers need to reflect a friendly, helpful, courteous, understanding, patient, truthful, enthusiastic, knowledgeable, and confident attitude. Customer service providers should use positive, strong words.

Verbal communication includes words, a set of symbols, and grammar, the rules for combining words. Words are symbols with meanings. A *meaning* is the interpretation a person gives to a symbol or word. No two people have exactly the same meaning for many words because they have had different experiences. "Very cold" in Tennessee means a temperature around freezing; "very cold" in Montana is below zero. A "buggy" in Tennessee is a grocery cart in Ohio. It's very likely that customers will not interpret all of our words the same way we meant them. We should check to make sure that customers understand us and that we understand the meaning of customers' words.[2]

Words do make a difference. If a person is a 13-year-old female, do we refer to her as a "child," "girl," "young person," "teenager," "young woman," "young lady," or "young adult"? It depends on the circumstances and to whom we are talking. We may inadvertently annoy a customer by using the wrong language. Each reference has a different *connotation,* the subjective or emotional meaning that people give a word, rather than the dictionary meaning. On the other hand, customers have their own language in their industry and lives. If an executive refers to her customers as "clients," use the same terminology to be more credible and likable. If a customer calls her child an "infant" or her "baby," using her word will develop rapport. The next sections will describe customer-oriented verbal communication and discuss negative and improper language.

Experience Discussion 7.1

What are some examples of verbal communication that are unacceptable in a business setting?

ACCEPTABLE VERBAL COMMUNICATION

The following are verbal communication skills that customer service personnel need to master. Do keep in mind that the words we use should be words we are comfortable with so we can be ourselves. Otherwise, we may be perceived as insincere and indifferent.

Positive, Powerful Language
* Use good grammar. Overly formal language is not necessary and may sound stilted, but "He don't" is incorrect grammar, which is irritating to many people. Poor grammar gives the impression that the person is uneducated or indifferent.
* Choose a short, simple word rather than a longer, overdone word or phrase. Otherwise, customers may think you are being condescending or pretentious. For example, say "help" rather than "facilitate," and say "use" rather than "utilize."
* Use positive, powerful words like "thank you," "appreciate," "yes," and "I agree." Always thank customers sincerely.
* Take the time to say, "You are welcome," when customers take the time to thank you.
* Let customers know you appreciate that they contacted you when they bring problems to your attention. Say, "Thank you for bringing this to my attention," "Thank you for documenting the information. It really helps," or "Thanks for understanding."
* Use the word "you." Why is it stronger to say, "You've asked a good question." rather than, "That's a good question"? The reason is that "you" is a more personal, attention-getting word. It tells customers that you are 100 percent customer-focused.

On the other hand, there are times when you should separate the person from the situation. Keep it impersonal. Personalizing negative messages irritates customers. This is not one of the times to use the word "you." Instead of saying, "Your payment is always late," say, "This payment is often late." Instead of saying, "You did not send in a payment," say, "There isn't a payment showing up on your account for June. The last one recorded was the 20th of last month." You are referring to an objective source, and the customer can react to the situation or computer, not to you.

* Do not say that a customer is wrong or has misunderstood. If the customer did something wrong, phrase it indirectly, "This form needs your signature right here." If a customer misinterprets, say, "I can see I did not explain that very well."

* Explain reasons for requests. For example, customers often complain about repetitive questions for information. If a patient says, "I gave you this information the last time I was here," you can say, "We've found that if we update information, we can make sure your medical information is accurate."

Here's an example of positive verbal and nonverbal language on the telephone. Lisa ordered a knit top from a well-known catalog company. When she received the package, the enclosed catalog showed the top on sale for 20 percent off. That didn't seem right to her since she had paid full price. Therefore, she called the 800 number and said, "I just received a knit top and was looking at the enclosed catalog and discovered that it is now on sale." The customer service representative, not hesitating, not even taking a breath, and she could tell from his voice inflection that he was delighted to do it, said, "Then we owe you some money. If you'll give me the item number and your credit card number, we will credit you for the difference." Notice the phrase "we owe you" was immediate, was very direct, took ownership, and was personal.

Names and Titles

* Use the customer's name. Practice remembering people and their names. Listen carefully when you are on the phone and when you are introduced. Look at a nametag. Use the name within the first 30 seconds. Write the name down. Repeat it more than once during the conversation, but do not overdo it. Using customers' names at the end of conversations helps us end on a positive note, with customers feeling good about us.

  If you see people you recognize and cannot remember their name, the best approach is to smile, extend your hand, and say something like, "Hello, I don't think we've seen each other in a while, but we met at. . . My name is. . . and I work at. . . " or "Hello. We've met before at. . . My name is. . . " The person will reciprocate with his name.

* Use a title, such as "Ms.," "Mrs.," "Mr.," or "Dr." Ask for the preferred title if you are uncertain. In most circumstances, it is best to use a title rather than a first name unless customers tell us otherwise. Be a little formal rather than overly familiar. If you are corrected about a title, apologize briefly and use what the person prefers. On the other hand, in some companies and regions of the country, first-name use is common. The best thing to do is ask permission, "May I call you Jim?"

* Use "Ms.," rather than "Miss" or "Mrs.," unless you are told differently. Since the title "Mr." does not indicate marital status, some women dislike titles that identify their status. Using "Ms." is safest.

UNACCEPTABLE VERBAL COMMUNICATION

Customer service providers need to be positive, competent, courteous, and clear. The following are examples of negative, weak, discourteous, and unclear language.

Negative Language
* Avoid using the word "no" at the beginning of a sentence. Say, "I can exchange it or give you a store credit. However, without a receipt, I'm not going to be able to give you a credit card refund."
* Three words that should never be used are "can't," "don't," and "won't." Do not say, "We can't do that." Say instead, "I wish I could, Ms. Stephens. That's a good idea. However, it's not an option. What else can we think of?"
* Avoid the word "problem," as in "What's the problem?" Say, "Please tell me what happened."
* Answer questions, rather than saying what a server said recently when asked about the ingredients of an entrée, "Beats me."

Weak Language
* Instead of just saying, "I don't know," or, "I'm not sure," say, "I don't know, but I'll find out," or "I'm not sure. Let me check."
* Say, "I'll find out," rather than, "I'll try to find out." "Try to" seems half-hearted.
* Avoid *clichés*—overused phrases—like "Have a nice day." They are lazy talk. Think of other expressions, such as "Thanks for buying at Fresh Market."
* Avoid overused business words, such as push the envelope, paradigm, virtual (anything).
* Avoid *euphemisms,* which are a positive or neutral expression used in place of a negative or unpleasant description, such as "downsizing" used for "laying off employees." Use euphemisms only when necessary for politeness. Another example is "She left the company to pursue other interests." People read this as "she was asked to leave." If you are using a euphemism to avoid confrontation, it's better to deal with it sooner rather than later. Don't use a euphemism if it leaves the person with only a vague idea of the truth.
* Eliminate personal overuse of any phrase, for example, "you know."
* Do not routinely say you are sorry unless you are apologizing for a true error. There is no reason to say you are sorry that someone is unavailable; it is not your fault if someone is out of the office. There is no need to say you are sorry that a customer had to hold if you asked permission. If you do need to say you are sorry for a customer's problem, do not say, "Sorry about that." It sounds insincere.
* Avoid the following weak terminology, which tells customers that you are uncertain, unprepared, or incompetent.
  * *Uncertainty expressions:* "maybe," "perhaps," and "I guess"
  * *Weak modifiers:* "I kind of like this" and "This looks pretty good."
  * *Tag questions:* "That's a good idea, don't you think?" and "That was a really good presentation, wasn't it?"
  * *Self-critical statements:* "I'm not very good at this. I'm new" and "I've never been good at math."
  * *Too many intensifiers:* "Really, this has been the greatest." or "It was truly phenomenal."
  * *Overpoliteness:* "Excuse me, please, sir" and "If it's not too inconvenient, would you mind stopping by my office this morning, please?"

Rude Language

* Avoid slang, terms used by subgroups of people. A 60-year-old male customer may consider "dude" disrespectful.
* Never use false terms of endearment or familiarity, such as "honey," "babe," or "buddy."
* Eliminate vulgar expressions and profanity.
* Eliminate words that customers hate to hear, like "policy" and "rules." Words like this make it seem as if you are ducking responsibility or you do not have a legitimate answer. It makes you appear more concerned about yourself than the customer's satisfaction.
* Avoid the word "should," as in "You should have told us about your coupon at the beginning." This sounds like you are blaming the customer for a mistake. Instead, say, "It would be best if you tell us about your coupon before you order." Do not say something like, "You should have read the directions." Customers realize this but they do not want to be reminded.
* Do not use other phrases that blame customers, like "You forgot to. . . " or "I can't believe the salesperson told you that." The latter implies either disbelief or blame of the salesperson. Customers may think you are accusing them of lying. At the least, it is calling the competence of your sales staff into question.
* Do not say, "You'll have to. . . ," as in "You'll have to wait." This sounds like an order or that the customers have no choice. The natural reaction to this message is, "No, I don't have to."
* Never say, "Calm down." It implies customers have no right to be upset and will make them more annoyed.
* Do not tell a customer to "Listen." We have all heard this when the person is interrupting and wants to give us an excuse.
* Do not use abrupt phrases, like "Who is this?" or "Who did you say you were?" Some experts recommend "Who may I say is calling?" However, this is becoming a cliché and irritates some people. Instead, say "Could I have your name please?" or "I didn't quite hear your full name."
* Avoid using the question "What may I tell her this is regarding?" It sounds formal, stilted, and arrogant. Try saying "Can I tell her what this is about?"
* Avoid one-word abrupt answers, such as "yes," "OK," and "sure" when customers ask questions. These can be perceived as a lack of interest or lack of communication skills.
* Never say, "It's not my job." Unbelievably, we have all heard this. If it's for a customer, it is our job.
* Be helpful. "It's somewhere back there (gesturing toward the back of the store)" is not helpful. Nor is a clerk telling customers that the product they are seeking is "somewhere on aisle 12 or 13." Some companies have this procedure down to a science. They either take you straight to the product or give you detailed instructions about where it is. "It's on aisle 16, about one-third of the way toward the front of the store, on the left middle shelf, about your eye level."
* Use *gender-neutral expressions*. While we do not advocate strict political correctness, there are some pitfalls. Men and women perceive some words differently, leading to breakdowns in communication. Using the generic "man" emphasizes maleness at the expense of femaleness, such as saying "mankind" rather than "humankind." Other examples are to use "police officer" rather than "po-

liceman," "salesperson" rather than "salesman," and "server" rather than "waitress" or "waiter." Another example is that many customers will think it is discourteous to automatically assume a physician is male and a nurse is female.

* There are also word-choice considerations related to people with disabilities, as will be discussed later in Chapter 12. In addition, by no means should we use derogatory racial terms.

Unclear Words

* Do not use in-house *jargon*, such as "four top" (dining table seating four) or "ops" (operations). Some people use jargon to impress customers, but it just confuses them. They feel like they should know the term and are too embarrassed to ask. Avoid technical terms that customers will not know.
* Avoid acronyms that customers won't understand. An *acronym* is using letters to represent the words such as the AAPP test. College admissions staff were in the habit of telling newly admitted students that they had to take the AAPP. Students had no idea what that meant. It's a combination of tests new students must take to measure their reading, writing, and math skills. The author doesn't know what the letters stand for.[3]

See Table 7.1 for examples of positive and unacceptable statements.

TABLE 7.1   Examples of Positive and Unacceptable Language

Positive	Unacceptable
Please	There's nothing I can do about that.
How can I help you?	I don't have time to do that.
What can I do for you?	That's not my responsibility.
Is there anything else I can do for you?	I couldn't help it.
I'd be happy to do that for you.	Hey, sorry about that. I got backed up and couldn't call you back.
Consider it done.	Well, I wasn't the one you talked to.
I can help with that.	I never said. . .
The best way to handle that is. . .	You're wrong.
The easiest way to do that is. . .	You must be mistaken.
The fastest way to do that is. . .	You don't understand.
I'm sure there's a way. . .	You don't see my point.
We can solve that issue.	You're not being reasonable.
Thank you for waiting.	You're not listening to me.
It was nice talking with you.	Listen to me.
Thank you for coming in.	I'm with another customer right now. You'll have to wait.
It's been a pleasure to serve you.	What you have to do is. . .
We appreciate your business.	Speak up please.
Thank you for letting us know.	Who are you holding for?
What we can do is. . .	What do you need?
I apologize for the inconvenience.	We never received that payment. Are you sure it was mailed?
You are welcome.	He doesn't work here any more. We let him go.

Source: Part of this section is based on Eileen O. Brownell, "Magical Words Create Customer Satisfaction & Loyalty," *Manage* 51, no. 3 (February 2000): 10.

Gender Differences

Differences in male and female language are attributed to socialization and responses to stereotyping. Other reasons are women's traditionally lower status and their greater concern with psychological states. In the United States, we expect women to use less intense language and more polite language.

Researchers have found several specific differences between men and women. First, women use more words about emotions, and their language is more conciliatory. Overall, women show more frequent use of fillers (hedges), a high degree of tentativeness or uncertainty, greater courtesy and sensitivity, frequent use of negations (what something is not rather than what it is), more references to emotions, and less assertiveness. Men's language is more direct, active, controlling, intense, nonstandard, egocentric [more use of first-person-singular (I, me) pronouns], aggressive, and focused on the here and now.

Some women have a tendency to add a tag question at the end of a sentence, such as "I think we might want to try. . . , don't you?" When men use tag questions and other tentative language, they are perceived as polite and other-directed. Unfortunately, women are seen as less powerful. Another tendency is using more weak qualifiers, words that modify, soften, or weaken other phrases, such as "It seems to me. . ." and "Perhaps. . ." Women are said to use more intensifiers, like "really," "quite," and "awfully." On the plus side, women use more civilities, words indicating politeness and courtesy, such as "please," "thank you," and "excuse me."

Men ask questions for information; women ask questions to show interest in people. If a coworker is talking about a problem, women will respond with empathetic words. Men will often respond with solutions. When women introduce a topic, they may not continue unless they are encouraged to do so by a comment or nonverbal signal. Men are more likely to introduce a topic and keep talking. They do not seem to need verbal or nonverbal expressions of interest. Women personalize their messages, emphasizing the emotional angle about how they feel. Men's conversations are more informal and impersonal. They will talk about events and emphasize the humorous parts.

Experts say that men are seen as more credible than women to other men, and, in fact, women perceive men as more credible than women. While women's style is not wrong, just different, it does sometimes lead to unfavorable perceptions, especially in business situations with internal customers. Women need to be aware of how their verbal communication influences others' perceptions of them. On the other hand, men need to be aware that women's verbal style has advantages and does not mean a lack of competence. We need to keep in mind that women's verbal style helps them connect with other people. Their style makes them good at increasing morale, developing teamwork, promoting empowerment, and building relationships. Women may want to modify their verbal style but keep the people-oriented language.

In addition, researchers have found that language often depends on the power position between the speaker and listener. Successful women who have acquired power through performance and occupational prestige or who work in traditional female or neutral occupations are less likely to be evaluated differently from men.[4]

Skill Development 7.1

Put a tape recorder on your desk or in your drawer or carry it in your pocket, and record yourself. Evaluate your verbal language.

DIFFICULT CONVERSATIONS

Many times it's tough to know what words to use. In service situations, representatives must balance the wants and expectations of the customers with their own understanding of what's right, acceptable, and doable.

One of the toughest jobs customer service representatives face is delivering bad news. The first key is viewing the information from the customers' perspective. Perhaps the company must institute a price increase. Tell customers, "I understand you don't want the prices to increase. We don't either." Then explain the reasons for the increase, whether due to supplier costs, increases in energy prices, or postal rate increases. Make the price increase logical and tangible for them.[5]

When customers call with questions, they like to tell their story before asking a question, and they may ramble. You need to listen and anticipate the information you need to provide help. While you need to hear them out, you also may have to interject questions to get the information you need. Use questions to get more control over the flow of conversation. For example, if they mention a date, you can jump in and say, "Let me make sure I have that. You said you bought that on January 15? . . . and would you give me the order number from the upper left-hand corner of your invoice?" Use probing questions, such as "could you tell me more about. . . " Probing questions imply conversation, convey understanding, and develop rapport. Learn how to ask quickly and smoothly without seeming to interrupt. Use a curious and helpful tone rather than an inquisitive tone. Data-gathering questions are more inquisitive and mechanical and can be used for specific information, such as address and telephone.

When customers are mistaken or wrong, do not tell them that. Express empathy and fix the problem. As you get more details about how the misunderstanding occurred, customers may realize they were wrong without you having to say anything. Since it is never expressed, customers will be less embarrassed. Another statement to use when customers misunderstand is, "If that's what you thought I said, I guess I didn't explain myself as well as I thought. Let me try again."

What do you do if the customer is right and the company was clearly wrong? Not saying, "We made a mistake," makes customers think we are hiding something or do not care. However, when admitting blame is not wise due to liability issues, respond with empathy, saying, "I am sorry about the inconvenience." If the problem is reasonably inconsequential, you can say, "I am sorry that happened." If it has the potential to get out of control, you should be careful what words you use. Some people will sue if they believe we admitted fault. On the other hand, if the company is wrong, telling the customer that the company is not to blame could be considered unethical. A company can get into a dilemma during a crisis if it denies it is at fault.[6] This is an issue that needs to be thoroughly discussed by frontline employees and management so everyone knows exactly what to say under various circumstances.

WRITTEN COMMUNICATION

A letter represents a company to a customer, just like a store, a receptionist, and the person who answers the telephone. Although letters have decreased as a contact method between customers and companies, they are still essential tools. In addition, anything in print represents the company. Written communication needs to be an asset that develops and increases customer loyalty. We can adapt our face-to-face verbal style to what we write.

Process

* Respond so that the customer knows you "listened."
* Picture a real person as you write. One expert suggests we pretend we are explaining to our mom so our language is less formal.
* Tell customers good news in the first line. If it's bad news, explain why. If they are right and the company needs to apologize, do so.
* Read the letter as if you were the customer before you send it. Reading it aloud will give you an idea of what the customer sees.
* Develop a selection of well-written standard letters to decrease the need for original writing. These are perfectly appropriate as long as they can be edited specifically for each customer.

Wording

* Use the active voice, "I appreciate your thoughts," rather than the passive voice, "Your comments were appreciated."
* Avoid old-fashioned business language, such as "Enclosed, please find. . ." Very formal, businesslike language can seem cold and unfriendly to customers. Use the simpler "Here is the information you requested."
* Avoid overworked, bland phrasing, such as "I enjoyed meeting you and Linda and hope we can have lunch soon." Be more creative. Say, "Talking with you and Linda about your new venture yesterday was intriguing. I look forward to hearing more about it."
* Keep the negative language to a minimum. Customers do not like to hear "We can't. . ." in a letter or in person.
* Do not use jargon, including technospeak, computerese, and legalese.
* Make sure your grammar, spelling, and punctuation are correct.[7]

Print Communication

Companies hand out, send, or post thousands of printed communications every year. Most stores have numerous policy signs. Some messages are perceived as cold or rude. A company can provide exceptional customer service in person and on the telephone, but if written messages are negative or rude, customers will be legitimately annoyed. Consider the store policy sign, "No returns after 30 days." While customers need to be aware of the policy, it is stated in a negative way. Stating it as "We accept returns up to 30 days" is more positive.[8] "This is the only notice you will get" is an example of a statement on an annual bill from an automobile insurance company with which the customer is otherwise very satisfied. Much better wording would be "We send out only one notice when your payment is due." Overdue payment notices like "It is necessary that you forward this delinquent amount. . ." are curt and overly formal. Customers would rather see "We have not received your payment. Please send it promptly."

Skill Development 7.2

1. Bring in a company bill or other printed communication that has an example of negative or rude language. How would you rewrite it?
2. What negative signage have you seen in retail stores? How would you translate the sign into positive language?

Companies should develop a way to correct rude and mixed messages. One thing they can do is to collect a sample of every printed document that goes out to customers, from bills, to shipping enclosures, to back-order notices, to overdue payment requests. If a company has outsourced functions, it should check what these outside resources are saying in written form and by telephone. Then revise all forms to make sure that they are polite and positive. Continue to monitor printed material as it is developed. If a lawyer needs to approve language, a customer service staff member should have a final review afterward so that the language is still customer-oriented.

According to a telephone company, customers view its bill as an important part of the company's communication. The company redesigned its bill to make it more concise and easier to read and understand. The company used larger paper, so the bill has fewer pages. The company also believes that consumers will rate the company as more helpful if it adds value to the bill. So the company provided customers the option to combine their local telephone bill with cellular, paging, and cable bills. It added a billing summary that shows all the companies that service their account so customers can easily find an incorrect billing.[9]

Other types of written communication can provide exceptional customer service. A heating and air-conditioning firm gives customers a "daily receipt" that outlines in lay language, no contractor-speak, what has been done that day, when and what time the crew will arrive next if the job is not done, and how much more work remains. In addition, the form has the date, order number, technician's name, serial and model numbers of the equipment, and payment information. This is much better than the wordless disappearing act common among repair and construction workers, leaving the customer wondering what was done and if the crew will ever be back.[10]

In addition to written documents, have you ever noticed signs in retail stores? "No soliciting." "No shoes, no shirt, no service." "No refunds without receipt." "No smoking." "No parking." "Parking for business only—Violators will be towed at their own expense." "We don't take credit cards." It's not surprising customers get the wrong impression. Stores should consider minimizing many of these negative, offensive signs. Change them to positive, polite requests. "We would appreciate it if you would not smoke" and "To help serve you better, please return merchandise with a receipt." See Table 7.2 for other examples of alternative language. Some signs are necessary and the language may be legally mandated, but companies should consider rephrasing what they can. Granted, the signs may be longer, but customers will be happier. A company can also add positive messages, like "Welcome" on the front side of the door and "Thank you" or "We appreciate your business" on the inside so customers see it when they leave.[11] These are much better than "Push" and "Pull."

TABLE 7.2   Retail Store Messages

Negative	Positive
No soliciting	Please do not solicit.
No shoes, no shirt, no service	Please dress appropriately—shirt and shoes.
No refunds without receipt	We request a receipt for all returns.
No smoking allowed	Please do not smoke.
No parking	Parking for [company] customers
We don't take credit cards.	We request cash or check only.
No pets allowed	Please do not bring pets inside.

Complaint Response Letters

Some complaints are not made in person or by telephone but by letter. Answering customer complaint letters requires special considerations. The company should have a staff member responsible for responding to these letters and design appropriate messages. A study of consumer perceptions of manufacturers' responses to complaint correspondence reported in the *Journal of Consumer Affairs* indicated four factors that are crucial to favorable customer reaction.

1. The first requirement is simply to respond. A 1988 study found that 18 percent of consumer packaged-good companies did not respond to letters. Over half, 53 percent, did not address the customers' specific issues.[12] For another example, out of 25 genuine complaint or compliment letters sent in March 1993 by the author's customer service class, only two companies had responded by early May.
2. The letter should tell customers that their input is appreciated, and it should tell them that more than once. Common sense would suggest that most companies do express appreciation; however, if it is buried in the middle of a paragraph or unless the appreciation is expressed multiple times, customers may overlook it.
3. The response should be sincere, specific, and accurate. A brief and clearly indiscriminate letter saying, "Thanks for writing. Sorry you were disappointed in our product. Here are several coupons," is not acceptable. Do not thank a customer for her comments about a brownie mix when she wrote about blueberry muffins.
4. Enclose a small gift with the letter, such as a coupon for a free box of crackers or $5 off a meal. While the higher the perceived value the better, a company can be creative without a big increase in monetary value. A company must weigh the benefits and costs associated with its response to customer correspondence, but what it does may make the difference between customers being merely satisfied or customers feeling that the company has gone the extra mile.[13]

One difficult job of customer service personnel is writing letters with negative messages to respond to a customer with a problem. Companies should apologize. Be specific about why the company cannot do anything. Explain what happened to cause the situation. Avoid absolutes, such as "We will make sure this never happens again." If the customer was wrong, make a suggestion to prevent it happening again, such as "In the future, I suggest you include your account number and a telephone number so we can reach you if there's a question." Always end on a positive note, "We value your business."

A research study of negative-message letters from consumer affairs departments to dissatisfied customers showed that the companies were not using standard business communication textbook principles. The letters were shorter than textbook examples, and the language tended to be direct, using "you" rather than the recommended third person. The letters usually began with a buffer, however the buffer was shorter than generally prescribed. A typical buffer included thanks, such as "Thank you for your recent comments about [product]."

The negative terms were not embedded or hidden in a paragraph. The negative message was never implied using positive terminology, which is what textbooks suggest. Most avoided using the word "no" but did contain negative phrases. Most of the letters, 92 percent, used negative language freely, including "We are unable to honor your request" and "Although our efforts have not met your expectations. . . " The researcher suggested that the negative language is intended to ensure customers are clear about the company's position.

Contrary to recommendations, apologies were common in words such as "We apologize for any inconvenience. . . " Research indicates that an apology adds pleasantness, avoiding an impression of rudeness. In addition, the theory of fairness suggests that customers want to believe that they have influenced the outcome. An apology shows the customer that the service person listened and paid attention to the customer's input.

None of the letters had sales information. If customers were satisfied with the response, the company assumed they would repurchase. If customers were not satisfied, sales information would make the situation worse.[14]

BUSINESS ETIQUETTE

Another type of communication in business is etiquette, which includes both nonverbal and verbal behavior. This section outlines a few principles of *business etiquette*.

Customers want customer service representatives to be polite and respectful. Knowing basic business etiquette will help us be more courteous. It goes a long way toward developing rapport with customers.

Many people think that etiquette is outdated. While not as formal as in the past, proper etiquette is still professional. People think that etiquette does not matter in a casual business environment. Manners still show respect. We also need to realize that manners have changed since women have entered the workforce. What our mothers taught us does not necessarily apply in today's business setting. Knowing the appropriate etiquette will help us make a positive impression and increase our credibility. This is particularly important with business-to-business customers and with internal customers. It will also make us feel more comfortable and confident.

Verbal and Nonverbal Etiquette

Introductions.   In the business world, introductions go by office seniority and age. Gender is not a factor. Make it a policy to know company titles and seniority. The correct order is introducing the lower status *to* the higher status as in:

* Client or customer, this is "coworker." For example, "Ms. Customer, this is Judy Graves."
* Senior executive, this is "junior executive."
* Older, this is "younger," unless the younger is a senior executive.
* Official person, this is "unofficial person." For example, "Ms. Mayor, this is Rick Morgan, our architect."
* Peer in another company, this is "peer in my company."
* Nonacquaintance, this is "acquaintance"—unless any of the above applies.

An example of what you should say is, "Mr. CEO, I'd like you to meet Ms. New Research Manager." Add information to acquaint people and get a conversation started. "Mr. CEO, I'd like you to meet Ms. New Research Manager. She has just joined us from Star Research in Atlanta." If you forget a name, just be honest, "I'm sorry. My mind just went blank and I've forgotten your name." Appropriate responses, using names, are, "Hello, Mr. CEO. It's nice to meet you." and "I'm pleased to meet you, Ms. Manager."

Don't fail to introduce people because of your uncertainty about how to do it. You may not know someone's title, position, or age. It is much better to introduce incorrectly than to not do it at all. Speak slowly and clearly so the names are heard. If no one introduces you, step forward and say, "Hello, I'm Judy Hamilton. I don't believe we've met."

If you are talking with a group and a newcomer approaches that you know but no one else does, it is appropriate to introduce the person to the others. A newcomer may be uncomfortable wondering how to become part of the conversation. You should also step back and turn your body slightly toward the person so he or she is part of the circle talking.

Titles.   Use a title when introducing people and when addressing mail. For an M.D. or Ph.D., use the title Dr. at the beginning of the name or M.D. or Ph.D. at the end, never both. For an attorney, use either Esq. or J.D. after the name with no title before the name. Avoid abbreviating business titles like Dir. of PR. Director of Public Relations is much more professional and respectful.

Handshake.   We form our first impression of people as soon as we see them. A first impression includes a handshake. This is important nonverbal communication, particularly in business-to-business customer service. One study found that a firm handshake indicated extraversion and expressiveness and was negatively associated with shyness. For women, a firm handshake was related to openness to experience. These associations suggest that a firm handshake is an excellent way for women to contribute to their perceived professionalism.

A handshake is appropriate when we are introduced, when someone from the outside enters our office, when we see a coworker we have not seen in a long time, when we enter a meeting and are introduced, when a meeting ends, when we see a colleague outside the office, when we say good-bye, and whenever we feel it is appropriate.

Poor handshakes include the limp or fish handshake, the tips of the fingers handshake, the bone-crushing handshake, the sweaty palms handshake, and the pumper. In business situations, a handshake should take place within the personal zone with both people stepping forward a little and then stepping back. The way to shake hands properly is to extend your hand at a slight angle with your thumb up. Aim so that the area between your thumb and first finger meets the other person's. Put your thumb down gently once contact has been made and wrap your fingers around the palm of the person's hand. There should be full palm contact. Use a firm grip with two to three pumps. A finger-grip handshake from a woman sends an unbusinesslike message. Eye contact and a smile further the impression of openness and confidence.

The higher-ranking person should extend a hand first, but if the person does not, it is acceptable for you to do so. It used to be considered polite for a man to wait for a woman to extend her hand. That is no longer true, but a woman might want to extend her hand so there is no confusion. If someone extends his or her hand, it is rude not to reciprocate. It is perfectly appropriate for two women to shake hands in today's business world. Both men and women should stand to shake hands when they are introduced.

The proper way to shake hands with someone who has lost the use of his or her right hand is to lay a hand on the person's hand, wrist, or forearm. Some people may offer their left hand. You can offer your left hand then or, if your right hand is already in motion, touch the person's left hand with your right hand. If you are the person with the loss of use, you can ease awkwardness that others feel by indicating what you prefer.[15]

Skill Development 7.3

Practice shaking hands with your instructor and other classmates.

Handshakes differ in other countries. In northern Europe, the handshake is a curt, firm, one-pump handshake. The French shake hands the most, in greeting, departing, returning, every day, in business and social situations. In Russia, a strong handshake is followed by a bear hug. In Islamic countries, unrelated men cannot touch women, and so they never offer to shake hands with women. A firm grip is not appropriate among Middle Easterners and Japanese; it should be gentle. Koreans and Japanese avoid direct eye contact when shaking hands.

In other countries, the proper greeting is not a handshake. People from other countries may have adopted the handshake as customary, especially when traveling; however, demonstrating their greeting is a sign of respect. For international customers, even if we do not know the language, learning proper signals improves communication. In Japanese society, a bow is the greeting. It signifies respect and humility and has several nuances, one of which is that the person of lower rank bows first and lowest. In other Asian countries, a handshake is more common, perhaps with a very slight bob of the head. In India, the hands are placed in a praying position about chest high and accompanied by a slight bow. In the Middle East, the salaam is the greeting. The right hand sweeps up, first touching the heart, then the forehead, and finally up and outward, perhaps with a slight nod of the head.[16]

Manners. The first person to arrive at a door should open it no matter what gender, age, or corporate position. It's polite for a host to open a door for a visitor. Always help people who need help, for example, if they are carrying something. You should always say thank you if someone holds the door for you. Hold the door for someone behind you to grab. If it is a very traditional company, then it is more appropriate for men to open doors for women and lower status to hold doors for higher status. Never embarrass someone for holding the door for you. Women should not act ungrateful.

In an elevator, wait until everyone exits before getting on. Move to the back to make room for people. Push the floor button for others at their request. Hold the elevator door open when appropriate. Move aside to let people in and out. If you must, step off and hold the door. If you are in the back and your floor is coming up, speak up.

When you arrive at a meeting, wait until you are directed where to sit. The host should do so. Do not sit until the host sits down. Do not put your belongings on the host's desk.

In an office setting, learn how to use the copier, printer, and other equipment properly so that you do not inconvenience others. Clean up the area before you leave. Do not leave a copier empty of paper. If the copier breaks, let the appropriate person know. Do not take or snoop through what is not yours. If someone has just a few copies, allow the person to interrupt or go before a larger job. Make sure you take your originals with you. Treat a printer similarly.

Conversation.   Do you have a coworker whom you would describe as a bore or obnoxious? Think about how you come across to people. Do you seem aloof, too serious, too flighty, nervous, rude, or insensitive? Do you talk too much, interrupt, or ignore others? Remember your listening, nonverbal, and verbal communication skills. For small talk, it's appropriate to talk about business events, the meeting place or city, traffic, sports, weather, or books, movies, or TV shows. Subjects to avoid are religion, controversial topics, personal misfortunes, health or diet, gossip, jokes of questionable taste, swear words, coworkers, or your spouse except in general terms.[17]

Experience Discussion 7.2

What examples of rudeness and incivility have you noticed in the workplace?

CIVILITY IN THE WORKPLACE

Civility is an essential element in internal customer service. *Incivility* is defined as the lack of courtesy, consideration, and respect for others. A survey of 2013 adults by Public Agenda in 2002 found that 79 percent thought that lack of respect and courtesy in America was a serious problem. Part of the speculated reason for rudeness is that it is a symptom of the decline of community and the collapse of social connectedness. In the workplace, experts believe that employee diversity, reengineering, downsizing, budget cuts, increased pressures for productivity, autocratic work environments, and the use of part-time employees have contributed to incivility. Another suggested reason is that civility is considered counter to Americans' belief in freedom, individuality, and self-expression. However, the lack of civility causes stress in our fast-paced, rapidly changing society. As one management author says, "The need for civility becomes greater when interactions among people increase in complexity and frequency."[18]

Little signs of workplace incivility are not saying please and thank you, dropping trash on the floor, not making coffee when the pot is almost empty, and walking away from a copier with no paper. Interpersonal incivility includes making sarcastic or condescending comments, talking behind another coworker's back, and using one's power over someone inappropriately. Another example is the attitude that "my life is more important than your life, and someone else can cover if I have to leave early for something at my son's school, never mind that it inconveniences someone else." Inconsiderate people always show up late, as if their time is more important than anyone else's.

If a workplace is uncivil, workers can become miserable or be aggressive. There are lost customers, higher employee turnover, and lower productivity, all of which affect the bottom line. Therefore, experts believe that managers must do something about interpersonal rudeness swiftly and justly. Otherwise, the situation lowers expectations and norms for the whole organization.[19]

One expert believes that civility is at an all-time low and causing productivity and morale problems. He thinks that employees feel they are easily replaced commodities. A study by a management professor at the University of North Carolina revealed that 100 percent of the respondents felt a coworker had treated them rudely, disrespectfully, or insensitively. Over three-quarters, 78 percent, felt incivility had increased over the past decade. Over half, 53 percent, said they had lost work time worrying about a confrontation with a coworker, and 28 percent had lost work time avoiding the person. Over one-fifth, 22 percent, had decreased their work effort, and 38 percent had reduced their commitment.[20]

Customer service jobs are known for their emotional labor. They are difficult and stressful and can lead to conscious and subconscious incivility. One interesting viewpoint is that service mediocrity actually requires more emotional labor than service excellence. Exceptional service efforts can minimize the hassles of a job, make a job easier, and in turn lower stress from emotional labor. Providing superior service lifts your spirits, is more satisfying, and raises your self-esteem.

TERMS

verbal communication

meaning

connotation

cliché

euphemism

tag question

intensifier

gender-neutral expressions

jargon

acronym

business etiquette

incivility

DISCUSSION QUESTIONS

1. Why are words important?
2. When should you use the word "you"? When should you not use it?
3. Why should you use a customer's name?
4. Give an example of unacceptable terminology. What words should be used instead?
5. Give an example of each of the following:
   a. Overused business term
   b. Cliché
   c. Euphemism
   d. Jargon
   e. Acronym
6. Give some examples of gender-neutral language. Do you agree or disagree about the use of gender-neutral language?
7. Give an example of verbally delivering bad news to a customer.
8. What are the key elements in responding to a customer complaint letter?
9. Describe and demonstrate a proper handshake.
10. What is incivility?

CASE—INSUFFICIENT SERVICE

On Friday, Jessica received a letter from the bank with an insufficient funds notice. The charge for the error was $25. She checked her account and realized that she had written a check for about $2000 the previous Friday and had forgotten to transfer funds from her money-market account to her checking account to cover it. She was really upset with herself for doing that, but she felt that the least the bank could have done was notify her since she had more than enough in her money-market account to cover it (more than $100,000 in her combined accounts). Transferring the money would have taken only minutes to do by the automated voice response system.

She called the local branch where she had done most of her business for the past 12 years. Sandra answered the telephone. Jessica proceeded to angrily tell her that the bank could have at least let her know.

> *Sandra checked the account and said:* "We did try to call you, but there was no answer."
>
> *Jessica:* "When did you call?"
>
> *Sandra:* "Tuesday morning."
>
> *Jessica:* "What time?"
>
> *Sandra:* "I don't know exactly."
>
> *Jessica, frustrated:* "Well, why didn't you at least leave a message on my voice mail?"
>
> *Sandra:* "We couldn't wait. We have to balance our accounts right away."
>
> *Jessica, angrily:* "I can't believe you wouldn't even let me know about it before I got this notice in the mail. Besides, you know I have more than enough money in your bank to cover it."
>
> *Sandra, impatiently:* "Now, just calm down. There was nothing we could do about it."
>
> *Jessica:* "There's plenty I can do. I can move my money to another bank."
>
> *Sandra, rudely:* "You should have asked for insufficient funds coverage."
>
> *Jessica:* "How much does that cost?"
>
> *Sandra:* "It's $25 a year."
>
> *Jessica:* "Why should I have to pay that much when I have four accounts at your bank!? Forget it." Jessica hangs up.

1. What happened here?
2. Would you have reacted as Jessica did?
3. What should Sandra have done differently?
4. What should Sandra do now?

NOTES

1. Jeanne D. Maes, Teresa G. Weldy, and Marjorie L. Icenogle, "A Managerial Perspective: Oral Communication Competency Is Most Important for Business Students in the Workplace," *The Journal of Business Communication* 34, no. 1 (January 1997): 67–81.
2. Roberta Turnbull-Ray, *The Power of Listening* (Dubuque, IA: Kendall/Hunt Publishing Company), 10.
3. Material for verbal communication is summarized from Chad Kaydo, "Start Making Sense," *Sales & Marketing Management* 152, no. 3 (March 2000): 88; Herschell Gordon Lewis, "All the Difference in the Word," *1 to 1,* August 2000, 64; Kristin Anderson and Ron Zemke, *Knock Your Socks off Answers* (New York: AMACOM, 1995); and Eileen O. Brownell, "Magical Words Create Customer Satisfaction & Loyalty," *Manage* 51, no. 3 (February 2000): 10.
4. Judi Brownell, "Communicating with Credibility: The Gender Gap," *Cornell Hotel & Restaurant Administration Quarterly* 34, no. 2 (April 1993): 52–62; and Kay E. Payne, *Different but Equal. Communication between the Sexes* (Westport, CT: Praeger Publishers, 2001), 103–114.

5. Debra Kahn Schofield, "Serving the Nightmare Customer," *The Weekly Guerilla,* available from http://www.gmarketing.com/tactics/weekly_106.html, accessed on October 12, 2000.

6. Anderson and Zemke, *Knock Your Socks off Answers,* 1995.

7. Vicki Clift, "Marketing via Correspondence," *Marketing News,* August 3, 1998, 7; and Donata D. Renfrow and Richard G. Hofmann, "Curing the Dr. Jekyll Phenomenon," *Mobius,* Spring 1986, 15–17.

8. Sandra Moore, "Customers Must Trust CS Message," *Marketing News,* May 7, 2001, 14–15.

9. Chrissy Moch, "Marketing Services: Better Communication through Bills," *Telephony,* April 19, 1999, n.p.

10. Irene Clepper, "Do Customers Know What You're Saying? Contractors Who Communicate Succeed," *Air Conditioning, Heating & Refrigeration News* 202, no. 13 (November 24, 1997): 1–2.

11. Jeffrey Gitomer, *Customer Satisfaction Is Worthless, Customer Loyalty Is Priceless: How to Make Customers Love You, Keep Them Coming Back and Tell Everyone They Know* (Marietta, GA: Bard Press, 1998).

12. Charles L. Martin and Denise T. Smart, "Consumer Correspondence: An Exploratory Investigation of Consistency between Business Policy and Practice," *Journal of Consumer Affairs* 23, no. 2 (Winter): 364–382.

13. Denise T. Smart and Charles L. Martin, "Manufacturer Responsiveness to Consumer Correspondence: An Empirical Investigation of Consumer Perceptions," *Journal of Consumer Affairs* 26, no. 1 (Summer 1992): 104–128.

14. Marcia Mascolini, "Another Look at Teaching the External Negative Message," *Bulletin of the Association for Business Communication* 57, no. 2 (June 1994): 45–48.

15. William F. Chaplin, Jeffrey B. Phillips, Jonathan D. Brown, Nancy R. Clanton, and Jennifer L. Stein, "Handshaking, Gender, Personality, and First Impressions," *Journal of Personality and Social Psychology* 79, no. 1 (July 2000): 110; and David A. Wesson, "The Handshake as Non-Verbal Communication in Business," *Marketing Intelligence & Planning* 10, no. 9 (1992): 41–46.

16. Roger E. Axtell, "Initiating Interaction Greetings and Beckonings across the World," in Laura K. Guerrero, Joseph A. DeVito, and Michael L. Hecht, *The Nonverbal Communication Reader,* 2d ed. (Prospect Heights, IL: Waveland Press, 1999), 395–405.

17. Marjorie Brody and Barbara Pachter, *Business Etiquette* (Chicago: Richard D. Irwin, 1994); and Dana May Casperson, *Power Etiquette: What You Don't Know Can Kill Your Career* (New York: AMACOM, 1999).

18. Matt Crenson, "How Rude: Americans Guilty on Most Counts," *The Knoxville News-Sentinel,* April 3, 2002, A1, A7.

19. Lynne Andersson and Christine M. Pearson, "Tit for Tat? The Spiraling Effect of Incivility in the Workplace," *Academy of Management Review* 24, no. 3 (July 1999): 452–454; and Joan Lloyd, "Increase Office Civility, Be Considerate of Co-Workers," *Minneapolis–St. Paul City Business* 18, no. 46 (April 13, 2001): 11.

20. Michael A. Verespej, "A Call for Civility. The Need for Dignity and Respect in the Workplace," *Industry Week* 250, no. 2 (February 12, 2001): 17.

CHAPTER

8

LISTENING

OBJECTIVES

1. Discuss the importance and effectiveness of listening skills.
2. Explain the stages of listening.
3. Explain the barriers to listening effectiveness.
4. Describe types of listening.
5. Discuss individual differences in listening skills.
6. Outline methods for improving listening effectiveness.

IMPORTANCE OF LISTENING SKILLS

Listening is an important factor in providing exceptional customer service. Not listening to customers costs companies time and money when customer expectations are not met and customers are dissatisfied. Customers want to be understood. When they have a problem, they want to vent, expressing their feelings and thoughts. One research study of dissatisfied customers found that dissatisfied customers who complained to a company about a problem were more likely to be loyal customers than dissatisfied customers who did not complain, even when they were not completely satisfied with the resolution to their problem.[1] Perhaps one reason is that someone at least listened to them.

We spend about 80 percent of our non-sleep time communicating in some way. We spend about half that time listening. A 1975 study of communication time showed that adults spent 55 percent of their communication time listening, 23 percent speaking, 13 percent reading, and 8 percent writing.[2] A 1980 study found that college students spent 53 percent of their time listening, 16 percent speaking, 17 percent reading, and 14 percent writing (see Figure 8.1).[3] A study of executives showed that they spend about 63 percent of their communication time listening.[4]

FIGURE 8.1 Amount of Time Spent in Communication Activities by College Students

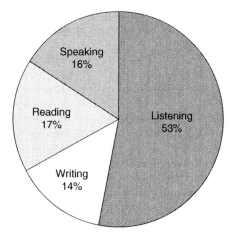

Source: Larry Barker, Renee Edwards, C. Gaines, K. Gladney, and F. Holley, "An Investigation of Proportional Time Spent in Various Communication Activities by College Students," *Journal of Applied Communication Research* 8 (1980): 101–109.

Given the amount of time spent listening, using effective listening skills is critical to job performance. Poor listening can lead to customer distrust, an overly emotional reaction, or a failure to resolve a conflict. Customers may believe we do not care and take their business elsewhere. Listening effectively allows us to respond to customer needs, recognize evidence of customer dissatisfaction, make fewer mistakes, gain trust and credibility, become more informed, and solve problems. Companies can be more productive, meet customer expectations, and increase sales.

Research has consistently shown that ineffective listening habits are the most common barrier to success in careers.[5] An analysis of 25 organizational communication research studies concluded that listening was considered the most important communication skill for entry-level workers.[6] A 1999 survey of American executives showed that effective listening skills were considered more important than technical skills.[7] Listening becomes even more critical as we move up the ladder to supervisory and management positions and job responsibilities increase. Experts contend that one of the primary causes of low productivity is that management does not listen to employees and customers. "Management by walking around," a management technique popularized by Tom Peters in *A Search for Excellence,* is all about listening—listening to customers, employees, and suppliers.[8]

A 2000 study of call center customers showed that effective listening in the form of attentiveness, perceptiveness, and responsiveness can help meet customer expectations. Attentiveness meant the extent to which call center agents showed they were listening by providing customers with nonverbal and verbal cues. Perceptiveness measured whether customers thought that a call center representative understood their message. Responsiveness meant that customers believed that the agents received, interpreted, and evaluated the customers' messages appropriately. Attentiveness and responsiveness were positively related to customer satisfaction, and perceptiveness and responsiveness were positively related to trust. In addition, the research found that satisfaction led to trust. Both satisfaction and trust were indicative of customers' intention to use the call center services again.[9]

EFFECTIVENESS OF LISTENING

How would you rate yourself as a listener? There is evidence that we do not do it all that well. Listeners overestimate how much information they remember. Research has found that average white-collar workers operated at only a 25 percent efficiency level; that is, they could remember only about 25 percent of what they heard.[10] A research study on retention found that most people remembered only about half of what was said immediately after a 10-minute talk. After 24 hours, they remembered less than 10 percent.[11] Other studies have found similar results. It is unclear exactly how efficient people are at listening, which is defined as comprehending and remembering what we hear, but most experts agree that our listening effectiveness is less than it should be.

Given your current listening skill, do you believe that you can listen better when you really need to? Can you "turn on" better listening for customers? According to communication experts, our listening effectiveness is only as good as we have developed our listening skills thus far. Listening harder does not necessarily mean listening better. Barker and Watson found that listeners could answer only four questions out of ten after watching a 20-second video even though they were told to imagine that the video was a life or death situation and remembering the information was critical.[12]

People receive very little training in listening compared with the amount of time spent in school learning to read, write, and speak. Consider for a moment which communication form is used first, from the minute we are born, and even before that. The answer, of course, is listening. Eventually we learn to talk, then read, then write (see Figure 8.2). How much time did you spend in preschool, grade school, high school, and beyond learning to listen? You probably spent far more

FIGURE 8.2 Learning Communication Skills

	Listening	Speaking	Reading	Writing
Learned	First	Second	Third	Fourth
Used	Most	Next to most	Next to least	Least
Taught	Least	Next to least	Next to most	Most

Sources: Larry Barker and Kittie W. Watson, *Listen Up: How to Improve Relationships, Reduce Stress, and Be More Productive by Using the Power of Listening* (New York: St. Martin's Press, 2000); and Madelyn Burley-Allen, *Listening: The Forgotten Skill,* 2d ed. (New York: John Wiley & Sons, 1995).

TABLE 8.1   Years Spent Learning Communication Skills

Writing	12 years
Reading	6–8 years
Speaking	1–2 years
Listening	0–1/2 year

Source: Madelyn Burley-Allen, *Listening: The Forgotten Skill,* 2d ed. (New York: John Wiley & Sons, 1995).

time learning to read, write, and speak. Burley-Allen contends that Americans spend 12 school years learning to write, 6 to 8 years learning to read, and 1 to 2 years learning to speak (see Table 8.1). We spend a half year at most learning to listen, often in bits and pieces with no structured format.[13]

A literature review by Pearce, Johnson, and Barker showed that in the 1970s and 1980s, universities and colleges, including business programs, had devoted very little time and effort to teaching listening skills.[14] A 1994 study concluded that most people entering the workplace in the 2000s would not have any training in how to listen effectively.[15] Ironically, our ability to learn to read, speak, and write depends on our ability to listen.

Perhaps our educational system assumes we learned to listen at home at an early age. However, we may have received negatively phrased reminders from our parents, such as "Listen to me when I'm talking to you" and "Pay attention to me." If you heard these comments, you may no longer have wanted to listen. Beginning in the home, we do learn our listening habits from others. If they were effective listeners, all well and good. If they were not, we have bad habits.

Some businesspeople believe that listening skills are worse than they used to be. In addition to lack of training, they say that today's news and entertainment media encourage short attention spans and poorer listening. According to Barker and Watson, members of Generation Y pride themselves on multitasking, doing several things at once. Because they may not seem to be paying attention, we might think they are not listening. Since they are adept at multitasking, they are probably listening more than we think they are.[16] Added to that is the possibility that some younger workers have never learned how to show that they are listening.

What might be clues that we are not good listeners? An example is the salesperson who always needs to ask, "Now, what was that name again?" Another is a customer service representative who interrupts a customer with a resolution to his problem only to be told, "No, that's not the problem." It could be a spouse saying, "Did you hear what I said?" Another clue is the realization that we are thinking about the dinner menu or any number of other personal issues instead of listening to our customers. The good news is that listening effectiveness can be improved with instruction on the importance of good listening in the business world and specific instruction in listening skills.[17]

Skill Development 8.1

Pick someone that you want to understand better. Listen to this person for 5 minutes, concentrating fully and eliminating all barriers. Encourage the person to talk by responding with good verbal and nonverbal responses. Report what you discovered.

FIGURE 8.3   Levels of Listening Effectiveness

Passive   ------   Superficial   ------   Active
                              listeners

--->

Increasing effectiveness

Levels of Listening Effectiveness

There are five main reasons we listen: to make contact and build relationships with other people, to enable others to express their feelings, to make decisions, to learn, and to be entertained. Our effectiveness will vary depending on our purpose in listening and our skills. Listening effectiveness can be described on a continuum from merely hearing, but not listening, to active, engaged listening (see Figure 8.3).

* *Passive listeners* are pretending to listen. People who are passive fake their attention; they tune in and tune out, and they are mainly thinking about other things.
* *Superficial listeners* are listening on the surface. They hear words, sounds, and parts of the message but not complete meanings. They do not expend any energy to listen. They are emotionally detached and pay no attention to the emotional content of messages. They do not make an effort to understand, and they frequently misinterpret, leading to workplace mistakes. If they provide any feedback at all, they give irrelevant, contradictory, or impersonal responses. They interrupt and change the subject. These listening behaviors may be appropriate when we are unwinding, but they can become habits.
* *Active listeners* pay attention to both the verbal and the nonverbal. They focus and concentrate on the communication. They try to understand the real meaning. They respond so that people know they are listening.

STAGES OF LISTENING

There are four stages of listening (see Figure 8.4):

* *Receiving.*   We sense sounds reaching our ears. We receive a message from a customer by focusing on the customer and paying attention to verbal and nonverbal components. We show the customer that we are listening and receiving his message through appropriate phrases and nonverbal behavior.
* *Interpreting.*   We assign meaning to the sounds. We process the information, relate it to our knowledge, and interpret it. Listeners interpret messages by watching for body language cues, paying attention to the tone of voice and other voice cues, and noticing if the verbal communication matches the nonverbal. We check to determine if we understand words and nonverbal language correctly.
* *Evaluating.*   We evaluate the information and decide what we need to do with it. This will depend in part on our purpose for listening.

FIGURE 8.4   Stages of Listening

---

  * *Responding.*   We provide feedback or respond to the message. We react by
    sending a message back or by taking an action. Feedback encourages a cus-
    tomer to continue communicating, develops rapport, and helps determine
    if understanding is achieved.[18]

LISTENING BARRIERS

Anything that distorts or interferes with communication is "noise." Noise may keep
us from accurately hearing a customer or, in the interpretation and evaluation
stages, prevent us from reaching an accurate understanding. Noise comes from *internal barriers:* psychological, personal, and physiological. *External barriers* are noise
from outside ourselves (see Figure 8.5).

Internal Barriers

We have numerous mental filters that act as internal barriers. They include our
needs and motives, values, beliefs, attitudes, and perceptions. Our emotions, biases,
emotional hot buttons, assumptions, past experiences, interests, and self-esteem affect our listening. Knowledge, intelligence, language and vocabulary capability, sensory acuity, and attention span are also factors. The following list illustrates how
these filters operate as internal barriers to listening.

  * Psychological barriers related to customers:
    * We have a prejudice against a customer based on past experiences.
    * We have a bias toward a customer due to age, gender, or ethnicity.

FIGURE 8.5   Barriers to Listening

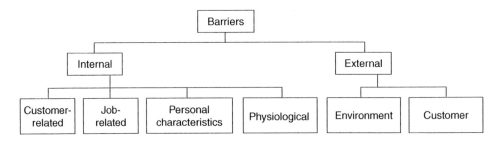

* We judge a customer as inept.
* We are distracted by customers' appearance, voice, or mannerisms, especially if we focus on their style rather than the content of their message.
* We interpret words differently from a customer based on our backgrounds.
* We misunderstand customers' nonverbal communication. We interpret it differently due to differences in age, gender, income level, culture, socialization, or past experiences.
* We react to customers' use of emotionally laden statements like "You cheated me."
* We respond negatively to a personal hot button, such as a customer calling us a "girl" or using words like "right," "wrong," "lie," "false," or "gay."
* We feel intimidated by a customer.

* Psychological barriers related to our job but unrelated to the customer:
  * We dislike our job.
  * We are bored with our job and daydream.
  * We are angry with our boss.
  * We are anxious due to work stress or information overload.
  * We are worried about our capability to handle a situation.
  * We are trying to do more than one thing at a time, resulting in inattentiveness or lack of concentration on a customer message, for example, listening to a customer on the telephone while finishing leftover paperwork.

* Personal characteristics:
  * We are preoccupied with personal problems.
  * We are preoccupied with everyday responsibilities.
  * We daydream.
  * We rehearse what we will say.
  * We prefer to talk rather than listen.
  * We have a habit of interrupting.
  * Words, like "chocolate" or "vacation," cause us to pursue other thoughts.
  * We are bored or uncomfortable with a topic.
  * We are self-absorbed and need attention or need to be right.
  * We like to disagree and argue.

* Physiological
  * We suffer from listening fatigue and burnout. Our listening energy is depleted.
  * Our listening effectiveness decreases when we are tired, ill, or hungry.

* We have a hearing impairment.
* We can process information faster than the average rate of speech. This is known as the *thought-speech differential*. Most people talk at an average rate of 125 to 150 words per minute. We can process information at the rate of 500 to 600 words per minute, about four times as fast as people speak. What do we do with the extra time? Many times our minds wander, or we think about what we are going to say.

External Barriers

External barriers include not only the workplace environment, but customers as well.

* Environment
  * One external barrier is workplace equipment noise, such as telephones ringing and copiers copying.
  * We are distracted by other employees or customers talking.
  * We are visually distracted, acknowledging a coworker's wave of greeting.
  * Our physical environment, such as an uncomfortable temperature, a confining workspace, an odor, or the color of the room, distracts us.
  * The disorganization of our desk or work area competes for attention.
  * The acoustics are not conducive to listening.
  * An external physical barrier is a desk or counter separating us from a customer, making it difficult to hear well enough to listen properly or making it appear we are not interested in listening.
* Customers
  * Sometimes our listening efficiency fails when customers mumble, talk too softly, talk in a monotone, talk too fast, or have an unfamiliar accent.
  * Customers use jargon, acronyms, or words we do not understand.
  * Customers deliver mixed messages, in which the nonverbal communication does not match the verbal communication.[19]

Skill Development 8.2

Try this experiment for 3 days. Pick one specific internal or external barrier, concentrate on it and only it when listening, and try to eliminate it.

Listening Energy

Listening requires physical, emotional, and intellectual *energy*. People experience listening fatigue and burnout from barriers. Feelings of irritability and hostility may surface.

Sappers are listening energy drainers. There are internal, external, and people sappers. Internal sappers include worrying, defensiveness, and physical fatigue. External sappers are conflict, interpersonal friction with a coworker, visual and noise overload, multitasking demands, and time demands. Our energy is sapped when we have to deal with difficult, overbearing people and their emotions. We suffer listening fatigue if we deal with people whose verbal style or appearance is offensive to us.

We should know what our energy sappers are and minimize them. We can replenish our listening energy by monitoring ourselves and realizing when our listening energy stores are low. We can take listening breaks. We can rebuild energy by reducing stimuli, changing our environment, doing something physical, or finding a new frame of mind. Granted, it takes time that we think we don't have, but we are losing time if we have no energy to listen when we need to. If we become exceptionally motivated by a topic or situation, we do have energy reserves, which is something like getting a second wind.[20]

TYPES OF LISTENING

The following are types of active listening. They describe ways of listening and are not necessarily mutually exclusive. We may move back and forth between the types. No one way is the best way to listen. Different purposes for listening, such as whether the purpose is to build relationships or to learn, require different skills. Unless they are taken to extremes, all types (except defensive listening) have positive value depending on when they are needed. The best advice is to learn and practice different styles and use whichever one is best for the circumstances.

Defensive Listening

When we perceive a threat, we tend to hear only what we want to hear and do not listen to the rest. If a customer is angry, we may misunderstand or distort her message. If we have a bias against a customer, we may resist communication. An older customer service provider may discount anything a younger customer says. Men may believe a woman can't explain what's wrong with her car. A customer's ethnicity may cause us to make wrong assumptions about her. *Defensive listening* shows in our nonverbal behavior—in our voice, facial expressions, and posture. We may use judgmental verbal responses, such as "Are you sure about that?" Both the nonverbal and verbal communication may result in customers becoming defensive. Then we have more conflict.

Detailed Listening

Detailed listening means concentrating and remembering specific instructions or facts accurately. We use clarifying questions to make sure we have the information straight. If we are not effective at this style, we may not be able to follow directions or remember dates or customers' names. Some people use this style if a topic interests them but not if they find the information boring. We may choose to listen to only the specific details of a presentation that relate to our interests. If we routinely use this type of listening, we may not be good comprehensive listeners. We miss the main points and the big picture. For example, students may be able to list and define the types of listening but not be able to explain their importance and use in customer situations.

Analytical/Critical Listening

The purpose of *analytical listening* is to understand the speaker's position and decide whether the position is justified. It is usually used when a decision is needed. We use the thought-speech differential to analyze the speaker's arguments. This is one of the least used types of listening and requires the most mental energy. This type of listening relies on the left brain, the analytical side, which may mean we miss the emotional part of the message. We need to use analytical listening with customers to understand their reasoning, say in terms of complaint resolution.

Comprehensive Listening

Comprehensive listeners want to understand and remember the central idea and main points. We use *comprehensive listening* to learn. To be a good comprehensive listener, we need to have a good memory and to be able to focus and concentrate for a long time. With a customer problem, we need an overall view of what happened. A downside to this type is frustration with speakers who are disorganized and ramble. If a customer tells a story that wanders from her problem with the DVD she bought, to her grandchild, to her drive to the store, to music, and back to the DVD, we may quit listening and not understand the overall picture.

Empathetic Listening

To empathize is to see the world as others see it and to put ourselves in their shoes. This is difficult since each one of us perceives the world based on our unique background and experiences. *Empathetic listening* means listening actively by attentive silence. We pay attention to customers' nonverbal communication. We use nonverbal communication, including eye contact, head nodding, and open posture to clearly show that we are paying attention. We convey understanding of their feelings. We are not distracted or concentrating on our response. Empathic listening tends to use both the right and the left brain. People who are left-brained, who do not pay as much attention to nonverbal cues, are likely to find empathetic listening more difficult.

Four goals in listening empathetically to a customer are:

1. To affirm a customer's feelings by responding to the customer as a person and demonstrating sincere concern
2. To understand the situation from a customer's perspective by paraphrasing—that is, by summarizing a customer's main points—and by clarifying with specific questions
3. To confirm the importance of a customer and the problem by responding with nonverbal and verbal communication to show empathy and concern
4. To help a customer find a solution[21]

Holistic Listening

This is listening with both sides of our brain. Americans tend to be left-brained due to the emphasis of our education system. However, a high proportion of meaning comes from nonverbal input from the right brain. *Holistic listening* uses all five senses working together and is an example of the concept of the whole being greater than the sum of its interdependent parts.

Hearing is the process of noticing incoming signals. Listening assigns meaning to the signals. We also listen beyond the words, hearing paralanguage, the nonverbal voice cues. Meaning comes from the volume of speech. A high voice volume may indicate anger. A low volume may indicate lack of confidence. Meaning comes from rate of speech. A slow rate of speech can mean confusion, tiredness, or thoughtfulness. A slow rate also can mean nothing at all except a learned cultural behavior. A fast rate can mean intelligence, anger, or compulsive talking. Meaning comes from pitch. A tight or high voice may indicate nervousness. A lower-pitched voice is thought of as being more credible. Meaning comes from the regularity of speech. Pausing for more than a second might tell us that the speaker is unsure or not prepared.

We also listen with our eyes to nonverbal language and derive meaning. We watch eye behavior and facial expressions. We are aware of body communication.

Our listening is affected by proxemics, the space around us. If a customer approaches us too closely, we may be distracted from listening. We are territorial about our space. We assign meaning based on physical appearance and artifactual communication. We notice body size and build, dress, accessories, and hairstyle. We interpret or misinterpret communication based on what we see. We listen by using touch in appropriate circumstances. We communicate with our noses. A smell may be pleasant or repulsive and may distract us.

Holistic listening also involves combining our senses with the effects of time and power. We listen to the speaker's concern for time. Is she in a hurry and impatient? Does he appear to be relaxed and have plenty of time? A person's psychological or physical power will have an effect on a conversation. A young entry-level service provider could have more difficulty communicating with a dissatisfied well-dressed businessperson than with an unhappy casually dressed customer his own age.[22]

Mindful Listening

Shafir, author of *The Zen of Listening*, suggests that listening is not "a technique to be learned." She says that it is a resource we already have and that effective listening requires a change in our mind-set toward listening, doing what she calls *"mindful listening."* She believes that if we are caught up in a list of listening "to-dos," we will end up not listening. Think about a time when you were completely absorbed in listening to the news about an event like the Super Bowl or something tragic like the 911 attack. You did not need to think about how to listen. Your innate listening reflex was there, and you could listen with great concentration. Shafir suggests we need to use this ability to improve our listening. She describes mindful listening as using our natural ability to listen and combining it with a sincere desire to listen based on our curiosity for information and a willingness to respect the speaker. Another way to illustrate mindfulness is "getting into the speaker's movie." When we watch a movie, we forget ourselves and naturally relax into a listening pose—we focus, and we get into it. This is what mindful listening is.

The opposite of mindfulness is *mindlessness*. A routine example is the attention paid, or lack of it, to driving. Have you ever driven home and when you got there, you did not remember driving? We find ourselves doing certain tasks mindlessly because they are procedures and habits that we do on "automatic pilot." The driving example is a little scary, but presumably, we become mindful if there is danger ahead.[23]

Experience Discussion 8.1

What type of listening skill or combinations of types is best for each of the college courses you are taking?

INDIVIDUAL DIFFERENCES

Preferences

Another way of looking at listening is to examine preferences. The types of information we want to receive most from others determine our *listening preferences*. The preferences include people, action, content, and time.

People-oriented listeners, as you might guess, are most concerned with how listening affects their relationships with others. They listen to recognize and understand emotional states and are nonjudgmental. They provide clear feedback signals. They may give overly expressive feedback and are sometimes intrusive. They can become overinvolved, lose their objectivity, and internalize others' emotional states.

Action-oriented listeners concentrate on the task. They focus on the main points and identify inconsistencies in messages. They also give clear feedback. They encourage people to stay on topic and focus on what is important. They may appear overly critical, jump to conclusions too fast, and minimize people issues. They can be impatient with and distracted by disorganized speakers. They could have a tendency to rush customers.

Content-oriented listeners evaluate everything they hear. They listen for all sides of an issue, enjoy details and complex information, and ask questions for clarity and understanding. They like listening to technical information and experts. They devalue nontechnical and nonexpert information. They may be too detail-oriented and may ask intimidating questions. They may get too involved in the reasons for customers' problems.

Time-oriented listeners' main concern is time. They set time limits for meetings and generally promote efficiency. They discourage long-winded speakers, are impatient, and often interrupt and rush speakers. By their devotion to the clock, they limit concentration and creativity.

Some people have more than one preference and use different styles in different circumstances. Which preference wins out depends on time pressure, interest in the speaker or topic, the communication setting, the presence of others, and the listening energy supply. For example, if the setting is informal and a relationship is highly desirable, people-oriented listening is dominant. Under stress, we tend to revert to our strongest listening preference.

Barker and Watson's research shows that about 40 percent of the U.S. population have a single listener preference, mostly people-oriented or action-oriented; about 25 percent have two preferences; and 15 percent have three or four preferences. These proportions do not hold true for other cultures. Women tend to have people-oriented preferences. Content and action orientations are more associated with men. More males than females report no preference.[24]

A recent research study suggested that customers were more likely to trust salespeople who were people-oriented or content-oriented listeners. A people-oriented listening style was associated with higher satisfaction and the customer's anticipation of future interaction. Customers were less trusting and less satisfied with salespeople who used a time-oriented listening approach.[25] Another study showed that time-oriented and action-oriented listeners were less empathetic. People-oriented listeners tended to be sympathetic but not empathetic. People using a content listening style demonstrated empathy without becoming emotionally involved.[26]

Listening Preference Cues. Service providers can watch for nonverbal cues to listening preference. People-oriented listeners make a lot of eye contact, smile and nod frequently, and vary their voice inflection. Action-oriented listeners will have a brisk firm handshake, tend to doodle or finger-tap, and speak more rapidly. Content-oriented listeners will have serious facial expressions and challenging or combative vocal tones. Time-oriented listeners will look at their watch frequently and display impatience.[27]

Styles

People with different responsiveness/assertiveness styles, described in Chapter 5, listen differently. While listening, analyticals sometimes look puzzled, questioning, thoughtful, or skeptical. They are evaluating and critiquing. They are content-oriented and obviously use analytical thinking often. Drivers want action and are impatient. They ask themselves the point of the information and how they can use it. They are often action-oriented listeners. Amiables are excellent listeners and will smile to encourage a speaker. They may have an expression of concern depending on the topic. They are people-oriented listeners and are very good at empathetic listening. Expressives like to be involved, and so they may become fidgety. They are easily bored with technical data. One way to communicate better with a different style from ours is to use style stepping, meaning to use some of the other person's style. This is somewhat like pacing, but remember that a little goes a long way.[28]

Gender

Listening experts have concluded that there are differences between the way some men and some women listen. Research has found that there is a biological basis for this. Brain researchers used an MRI to measure blood flow in the brain while participants were listening. The research on hemispheric processing showed that right-handed men listened mostly with the left hemisphere of their brain and right-handed women processed language with both sides. Hemispheric processing is less clear with left-handed men and women. This does not mean one way is better than the other; it means their listening can be different.

While certainly not true for all men and all women, certain patterns have been shown. Many women have a more people-oriented listening preference. In addition to the biological reason, socialization also has an effect. When they use the right brain, women notice both verbal and nonverbal cues more frequently than men. Women often read emotions faster and communicate empathy. They may listen more responsively than men. They will use questions to connect with the speaker. Men who have occupations in which a more responsive style is needed, such as nurses, psychologists, pastors, or teachers, make an effort to learn more people-oriented listening skills. Men sometimes feel that women's questions are intrusive rather than motivated by concern. Women may interpret men's responses as more negative than they are because men may not be as visually responsive, may not show empathy, and may change the subject. As a result, women are not sure they are understood.

Men tend to focus on one message at a time. Men tend to remember what they hear; women remember what they hear and see. Men retain only general ideas about a conversation, whereas women recall exact phrases and details. A man might relate that a salesperson was indifferent or rude; a woman might tell exactly what the salesperson said. Another difference is that research has found that people remember more when they listen to men, and both men and women say they would rather listen to men speakers than women speakers. Part of the reason could be the stereotype that men are more powerful than women. Women's voices are softer and higher-pitched, reinforcing the stereotype.

Research has found three ways that one gender may actually be better than the other: accommodating others, handling distractions, and interrupting others. First, on the positive side, women are viewed as more accommodating, cooperative, considerate, and helpful. Women avoid confrontation and conflict. Unfortunately, if this behavior is carried to an extreme, women are seen as too submissive and lacking credibility. Second, since men may listen mostly with the left side of their brain, they can be better at tuning out distractions. Women may be more able to listen to two messages at once, so they can be more distracted by a competing message than men are. In a telephone center, women may have more difficulty tuning out room and voice noises than men do. Third, men interrupt more than women do. They often interrupt women or overlap them, starting to say something before a woman finishes.

Both genders can improve the quality of their listening by making the most of their positive skills and strengthening the skills associated with the opposite gender. With customers, men could use more people-oriented listening skills. Their active listening should include looking for unspoken meanings behind the words, working on interpreting feelings in conversations, and asking questions to check their perceptions and interpretations. Listeners must try to be empathetic and see the world from the other person's perspective. Empathetic responses are "It sounds like you. . . " and "I get the impression that you. . . " Men should also refrain from interrupting.

Women could use more action-, content-, and time-oriented listening skills. They could be more assertive, not be intimidated by men's voices and volumes, and avoid reading too much emotion into men's verbal and nonverbal messages. They should be patient when men interrupt too much. On the other hand, experts also advise us against being ruled by male and female stereotypes. We can use the stereotypes to help figure out how people will respond but allow for individual differences.[29]

Experience Discussion 8.2

What have you noticed about the differences in listening behavior between men and women?

DEVELOPING BETTER LISTENING SKILLS

Listening skills can be practiced and learned. Listening is not instinctive. Listening well is hard work. It takes energy and focus. We need to understand the complexity of listening and the barriers to effective listening. We should understand the different types of listening and when to use them. Effective listening also must be goal-oriented so that we know how and why we will listen. Each listening type or preference is more useful in some circumstances than others. We need to determine our goal in listening and use the appropriate style. We need to develop flexibility in our listening style to adapt it to the needs of the situation.

Although we can't listen better by just mentally telling ourselves to, Barker and Watson say we can jump-start listening improvement. Interestingly, research shows that when we put our minds and bodies in positive listening mode, our effectiveness actually increases. Readiness is the key and somewhat like being mindful. Barker's advice is to look and sound as if we are listening. Use eye contact, nod, lean forward slightly, and respond verbally if possible, and we will listen better.

Listening to Customers

1. *Remember that listening is an active process, not a passive one.*   Listening will improve if you are motivated to listen, expend the energy to listen, and focus your attention on customers and their messages. Be present in the moment.
2. *Recognize when you don't listen.*   Identify your barriers. Figure out what you need to do or stop doing.
3. *Ignore or remove external distractions.*   Tune out other people talking. Move to a place where there is less noise.

4. *Provide appropriate nonverbal and verbal feedback while customers are talking to demonstrate that you are listening and understand, to build rapport, and to encourage customers to continue communication.*   Focus only on the customer. Make eye contact, nod, and have an open posture. Smile when the conversation is positive. Show concern if customers are upset. Use phrases like "I see" and "Uh-huh." Do not use negative nonverbal language or adapters that suggest you are impatient.

5. *Quiet your inner voice so you are more customer-centered than self-centered.*   Be empathetic, acknowledging a customer's inconvenience or saying, "That must have been frustrating." Understand that listening does not mean agreeing. Stephen Covey writes, in *Seven Habits of Highly Effective People,* "Seek first to understand, then to be understood."[30]

6. *Take brief keyword notes and fill in details later.*   If you are visual, draw pictures or diagrams.

7. *Use the thought-speech differential.*   Use the extra time to summarize what a customer is saying, to relate the information to what you know, and to formulate questions.

8. *Resist the urge to interrupt.*   Concentrate on what is being said, not on your response. Repeat silently what you just heard. In fact, it sometime helps to stop paying attention to what you are thinking.

9. *Pay attention to nonverbal communication.*   Listen between the lines. Interpretation will improve if you verify and clarify nonverbal cues.

10. *Words will never have exactly the same meaning to two people, and so you must make sure that you understand what a customer means.*   You can use responses like "Tell me more about. . . " or open-ended questions like "What do you mean by. . .?" Paraphrase to ensure understanding, "So what happened is that the couch you ordered didn't arrive on time." If you can paraphrase what a customer says without changing the meaning, you are a good listener.

11. *Be patient.*   Not everyone is a good communicator.

12. *Remain objective about customers and their topic.*   Keep an open mind. Otherwise, your emotions or biases may take over and you will hear what you want to hear. Don't assume you know what a customer is going to say; you may miss the real point.

13. *Identify your hot-button words and learn how to ignore them.*   Don't let yourself react when a customer refers to you as a waitress when you prefer "server."

14. *Recognize your biases.*   Avoid prejudging customers by what they wear, do, or say. For example, put your dislike of body piercing on the back burner.

15. *Don't assume that you know a customer's motive.*   Just because customers seem nervous or act suspiciously does not necessarily mean they are problem customers. Put your tendency to evaluate them on hold. Listen to the content.

16. *When you attempt to do more than one thing at the same time, such as checking your computer for e-mail or waving at a coworker while listening to a customer on the telephone, your attention is divided and you will miss essential information.*   While women may be able to listen to two conversations at the same time, it does not mean that they get every nuance of both conversations. If you are so overloaded that your job requires you to multitask when talking to customers, think about how you can reorganize it so you can listen attentively. Have a customer service team discuss stressful situations in which they were trying to multitask and come to some conclusions about how to handle the expectation that you have two heads and four hands.[31]

Skill Development 8.3

This chapter approaches listening skills from several points of view. Use what works for you. You don't have to know everything about listening, your listening style, and barriers to improve. Pick one barrier. Develop a goal and plan to eliminate the barrier. Practice. Then, with each success, reward yourself.

Use the following outline to improve your listening:

My current listening skills are effective in the following areas:

I need to improve in the following area:

I will implement an action plan for improvement as follows:

My listening goal is:

My plan for reaching my goal is:

My timetable is:

The following people will benefit:

They will benefit in the following ways:

Memory

Memory has three processes: encoding, storage, and retrieval. During encoding, when we listen, information goes into our sensory memory, where it is held for about 1 second. If we need to remember the information, for example, a telephone number, we need to store it in short-term memory. For this to happen, we need to repeat or rehearse it to ourselves for about 15 seconds. Our short-term memory can hold about seven bits of information at one time. If we want to retain this information for the future, we have to take it to long-term memory. Methods for doing this are associating it with something familiar or previous knowledge. This does not take very long, about 60 seconds, but we need to be able to concentrate to do it.[32]

Say we want to remember a customer's name, Sandy Willow. We should give ourselves a quick reminder to listen for the name. We should say the name aloud immediately. We will then know if we heard it correctly. To store it in short-term memory, we repeat it to ourselves several times. Write it down if possible. Then use it within the first 30 seconds of the conversation. If we want to store her name in long-term memory, we can associate her face with her sandy-colored hair and note that she is tall and willowy. We picture her standing in front of a willow tree on a sandy beach, and we remember her name from our associated picture the next time we see her.

Teamwork Listening

One of the barriers in teamwork is the lack of effective listening, in particular the tendency of some team members to interrupt others. By watching body language, we can tell that people are thinking of their response long before a speaker has made his main point. The team facilitator should create an environment for effectively sharing ideas. Team norms can be used to remind team members to take turns. Team members can use body language to indicate their desire to contribute. The facilitator can literally insist team members wait until the speaker is finished to start their response. Occasionally, several people will be talking at the same time. This is fine, but at some point, the discussion has to be back in control so everyone can contribute and listen.

TERMS

passive listeners
superficial listeners
active listeners
internal barriers
external barriers
thought-speech differential
listening energy
sappers
defensive listening

detailed listening
analytical listening
comprehensive listening
empathetic listening
holistic listening
mindful listening
mindlessness
listening preferences

DISCUSSION QUESTIONS

1. How can you benefit from listening more effectively?
2. What are the four stages of listening?
3. Name a barrier to listening effectiveness. How can you eliminate or reduce the barrier?
4. What is the thought-speech differential? How can you use it to improve your listening?
5. Describe a situation that depletes listening energy. How can a customer service provider recover from this energy drain?
6. Describe the differences among detailed, analytical, and comprehensive listening.
7. Describe a situation in which you used empathetic listening with a customer.
8. What are the similarities and differences between holistic and mindful listening?
9. Explain listening preferences.
10. What are some differences between men's and women's listening? In what circumstances should you change gender-related listening habits?

CASE—NOT MULCH LISTENING

Ben James was building a house on 5 acres in Hayes County. He called four nurseries to check on the price and delivery of 12 yards of mulch. The price ranged from $12 a yard to $18 a yard. Two companies also had a $15 delivery charge, and two could not deliver the mulch for 2 weeks. So he decided to purchase the mulch from Lee Nursery, which offered a price of $12 and immediate delivery. On Wednesday, he called, ordered the mulch, and charged it to a credit card. He discovered at that point that the price he had been given was a sale price that had expired and that there was a $15 delivery charge the nursery had neglected to mention. He ordered the mulch anyway for $15 a yard.

Carrie, the service representative and owner's daughter, said it would be delivered on Friday. He told her that a construction supervisor would be on-site. He also stressed that the delivery person should not drive on the ground over the septic tank next to the driveway because the dirt had not settled yet. He told her that it was marked with a post. Carrie assured him that their delivery person, who was her father, the owner, would never go off the driveway.

Late Thursday he received a phone call telling him that the nursery would not be able to deliver the mulch on Friday due to a truck breakdown. It would be Saturday. The mulch did not show up on Saturday. No mulch on Monday. Lee Nursery called and promised Tuesday. No mulch and no call on Tuesday. He called late afternoon on Tuesday. Carrie was very apologetic and promised a $25 gift certificate with the mulch as compensation for the problem.

The mulch was finally delivered on Friday. When the delivery person, Mr. Lee, the owner, arrived, he did not check in with the construction supervisor, whose van was parked out front. He proceeded to back up off the driveway, into the lawn, past a well-marked post, right over the septic tank. He did not deliver a gift certificate.

Ben stopped by the nursery about a week later to complain. The nursery was a family-owned and-run business. Mrs. Lee, who owned the company with her husband, and Carrie, her daughter, were in the store. He went up to the counter and explained to Carrie, who was behind the counter, and Mrs. Lee, who was standing at the end of the counter making a ribbon bow, all of the difficulties he had experienced. Carrie listened and reexplained about the equipment problem and said that her mother had been out of town. She said that the gift certificate was around someplace but she could not find it. She seemed concerned but didn't seem to know what to do. Mrs. Lee proceeded to finish making the bow, not making eye contact and turning her back on Ben at one point. The daughter asked, "Mom, did you hear all that?" Mrs. Lee said, "Only the first part."

Ben continued to express his dissatisfaction. Eventually, Mrs. Lee said, "Well, what do you want?" Since the gift certificate amounted to a 10 percent discount and he really did not want to buy anything else at this nursery, Ben said he thought a 20 percent reduction in the bill was in order. Mrs. Lee then decided that she was not the owner, but that her husband was, and that Ben would have to talk to him. Carrie took Ben's phone number and said, "My dad will call you." Mr. Lee never called.

1. What are the customer service problems?
2. Do you think Ben was justified in asking for a 20 percent discount?
3. What should Ben do now?

NOTES

1. U.S. Office of Consumer Affairs, *Increasing Customer Satisfaction through Effective Corporate Complaint Handling*, 1986.
2. Joseph A. DeVito, *Messages: Building Interpersonal Communication Skills* (New York: HarperCollins College Publishers, 1996).
3. Larry Barker, Renee Edwards, C. Gaines, K. Gladney, and F. Holley, "An Investigation of Proportional Time Spent in Various Communication Activities by College Students," *Journal of Applied Communication Research* 8 (1980): 101–109.
4. Lyman K. Steil, Larry L. Barker, and Kittie W. Watson, *Effective Listening: Key to your Success* (Reading, MA: Addison-Wesley Publishing Co., 1983).
5. Larry Barker and Kittie W. Watson, *Listen Up: How to Improve Relationships, Reduce Stress, and Be More Productive by Using the Power of Listening* (New York: St. Martin's Press, 2000).
6. Vincent S. DiSalvo, "A Summary of Current Research Identifying Communication Skills in Various Organizational Contexts," *Communication Education* 29 (July 1980): 283–290.
7. Jennifer J. Salopek, "Is Anyone Listening?" *Training and Development* 53, no. 9 (September 1999): 58–60.

8. Thomas D. Hinton, *The Spirit of Service: How to Create a Customer-Focused Service Culture* (Dubuque, IA: Kendall/Hunt Publishing Company, 1991).

9. Ko de Ruyter and Martin G. M. Wetzels, "The Impact of Perceived Listening Behavior in Voice-to-Voice Service Encounters," *Journal of Service Research* 2, no. 3 (February 2000): 276–284.

10. C. Glenn Pearce, Iris W. Johnson, and Randolph T. Barker, "Enhancing the Student Listening Skills and Environment," *Business Communication Quarterly* 58, no. 4 (December 1995): 28–34.

11. Barker and Watson, *Listen Up.*

12. Barker and Watson, *Listen Up.*

13. Madelyn Burley-Allen, *Listening: The Forgotten Skill,* 2d ed. (New York: John Wiley & Sons, 1995).

14. Pearce, Johnson, and Barker, "Enhancing the Student Listening Skills and Environment," 28.

15. J. Brownell, "Managerial Listening and Career Development in the Hospitality Industry," *Journal of the International Listening Association* 8 (1994): 31–49.

16. Barker and Watson, *Listen Up.*

17. Nelda Spinks and Barron Wells, "Improving Listening Power: The Payoff!" *The Bulletin,* September 1991, 75–77.

18. Roberta Turnbull-Ray, *The Power of Listening* (Dubuque, IA: Kendall/Hunt Publishing Company, 1994).

19. Compiled from Dennis M. Kratz and Abby Robinson Kratz, *Effective Listening Skills* (Chicago: Richard D. Irwin, 1995); Turnbull-Ray, *The Power of Listening*; and Barker and Watson, *Listen Up.*

20. Barker and Watson, *Listen Up.*

21. Barker and Watson, *Listen Up.*

22. Paul J. Kaufmann, *Sensible Listening: The Key to Responsive Interaction,* 3d ed. (Dubuque, IA: Kendall/Hunt Publishing Company, 1994).

23. Rebecca Z. Shafir, *The Zen of Listening: Mindful Communication in the Age of Distraction* (Wheaton, IL: Theosophical Publishing House, 2000): 21; and Tom Bruneau, "Empathy and Listening: A Conceptual Review and Theoretical Directions," *Journal of the International Listening Association* 3 (1989): 14.

24. Barker and Watson, *Listen Up.*

25. Megan Jefferson Verret, "The Impact of Buyer/Seller Listening Styles on Mutual Trust, Satisfaction, and Anticipation of Future Interactions," *Dissertation Abstracts International: Section B: The Sciences & Engineering* 61, no. 6—B (January 2000): 3328.

26. James B. Weaver, III, and Michelle D. Kirtley, "Listening Styles and Empathy," *The Southern Communication Journal* 60, no. 2 (Winter 1995): 131–141.

27. Barker and Watson, *Listen Up.*

28. Jacquelyn Wonder and Priscilla Donovan, *Whole Brain Thinking: Working from Both Sides of the Brain to Achieve Peak Job Performance* (New York: William Morrow and Company, 1984).

29. "Men Use Only One Side of Brain When Listening; Women Use Both: Study," *Jet* 99, no. 2 (December 18, 2000): 20; Marjorie Brody, Presentation at the Society of Consumer Affairs Professionals Spring Conference, Atlanta, GA, Spring 1993; and Barker and Watson, *Listen Up.*

30. Stephen R. Covey, *Seven Habits of Highly Effective People* (New York: Simon & Schuster, 1989).

31. Summarized from Barker and Watson, *Listen Up;* and Turnbull-Ray, *The Power of Listening.*

32. Shafir, *The Zen of Listening.*

TELEPHONE COMMUNICATION

OBJECTIVES

1. Explain the importance of effective telephone communication.
2. Describe and illustrate best practices for pre-greeting, greeting, conversation, and closing.
3. Describe and illustrate best practices for telephone actions.
4. Discuss effective use of telephone specialty features.
5. Outline best practices for wireless telephone communication.

EFFECTIVE TELEPHONE COMMUNICATION

Importance

An important aspect of customer service is telephone interactions. A telephone is a critical business tool since a substantial proportion of business is conducted over the telephone. Many times a telephone call is the first impression customers have of an organization. Companies spend millions of dollars on marketing so that potential customers will buy their products and services. When customers contact the company by telephone, the marketing money is wasted if calls are handled badly and the company loses customers. This chapter covers verbal communication, specific telephone actions, and the use of specialty features by a customer service provider. Chapter 10 deals with the broader issue of interactive telephone systems and other electronic communication.

Experience Discussion 9.1

When you call a business, what annoys you? What are your pet peeves?

FIGURE 9.1   Percent of Customers Who Dislike Selected Telephone Practices

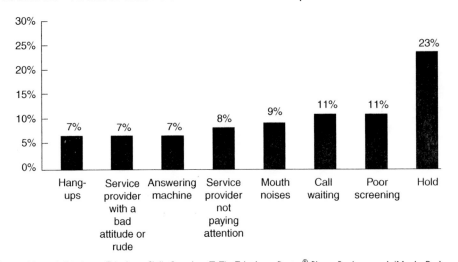

Source: Nancy J. Friedman, *Telephone Skills from A to Z: The Telephone Doctor® Phone Book,* rev. ed. (Menlo Park, CA: Crisp Learning, 2000), 19.

Several years ago, the Telephone Doctor, Nancy Friedman, asked customers what they disliked most about telephone calls. Figure 9.1 illustrates what they said. The procedure that was disliked most was being put on hold. In a recent repetition of the study, hold was still first and voice mail was second.[1]

A Federal Communications Commission survey showed that 41 percent of consumers complain about receiving inaccurate information on the telephone. Sixteen percent complained about unresponsiveness. Other problems were waiting too long on hold, rudeness, poorly trained representatives, minority bias, and blind transfers.[2]

How many times a day do you talk to someone on the telephone? Are the businesses you call providing exceptional telephone communication? We are inclined to take our telephone procedures for granted since they have become habits in our personal and business lives. We generally learn our telephone behavior in our personal lives and then transfer it to our business lives. It does not always transfer well. Do you know how to use the telephone effectively? Are you making a favorable impression on your customers? Telephone usage is often misguided and mismanaged, because people assume they know how to use a telephone. However, many employees have never been thoroughly taught the proper telephone skills and behavior. Although companies assume their employees know how to use the telephone, customers can tell us that many do not.

In addition to not having good telephone communication skills, sometimes employees' attitudes interfere. For example, one customer reported that he saw a receptionist put all her lines on hold and take a coffee break. Another time he observed calls stacked on hold while the office workers finished their personal conversation. At another company, when he told the receptionist that he was calling long distance, the receptionist put him on hold for more than 7 minutes.[3] Employees sometimes consider the telephone an interruption of their jobs. Finishing paperwork takes precedence over answering a telephone. Other times employees caught up in orders and details do not even realize that they have stopped being polite.

Another problem is what could be labeled "phonephobia." Some people avoid telephone communication. Some are just telephone shy for some reason. Perhaps they would rather talk face-to-face. They may feel awkward with the technical features. Others are uncomfortable because they do not know what to say and do in many situations. Companies must make sure that everyone clearly understands that all telephone calls are important and recognizes that customers' calls are essential to business success.

Communication on the telephone is hindered because we cannot see our callers and their body language. It is generally believed that we must rely on voice cues for about 85 percent and words for 15 percent of the communication meaning (see Figure 9.2). It is much more difficult to develop rapport and understanding when we cannot read our customers' body language. When customers call a company, their perceptions are determined only by what they can infer from the voice and the words they hear. Employees need to be conscious of their voice and must choose their words carefully.

Telephone Communication Training

All company employees who answer and use the telephone, including executives and temporary help, should be trained in telephone communication behavior and protocol. We would expect upper-level management to communicate effectively on the telephone, but they may well have developed some careless telephone habits. If you have ever heard a telephone answered, "[mumble] Company," you know that the employee was not taught even the most basic convention of how to answer.

The training that is often provided is the technical aspects of the telephone system—how to operate the features, such as the intercom and memory programming. Companies need to instruct and inform employees about verbal communication, the actual words they should use, and nonverbal voice cues, such as their volume, pitch, rate of speech, and articulation. Telephone greeting, conversation, and closing should be reviewed. In addition, content is important. All employees

FIGURE 9.2   Distribution of Meaning Communicated in Telephone Communication

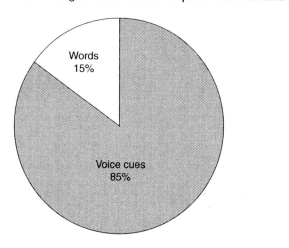

should be able to provide contact information, such as address, fax number, website address, and business hours. They should be able to answer basic questions about the company's products and services. They should know to whom calls should be directed for any customer request. An excellent way for a company to assess the quality of its staff's telephone skills is to use mystery telephone shoppers.

An operations problem can be the telephone number itself. Word pictures for telephone numbers are very helpful for remembering the number, for example, 1-800-FLOWERS. However, think about how long it takes you to dial a number if all you have are the letters. Have you ever wondered how it works when the letters add up to more than seven? To save time for customers, companies should always include the telephone numbers along with the words in all messages. By the way, FLOWERS is 356-9377.

BEST PRACTICES

The following are *best practices*, methods of accomplishing business functions that are considered to be superior to all other known methods, summarized from telephone communication training experts. The better we are at telephone skills, the more valuable we will be to our company. The best practices are intended for all company employees. A role may have specialized duties, for example, requiring a headset, so all the guidelines will not apply. The information is organized in chronological sequence: pre-greeting, greeting, conversation, and closing.

PRE-GREETING BEST PRACTICES

Know how to use the telephone system. For instance, learn how to transfer calls flawlessly so that you never cut customers off. Customers do not like to hear, "We've just put in a new telephone system, and I'm not sure how to use it yet."

Arrange your environment so that your telephone conversations are customer-oriented, convenient, and efficient. Figure out how to reduce distractions. If you do not have a private office, there is always office noise. Learn how to tune it out.

You should always have paper and pencil handy to take notes if necessary. It is unacceptable for a businessperson to say, "Hang on a sec. I have to find something to write with." It appears very incompetent. Do you need to switch hands to take notes, creating a break in the conversation? Try answering and talking with the receiver in your left hand if you are right-handed and vice versa.

Be prepared to answer the telephone. Ask yourself if it is within easy reach. It should be no more than an arm's length away. Will you knock over a stack of papers or, worse, a soft drink, reaching for the receiver? Will the receiver hit anything as you retrieve it? Will the cord get tangled?

Maintain good posture. It shows on the telephone. A slouched posture will affect your voice quality and perhaps cause customers to think you are apathetic or stressed. An alert posture reflects positive energy and confidence. If you are angry or frustrated, that will show as well. Stand up to relieve stress if you are talking to an angry customer. Standing for the next call is also a good way to relieve tension if you have just hung up from a tough call.

Make sure that the receiver is in the proper position before you start talking. It should be about 1 to 2 inches from your lips for the clearest reception. An example illustrates this point. An advertising account executive often had considerable difficulty understanding one of her clients. She would frequently need to ask the client to repeat what she said to the point that it was embarrassing. She eventually learned from a mutual business associate that the client was in the habit of holding the telephone receiver below her chin as she sat at her desk. In addition, pay attention to your posture. The telephone should not be jammed between your shoulder and ear. At a minimum, this puts a strain in your voice. If you are a heavy telephone user, a headset is a valuable investment.

Smile; customers can "hear" it. This sounds odd, but like posture, a smile shows in your voice. Customers will react positively. Smiling will also affect your attitude in a positive way. The best approach is to smile before you answer the call. That way all customers, no matter who they are, will get a smile. Putting a mirror on your desk helps to monitor your smile. Smile during the conversation when appropriate.

Skill Development 9.1

Try this experiment. For several days, concentrate on smiling before you pick up the telephone. See if you can detect any change in how customers perceive your attitude and how they react.

Be prepared when you answer the telephone. A telephone call can be an interruption of what you are doing. You do not want customers to ever have that perception. A call is frequently an interruption of your train of thought. Put what you are doing aside. Do not pick up the telephone while finishing another conversation; callers may hear this. Be mindful; be present in the moment. Clear your mind and focus on the caller.

You should normally not take a call if you are in a meeting in your office. Forward your telephone calls. Instruct someone to handle your calls or take messages. If you absolutely must take a call because no one else is available, excuse yourself, find out what the call concerns, tell the caller you are in a meeting, and ask when is a good time to call back. If you are expecting an important call, let your visitors know that when the meeting begins.

Pay attention to your frame of mind and self-talk. Sometimes a difficult call leaks into the next one. Let the telephone ring one more time, take a deep breath, focus on the new customer, and answer the telephone.

Depending on your job duties, focus on each caller's needs and what you can do, rather than assuming that you will be taking a message or transferring the call. Some experts recommend that whoever picks up the telephone "owns" the call and should do whatever is necessary to serve the customer. We will cover this in more detail later in the chapter.

Do not be too busy. If internal customers ask how you are, never say, "I've been soooo busy." They will get the impression that you think you are too busy to help. Besides, everyone is busy. Say, "Great! What can I do for you?"

Most of the time, you should answer the telephone promptly, between one and three rings. Customers expect a business to be open and the telephone to be answered. They begin to wonder whether the company is indifferent or understaffed after about the third ring. Some customers know that they cannot tolerate letting

TABLE 9.1   Summary of Pre-Greeting Practices

Know how to use the telephone system.
Arrange your environment.
Always have paper and pencil handy.
Be prepared to answer the telephone.
Maintain good posture.
Make sure the receiver is in the proper position.
Smile.
Be prepared when you answer the telephone.
Check your frame of mind.
Focus on each caller.
Answer the telephone promptly.

their own telephone ring, and so they cannot imagine why other businesspeople would. If they do not receive timely service, customers may hang up and call another business. If a company finds that answering the telephone quickly is not possible, it should consider adding personnel or adjusting its systems so that it is possible. On the other hand, answering too quickly, so that the caller does not hear the telephone ring once, is also undesirable. Customers are usually taken aback when this happens. Between the second and third ring is best. If it is an automated system and a person will not answer, an answer before three rings is essential.[4]

There are exceptions. Studies have shown that customers care more about receiving assistance than how many times the telephone rings. For example, if you work in a retail store, are helping a customer, and can finish before answering the telephone, more than three rings is acceptable. Then you will not immediately have to ask customers if they can hold. If the phone does ring longer than it should, you can say, "Hello, I'm sorry it rang so long. This is Shoe Palace. How can I help you?" This defuses the situation. Then be sure you can help the customer.

One problem that may happen is receiving calls that are wrong numbers. Rather than just telling callers that they have reached the wrong number, a helpful company practice is to direct them to the right number. If you receive numerous calls for a number that is similar to your company's, for example, one with the numbers transposed, have it on hand to give the callers.

Table 9.1 sums up pre-greeting best practices.

GREETING BEST PRACTICES

When you answer the telephone, give a strong *verbal handshake*. The first 4 to 6 seconds are critical. The words you use depend on many factors: the type and size of the organization, your role in the company, your responsibilities, and the operation of your telephone system. The major consideration is to make sure you provide customers with what they need and expect. They need courtesy, assistance, and positive feedback. They need to know that they have reached the right company and/or the right person. They often want assistance as soon as possible.

Buffer Words

Start out with *buffer words*. Oddly enough, telephone communication experts tell us that callers often do not hear the first two words even though they are expecting someone to answer. In addition, sometimes the first two words are cut off if the telephone is not positioned properly when you answer. So consider your first couple of words "throw-aways." This means that you should not start out with the company name. If you do, you may find that customers will ask, "Have I reached [company]?"

Say something like, "Thank you for calling. . . ," or "Good morning, this is. . . " Be careful using the time of day lest you say good morning when it is afternoon. That would make you seem less competent. Never say "Hello" and then be silent.

Company

The next words should be the name of the company the customer has reached. Say the name very clearly. Do not mumble. Do not run the words together. Do not say it in a monotone or singsong voice. If a receptionist says, "Ottawa State College," in a bored, singsong voice, customers can tell that she has answered the telephone 50 times a day for months. Avoid the temptation on a busy day to shortcut the greeting. Every caller is as important as the last.

Do not rush, especially if the company name is more than a couple of words. If you say "Winter, Walker, Chamberlain, and Carpenter Law Offices" too fast, customers will not be sure what you said. Remember, even though you have said it many times that day, it is the first time customers have heard it. Customers want to know they have reached the right company.

Make the greeting as short as possible. If the name of your company is long, it is best to shorten it in some way if you can, perhaps to the words your customers use. An example of what not to say is "Thank you for calling First Federal Bank of Elizabethton County." This is hard to say, is hard to understand, and takes too long. Use what your customers say, "Thank you for calling First Federal. How can I help you?"

Offer of Assistance

There are two schools of thought on offering assistance, which depend partly on who answers the telephone. Some experts believe that you should always show a willingness to help by offering assistance, saying, "How can I help you?" Others say if your job is to transfer the call or take a message, offering help gives customers the wrong impression, that you are the person who is going to help. If you are directing calls, you can say, "How may I direct your call?"

If you are the person who will help, you should offer. Say, "Thank you for calling Twilight Company. How can I help you today?" "Can I help you?" is not the best wording to use. Customers subconsciously think, "Yes, that's why I called." In their mind, they think, "Yes," and then you have to ask, "How can I help?"

Name

Tell the caller who you are if appropriate. Depending on the type and size of the company, the receptionist's name may not be necessary. If you are first to answer the main telephone line at your company and there is a good reason for customers to know your name, by all means, tell them. Perhaps as a receptionist, customers know you. Perhaps it is a retail store and customers know or want to know with which salesperson they are speaking. Offering your name does build rapport. In this case, say, "Thank you for calling Walden's Hardware. This is Jill. How can I help you?" One disadvantage of the sequence of your name and then an offer of assistance is that if you say anything after your name, the caller is less likely to hear your name.

If a receptionist has connected a call to you, use a greeting, your department, your name, and an offer of assistance. You do not need to repeat the company. If the call comes from outside, then you do need to say the company name.

Do say, "Hello, Sales Department. This is Dan Spencer. How may I help you?"

It is better not to say, "Dan speaking." This could sound as if Mr. Speaking answered. You should also be aware that using just your last name, "Hello, Sales Department. Spencer," is too abrupt. Plus, now the customer is not sure whether it's your first or last name.

If you can distinguish between external and internal calls on your telephone system, change your greeting to less formal and more appropriate company language for internal calls, such as, "Hello, Accounting. This is Sam Young." Do not answer with just "Hello." Do not say, "This is Sam." Callers cannot always be sure they have reached the right department or person. Remember, internal calls are customers, too. If you receive both internal and external calls on your telephone, use a more formal greeting.

If you answer someone else's telephone, say, "Hello, Ms. Kirkland's office. This is Mary Stockton, her assistant. How can I help you?" If you are answering the phone just to take messages and your name or relationship to Ms. Kirkland is not germane, your name is not necessary.

Change the greeting occasionally or have alternatives so you do not begin to say it too fast or sound like a robot. A business should develop several acceptable phrases to use.

Do not turn your greeting into an advertisement. It becomes too long, and research shows that it is irritating to customers. Do not say, "Thank you for calling Pizza House. Our special tonight is two large pizzas for $. . . Would you like to order?" You get the idea.

Skill Development 9.2

Give some examples of how you answer the telephone at your company. Is there a better way to do it?

What do you do if the company requires you to say something that is not a best practice?

CONVERSATION BEST PRACTICES

Since automated systems are common, when customers reach a human being, they want courtesy, helpfulness, and sincere friendliness, not machinelike efficiency. You will get back what you give. Customers respond in kind.

An 800-number study of 121 calls to 109 different companies found that satisfaction with the call and the likelihood of repurchase were positively related to the

TABLE 9.2 800-Number Telephone Communication Study

Customers were more satisfied if representatives:
  Were courteous
  Were interested
  Were knowledgeable
  Gave an apology for a problem
  Answered questions effectively
  Thanked customers for comments
  Encouraged customers to call again
Customers thought representatives should be:
  Better listeners
  More courteous
  More personable
  Less impatient
  Less apathetic
  More appreciative of customers' comments

Source: Charles L. Martin and Denise T. Smart, "Consumer Experiences Calling Toll-Free Corporate Hotlines," *The Journal of Business Communication* 31, no. 3 (July 1994): 195–213.

service representative's communication. If the representative was perceived to be courteous, interested, and knowledgeable, callers were more likely to be satisfied with the call. For those with a complaint, a verbal apology increased satisfaction. Other verbal responses that were related to higher satisfaction were answering questions effectively, thanking customers for their comments, and encouraging customers to call again if they needed to. In terms of what could be better, about 17 percent of the customers thought the representatives should be better listeners, more courteous, more personable, less impatient, less apathetic, and more appreciative of customers' comments (see Table 9.2).[5]

The recommendations below for conversation apply in a general sense and are not specific to dealing with customer complaints or other specialized situations. Those aspects will be covered in Chapter 13 on problem resolution and recovery.

Customer Names

Customers' names are vital. Be paying attention from the beginning so you hear their name. Be ready to write the name down. This is actually rather hard to do, and many people miss it. Practice. Write the name down, use it, and remember it. Customers will feel more like they are being treated as people instead of their account number. Use customers' titles until asked to do otherwise. If customers do not tell you their name, ask for it early in the conversation, even if you do not necessarily need it. If you need the spelling, check later in the conversation. Ask how a name is spelled even if it seems simple.

It is often impolite to make a comment about an odd or difficult-to-spell name. You may offend. This does depend on what is said, the context, and the type of company. Just remember that a person's name is the person. Moreover, the customer has heard similar comments a thousand times.

Listening

Listen attentively. Do not do something else while you are on the telephone. You should not eat, chew gum, smoke, file papers, or fiddle with a pencil. Use your keyboard only if it is related to the call. Do not let another employee's wave from across the room distract you. Learn to tune out office noises. If coworkers walk up to you, acknowledge them but silently indicate you will be with them shortly. If you absolutely must respond to a coworker or ask a question, ask if you may put the customer on hold. Do it only at an appropriate juncture. Customers who hear you communicating with someone else are rightfully offended.

During the call, do not rely on your memory. Record necessary details. Use or construct an appropriate form. Double-check vital information by repeating it.

Nonverbal Communication

Since about 85 percent of the message is communicated by nonverbal language on the telephone, consider the information covered in Chapter 6. Be aware how facial expressions, body movements, and voice cues affect your telephone delivery. Project a friendly, confident, and polished manner. Remember to smile and have good posture.

Use the voice skills discussed in Chapter 6 on nonverbal communication. Consider how your voice sounds. Most of us do not have a clear, objective sense of what we sound like on the telephone. Telephones do change or distort voices, and as you know, the voice you hear is not the voice others hear. Test your telephone voice with a tape recorder or a coworker's help. Listen to your voice-mail message. Your voice volume should be appropriate. Check to see how your telephone amplifies your voice. Your rate of speech should be in the range of 130 to 160 words per minute. In language or hearing difficulty situations, you may need to slow down. Check to see if the quality of your voice is natural and clear. Since voice cues are so important on the telephone, your voice should reflect an alert, positive, and helpful manner. Make sure your pitch does not inadvertently make you sound like you are impatient, irritated, or stressed. Do not speak in a monotone. Be expressive and conversational. Articulate distinctly.

Listen with your ears, and listen for nonverbal communication. When customers are talking, make sure they know you are listening. Respond with "Yes," "uh-huh," "I see," and other positive listening response phrases. Do not allow excessive dead air space. Never ever interrupt customers. If you need to move the conversation along, wait until the customer pauses or takes a breath. Get in the habit of recognizing customers' mood and style from their voice and other nonverbal clues and respond appropriately. Ask yourself if the customer is in a hurry. Is he analytical? Is she hesitant? Consider why and how you can help.

If a customer is talking too fast, politely say, "Excuse me, Ms. Allen, I'm struggling to write down all of your information. If you could slow down a bit, I can get it all correct and take care of this for you." If a customer is talking softly, say, "Excuse me, I'm having some trouble hearing. Could you speak a little louder?"

Verbal Communication

On the telephone, about 15 percent of the meaning is delivered by words. Recall the use of positive, strong language from Chapter 7. Be courteous. Say please, thank you, and you're welcome. Use good grammar.

Learning to understand foreign accents is good business. Customers may speak good English but have an accent. If you cannot understand the words, do not pretend. Ask them to slow down so you get everything correct. Listen to the speech pattern to pick up key words. Repeat back to clarify. Do not talk louder. In some cases, conversations will take a little longer because customers have to translate what you say and then translate back to English to reply. Sometimes customers understand English better than they speak it. Keep a language aid available for a few common phrases, even if you pronounce words wrong. Customers will appreciate your effort. Another alternative is to ask them to wait for a moment and find someone to help.[6]

What do you do and say when customers keep talking and you cannot get them off the telephone without being rude? First, if the call is about a problem, listen more to make sure they are finished and satisfied with the solution. Perhaps they are trying to tell you something that you are not getting or that they think you do not understand. Perhaps you have jumped to the wrong conclusion and offered the wrong solution because they are not explaining well. Paraphrase to confirm your understanding. Second, some customers just like to hear themselves talk and do not know or care if you are listening. If you end the conversation courteously and directly, they will not care. Say, "I'm so glad you called about this. I'm going to go now to take care of the situation. I'll let you know this afternoon. OK?" Customers would hardly say no to this. An alternative method is to say, "I need to take some time to review the information you've given me so I can correct this. I appreciate your letting me know. Thank you for calling. Good-bye." Do not say this too fast or in a dismissive way. If you are the caller, clarify on the front end, "Do you have 10 minutes to talk about the situation you called about this morning?" Then later say, "I promised I was going to take only 10 minutes, so thank you for your time, and I will take care of it."

Disconnections

If you are disconnected, the general rule of thumb is that the person who made the call should call back. If you do not have the customer's telephone number, the customer will need to call back. However, if you do have the number, we advise the service representative to call back. If customers are annoyed, they could think the disconnection was intentional. Use your own judgment based on the circumstances.

CLOSING BEST PRACTICES

Close the conversation properly.

Summarize the conversation.

Confirm what will happen next. Say, "I understand. I'll let Sally know. She will call you back when the information reaches her desk."

Ask if there is anything else you can do to help. This is viewed as helpful behavior and may remind the customer of something.

Thank the customer for calling. Be formal. Say, "Thank you for calling." Other phrases to use are "We appreciate your call" and "Thank you for your order."

Encourage customers to call back again. Research shows that this is appreciated.

Say "Good-bye." Do not use the informal "Bye-bye."

Let customers hang up first so they do not hear your click or half of a message.

If the call requires you to take action, do so as soon as you can. At the very least, write it down on your to-do list right away. You may think you will remember in an hour, but you may not remember until it is too late.

Use these skills for internal calls as well. In smaller companies where everyone knows everyone else, you may be somewhat more casual, but courtesy, helpfulness, and professionalism are still essential.

Hanging Up

Never hang up on a customer, external or internal. For example, a faculty member, Susan, once received a call from another faculty member about a student. Susan politely responded that she did not recognize the student's name and did not know her, but the other instructor kept insisting that the student was one of Susan's advisees and in one of her classes. Susan said, "No, I'm sure she isn't." The instructor became rude, claimed that Susan was not being helpful, and hung up on her. Susan was justifiably insulted and never did figure out what the problem was. It may have been a case of mistaken identity.

TELEPHONE ACTIONS

You may take one of several actions when you pick up the telephone. Handle or own the call yourself. Put the caller on hold. Take a message. Take a call for an unavailable employee. Connect the caller with another employee. Screen the call. Make a call yourself.

Handling Calls

In terms of handling calls, who is the most important person at your company? Exactly. The receptionist is. This is truly a frontline job. The receptionist is often the first person with whom potential customers talk. It is a vital role and a tough one. Juggling calls while remaining courteous, proficient, and upbeat all day is demanding. The image, welcome, and competence that the receptionist conveys are a customer's first impression of the company. Receptionists need to have exceptional telephone skills, among the most competent in the company.

Sometimes other employees need to take over the receptionist's responsibility when it is not part of their normal duties. Here are several suggestions. Be sure you are very clear on how to operate the system. Get instruction from the receptionist. Devote your full concentration to the receptionist role so you represent the company correctly. Whether it is the main line or a department line, use the question "May I direct your call or take a message?" to make clear to customers what you can and cannot do. If you say "How can I help you?" customers will tell you and you may need to connect their call or take a message anyway. Make sure you have a company directory for transfers. Find out if anyone is expecting a call during your duty time or any other details that only the receptionist knows. Receptionists should be willing to provide all the information a substitute needs since the employee is really representing them.

Owning Calls

Customers dislike being passed from person to person and not being helped. They dislike poorly handled transfers. Friedman says, however, that only 25 percent of customer calls are handled on the first call. One study showed that 66 percent of customers who call a call center expect the first person they speak with to handle their call.[7]

Skill Development 9.3

Read the following telephone conversation. What unacceptable telephone behaviors and procedures can you identify?

Operator: "Any State Retirement System."

Customer: "Hello, I need to change my address."

Operator (sounding confused): "Um, I think that's Personnel. One moment please."

Voice 1 (incorrect department): "Hello, may I help you?"

Customer: "Yes, I want to change my address."

Voice 1 (abruptly): "This isn't Personnel." Click. Customer put on hold and transferred.

Personnel 1: "Hello, Personnel."

Customer: "I want to change my address."

Personnel 1: "I don't think we do that in this office. I don't have the forms. Hold on."

Personnel 2: "Hello."

Customer: "Can you help me get my address changed?"

Personnel 2: "Of course, I'll need to send you a form."

Customer: "Can't I just change it over the phone?"

Personnel 2: "Oh, no, that's against the rules. If you'll give me your name and the address, I'll send you a form."

Customer: "Well, my new address is. . . "

Personnel 2: "No, no, I have to send it to the address I have. I just want to verify it."

Customer: "But this doesn't make sense. I've already moved. Never mind, I am sure it will be forwarded. My address was. . . "

Do own the call if possible. This means either take care of the customer yourself or "sell" the question or problem to someone else in the company. Sometimes *owning the call* means you can take care of it quickly and it is done. Have you ever wanted to know something as simple as the company address and the receptionist sends you to someone else? Everyone in the company should be able to provide basic information about the company.

"Selling" the customer's call does not mean delegating it. It means that you will find the right person to accept responsibility for the customer's need and agree to take care of it. Then you make sure the person follows up. If you cannot handle the call and the person the customer wants is unavailable, find out what the customer needs and get all the necessary information. Then you can pass the customer's information on to the right person. If you cannot handle the call and it is for another department, ask the caller to hold and find the right person in that department, explain what the customer needs and the details, and then transfer the call. Do not transfer until you have "sold" the call. If you have no idea who is qualified to help the customer, ask for all the information you need, write it down, and tell the customer that you or someone else will call him back within a certain time frame. Then get on the telephone yourself and find the answer or the appropriate person. If it is going to take longer than the time you promised, call back and explain.

Absolutely do not transfer if customers say that you are the third person they have talked to. Help customers yourself. Get the needed information and call them back with it or find the right person to do so. Each telephone call may take a little longer, but overall the company will receive fewer calls because customers are taken care of the first time.[8]

Using Hold on Calls

As mentioned earlier in the chapter, a survey that Nancy Friedman, the Telephone Doctor, conducted found that being put on hold was the number one telephone procedure that customers disliked.[9]

A recent research study, which explored customers' attitudes about being put on hold, found the following:

1. Almost all respondents were frustrated with automated menu systems. If they heard, "...Can you hold please? Click," they felt irritated, aggravated, annoyed, and unimportant. The "click" causes uncertainty and a feeling of lost control. Many customers reported that they would hang up.
2. If consumers were calling about a problem of some importance to them, automated menu systems increased their anxiety.
3. Talking to a person made them feel more important.
4. If the reason for being put on hold was explained, callers were more willing to wait.
5. They were dissatisfied if they thought a wait was unjustified, such as being put on hold while a representative took other calls.
6. Callers often think of being put on hold as a necessary process. Therefore, they did not mind being on hold if they knew that the representative was taking care of their request.
7. If the call is for something very important to consumers, they were willing to wait longer.
8. Time went faster if callers heard music they liked.
9. Informational messages made the time seem less wasted.

The consumers in the study believed that being put on hold meant that the company had too few employees, poorly trained representatives, and poor management. Although advanced telephone technology increases productivity and reduces costs, a negative result is the perception that the technology is replacing personal relationships.[10]

The best advice is to use *hold* as little as possible. Customers hate it. Saying "Hold please" comes across as an order. Since using hold is often necessary, the best procedure is to ask if the customer can hold. Then—this is essential—wait for the customer to answer. Then say thank you. One study found that asking if customers can hold was the second most overused and misused expression precisely because the asker never waited for an answer.[11] The question means nothing if you do not wait for an answer. Perhaps the customer is calling long distance. If customers object to holding, ask for their name and number and say you will call back at their convenience.

Do not say, "Hold on." or, "Hold please." and then click!

Do not say, "Hang on a second. I'll be right back." This is not realistic.

Do say, "Can you wait while I check on that?" Wait for an answer.

Do say, "Would you mind holding a moment while I get your file?"

Give customers an estimate of how long a hold will be. You should not leave customers on hold longer than 60 seconds without checking back. Hold should not ever be used for more than 3 minutes. You should not use hold when a callback will serve equally well or better. If the hold time is so long that customers put the call on speakerphone, it's too long. A call center director asserts that, for 800-number calls, customers with serious problems will usually hold for 60 seconds, while those with questions will not tolerate a 20-second delay.

Do say, "It may take me 2 or 3 minutes to get that information. I'll be happy to call you back, or you can wait if you prefer."

The 800-number study, mentioned earlier, also found that decreasing the amount of time customers waited was the most frequently suggested improvement. In this study, the wait included waiting for calls to be answered, time on hold, and time spent reexplaining the reason for the call to more than one representative.[12]

When you are back to the phone, thank customers for waiting. This acknowledges customers' understanding and patience. Avoid the word "hold." Do not apologize. First, there is no need to apologize; you received permission. Second, it is needlessly negative.

A complete conversation for a hold would be:

Assistant: "I think Mr. Carson may be in a meeting. Are you able to wait while I find out?"

Customer: "Yes, I can."

Assistant: "Thank you."

10 second wait

Assistant: "Thank you for waiting. He just finished his meeting. I'll connect you."

Customer: "OK."

If the person a customer wants to speak to is on another line, say, "Ms. Johnson is on another call. I'm not sure how long she will be. If you'll tell me your name and number, I will make sure she gets the message." Saying you do not know how long it will be, which is true, prevents customers from asking. Asking for a name and number is much more effective than asking if customers would like to leave a message. Many customers decide their message is too complicated, or they want to be the originator of the call and will not leave a message. They may call the next business on their list and never call back.

One exception to asking if the caller can wait is if you are the receptionist. If customers ask to speak to a specific person, they expect the receptionist to put them on hold to connect the call. The receptionist should be polite, but not curt. One method that works well is:

Receptionist: "Thank you for calling Blanken Books. How can I help you?"

Customer: "I'd like to speak with Jan Billings in sales, please."

Receptionist: "I'll be happy to connect you."

The receptionist or employee taking the call should have a system for making sure that the transferred call is answered. Do not go back to a customer on hold and say, "Who are you holding for?" Customers will think that you are very inexperienced or incompetent. It is a receptionist's job to keep track. If an employee is not available, the receptionist should get back to the customer and ask for a name and telephone number or ask if the caller wants to leave a message on voice mail. It is also helpful to give the customer the person's direct line or extension if there is one. One of the biggest problems as a receptionist is dealing with many different things at once and handling multiple calls. If you know exactly what you should say and do, it will prevent you from becoming confused and stressed and will enable you to handle situations better.

Here is an example of a confused receptionist. Amy called her local chamber of commerce to speak to a specific person.

The receptionist answered, "Any City Chamber of Commerce. Hold please." Click!

About 60 seconds later, Amy heard, "The best thing for you to do is to call the library for that information."

Amy said, "I haven't even asked a question yet."

The receptionist said, "Well, excuse me!" She put Amy back on hold.

This was a chamber of commerce! Amy hung up.

Music.   What about playing music or other audio while someone is on hold? A 1999 research study found that callers waited longer if they liked what they heard than if they did not like it. The study used panpipe and Beatles' music. The panpipe music fit their expectations better than the Beatles' music, and so they tended to wait longer when listening to panpipe. They also waited longer if they heard music as opposed to a message, "I'm sorry, the line is busy. Please hold" repeated every 10 seconds.[13]

If customers hear nothing, they may begin to think they have been disconnected. Silence is probably acceptable for a few seconds. If you do use music, make sure it is compatible with most of your customers' preferences. A radio station may not be appropriate because it includes commercials. A recording that tells customers repeatedly during the hold time that their call is very important makes them wonder if they really are. Recordings that tell customers an approximate wait time and how many callers are waiting can be helpful if they decide they would rather not wait. However, hearing it repeatedly is irritating. You can also use prerecorded information, but our advice is not to use prerecorded company commercials. Some companies record tips about their products and play those. For example, one appliance manufacturer has an extensive audiotape on its 800 number that gives tips on laundry, cooking, baking, microwaving, and other household activities. It's useful advice, and customers never hear repetition.

Taking Messages

Taking messages seems so easy, but many entry-level employees have never had the procedure explained.

A writing tool and a pad of paper should be available near every telephone. These often seem to have legs and disappear, but there are many products available to solve this problem. Many organizations use preprinted telephone message pads (see Figure 9.3). If those work, that is fine. Without a form, many people will be in a hurry and leave something out. If the message pads do not have space for the appropriate message or designations at your company, buy or devise a new form. Perhaps the message page needs room to include more detail or impressions, such as "I

FIGURE 9.3   Example of Telephone Message Content

```
                    Telephone Message
     Date _____            Time _____

     Message for _____

     Name_____

     Company_____

     Department _____

     Phone number ( )_____

     Message_____

     _____

     _____

     _____

     _____

     Callback time_____
     Initials_____
```

think he's getting impatient." The form may need a space for a priority rating or for the action needed. You can also consider keeping a telephone log for record and time management purposes.

At a minimum, record:

* *Person the message is for.*
* *Date and time of day*—This is critical so calls are returned in a timely manner. The person called should return calls preferably by the end of the business day, at least within 24 hours, or by the time specified.
* *Customer's complete name, spelled correctly*—It should be spelled phonetically if there is any question, and gender should be indicated if there might be confusion. "Bill called" works only if you know only one Bill. How do you pronounce "Hani?" Is "Jamie" a man or a woman?
* *Company name and/or department, if applicable, again, spelled correctly*—This will help the person know what the call may concern and act as a backup in case the telephone number is wrong.
* *Phone number, including area code if needed, legibly*—If customers tell you that the person has the telephone number, get it anyway. Just say, "I'm sure she probably has your phone number, but for 'easy reference,' would you tell me so I can write it down right on the message?" This will save time and prevent a mini-crisis if she does not have it.
* *Message, clear and accurate*—If no message is offered, you might ask, "Is there any information you would like to leave that may be helpful when she calls you back?"
* *When the caller wants to be called back, if specified*—You can tell the customer when the person normally returns calls if you know.
* *Verify all vital information.*   Read the last four phone numbers back in word pairs, 525-5015 is 525-fifty-fifteen, to avoid transposing them.

* *Say thank you for calling and assure customers that you will give the person the message as soon as she is available*—Remember, do not say, "I'll have her call you back." You have no control over that.
* *Your name or initials, in case there are any questions*—It is very frustrating to receive a message with a telephone number you cannot decipher, or the number turns out to be long distance and you do not know the area code location, and the message has no initials. It's an irredeemable error.

Taking Calls for Other Employees

When the employee the customer is calling is not there, do not say anything unprofessional. Do not tell customers anything personal about the person, such as the person is out sick, has a doctor's appointment, or is on vacation. Customers do not need to know that. If you tell customers that the person has not come in yet this morning, is not back from lunch yet, or has disappeared from his desk, it will give entirely the wrong impression. Saying someone had an emergency either makes the company look bad or implies the employee has personal problems. This is not a good idea.

Experience Discussion 9.2

What unprofessional comments have you heard?

If you know the person will be back and will return calls, say, "She'll be back at 4:00. If you will give me your name and number, I will give her the message," or "He will call for messages this afternoon," or "She'll be back at her desk soon. I will be happy to give her your name and number to call you back." This is even more effective if you already know the customer's name. Do not say, "I'll have him call you as soon as possible." You are implying that you have control over whether he does or not. If the employee is gone for the day, callers may want to know that. "He will be out of the office at a meeting the rest of the afternoon." or "She is out of the office today." You do not say, "He left early."

As mentioned above, asking "Can I take a message?" is often ineffective because callers may say, "No, that's OK. I'll call back." They may go right to the next number and call a competitor. Another possibility is that callers may believe people will not return telephone calls from unknown people and would rather reapproach the intended recipient themselves. Ask for a customer's name and number instead.

If you have been instructed that you can send the caller to someone else, say, "She is out of the office this week and next, but John Reynolds is answering her calls. May I connect you with him?"

If you are an assistant and you do have the experience to help, the best response is, "He's not available right now [or not in at the moment]. This is Susan, his assistant. If you'll tell me more about the reason for your call, perhaps I can help." When you repeat your name and identify your relationship, you establish your credibility. Customers will often venture a question. Frequently it is a question that you can answer or a task that you can handle. If customers want to leave a message at this point, they will. You could also suggest connecting customers to another employee who can help them.

Connecting Calls

Anecdotal evidence tells us that customers do not like to be transferred to the wrong person, transferred multiple times, or disconnected.

Learn your company well enough to transfer calls to the correct department or person every time. Develop a call transfer guide for yourself or department using the way your customers ask for departments and topics, not the way your company refers to them.

Let customers know that you are going to transfer the call. Give customers a reason why. Do not make it sound like you are trying to get rid of them. Let them know that you are sending them to someone who can help them faster or sending them to an "expert."

It is better to not use the word *"transfer."* Say *"connect."* Due to their experiences, many customers instinctively dread what happens next when they hear the word "transfer." If your phone system has any unusual noises, warn customers so they don't think they've lost the connection.

Give customers the employee's name, department, and extension or direct telephone number before you transfer them. Customers can call back more easily if need be.

Do say, "Mr. Wood, I'm going to connect you with Bob Andrews in Technical Support at extension 547 for that question. He will know exactly how to help you."

Although it is not always possible in these days of high-volume calls, it is a good idea to tell the employee the customer's name and any information he told you so he does not have to repeat. An example is, "Bob, I have Mr. John Wood on the line. He needs some help installing his water heater." Bob can say, "Hello, Mr. Wood. I understand you have a question about installing your water heater." If customers are greeted with their name and basic question, they will feel much more taken care of and important to the company.

If it is possible on your telephone system, make sure the call is transferred. If it is not possible to track calls, perhaps your company should consider how many calls it loses and modify its system.

It is often necessary and acceptable these days to transfer customers to an employee's voice mail. Make sure that it is acceptable to customers. Say, "Would you like me to connect you with her voice mail, or may I have your name and phone number for her to return your call?"

Screening Calls

To most people, *screening calls* means having someone else answer your telephone line and take messages or put callers through depending on who they are. Having calls screened is an extremely useful option. It enables businesspeople to organize work and manage time. However, it is a tricky and awkward assignment. Customers perceive screening as a dodge. If you have ever been screened with the question "Who's calling?" and the screener returns to tell you the employee is unavailable, you know you wonder if he does not want to talk to you or he can't talk for another reason. It is even less pleasant if the screener grills you about who is calling—what company you are with and what it is in reference to. It's intimidating. One of the most awkward situations is getting the customer's name and then having the employee ask you to tell the customer he is not there. Do not lie. Say, "Mr. Matthews, I thought Ms. Connor was available, but isn't right now. What can I do to help?"

If you need uninterrupted time, the best practice is to have your assistant take messages from everyone. If a caller is someone the screener knows you want to talk to, she can deliver the message immediately.

If you must screen calls, find out how you should do it.

* Find out if there are any callers who should always be put through.
* Find out if there are any callers who should never be put through.
* Find out if someone might call about a current project.
* Find out if the person is expecting particular calls.
* Find out when and where you should report messages—as they occur, at certain times during the day, in a special place.
* Find out when you should tell callers that their calls will be returned.

If you are having calls screened, give your call screener a list of questions or guidelines to use as above. Have the screener tell the truth, tactfully. Asking "What is this in regard to?" is a question best scrubbed from memory. Customers and salespeople are beginning to hate it. If you intend not to take cold calls from salespeople, have your screener tell them that you do not have time right then to talk with them. For a salesperson, a no is better than a maybe that means no. The screener can request that information be mailed and tell the salesperson he will make sure the intended person gets it. You can also empower an assistant to handle sales calls.

It really is best for all businesspeople to return all calls themselves. It is useful to remember that every call is important. Perhaps you do not have time for a salesperson. However, it's good business to recognize that salespeople are doing their job. Otherwise, you are disregarding their effort and time. You can pleasantly and assertively say you do not need their product right now. What if you need precisely that company's product in 6 months on short notice? Another caveat is that you do not know when you may encounter that caller again. You never know who may offer you a job someday or who your boss will be 5 years from now.

An example of a good way to screen calls is the system used by the CEO of a travel and convenience center company. When someone calls the CEO, Lynn, his administrative assistant, answers the telephone and very diplomatically finds out who callers are and what they need. She is so familiar with the CEO's schedule and activities that she can often assist the caller. Jennifer sent the CEO a job inquiry letter and called to follow up. Lynn acknowledged that she remembered the letter and that it was on the CEO's desk. She said she would check on it and asked Jennifer to call back in a few days. When Jennifer did, Lynn told her that the CEO had written her a letter that she would be receiving shortly. She thanked her for her call and interest. Even though she was not able to talk with the CEO, Jennifer thought that Lynn was exceptionally helpful, courteous, friendly, and professional.

Making Calls

If you are away from your desk quite a bit during the day, block out a time or times of the day to return calls, perhaps late morning and late afternoon. Do try to return calls the same day or at least within 24 hours.

Whether you leave a message or reach the person, you should always plan calls in advance. Otherwise, you may forget an important point or question or, worse, sound incompetent. If you leave a message, always give your telephone number even if you know the person has it. It speeds things up for everyone.

As the caller, you should give your name and your company, if applicable, to the receptionist. This method is more courteous and avoids the screening process. Say, "Hello, Matt Collins calling. Is Debra Pendleton available?" It is irritating to have to repeat your name if the person taking the call misses it (and he or she will), but it is more polite and may save time.

A screener may ask, "What is this in regard to?" Again, this question is best deleted from everyone's memory. Still, if you are asked this, come up with a safe phrase, such as "I'm interested in doing business with your company."

When you reach the person, say your full name even for someone you call routinely. The person may or may not recognize your voice.

It is best to check if it's a good time. For example, say, "Hello, Mr. Denton. This is Cindy Williams with LFC Tools. I would like to discuss our recent proposal with you. Do you have time to talk?" If the person does not have time to talk, arrange a callback time.

When you are on hold for a long time, do simple tasks, like quick reading or computer housekeeping until the party comes back on the line. You can also put your telephone on speakerphone although it is somewhat rude when you have to grab it to talk.

Sometimes executives have their assistants place calls for them. Because this can appear somewhat arrogant, executives should reconsider this action.[14]

Telephone Tag.   With voice mail and e-mail, telephone tag has been greatly reduced. You can minimize it even further by following a few guidelines. Leave a specific message. "I need to know. . . Just leave a message on my voice mail." Make return calls unnecessary. "Call me back only if you can't make the meeting on Thursday." Schedule a callback with a specific day and time. Find out if someone else can help.

TELEPHONE SPECIALTY FEATURES

Voice Mail

Voice mail can be a real timesaving advantage. From customers' viewpoint, they do not have to wait on hold and then discover the person is unavailable. They can leave a detailed message directly rather than relying on someone to write it down. There's less telephone tag.

From employees' perspective, they can get messages faster than if an assistant puts messages in a mailbox or some other common place. It saves time since you can find information or an answer to a question before calling back. Voice mail is helpful if you are in a meeting and do not want to take calls.

However, make sure you and your company are using voice mail for the right reasons and are using it wisely. Make sure your staff is not using voice mail as a shield or call-screening device to avoid work or customers. If every time customers call a businessperson and her voice mail is on, customers begin to wonder. Carefully consider customers' perception of the company's accessibility. Voice mail is intended as a way of making you available when you are not and is meant to expedite calls. Since the purpose is improving accessibility, users must return voice-mail calls promptly. Remember that some customers do not like talking to a machine. Voice mail removes the company's personal touch. Do not make voice mail an obstacle to customers; it's supposed to be the opposite.

Experience Discussion 9.3

What voice-mail practices do you like and dislike?

Recording a Message.   Some suggestions for voice mail:

* If the company message outside office hours gives the hours the office is open, make sure someone answers the telephone during open hours. Calling at 9 A.M. and hearing on voice mail that the office is open from 8 A.M. to 5 P.M. is frustrating for customers.
* If you are in your office, unless you are in a meeting with someone or genuinely need uninterrupted time for a task, always answer your phone.
* For personal voice mail, set the telephone system so it picks up after no more than four rings. That's convention, and it is long enough for people to decide you are not available so they can hang up if they do not want to leave a message. Any longer than that, most people will decide that you do not have voice mail or that it is not working. Consider your customers' needs before you decide.
* The message should be an exceptional one so that it is personal and welcoming. If you are using the standard, "I am either on the phone or away from my desk," think again. These days that is obvious to the caller. Be more creative. Record the message, listen to it, and re-record it as many times as necessary. Listen until you are satisfied that it is the best it can possibly be. The message represents you.
* Smile or have a pleasant expression on your face when recording the message.
* The basics for a personal voice-mail message are a greeting, your first and last name, and a way to reach a real person or an alternate number if appropriate. Also include where you are if applicable (at least do not tell where you are not) and when you will return calls.
* Always give customers a way to bypass the voice mail early in the message. Tell them how to reach a real person first rather than last. If you give a customer another employee's number, make sure the person is answering that number and can help. Have the alternate ready to give your e-mail address, fax number, pager or cell number, and mailing address if the customer needs it.
* Give customers sufficient information, but make it simple. Script it carefully so that the message is no longer than 15 seconds.
* Make sure the message is clear. Do not say the message too fast. Use your best voice. However, try not to sound so real at the beginning that the caller does not realize that it is voice mail.
* Make it timely. It takes only 10 to 15 seconds to record a message once you have a script and get the hang of it. Do be careful to change the message if you have said that you will be back in the office on Wednesday after Labor Day.
* Prompt callers for any specific information that you need, such as the best time to call them back. You might remind callers to leave their phone number.
* Be specific about when you check messages and when you will call back, something more than, "I'll call you back as soon as possible." A customer's version of as soon as possible may be within the hour; yours may be within

24 hours. Pay attention to time management, and do give yourself some lee-way in case it is impossible to call back by the time you specified.

* Avoid the obvious, "Please leave a message after the beep." Everyone knows this by now, and "beep" is not a soothing word. If you have an unusual tone configuration, like a short tone, followed by a long tone, you should warn people. Better yet, change it.
* Check your voice mail regularly.
* Always return calls when you say you will.
* A nice feature is to offer a way for callers to review their message. Then they will not wonder if they remembered to give you their telephone number.

The following are examples of appropriate short messages:

"This is Sally Summers. I am not available to answer the phone. Please leave a message, and I will call you back after 4 this afternoon."

". . . I am out of the office for the afternoon. Please leave a message, and I will return your call tomorrow morning."

". . . I will be out of the office on Tuesday and Wednesday. If you would like to talk to someone now, please press zero. Otherwise, please leave a message, and I will return your call on Thursday."

". . . I am out of the office the week of April 12, but I will be calling in for messages, so please leave one if you like. If you need to speak with someone now, press 0."

". . . I will be out of the office the week of April 12. Mike Hall is handling my calls; his number is 000-0000."

Leaving a Message on Voice Mail.   There are also good and not-so-good ways to leave a message on voice mail. When you make calls, expect to reach a voice-mail system and be prepared. The author once had the opportunity to review a message that she had left on voice mail before she hung up. She was embarrassed at how she sounded and what she said and quickly changed it. Be sure you know what you want to say so you are coherent. Otherwise, your message may be disorganized and hesitant. Make your message great. It represents you. Smile. Speak slowly and clearly. Be personable and upbeat. Talk as if the person is listening.

Give your full name and telephone number at the beginning. Then indicate the subject so the listener can judge its priority. Do not assume the person recognizes your voice. You may need to spell your name if it is difficult to understand on the telephone like the author's. Don't assume the person has your phone number handy. Be specific to avoid wasting time. If your message is more than a few sentences, give your name and number again at the end. Keep the message to 60 seconds or less. If needed, give a time by which you need a response. If you do not hear back, follow up with a fax or an e-mail rather than calling again. Be aware of possible interference from external noise.

If you need to talk to a person, a zero (0) will often get you to the operator although many systems no longer have this feature. The pound (#) key may bypass the person's voice-mail message if it is someone you call routinely.[15]

Call Waiting

You may have *call waiting* if you work out of your home. The best advice is do not use it, especially if you have made the call. If you must have call waiting for some reason, figure out the least rude thing to say to your current caller, something like, "Martha, could you please hold for a moment while I see if that call is an emergency?" Then get the second caller's name and number, and call back later. If it is not an emergency, do not tell the first caller that you have to take it. Obviously, you will imply that the second caller is more important. Call waiting is a convenience for you. It is an inconvenience to your caller.

If you do not want to miss a call while you are on the telephone, use an answering service that goes to voice mail when the telephone is busy. Another option is to use a telephone company service that allows you to cancel call waiting by pressing a sequence of keys (for example, *70) before you make a telephone call.[16]

Speakerphones

Speakerphones are very useful for three-or-more-way conversations, so that everyone is informed and understands a situation. However, there are some ground rules. Do not use a speakerphone if you're the only person in the room. It is rude to work at your desk while you talk, and it's an implied power play.

Assume you and two company personnel are in your office having a conversation with a client in another city. Speakerphones should not be used at the beginning or end of the conversation. You should never put a call on speakerphone without asking permission. Introduce the client to the company personnel in the room. They should identify themselves when they talk. It will be confusing if the client does not know who is speaking. The client should identify to whom she is addressing a question or comment. Do not do other things while you are on a conference call. The person at the other end may be able to tell you are not paying attention.

As mentioned before, a speakerphone is helpful to use if you know you will be on hold for a long time. Perhaps you are calling a particular company and know that it will take 15 minutes to get through. Use the speakerphone to hear when the call is answered and then pick up, quickly, with no fumbling.[17]

WIRELESS COMMUNICATION

Cell Phones

Miss Manners says, in public areas, cell phones are not "a passport into an etiquette-free zone."[18] We advise that you do not take calls in quiet areas, such as libraries or churches. It's not a good idea to talk on cell phones during public presentations and meetings, at restaurants, and in other public places. It is annoying to others. Casperson in *Power Etiquette* says, "Having a cell phone is not a status symbol; in fact, it may be a rudeness badge."[19] Some people consider it pretentious when people use cell phones in public places. During a presentation in a meeting, if you are asked to turn a cell phone off, leaving it on is selfish and self-important. Think about it. Are you using the cell phone because you have to or because you can? *Can* does not make it right.

On the other hand, for some businesspeople it is essential that customers or other employees be able to reach them at any time. If you receive a call while with a group of people, be polite. Excuse yourself and step away before taking it. In addition, it is impolite to make a call while in a group of people. When you must talk in public, talk quietly. Do not force others in the vicinity to listen to your cell phone conversations.

It depends on company style and policy whether you keep your cell phone on in meetings. If a cell phone rings in a meeting, everyone scrambles to figure out whose it is, disrupting the meeting. It's better to use the silent mode if the ring will disturb others.

You should also remember that cell calls are not secure.

It seems like plain common sense, but you may physically run into someone if you walk while talking, especially down stairs or through doors.

Distraction has become a major concern about using a cell phone in a car. In 2001, the state of New York passed a law against cell phone use in automobiles unless it is hands-free. At this writing, other states and cities are considering passing similar laws. There is some evidence that using a cell phone while driving can cause accidents. Proponents of cell phone use say that it's no different from eating, reading a map, putting on makeup, or doing many other activities while driving. One research study has found that changing a CD and reading a map were more distracting than using a cell phone. We do not know for sure. Experts tell us that if you have a car accident, insurance companies will ask if you were on the telephone. Telephone records will show if you were or not.

The wireless industry has suggestions for safe use. It recommends that drivers use a hands-free phone or speakerphone and a speed-dialing feature or voice-activated dialing. The industry suggests dialing manually only when stopped. Use voice mail to pick up calls when it is not safe to answer. Taking notes during a call while driving is also not considered a good idea.

It's even better not to talk while driving. One study found that even hands-free phones were unsafe. Especially if you are negotiating or involved in a complicated conversation, you might consider pulling off the road to talk. When you are stopped, it's considerate to minimize noise: Close windows, turn off the radio, and turn the air conditioning down. It is a good idea to let the person know you are using a cell phone in case the connection is lost.

Pagers

Pagers are handy if you are on call 24 hours a day. A pager should usually be on vibration mode unless you are at home. Make sure coworkers who give out the pager number know why and when they should offer it. Is it for emergencies only? What times of day are you available by pager? That way customers won't use it and not reach you. Let coworkers know how long it usually takes you to return a telephone call. Make sure potential callers know what type of message the pager will accept, whether it will take a phone number only or also voice or text.[20]

TERMS

best practices	transfer
verbal handshake	connect
buffer words	screening calls
owning the call	voice mail
hold	call waiting

DISCUSSION QUESTIONS

1. Why are exceptional telephone skills important to a company?
2. What should you consider before you pick up the telephone?
3. Think about the greeting that your company uses or one you have heard as a customer. Is it effective? If not, how would you change it?
4. What nonverbal communication skills should you use during a telephone conversation?
5. Outline best practices for closing a telephone conversation.
6. What does it mean to "own" a telephone call?
7. Explain best practices for:
   a. Using hold
   b. Taking a message
   c. Taking a call for someone else
   d. Connecting a call
   e. Screening a call
   f. Placing an outgoing call
8. Listen to your voice-mail message. Write it out. Critique it. How would you revise it if necessary?
9. Do you believe that government should pass a law against using a cell phone while driving?
10. What are best practices for cell phone use?

CASE—LACK OF ALL AID

Barb called a home repair and remodeling franchise company to request an estimate for a painting job. The customer service representative answered with the company name and her name and offered assistance. The name of the company was not clear, and Barb couldn't understand the representative's name. It was Karen. Barb told her what she needed and noted that the house was new, not-quite-finished construction. Karen immediately said, "We don't work with contractors. We only do remodeling jobs." Barb explained that she and her husband were the owners and builders and that they needed a couple of rooms painted and that the outside siding needed to be painted.

Karen transferred Barb to the owner of the franchise, who eventually agreed the company could help Barb after all and transferred her back to Karen. Barb explained in more detail what they needed. Karen asked several questions and told her it would be 4 to 7 days until someone would call about an appointment for an estimate. Barb asked if the estimator could come in the evening. The answer was no. Barb asked about a Saturday. Again, Karen said no, that their people didn't work at night or on weekends. Karen asked Barb for the address and other information.

Then Karen went into an extended spiel about all the company's procedures, insurance, etc. She talked very fast. Barb could not get a word in edgewise. Karen garbled her words together, but Barb caught a word here and there. Barb had already told her early in the conversation that she had a hearing problem and had asked her to please speak a little louder. At the end of this monologue, Karen said,

"Did you get all that?" Barb told her, "Not really, but never mind." She didn't care by then. Nor did Karen, who then said someone would call in 4 to 7 days and make an appointment for the day after.

After Barb thought about the conversation overnight, she decided that she did not want to hire the company after all. The next day she called about 10:30 a.m. She had to ask again for the service representative's name because she could not understand it. This time it was Jenny. Barb explained that she had changed her mind because the estimator could not do an estimate in the evening or on a Saturday. She asked to speak to the owner. The owner wasn't there, but Jenny asked for her name and phone number for a callback.

Then Jenny asked, "What is this phone call regarding?"

Barb said, "I'll tell the owner."

Jenny flatly said, "Unless I can tell her what it's about, she won't call you back."

Barb, exasperated at this point, said, "It's about customer service."

Jenny called back within 15 minutes and wanted to know if the company could do an estimate on Saturday. When Barb hesitated, Jenny asked if she'd rather talk to the owner first. Barb said yes. Jenny said she would see if she was available. The telephone was disconnected.

A few minutes later, the owner, Ms. Jones, called and said she understood Barb had a complaint. Barb explained that she thought that the conversation she had had with the representative the day before had been very negative.

Barb started to tell Ms. Jones that she thought that being informed that the owner did not return calls unless she knew what the call was about was not very good customer service.

Ms. Jones interrupted her and said, "Listen. Let me explain. I have to have the girls ask because I receive 50 calls all day long from salespeople. If I took all those phone calls, I wouldn't be able to return any calls to customers and I wouldn't be talking to you."

Barb said, "I understand that can happen, but. . . "

Ms. Jones interrupted again and asked about the conversation the day before.

Barb began to explain that it was very negative when she asked about evening and Saturday estimates.

Ms. Jones interrupted again and said, "Let me explain something. We have independent contractors, and I can't make them come in the evening. I can't make them come on a Saturday. It's obvious we can't service your needs. Have a nice day." She used a very rude tone of voice. The "Have a nice day" part was very snotty.

Barb found the 800 number for the corporate office on the Internet and got an automated system when she called. After hearing about 10 options, she pressed 41 for Customer Relations. The telephone rang over 50 times; no one answered it.

She called back and pressed zero. She got voice mail for the owner of the local franchise. She quickly hung up.

She called back a third time and pressed 12 for one of the founders of the company, Mr. Samuel.

About 2 hours later, he called Barb back. She explained everything that had happened. He listened until she was finished talking. He apologized. He asked several questions. He assured her that if she had called any other franchisee, it wouldn't have happened. He said he hoped she would try the company again sometime. He apologized several times. He thanked her for calling.

1. Evaluate Karen's and Jenny's customer service.
2. Evaluate the customer service of Ms. Jones, the franchise owner.
3. Evaluate the automated telephone system.
4. Did you think Mr. Samuel provided good customer service? Explain.

NOTES

1. Nancy J. Friedman, *Telephone Skills from A to Z: The Telephone Doctor® Phone Book,* rev. ed. (Menlo Park, CA: Crisp Learning, 2000), 19.
2. Dartnell Corporation, "Inaccuracy, Unresponsiveness Top Complaints about Phone Service," *Inbound Service & Selling,* sample issue, 2002, 4.
3. Joseph R. Schmitt, "Callers Held Hostage on 'Hold'," *Contractor* 38, no. 1 (January 1991): 38.
4. Dartnell Corporation, *The Telephone Success Express,* booklet (Chicago: Dartnell Corporation, 1997).
5. Charles L. Martin and Denise T. Smart, "Consumer Experiences Calling Toll-Free Corporate Hotlines," *The Journal of Business Communication* 31, no. 3 (July 1994): 195–213.
6. Friedman, *Telephone Skills from A to Z.*
7. Roger Shank and Jon Anton, "Natural Learning: The X-Factor in TSR Performance?" *Call Center Solutions,* July 1998, 118–125; and Friedman, *Telephone Skills from A to Z.*
8. Michael Ramundo, "If You Pick Up the Phone, You Own the Call," reprint from *The Apex II,* no. 8, MCR Marketing, Inc., 1990.
9. Friedman, *Telephone Skills from A to Z.*
10. D. K. Unzicker, "The Psychology of Being Put on Hold: An Exploratory Study," *Psychology & Marketing* 16, no. 4 (July 1999): 327–350.
11. Dartnell Corporation, *The Telephone Success Express.*
12. Martin and Smart, "Consumer Experiences."
13. Adrian C. North, David J. Hargreaves, and Jennifer McKendrick, "Music and On-Hold Waiting Time," *British Journal of Psychology* 90, no. 1 (February 1999): 161–164.
14. The best practices material is summarized from Kristin Anderson, *Great Customer Service on the Telephone* (New York: AMACOM, 1992); Friedman, *Telephone Skills from A to Z;* Karen Leland and Keith Bailey, *Customer Service for Dummies,* 2d ed. (New York: IDG Books Worldwide, 1999); Paul R. Timm, *Winning Telephone Tips, 30 Fast and Profitable Tips for Making the Best Use of Your Phone* (Orem, UT: Paul R. Timm, Inc., 1994); and Terry Wildemann, *1-800 Courtesy, Connecting with a Winning Telephone Image* (Newport, RI: Aegis Publishing, 1999).
15. From Leland and Bailey, *Customer Service for Dummies;* Joel Gruber, "Voice Processing: A Fine Line between Customer-Friendly and Customer-Deadly," *The Service Edge,* March 1992, 7; and Wildemann, *1-800 Courtesy.*
16. Wildemann, *1-800 Courtesy.*
17. Friedman, *Telephone Skills from A to Z.*
18. Kendall Hamilton and Stacy Sullivan, "Netiquette: A Guide to Manners in the New Age," *Newsweek* 130, no. 9 (September, 1 1997): 14.
19. Dana May Casperson, *Power Etiquette: What You Don't Know Can Kill Your Career* (New York: AMACOM, 1999), 109.
20. Dartnell Corporation, *The Telephone Success Express;* Friedman, *Telephone Skills from A to Z;* Hamilton and Sullivan, "Netiquette: A Guide to Manners," 14; and Wildemann, *1-800 Courtesy.*

CHAPTER

10

ELECTRONIC COMMUNICATION

OBJECTIVES

1. Describe best practices for automated response systems.
2. Explain the importance of e-mail communication to customers and businesses.
3. Discuss the legal and societal issues concerning e-mail.
4. Explain e-mail management.
5. Describe best practices for e-mail format, composition, and operations.
6. Describe best practices for e-mail response management systems.
7. Outline best practices for customer-oriented company websites.
8. Explain best practices for outbound and inbound fax communication.

TECHNOLOGY

This chapter discusses automated telephone and other electronic systems used by customers and companies to communicate. According to experts, customer telephone contact will not decline much for companies, although it may not increase much either. E-mail contacts will increase, and letters will continue to decrease. Automated telephone systems need to be planned with customers' convenience and satisfaction in mind. Knowing best practices for e-mail and fax communication will improve relationships with external and internal customers. New technologies related to phone and computer use will continue to provide opportunities for companies to improve productivity and, more important, their customers' experiences. In fact, by the time students read this, given the rapid change, there will be additional changes and technology combinations.

189

AUTOMATED RESPONSE SYSTEMS

You will recognize an *automated response system (ARS)* if we say, "press 1 for . . . " It is used here as a generic term for an automated attendant that routes calls based on digits that callers enter on Touch-Tone phones. Some systems have speech recognition.[1] Automated systems are an advantage to companies and to customers. The Society of Consumer Affairs Professionals (SOCAP) 1998 Customer Contact Study found that 61 percent of toll-free numbers had an automated response system. By 2003, the proportion was probably much higher. In 1998, ARSs allowed companies to increase customer satisfaction, handle more calls, reduce staffing requirements, lower cost per call, and, consequently, allow service representatives more time to handle the more complex calls. The median cost of a live call was $1.00 per minute and an ARS call was $0.25.[2]

Experience Discussion 10.1

1. What do you like about automated telephone systems?
2. What do you not like?
3. For what functions are you willing to use an ARS?
4. For what functions would you prefer to speak to a person?
5. How long are you willing to wait on hold?
6. What do you want to hear while on hold?

From a customer perspective, ARSs can be anywhere from a blessing to exasperating. For many, customers simply press 1, 2, or 3 to reach their goal. For others, customers have a choice of six numbers or more, which are not always consecutive, then another set of numbers, and sometimes more choices after that. Some systems want customers to know an employee's extension number. Sometimes, if no key is punched, the system hangs up, frustrating customers even more. Some customers pretend to be using a rotary phone to avoid the systems. According to one report, 39 percent of Americans could not find the pound (#) key, and customers made a mistake in 1 in 10 transactions when punching in a 10-digit account number. When they did reach a person, 29 percent spent time venting their frustration.[3] The systems can be difficult to use and aggravating and drive even loyal customers away.

A 1998 IVR (Interactive Voice Response, which is a specific type of ARS) Consumer Satisfaction Study conducted by the Center for Client Retention for SOCAP surveyed 6000 consumers who had contacted the consumer affairs departments of SOCAP's membership of *Fortune* 500 companies. The researchers found that 53 percent of the respondents said that the way a company's ARS system works would affect their decision to buy the company's products. What they liked about automated telephone response was that it allowed 24-hour access, was fast and convenient, and connected them to the right person. What they disliked most was that they would rather talk to a live person. They also said that systems had too many options, did not have the options they needed, kept them on hold too long, made it difficult to opt for an operator, were too confusing, and were too impersonal. Table 10.1 shows other findings of the study.[4]

Jeffrey Gitomer figures that "if companies would make the first option, 'press 1 if the computer phone attendant [makes you mad]' and send it to the CEO," automated telephone systems would be "ripped out of the walls" worldwide.[5] Naisbitt, author of *Megatrends,* says telephone automation, which moves customers another step away from service providers, is the opposite of what he had in mind when he

TABLE 10.1 SOCAP 1998 Interactive Voice Response Consumer Satisfaction Study of 6000 *Fortune* 500 Call Center Customers

Usefulness

53% say the way a company's automated system works will affect their decision to buy

80% would rather use IVR than get a busy signal

What Customers Like

29% fast

18% convenient

17% getting them to right person

13% 24-hour access

Pet Peeves

22% would rather talk to a person

16% too many options

13% impersonal

10% keeps you on hold too long

8% doesn't have options you need

7% not easy to opt for an operator

7% too confusing

Options

92% said the option to speak to a live representative was essential

72% said the ability to make a selection at any time was essential

64% said the system should provide an estimated wait time

47% wanted to speak their option

35% wanted to press a button

Talking to a Person

38% would opt for a person almost all the time

33% would opt for a person at least half the time

29% would opt for a person less than half the time

52% who were 65 and older wanted to speak to a person

14% of those under 18 preferred to speak to a person

Hold

21% would stay on hold under a minute

27% would wait 1–2 minutes

38% would wait 2–3 minutes

14% would wait over 3 minutes

94% would prefer anything but advertising, including silence

60% wanted music

Functions

52% would be satisfied to get a programmed answer to a specific question

13% were very willing to purchase a product using ARS

54% would not be very willing to purchase a product

13% were willing to register a complaint

36% were willing to give a compliment

44% were very willing to request a fax

31% would be very willing to leave their name and address

50% would complete a survey after their request had been completed

88% expected not to have to key in an account or Social Security number twice

Return Calls

46% would leave a telephone number for a return call if they heard back the same day

13% expected a call back within 2 hours

17% wanted a call back within an hour

19% were willing to wait until the next day

Source: Society of Consumer Affairs Professionals, "Consumer Acceptance of Automated Telephone Systems Is Mixed: Can Lead to Hang Ups, New Report Finds," [news release online], November 10, 1998, available from http://www.socap.org/Publications/ivrstudy.html, accessed July 3, 2001.

coined the phrase "*high tech, high touch,*" meaning the more advanced the technology, the more we need human interaction.[6]

Companies need to figure out what functions can be effectively automated from their customers' point of view and determine what level of service customers expect. The overriding concern is developing ARSs with customers in mind. If customer loyalty is a concern, too much technology may alienate customers. Goodman says that if a call is picked up within six rings and a service representative is taking care of the call within a minute, there is no negative impact on customer satisfaction. If the system is perceived as a barrier, loyalty can drop 10 to 15 percent immediately.[7]

Automated customer service functions, such as call routing and account inquiries and transactions, have been the most successful implementation of this technology. It is best for routing customers to the appropriate service representative group, providing basic information like account balances and rate quotes, and allowing simple transactions such as funds transfers and payments. ARSs are not suitable or customer-oriented for time-sensitive data or complex technical assistance. If customers need customization or after-sales support, have purchased a big-ticket item, or have a relationship with a specific customer service representative, they should be able to reach a person. Companies have also found that older customers are more wary of and less likely to use automated telephone technology than younger customers.[8]

A SOCAP study conducted by Yankelovich Partners in early 1998 found that less than 1 percent, 0.8 percent, of the 1004 respondents had never called an 800 number. Of the 99.2 percent who had placed calls, 72 percent placed an order and 68 percent asked for specific information. Forty percent called to complain, and 26 percent to compliment. Consumers said they were the most frustrated when they had to wait a long time to speak with a representative (81 percent) and when they were unable to reach a human voice from the automated system (76 percent). About three-quarters said that an unsatisfactory experience with a representative would affect whether or not they continued to buy the company's products. Still, only 13 percent were completely opposed to automated systems.[9]

System Design

John Goodman, of Technical Assistance Research Programs, says that most systems were designed by engineers with no thought of customers. Recently "human factors" specialists are redesigning systems to be more customer-oriented. Those that use human factors experts to design and test their systems with customers have lower *opt-out* rates, meaning that fewer customers hang up.

Before making the decision to use an automated telephone system, companies need to find out if their customers will accept it and what their needs and expectations are. Before beginning to use the system, companies should conduct customer pretests for feedback. In addition, companies should monitor the system to find out the causes of customer frustration.

The system should not be too complicated. Goodman (of TARP) says that customers who are not expecting automated call routing will tolerate three choices, maybe four. If they have to choose from five options, half of the customers hang up or go to the operator. If customers expect an ARS, they are more likely to try the script.

A majority of customers want to talk to a person, so the ARS should be optional and allow the customers to exit the system and reach a service representative at any time. When customers encounter a choice of six numbers to press, then the choice of three more, then three more to reach a person to solve a problem, they do not feel very favorably toward the company. Many customers learned that pressing zero would get them to a person, but now they often hear, "That is not a valid option." Customers should have access to a person early in the message and, thereafter, be reminded what key to use. If customers opt for a person, they should be queued to a service representative at the point they would be if they had been waiting already. Customers should be informed how long the wait will be in case they choose to return to automated service.

The scripting must be customer-driven and clear. The automated attendant should be a friendly, positive voice. Most systems use a female voice. Robotic voices are not acceptable. Experts recommend that the menu descriptions be brief and simple. Menu options should be the same throughout, for example, using the same key for reaching a customer service representative at each level. The options should use the words that customers are familiar with, such as "checking account" rather than the banker's term "demand deposit account." Some companies have been successful with conversational-like scripting.

Experts also suggest that customer input be simple. Asking for a zip code or a Social Security number is acceptable. Anything longer or anything customers must look up is not. Systems should verify information input and make it clear to customers how to correct errors. Remember, one study showed that customers do make errors when keying in 10 numbers. Information that has already been input should be transferred to the service representative rather than asking customers for their account or Social Security number again.

Certain features enhance usage by service representatives and increase customer satisfaction. For example, most systems include a screen pop of the customer account. In addition, systems can provide flexible entry so service representatives can go to any field and enter information in the order customers provide it. Another useful function is access to appropriate response guidelines, for example, if customers ask the reason for a policy. It is also helpful to have automatic fulfillment so that service representatives know and can tell customers their request will be taken care of.

Customer education leads to more customer use, a higher rate of completion of transactions, and higher customer satisfaction. Education before use decreases the opt-out rate from more than 30 percent to about 10 percent. Education can be delivered by printed material prior to use or training during use, such as when a live service representative walks customers through the system. If the ARS is easy to navigate and customers find it does save them time, they begin to accept it, as in the case of automated prescription refill.

Companies should resist the urge to immediately cut staff upon installing the ARS. Reduction of the number of calls to live service representatives does not happen all at once. ARS adoption rates can be slow. If customers get frustrated with the ARS, they will be even more so if they have to wait to reach a person.[10]

A few companies have decided that an ARS and voice mail are not acceptable. One company's competitive advantage is its call center, which does not use an automated response system. The centralized center has all order processing employees, technical repair personnel, and applications engineers in one area with glass partitions. No one is transferred to an unmanned telephone. Customers get a return call within 30 minutes if a representative needs to find out an answer to a question. This company's surveys show that 90 percent of its customers are satisfied.[11]

Experience Discussion 10.2

Call two toll-free numbers with a legitimate question or need. If a number does not go to an ARS, find one that does. Count the first set of options. Count any additional sets of options. Make a note of each option.

1. Were there too many options? Were there too many sets of options?
2. Were the options clear?
3. Was the option you needed available?
4. How did the automated voice sound?
5. Were you put on hold? How long were you on hold?

E-MAIL COMMUNICATION

In recent years, customers have favored contacting companies by telephone due to easy access using toll-free numbers. With the advent of the Internet, that is changing. More and more customers are using e-mail to contact companies. Access to companies through e-mail interaction has become a competitive necessity. Proactive development of customer-focused systems will create positive impressions about companies and their products and promote customer loyalty. The systems and personnel must reflect company strategy and be designed and managed to provide customer-oriented, effective, efficient, and flexible customer experiences.

IMPORTANCE OF E-MAIL COMMUNICATION

E-mail communication is an opportunity for both customers and companies. E-mail is a fast, reasonably easy, and inexpensive way for customers to contact companies. Customers have no time constraints. They can write a message to a company and send it 24/7. They do not have to call a 10-digit number, punch multiple-choice phone buttons, wait with the phone at their ear, and listen to advertising or "your call is very important to us" over and over.

Datamonitor, an industry analyst group, predicted that, by the end of 2003, companies would get 20 percent of all customer contacts through e-mail and web forms. SOCAP member companies were receiving 7 percent of consumer contacts by e-mail in 1998. That increased to 12 percent in 1999. According to Forrester Research, 50 percent of the U.S. population would be using e-mail to communicate by the end of 2001.[12] A 1998 SOCAP study found that 68 percent of member companies surveyed were using e-mail for customer contact. Twelve percent of the companies had surveyed customers, and of those companies, ninety-four percent reported that customers found the e-mail contact acceptable. Thirty-five percent of the companies receiving e-mail required customers to use a web form.

For companies, internal e-mail communication minimizes differences in location and time zones and increases productivity. It provides the capability to keep records of all outgoing and incoming messages. It provides access to people who are often unavailable by telephone and is a very easy method of sending a message to multiple people.[13] An international study of 1400 middle- and senior-level executives, conducted in early 2001, found that the executives were spending an average of 120 minutes a day receiving, checking, preparing, and sending e-mails.[14]

E-MAIL ISSUES

Concerns about e-mail communication include legal and societal issues. Users should follow current law and e-mail provider rules and conduct their communication in an ethical, legal manner.

Confidentiality

Remember that e-mail communication is not private or confidential. Companies and organizations have the right to and do check internal e-mail content. The Electronic Communications Privacy Act ruled that internal e-mails are the property of the organization that pays for the e-mail system. Software programs are available that will search all e-mails for specific suspicious and undesirable key words to detect and prevent harassment and threatening situations. Online harassment, such as sexual innuendoes or intimidation, is illegal. Threatening e-mails should be reported. Specialists can recover deleted e-mails. E-mails can be used as evidence in civil and criminal court cases. For example, e-mails may be searched and retrieved for situations involving promotion, termination, product negligence, price fixing, patent infringement, or discrimination. They have been disclosed in more than one lawsuit and in the news. In fact, there are rumors of companies that specialize in mining e-mails to develop class-action lawsuits.[15]

People should not send anything they would mind seeing during a performance appraisal or in a newspaper headline. Customers or coworkers other than the addressees may also read the e-mails. E-mails are easily copied, printed, or forwarded, perhaps to someone the writer insulted. Be professional and careful about what you write. If the content is confidential, use another method of communication. If you are tempted to fire back a rude reply, think twice before you do so.

Privacy and Security

Privacy of personal information is a significant issue to customers using a company website. This is important for conducting transactions but also relevant for problem or inquiry e-mail transmissions. The best way for companies to gain customers' trust is to use third-party verification of online privacy and security.[16]

Be careful opening messages that may contain a virus. Be alert to current warnings and keep security software up to date. Do not open anything that looks suspicious. Senders should use clear subjects so recipients do not automatically delete messages. An e-mail from unknown@company.com with an unclear subject may be deleted even if it's legitimate.

Legal Document

The use of an e-mail transmission as a legal document is being studied. Two major points to consider are the authentication of the party sending the e-mail and verification that the document came from and was written by that party. One possibility is to treat e-mail like federal mail. Then, tampering with it would be illegal, and e-mails could be used as legal documents.[17]

Appropriate Use

One undesirable outcome arising from our increasing use of e-mail and voice mail is that we talk less with colleagues face-to-face. In fact, business is often conducted by people who have never met in person. E-mail can be overused to substitute for a face-to-face conversation or a telephone call. It is not as secure, private, and confidential as people think or might want. Some people hide behind the technology to avoid speaking to people. When we consider that with e-mail we have lost all nonverbal communication, it is much harder to make the meaning of the message clear. An e-mail consists of words only, and that can lead to misunderstandings. In the international survey mentioned previously, the executives believed that e-mail had improved the effectiveness of routine organizational communication, but more than two-thirds of the executives said that important and bad news should be delivered face-to-face.[18]

One physician, whose patients are senior business executives, believes that "human moments" are fast disappearing, causing anxiety, isolation, and confusion at work. What the physician calls "toxic worry," which is worry that has no basis in reality, happens due to the lack of cues that reduce it. An e-mail may be abrupt, so that the recipient is offended or intimidated; or the e-mail is ambiguous, and thus the receiver misunderstands. Nonverbal language is limited in voice mail, and body language and voice cues are totally absent in e-mails. Little misunderstandings increase. An abrupt e-mail message is misconstrued—what did I do? You are not included on a distribution list—was it an accident? Usually only a face-to-face conversation can resolve the questions.

We recommend that e-mail not be used when face-to-face would be better. There are many topics better discussed on a personal basis since so much of the message meaning is missing, even more than with the telephone. One company has a policy that no one should send an e-mail to someone within walking distance from the person's office.[19] We should talk person to person or use the telephone when privacy is a concern, when negotiations require a give-and-take, when we need the nonverbal input or voice cues, when we need an immediate answer, and when the information is complex.[20]

Spam

Spamming, sending unsolicited advertisements by e-mail, is unlawful in some states and under consideration for banning by federal legislation. Many Internet service providers will deny access to companies that send spam. The delivery of e-mail advertisements is acceptable if customers have requested them, so the best procedure is to adopt an opt-in policy, meaning that if customers want the ads, they can sign up for them on the company's web site. Every e-mail advertisement a company sends, even to those who have requested it, should include easy-to-use opt-out instructions.

Junk

Do not send jokes or other "junk" to people who may not want it. We should not indiscriminately send what we perceive as humorous content from the Internet or e-mail to a laundry-list distribution list. Too much of it wastes time and some of it may be objectionable. A case in point occurred in an online college course in which the instructor and the students received an e-mail from one of the other students enrolled in the course. The e-mail was an illustrated list of rather vulgar emoticons. Some of the recipients did not find the content amusing.

Do not send along a chain letter. First, many people open every e-mail, and it is time-consuming to look at non-job-related mail. Second, if a chain letter involves money, it is illegal. Third, you may start getting too much e-mail in return and e-mail that you do not want to read.

Skill Development 10.1

Research an e-mail issue, such as confidentiality, security, privacy, or spam. Report to the class what you have discovered.

E-MAIL MANAGEMENT

Learn your e-mail software so you can be efficient and not make embarrassing errors. You might accidentally send, reply, or forward a message. The software may automatically send a reply back to everyone if it is sent to a distribution list. On some software, you can set an option that always asks if you want to reply to all or just the sender, making mistakes less likely.

Plan e-mail time just like you do telephone time. Do not get in the habit of dropping everything when the beep tells you that you have a new e-mail. That may be somewhat inefficient for getting things done. Turn the alert off and schedule time for checking e-mails. Know the difference between urgent and important. Experts suggest checking once in the morning and once in the afternoon, depending, of course, on the type of job you have and the average volume of your e-mail.

Some jobs require hourly attention to customer and internal e-mail. In these cases, check your e-mail often. People view it just like they view a telephone. They expect you to respond. Since e-mail is instantaneous, a coworker may need an instantaneous answer. There are surveys showing that some companies take days or weeks to answer customer e-mails. Sometimes the companies never answer. Give your company a competitive advantage by replying quickly. We will discuss this more later in the chapter.

You should expect a range of response times from people to whom you send e-mails. As mentioned, some people read their e-mails whenever they hear a beep announcing one, just like when the telephone rings. Some are at the other extreme and read their e-mails only once a week or less. In addition, some people receive dozens of e-mails a day, and so answering them takes awhile. Be patient if you expect a rapid answer; the recipient may not be available. You should let people know in the e-mail when you need a response. Use the telephone if it is urgent. Do not keep sending e-mails. As you use e-mail, you will begin to know who answers quickly and who never answers.

To be efficient, manage your e-mails. In other words, use a system. According to time management principles, when we complete a task, we generate a feeling of accomplishment and satisfaction. Here are some good ideas. Reply immediately to those e-mails that you can. Respond promptly to requests. If it will take longer than a quick message, leave it to take care of later, but, if appropriate, let the person know when that will be. If you cannot help, in some circumstances, you should still respond to a sincere individual request. However, if you do not know anything about the topic in question, it is not necessary to e-mail back, "I don't know anything about that." The e-mailer does not want to read 50 of that type of response. Delete a message if it does not apply to you or you are not interested. Save messages to another folder or hard copy if it is information you will need later. Download messages that need to be saved to a disk or a hard drive to keep disk storage to a minimum. You know that if you do not do this, you will end up with a hundred messages in your inbox. It's also a good plan to save e-mail or hard copies of everything important that you send.

NETIQUETTE

The pioneers of the Internet and electronic communication developed workable guidelines for cyberspace communication. The rules, often called *netiquette*, about acceptable electronic communication conventions and practices are intended to make e-mail a timesaving, productive communication method. Longtime users question why new e-mail users waste everyone's time by sending a reply to an entire distribution list when the reply should have been sent just to the originator, "shouting" by capitalizing all letters, or not using a subject. Jeff Johnson, Computer Professionals for Social Responsibility, reminds us that new users will not automatically know what longtime users have learned.[21] Just as certain practices work better on the telephone and in person, netiquette rules will increase the effectiveness of our e-mail communication.

The following are the rules of the road for individuals. E-mail communication netiquette applies to external customers, both consumer and business, and internal customers.

E-MAIL FORMAT

E-mail Heading

The sections of the heading information are your e-mail address, the subject, the recipient's e-mail address, the date, and the cc (copy to) information.

* *Address.*   If your name it is not obvious from your e-mail address, add it so that it is automatically generated. Companies really should try to make the username easy for customers to use. In the author's experience, having the username "aswartzlande@pstcc.edu," because the system cannot handle more than a 12-letter username, makes life difficult. Not having the "r" at the end has caused many an e-mail to go astray. It would be much better for usernames to be complete names, for example, "anne.swartzlander." In addition, be aware that people will make assumptions about you from your username and domain name. The domain names ".edu," "aol.com," ".org," and "yahoo.com" convey different images. Think carefully about your personal e-mail address if you ever use it for business messages. Addresses such as "*barbiedoll@yahoo.com*" and "*GoBuckeyes@aol.com*" are not appropriate.
* *Subject.*   Always include a clear, short (25- to 30-character limit), pertinent subject on the subject line so the recipient knows what the e-mail is about and how to prioritize it. Keep it short, like a newspaper headline. Start out with "Urgent:" if it is really time-sensitive. Note in the subject if a message is long, over 100 lines, so a receiver can prioritize it. It's best to write about only one subject per e-mail. Nine times out of ten, a question or paragraph at the end of the e-mail about a completely different topic will be missed. In addition, sending separate replies to separate questions will be easier to categorize, save, sort, and find for both customers and computers.
* *Recipient's Address.*   Be sure the e-mail is addressed to the correct person and is typed accurately. Many people maintain distribution lists of groups of people they send messages to. Make sure yours are appropriate and accurate. Eliminate people that really do not need to see the message. Make sure that all the addresses are correct and professional. For example, do not use a title inappropriately: Dr. Mack Williamson, M.D. As noted in Chapter 7, using both "Dr." and "M.D." is incorrect form.
* *Date.*   The e-mail software will automatically generate the date and time.
* *CC.*   Use the cc, copy to, just as you would in a business letter. Use bcc, or blind copy, to keep everyone's e-mail address private and prevent the unscrupulous from collecting addresses and selling them to companies that send junk e-mail.

E-mail Message

The message section should include a salutation, the body of the message, a closing, and, optionally, a signature line.

* *Salutation.* It is best to use a salutation or greeting at the beginning just as you would in a business letter. It's more professional and at the same time more personal. One good way is to use the person's name, either a title with a last name or just a first name, depending on the situation, and then a comma or dash. Examples are "Mary," or "Ms. White—". Since e-mail is somewhat more informal, "Dear Ms. White:" (including the colon) is more appropriate for a regular business letter on letterhead, but still it's not entirely improper for e-mail.
* *Body.* This is the message. Composition is covered in the next section.
* *Closing.* Use a closing, at the very least, your name. "Thank you" is appropriate in many circumstances. Many letters from companies use real names. Another alternative is [company] Customer Relations.
* *Signature Line.* Include *signature lines* when communicating with people who may need the information—your position or job title, department and company or organization, mailing address, and phone and fax numbers. You may need to include your e-mail address since some software deletes the heading information. Netiquette experts recommend a maximum of no more than four to five lines for your signature lines. Most e-mail software allows you to automate this. If an inspirational quote is appropriate, keep it short and change it frequently.

E-MAIL COMPOSITION

Style

Many people are treating e-mail as a very informal type of communication. It is often filled with typos, poor grammar, vagueness, and discourtesy. The sheer volume of e-mail seems to engender quick, sometimes sloppy, responses. In her netiquette rules, Virginia Shea claims that people will judge us based on our written e-mail communication just as they do by our other communication skills. We cannot tell much about people and vice versa from e-mail compared with the way we can in person and even on the telephone. Therefore, people *will* make assumptions about us.

While some believe that instantaneous electronic communication is supposed to be a timesaver and, therefore, should be less regimented, we believe that e-mail should reflect our professionalism. A careless e-mail may give the impression that we are inexperienced, too stubborn to learn, incompetent, uneducated, or indifferent. In fact, proper writing is even more critical because an e-mail must be concise yet clear. Many e-mail users are well educated. Use good grammar. Grammar mistakes are not as noticeable on the telephone, but they will be in writing. This does not mean that we must be as formal as in a business letter. It does not mean that we have to spend an hour on each message so it's perfect. We don't have time to do that, and most of us are not perfect writers. Nor does it mean that an easy, friendly style is inappropriate. One trainer has called it "business casual." It depends partly on who the recipient is. It does mean that certain conventions should be honored, particularly with customers. One study found that more than half of company e-mail responses were as formal as written correspondence. The rest were less formal, but still conservative in their responses.[22]

When you are considering the formality and correctness of your e-mails, ask yourself (1) if the recipient is likely to care about your competence and (2) what the e-mail's objective is. If you are trying to win and keep customers, style matters more than if you are corresponding with a business friend.

Layout

A message on a computer screen is harder to read than on paper. The resolution is not as good, sometimes there's a flicker, and sometimes the font is hard to read. Therefore, good e-mail page layout is different from paper layout. Write complete sentences but keep them short. Experts recommend no more than 15 to 20 words per sentence and no more than four lines of type without a paragraph break. Use a single space between lines and a double space between paragraphs. Use paragraph headings if there are different parts to the message. Doing all this makes your message clearer and much easier to read.

Screen sizes, width and height, are different. Limit line length to 80 characters or even less. Newspaper columns are only a couple of inches wide because it's easier for the reader.

Word wrapping can also be a problem. Otherwise,
the lines may break
in odd places, and it
can become very annoying
to try
to read the message.

There are numerous software packages for e-mail. The message you send may not look the same when displayed on the recipient's screen. If your software allows you to use bold and italics, be aware that your recipient's software may not have the same capability. A message like this:

Hello! **Thank you** for letting me know about. . .
may look like this on the other person's screen:
<B><I>Hello!<I><Thank you<B> for letting me know about. . .

Do not put several spaces between words, use the tab key, or use a bullet and expect the message to look right when the person receives it. These methods do not work on dissimilar software. For example, Figure 10.1 shows what tabs might look like.

FIGURE 10.1   Incorrect Format

Subject: Tabbed E-mail
Date: 2-15-02
To: Readers
From: CS Communications

Percent	Length of Time
25%	1 day
29%	2 days
34%	never
12%	no e-mail address

Content

Because e-mail is read quickly, deliver your message in the first sentence or two. Do not make customers hunt through paragraphs of text to understand your e-mail. Most e-mail users use it extensively in business, and so they are used to a just-the-facts style. They want a direct yet friendly answer. Try to keep e-mails to one page, which is 25 lines of text.

Keep the message short and to the point while being careful not to be abrupt and rude. Do not forget that a person will read the e-mail you send. E-mail is a very useful, quick way to contact someone or respond. However, do not let speed drive content, firing off replies without thinking. Read e-mails actively, as if you were listening. Also, do not be guilty of dispatching a message with no thought for courtesy. What may sound fine as you type it may come across as blunt and surly on the other end (see Figure 10.2). Pay attention to the tone of your e-mails. If you are requesting information, be sure to say thank you in advance.

FIGURE 10.2   Abrupt E-mail Message

> Subject: Forms
> Date: 1 May 2002
> To: Employee
> From: Payroll
>
> Use an ink pen to sign leave forms, not a pencil!

Think twice—or even better, three times—before sending an irate response. Cool off for a day before pressing send. If you need to confront someone, do it in person. Sometimes people are rude in e-mails because they can be. They do not have to answer face-to-face. One expert's analogy is "just as in the anonymity of an automobile, where people can behave like crazed maniacs, so too on a keyboard courteous people can become rude and abrupt."[23] E-mail and voice mail are very efficient and save an enormous amount of time, but perhaps Naisbitt was right in *Megatrends* when he predicted that high tech would require high touch, the need for more personal relationships.

Skill Development 10.2

Bring an example of a rude, ambiguous, or otherwise unprofessional business e-mail (with identifying names removed) to class for discussion.

1. What is unprofessional about the e-mail?
2. Why do you think it is inappropriate?
3. How would you rewrite or change it?

An e-mail has no nonverbal communication, and so the meaning is delivered 100 percent by the words. We are not used to communicating this way. Avoid ambiguous words subject to personal interpretation. Be explicit when agreeing or disagreeing so there is no confusion—say, "I agree," "Yes," or "I did not quite understand." It helps to use active, sensory words, for example, "I see what you mean," "I get the picture," "I hear what you're saying," "That sounds good to me," and "I have a feeling. . ." Reread to make sure you are not being wordy and repetitious.

Be careful when using humor, sarcasm, irony, and double meanings. With no face-to-face communication and nonverbal language, your comment might be perceived as criticism or might be misunderstood. The recipient will not be able to tell if you are serious or kidding. You may be "*flamed*" by a return e-mail, which means you are the recipient of antagonistic criticism. If you are flamed, the best thing to do is ignore it.

In a professional situation, it is best not to use *emoticons,* such as :-) to express humor. Many customers will not understand the symbol or appreciate the effort to interpret it. You would not want to receive an e-mail with <:-) because this might mean you asked this person a dumb question. It is also best not to use acronyms, such as IMHO (in my humble opinion) or LOL (laughing out loud), to excess, certainly not with customers. Use creative wording to convey your meaning and style.

Grammar

Capitalizing the entire e-mail and even whole words is considered SHOUTING. Not only are capital letters considered rude, but all capitals are also more difficult to read. Asterisks surrounding a *word* can be used for light emphasis. You can use all caps for a couple of words if you REALLY need to emphasize something.

On the other hand, not capitalizing the first word of sentences and proper nouns is confusing—for example, "i can assure you that i will take care of it on mon may 15." We could call a message with no capital letters, "whispering." It is just as irritating as shouting. There may be times when you want to whisper or lower your voice to indicate that your comment is an aside or private. If you are in the habit of using no capitals or putting two parentheses around a ((word)) to show that, make sure the recipient is familiar with what you are doing. The lack of punctuation is even more confusing. However, extra punctuation like "Wow!!" or extra letters, as in "Soooo," can be used to create more expressive language.

Most of the world uses MM DD YY for listing dates. To avoid misinterpretation, spell out the month as in "Jan 2 03" or "2 Jan 03," rather than "010203." Computer people use yy mm dd, 030102, which could tend to confuse.

Spell-check. Proofread to eliminate typos, misspellings, and grammatical errors. Reread the message before you send it. Make sure that it's understandable. It is very easy to leave out a word, such as "not," which changes the meaning of a sentence completely. The use of "resent," instead of re-sent, meaning "to send again," looks like resent, meaning, "to feel annoyed by." You will make whatever typing mistakes you normally make, such as "you" for "your" or vice versa or "the" instead of "to," so proofread line by line to check for clarity.

URLs

Web addresses, *URLs,* are recognized by either http:// or www. It's best to use the http:// if you want to make the address "live." Be careful about putting a period at the end of a URL if it's the end of the sentence. The software will recognize the period as part of the address. Skip a space as below:

The college's website is ***http://www.pstcc.edu***

You can also put the URL on the next line without the period. This also makes it easier to cut and paste.

The college's website is

http://www.pstcc.edu

If you want to make a long URL clickable and it ends up on two lines, the software will probably not read the second line. Using angle brackets will solve this problem most of the time:

<http://www.pstcc.edu/webct/public/mkt2420_anne_swartzlander_spring03/ welcomepage>

E-MAIL OPERATIONS

Attachments

If you are in the habit of composing messages with word processing software, do not send a short word-processed message as an *attachment*. Cut and paste it to the e-mail rather than attaching it. It takes extra time for recipients to open attachments; the recipients would rather just read the message.

Check the address, subject, and attachments, if any, before hitting send. We now use e-mail so quickly that mistakes are easy to make. You've seen them—"Oops, I forgot to attach the attachment." Make sure you know the exact procedure to send attachments. If you are not sure, do not waste the receiver's time. It's easy to send a test message to yourself or use "preview." One way to keep yourself from sending a message prematurely is to put the address in last. That way, if you hit the send key too quickly, the e-mail will go nowhere.

Think twice, or several times, about broadcasting a message to a distribution list with graphics or a long document attachment. A good rule of thumb is not to send a file larger than 50 kilobytes. Otherwise, it takes too long to load and clogs up networks. Send long messages only to those people who expect it. You can also put a large document on the web and e-mail the URL instead of the file.

Reply

To respond to an e-mail, use "*reply*" so the original message is quoted and the person knows to what topic you are replying. We once received a message from a colleague that said, "OK." The original message had been sent several days previously, and so by the time we got the message, we had no idea what "OK" meant.

When you use reply, the best place for your message is at the top so the recipient does not have to scroll down to find your message. To save time for everyone in a reply, edit the original message to only what is necessary to provide context. If the message is bounced back and forth several times, it gets longer and longer.

Be careful to whom the reply goes. Set your e-mail software to ask before you send it to everyone who received it initially rather than just the sender. Unnecessary e-mails add to the glut of e-mail everyone receives. There is also a chance your reply could be embarrassing or, worse, detrimental to your reputation and job. If you want to forward an e-mail to someone else, respect the sender's privacy and ask permission first.[24]

Skill Development 10.3

Write a legitimate e-mail message of complaint, compliment, or inquiry to a company with which you do business. When you receive a response, print a copy of both e-mails (yours and the response) and turn them in with the answers to the questions below.

1. How many minutes, hours, or days did it take to receive a response? Was the length of time acceptable?
2. Was the response appropriate in terms of content?
3. Did the response follow netiquette guidelines?

E-MAIL RESPONSE MANAGEMENT SYSTEMS

The number of customers who use e-mail has been growing at an exponential rate. At this writing, few companies have been prepared to handle this communication. In December 2001, Jupiter Media Metrix conducted a study of 250 online and off-line retail companies, including the consumer packaged-goods, music, automobile, and travel industries. Jupiter found that 30 percent replied to consumers within 6 hours, 18 percent in 6 to 24 hours, 18 percent in 1 to 3 days, and 33 percent in more than 3 days or never. In November 2001, Jupiter surveyed 2000 consumers nationwide and found that e-mail response times were an important factor in future purchase decisions.[25] In May 2001, Jupiter reported that only 41 percent of business-to-business companies responded to e-mails within 6 hours, and only half of those provided an acceptable response. In addition, 29 percent never responded.[26] A 1999 SOCAP member benchmark survey found that the standard for e-mail turnaround time was 24 hours for 51 percent and 48 hours for 20 percent of the companies.[27]

Companies need to develop *e-mail response management systems* with procedures and standards for handling e-mail messages from customers. Automation provides efficiency and cost-effectiveness. One of the first objectives should be to integrate and link the company databases so that a customer's account and complete telephone call and e-mail history are easily accessible by the employees.

So that responses are fast, courteous, and helpful, contact centers should designate specific staff members to be responsible for customer e-mail. The staff should be hired with the same rigor as the telephone representatives. They should be customer-oriented, genuinely care about customers, have strong reading and writing communication skills, and have thorough product knowledge. Along with designating e-mail specialists, companies should train all personnel in basic e-mail communication.

Conventional wisdom says we do not write as much these days as we used to. E-mail has changed that. If the writing in e-mails and on websites is poor, customers may assume products are poor as well. Exceptional written communication in e-mails and on a website can now be a competitive advantage. The words need to clearly answer customers' questions, provide information, and solve problems. If representatives need to ask the customer questions in order to respond, they should be asked all at one time or e-mail tag will begin. Tell customers that if the response does not answer their question, they should e-mail back. Include the toll-free number so they can call instead. A company's credibility is at stake.

E-mail from customers is a critical link to their feedback, questions, and problems. If companies have a policy to answer telephone calls within three rings, what is the standard for answering e-mails? Customers expect quick turnaround, at least within 24 hours, the information they are seeking, and easily understood responses. Companies need to let customers know what the expected turnaround time is. Customers can choose whether a telephone call would be better. They will use the telephone in critical situations. They will use e-mail for important but not urgent situations. If a backlog of messages occurs, companies can use *auto-acknowledgment,* letting customers know that they received the e-mail and that they will respond within an explicit time frame—as long as they do so. Customers will be very dissatisfied if all they ever receive is the acknowledgment, which happens all too often.

New technology improves productivity. *Auto-suggest* provides standard phrases, templates, and attachments to cut and paste. *Auto-reply,* which can provide boilerplate for customers with similar questions, automatically sends a reply back to a customer. When auto-reply is used, e-mails should be checked before they are sent so that responses are accurate, relevant, and personalized. Someone still needs to read e-mails, or a catalog may be sent to a customer whose message actually said, "I hate your catalog."[28]

Another technological answer is *queuing and routing software.* To prioritize messages and increase response speed, messages can be sorted, routed, and queued into categories. The routing categories can be based on the topic, the urgency, and the best company representative to answer the e-mail. There are five recommended content and priority categories. The first one is suggestions or compliments that deserve thank-you e-mails. The second category is standard questions that need a response within 24 hours. The use of boilerplate is often possible. Third are issues involving an answer outside the norm that must be analyzed by a specialist, such as a technical question. Fourth are e-mails designated as critical because they could escalate, which require rapid resolution, highly skilled customer service representatives, and possibly higher management. An example is a customer complaint to an automobile manufacturer about her car, which she is convinced is a lemon. The final category is red alerts, which are worst-scenario crises and need higher management and the legal department involved. Perhaps a customer is threatening to sue due to a product safety problem.

Using the categories and content codes, companies can track and analyze messages so they can identify patterns and trends just as they do with telephone calls. They can update their knowledge base and FAQs (frequently asked questions) on the website based on frequent customer questions. E-mail response should also be tracked to measure volume, response time, and user metrics to determine service quality and productivity.[29]

COMPANY WEBSITES

Customers have started to use company websites before calling or e-mailing. The biggest difference between contact through websites and toll free numbers is that the website is used more as an information source. This does not necessarily mean call volumes will decrease, because the web users may well represent a different segment of a company's market.

According to Forrester Research, a telephone conversation between a customer and a service representative averaged about $33 per transaction. E-mails averaged about $10. Live e-mail chat was $7.80, and self-help via a website averaged $1.17. Doculabs reported that out of 3.7 million customer service requests on company website self-service in the first quarter of 2001, 87 percent were handled without escalation. Self-service websites with searchable knowledge bases of FAQs and automated e-mail replies not only speed customer assistance but also save money.[30]

The following are some suggestions for improving online customer service.

1. Make your company easy to find online in order for customers both to find the information they need and to contact your company. Companies should put the web address in all its marketing vehicles.

2. Have a Contact Us section on the website with a menu of all communication options—e-mail, fax, telephone, address, and location. Put the exact address for e-mail next to the toll-free number on product, package, and information materials so it is easy to find.

3. Use a structured e-mail web form rather than free-form e-mail to increase efficiency. Make sure the form is easy to use and asks for necessary, but not any more than necessary, information. If there are too many required fields or customers are concerned about privacy, they will abandon or avoid it. Another advantage of using e-mail web forms is that companies can capture customers' names, which is not always possible with typical consumer e-mail addresses, like *joey@icx.net*. Allow customers to opt in and opt out of e-mail and any other advertising. If the company requires an e-mail address, do not automatically begin sending e-mail advertising.

4. Provide a telephone number for customers, and be sure to staff the phones with representatives that know the website. Customers, who are unfamiliar with the Internet or your specific website and cannot find what they want, become frustrated and want to speak with a person. Many customers leave their shopping cart because they need an answer to a question. Perhaps a product description is unclear or incomplete, or perhaps they got lost trying to find what they needed on your website. Your website should not be a barrier for those needing the human touch. If it is, customers will think the company does not care about its customers.

5. Keep your site navigation simple and clear. Use consistent design and color. Customers use the web for speed and convenience. Provide a way for customers to know where they are. Offer a broad selection of options to click on. Use clear names; cleverness is cool, but do not make users have to figure out what the choices mean. Give text descriptions of what a link has to offer.

6. Give your customers a reason to visit your site. Web marketing experts say that a "brand" is created by the quality of experience customers have. Offer more than dry, static information. Give added value in the form of relevant links, free newsletters, articles, and discussions.

7. Use FAQs and searchable knowledge bases for informational brochures, owners' manuals, and troubleshooting guides for customers who prefer self-service. If customers need help using your site, offer to walk them through it so they can use it easily next time.

8. Test your system over and over if necessary. Developers of websites are too familiar with the site and tools, and so they do not look at them as customers would. Use people who are not likely to be very good at it, not tech-

nical people. Have service representatives ask customers about the usefulness of the site. Use website surveys to ask.

9. Monitor newsgroups, bulletin boards, and other places that customers frequent for comments about products and the company. Problems and criticism can be addressed proactively on a website to reduce e-mail volume and resolve problems.[31]

Instant Messaging

One technology that is useful on company websites is instant messaging (IM), also called live text chat, between customers and service representatives. E-retailers have discovered that answering questions via chat is less expensive than answering by e-mail and telephone. Customers with only one phone line are able to stay online to shop. Representatives can also help customers navigate by cobrowsing during a chat. There is skepticism about instant messaging's future. Customer service agents can juggle multiple conversations at the same time, but the quality of responses is an unknown. It does offer customers an alternative. Businesses need to determine their expectations and satisfaction with live chat.[32]

FAX COMMUNICATION

Fax communication is common internally and in business-to-business situations. The following are guidelines for fax communication.

* For the cover sheet, use letterhead with the company address, telephone number, fax number, e-mail address, and any other vital information. The cover sheet should also have the recipient's name, the recipient's fax number, and the number of pages, including the cover sheet. In addition, note if the fax is urgent. Handwritten notes should be in black ink. Blue ink does not always transmit.
* Be sure the copy is neat and clean. You should not send anything you would not mail.
* Use larger margins than usual.
* Make sure the type is large enough to read easily. Use a readable font, 12- to 16-point size. A computer graphics company study, reported in *Communication Briefings,* found Palatino, New Century Schoolbook, Courier, Helvetica, and Bookman were the easiest fonts to read. Times Roman and Avant-Garde were the most difficult.[33] If the original is small typeface or illustration, enlarge it before faxing. Faxing a copy of a fax will often make it unreadable.
* Calling ahead about a fax remittal depends on the recipient's needs and company office practices. If faxes are routinely delivered, it may not be necessary. If the recipient is waiting for the fax, then call before sending it.
* Do not send faxes that are more than five pages. They can tie up a machine. It is better to mail the material or send it by e-mail attachment unless the fax is urgently needed.

* If the document is for information purposes that will become part of a permanent record or one that requires signatures, follow up with a mailed hard copy. Fax printing will not last over time.
* Avoid sending anything personal. Fax machines are often shared, and so someone else could read it. Because a fax is somewhat like a private communication, a fax addressed to someone else should not be read.
* It is not a good idea to send unsolicited advertising.[34]

TERMS

automated response system (ARS)	URLs
high tech, high touch	attachment
opt-out	reply
spamming	e-mail response management system
netiquette	auto-acknowledgment
signature lines	auto-suggest
flamed	auto-reply
emoticons	queuing and routing software

DISCUSSION QUESTIONS

1. What are the advantages and disadvantages of automated response systems for customers and companies?
2. Outline best practices for automated response systems.
3. Why do you think an increasing number of customers are using e-mail to contact companies?
4. Explain the societal and legal issues concerning e-mail communication.
5. Describe how to manage e-mail.
6. Describe best practices for e-mail format.
7. Discuss the requirements for professional e-mail composition.
8. Explain best practices for e-mail response management systems.
9. Locate a company website and evaluate it according to the website guidelines.
10. Outline best practices for fax communication.

CASE—TAXING OBFUSCATION

This is a case about a customer who had downloaded an income tax software program from the company's website. Her goal was to finish and file her tax return as quickly as possible. She was seeking a fast, simple product. The download had taken about 2 hours. Everything worked fine until the customer tried to electronically file the income tax return. She had been provided with an ECN, a number from the IRS, so that she could file electronically. It didn't work. She e-mailed technical support; copies of the e-mails are below. The customer eventually printed and mailed her income tax return to the IRS.

Subject: Electronic Filing of Income Tax Return
Date: 20 Mar 2001 13:45
To: [Company]
From: Customer

I downloaded your program a couple of days ago.

When I tried to electronically file (I have an ECN number), the tax return could not be submitted. This was the message: error occurred when converting to IRS/State format.

Please help. Thanks.

Subject: Re: Electronic Filing of Income Tax Return
Date: 20 Mar 2001 15:30
To: Customer
From: [Company]

Is this a macintosh version for [software] or is it the windows version???
If it's mac and if you are trying to send the state of california independantly and getting this error the you will have to send the return with the federal return (joint return).
If you have not previously filed the federal return electronically with [company], please be aware that there is a 9.95 charge for the federal and a 9.95 charge for the state. If you don't want to be charged for the federal portion you may want to send the state of CA on paper instead.

thank you
Support

Subject: Re: Re: Electronic Filing of Income Tax Return
Date: 20 Mar 2001 15:50
To: [Company]
From: Customer

It is a Windows version.

I live in Tennessee and we do not have a state income tax.

Subject: Electronic Filing of Income Tax Return
Date: 21 Mar 2001 9:30
To: Customer
From: [Company]

was there more to the error message than what was in the email you sent.

If there was try and get the program to recreate the error message again and then copy the whole thing down and forward it to us. It might contain vital clues as to how, why, when and where the error is generating from within the program.

Subject: RE: Electronic Filing of Income Tax Return
Date: 21 Mar 2001 10:15
To: [Company]
From: Customer

No, before the error message, the Transmitting Tax Return box says it was completed. Then I get a box entitled [company] Filing Edition that says, as I included in my first message, "Your return was not submitted because an error occurred when converting to IRS/State format."

Subject: Electronic Filing of Income Tax Return
Date: 21 Mar 2001 14:30
To: Customer
From: [Company]

Have you tried resending since this error occurred??
If you have and got the same error, make sure you got all the updates before transmitting. If this error still occurs, uninstall and reinstall [software]. (you should make sure to back up the actual return on a disk, although the program will not uninstall the return portion, it is a safety precaution.)

Subject: RE: Electronic Filing of Income Tax Return
Date: 21 Mar 2001 14:45
To: [Company]
From: Customer

Yes, I have tried to re-send it several times.

I just bought [software] on Wednesday, March 19, and tried to efile on Thursday. Are you telling me there have been updates in one day?

It takes forever to install. I bought [software] so I could efile to save me time, and it's not saving me time. I'm not getting much help here, and I am starting to regret buying [software].

Subject: Electronic Filing of Income Tax Return
Date: 22 Mar 2001 10:30
To: Customer
From: [Company]

Your program may ahve been sitting on a shelf for several weeks or months before you purchased it. So yes, you should get the updates. We don't write the program, we only file the returns to the IRS. this problem may be caused by an update you need in the preparation portion. With out it you may never get this electronically filed.

Subject: RE: Electronic Filing of Income Tax Return
Date: 22 Mar 2001 11:00
To: [Company]
From: Customer

If you will pay attention and go back to my first e-mail, I downloaded it!

Subject: Electronic Filing of Income Tax Return
Date: 22 Mar 2001 12:30
To: Customer
From: [Company]

Contact [software company], you could have gotten a corrupt down load. They may need to send it to you on disk.

We are only the electronic filer to the irs, and we do not handle software issues.

At this point, the customer gave up and mailed her tax return. She e-mailed the software company to get a refund. It took until July to get a refund. The company promised to send the appropriate paperwork but never did. She eventually called an 800 number. The company required her to fill out a form saying that she had destroyed the software, and then she had to fax the form. Once the form was faxed, it took more than a billing cycle for the refund to show up as a credit on her statement.

1. What did the technical support representative do correctly and incorrectly?
2. How would you characterize this company's e-mail response management system?
3. What could the customer have done to improve the situation?
4. How do you suggest the company improve its response?

NOTES

1. Society of Consumer Affairs Professionals. Customer Care Glossary, available from http://www.socap.org, accessed March 16, 2002.
2. Cynthia J. Grimm, "Customer Contact: More Is Better," *Customer Relationship Management,* June 1998, 9–11; and Cynthia J. Grimm and Dianne S. Ward, "Competitive Edge or Over the Edge? Best Practices for Automated Response Systems," *Customer Relationship Management,* September 1997, 5–7.

3. Mark Albright, "Dial One for Trouble," *Knoxville News-Sentinel,* August 1999, C1.

4. Society of Consumer Affairs Professionals, "Consumer Acceptance of Automated Telephone Systems Is Mixed: Can Lead to Hang Ups, New Report Finds," [news release online], available at http://www.socap.org/Publications/ivrstudy.html, accessed July 3, 2001.

5. Jeffrey Gitomer, "Add a Human Touch to Your Web Site and Phone Setup," *Sacramento Business Journal* 18, no. 9 (May 11, 2001): 22.

6. Albright, "Dial One for Trouble."

7. Kevin Heubusch, "Welcome to the Machine," *Marketing Tools,* January/February 1998, available from http://www.demographics.com/publications, accessed May 27, 2001.

8. Grimm and Ward, "Competitive Edge or Over the Edge?"

9. Society of Consumer Affairs Professionals, "New Survey Finds Consumers Have High Expectations When Calling a Company 800 Number," [news release online], available from www.socap.org/Publications/tollfree.html, accessed July 3, 2001.

10. Summarized from Grimm and Ward, "Competitive Edge or Over the Edge?"; Heubusch, "Welcome to the Machine"; Joel Gruber, "Voice Processing: A Fine Line between Customer-Friendly and Customer-Deadly," *The Service Edge,* March 1992, 7; and Aimee Blanchard, "Using Technology to Target Personalized Service," *Customer Relationship Management,* September 1999, 43–45.

11. Larry Maloney, "No Voice Mail Allowed," *Design News* 53, no. 23 (December 7, 1998): 71.

12. Carol Drzewianowski, "Instant Gratification via E-mail Management," Column, March 1, 2001, available from http://www.tmcnet.com/tmcnet/column/carol1030101.htm, accessed March 16, 2002.

13. Grimm, "Customer Contact: More Is Better."

14. Rogen International, "First International Study on Impact of E-mail, E-mail—Tool or Torment?" [news release online], available from http://www.rogenint.com/study.htm, accessed June 23, 2001.

15. June Langhoff, "Telecommuting and the Law," *Customer Relationship Management,* September 1997, 30–31.

16. crm-forum, "Promises Don't Earn Consumers' Trust," June 25, 2001, available from http://www.crm-forum.com, accessed July 3, 2001.

17. Jim Sterne, *Customer Service on the Internet,* 2d ed. (New York: John Wiley & Sons, 2000).

18. Rogen International, "First International Study."

19. Gary Stern, "Tact, Details in E-Mail Build Virtual Trust," *Investor's Business Daily,* October 31, 2000, A1.

20. Dianna Booher, "Practical Tips for Effective E-Writing," *Customer Relationship Management,* December 2001, 34–36.

21. Jeff Johnson, "Netiquette Training: Whose Responsibility?" *CPSR Newsletter* 16, no. 3 (Summer 1998): 14–18, available from http://www.cpsr.org/publications/newsletters/issues/1998/netiquette.html, accessed September 25, 2000.

22. Dennis C. Morgan, "Benchmarking Cyberservice, Initial Findings and Implications for Continued Research," *Customer Relationship Management,* September 1997, 8–11.

23. Edward M. Hallowell, "The Human Moment at Work," *Harvard Business Review* 77, no. 1 (January–February 1999): 58.

24. E-mail best practices from Martha Irvine, "E-mail Writerss [sic] Delete De Rules. Trend Favors Sloppiness," *Knoxville News-Sentinel,* n.d.; Terry Wildemann, *1–800 Courtesy, Connecting with a Winning Telephone Image* (Newport, RI: Aegis Publishing, 1999); Arlene Rinaldi, "The Net: User Guidelines and Netiquette," available from http://www.fau.edu/rinaldi/net/user.html, accessed March 20, 1997; Kaitlin Duck Sherwood, "A Beginner's Guide to Effective Email," rev 2.0, available from http://webfoot.com/advice/email.top.html, accessed July 27, 2001; Sterne, *Customer Service on the Internet;* and "Netiquette," available from http://www.albion.com/netiquette/book/0963702513.html, accessed on July 27, 2001.

25. Steve Jarvis, "Yes, I Would Like Some Help, Thank You," *Marketing News,* February 18, 2002, 3.

26. "Customer Service Found Deficient," *eWeek*, May 28, 2001, 51.

27. Society of Consumer Affairs Professionals, "SOCAP 1999 Member E-mail/Internet Benchmark Survey Results," available from http://www.socap.org, accessed March 16, 2002.

28. Debbie Baer, "How to Manage E-mail Effectively," *Customer Relationship Management,* March 1999, 18–19.

29. Baer, "How to Manage E-mail Effectively," 18–19; Christine Timmins and Lisa Mild, "The Avalanche of E-Mail: How to Manage and 'Mine' Customer E-Mails," *Customer Relationship Management,* September 1999, 37–39; Karen Leland and Keith Bailey, *Customer Service for Dummies,* 2d ed. (New York: IDG Books Worldwide, 1999); and Sterne, *Customer Service on the Internet.*

30. Greg Gianforte, "Web-Based Self Service: The ROI 'Sweet Spot' for Customer Care," *Customer Relationship Management,* September 2001, 8–9.

31. Baer, "How to Manage E-Mail Effectively"; and Leland and Bailey, *Customer Service for Dummies.*

32. Charles Waltner, "Live Internet Service Set to Capture Customer Attention," available from http://www.InformationWeek.com/815/live.htm, accessed on April 28, 2003; and Stephanie Sanborn, "Instant Messaging Enters Realm of Online Customer Service," *Network World,* January 31, 2000, n.p.

33. Dartnell Corporation, *The Telephone Success Express,* booklet (Chicago: Dartnell Corporation, 1997).

34. Audrey Glassman, *Can I Fax a Thank-You Note?* (Berkeley, CA: Berkeley Books, 1998).

II

PROBLEM SOLVING

OBJECTIVES

1. Describe how right-brain and left-brain dominance affects our thinking style.
2. Explain how our styles affect thinking and problem solving.
3. Describe how our environment affects thinking.
4. Explain the importance of creativity and the factors that block creativity.
5. Discuss how to increase creativity using creativity tools, mind mapping, and brainstorming.
6. Explain consensus decision making.
7. Illustrate conflict resolution strategy.

CUSTOMER SERVICE PROBLEMS

Customer service providers are faced with numerous problems to solve. Customers bring problems when they need information or have a complaint. Knowing how to resolve problems creatively and fairly is essential. The goals of companies and customers are often different and sometimes opposed. Companies need to make a profit to stay in business, and customers want their money's worth when they buy products and services. It appears that one or the other loses. Creative problem solving can be used to reach win-win solutions rather than win-lose answers. Within organizations there are also problems and conflicts. Hundreds of decisions are made concerning customer service strategies, procedures, and policies.

Problem solving is an active resolution to a challenging situation. This chapter will explain aspects of thinking styles and creativity in order to improve the ability to solve problems. We will also discuss consensus decision making and conflict resolution to provide insight when opposing goals are involved.

THINKING

The good news about our brains is that we can sharpen our mental skills. Our brains can grow new brain cells and connections between existing cells throughout life. In addition to a good diet and physical exercise, we can improve our mental capability with social contact and challenging mental activities. Much research has been conducted on the brain and its functions. Keep in mind that, as would be expected, there is controversy among researchers about whether some of the brain theories have been scientifically proved. This section provides an overview of how we think, how our left and right brains function, and how using both sides can improve listening and problem solving. In addition, the section covers individual personality and perceptual styles and productivity.

Hemispheric Dominance

Researchers do know that each half of the brain controls the opposite side of the body's movements and sensations. They also believe that the brain has two different but overlapping ways of thinking. An EEG can be used to measure brain activity to determine which side is dominant in an activity. Study of the brain has found that both hemispheres are skilled in all areas and that the mental skills are distributed throughout the cortex. However, each hemisphere is dominant in certain activities, which is called *hemispheric dominance*. According to Carl Sagan, left-brain skills are more specific to the human mind and right-brain abilities are similar to animal abilities. This could be one reason why our education system stresses left-brain skills.[1]

The two sides have complementary approaches to solving problems. Our left hemisphere solves problems in a verbal, linear way, and our right hemisphere approaches problems in a visually based, configurational way. Some problems are more easily solved by left-hemisphere dominance and some by right-hemisphere dominance. The left hemisphere focuses on verbal communication, and the right hemisphere processes nonverbal communication. However, to interpret communication the two sides must communicate with each other. Researchers believe that men have a strong left-hemisphere specialization for language and that women's verbal and spatial centers are more evenly distributed in both halves.

The left brain is dominant in words, numbers, and lists. *Left-brain dominants* are analytical, verbal, linear, rational, orderly, logical, and goal-oriented. Left-brain dominants process information one piece at a time, sequentially. Our left brains take in new information and compare it with data we have in order to organize the new information into meaningful categories. Left-brain dominants focus on the parts that make up the whole, like taking a clock apart to see why it is not working and being able to put it back together.

The right brain is dominant in rhythm, color, dimension, spatial awareness, imagination, daydreaming, and gestalt (the whole is greater than the sum of its parts). The right brain controls intuition and creativity. *Right-brain dominants* are visual, artistic, emotional, physical, symbolic, relational, and holistic. They process information simultaneously. They emphasize integration and wholeness and are able to visualize how a room will look decorated.

Lateralization is the degree to which tasks are performed in the task-appropriate hemisphere. The highly lateralized, usually the case with men, shift back and forth depending on the skill needed. The less lateralized, usually the case with women, will use both hemispheres at the same time.

We all are capable of using both sides of our brain at the same time and of shifting back and forth, but people often prefer using one side or the other. It depends on the skills needed at any particular time. We learn to develop the skills of the less preferred side. Dominance can change with age, experience, and training. Our education system encourages left-brain thinking. We often become more left-brain oriented as we get older just because we have more responsibilities. Keep in mind that saying one is left- or right-brained can be counterproductive. It may limit the development of new strategies. If we use one side less, we need to develop the mental skills associated with that side.

One test to determine if a person is left- or right-brain-dominant is to see if it is easier for a person to tap rhythmically with the right or left hand while talking. If a person is left-brain-dominant, it's easier with the left hand. Using the right hand, which is controlled by the left side of the brain, is more confusing and difficult.

Skill Development 11.1

Do each one of these exercises and mark right or left on the chart shown in Figure 11.1.

1. Clasp your hands, with your thumb on top. Which thumb is on top? That's your dominant thumb.
2. When you applaud, which hand is on top? That's your dominant hand.
3. Cross your arms with one arm on top of the other. The one on top is your dominant arm.
4. Wink one eye and then the other. Does one eye feel more natural? If so, that's your dominant eye.
5. Hold your thumb at arm's length in front of you and use it to block a small object on a far wall, such as a light switch. Close your right eye. If your thumb is still blocking the object, your left eye was dominant in focusing. If the object moved, then you focused with your right eye.
6. Smile at yourself in a mirror. Which side of your mouth is higher? Look for the side with more wrinkles. The higher side is your dominant one.
7. Sit down and cross your legs. Which leg feels more comfortable on top? That's your dominant leg.
8. If someone rolls a ball to you, which foot would you use to kick it?
9. Draw a dog or horse on a sheet of paper. Which way is it facing? If it's facing right, mark that down. Left-brain people will draw the animal facing to the right.
10. This one will require help from another person. Have a friend ask you a question. Ask the friend to observe whether your eyes move to the right or the left as you think about the answer. Don't stare. Your eyes need to be relaxed to move. If your eyes go up or down first, that's natural. When you visualize an answer, your eyes will go right. If you are feeling an answer, your eyes will go left. If your eyes don't move, ask your friend to observe you when you're not aware of it. Mark down whether your eyes moved left or right.

Foot preference is correlated with brain dominance, but handedness is unreliable. One reason is that there are many people who are really left-handed but were taught to use their right hand. About 54 percent of the population are right-eyed,

FIGURE 11.1   Determining Hemispheric Dominance

	Left	Right
1. Thumbs	———	———
2. Hands	———	———
3. Arms	———	———
4. Wink	———	———
5. Eyes	———	———
6. Smile	———	———
7. Legs	———	———
8. Feet	———	———
9. Drawing	———	———
10. Eye movement	———	———
	Right Brain	Left Brain

If you marked mostly right on the chart, you are mostly right dominant. If you are mostly right dominant, you are left-brained. The opposite applies if you are left dominant. If your preferences are mixed, you are neither right- nor left-brain dominant.

Source: Jacquelyn Wonder and Priscilla Donovan, *Whole Brain Thinking: Working from Both Sides of the Brain to Achieve Peak Job Performance* (New York: William Morrow and Company, 1984); and Charles Thompson, *What a Great Idea! The Key Steps Creative People Take* (New York: HarperPerennial, 1992).

5 percent are left-eyed, and 41 percent are neither strongly left-eyed nor right-eyed.[2] It is said that a hypnotist looks at people's clasped hands to judge their susceptibility to hypnotism. If the left thumb is on top, the person is right-brain-dominant, more suggestible, and more easily hypnotized.

When listening, left dominants focus on words and the message; right dominants notice body language and emotional tone. Rights recognize faces and associate faces with what people wear, what they ate, or whom they were with. Lefts need to repeat a name, spell it, and use it; otherwise, they will forget it. Right dominants prefer visuals, charts, diagrams, and maps. Lefts like analysis and verbal directions. If in need of directions to a location, left brains need specific directions, like three blocks north, one south, and the names of streets; rights prefer visual or emotional cues, a white house with blue shutters and a Wendy's on the corner. Lefts like algebra; rights like geometry. Lefts are time conscious; rights are not.[3]

In studies of occupations, researchers have found that accountants and chemists tended to be left dominants, and athletes, musicians, and painters were more likely to be right dominants. Actually, both sides are responsible for musical skills, with more left-brain involvement as the skill level rises. Lawyers in corporate or contract law were left-brain-dominant, and lawyers in domestic or criminal law were right-brain-dominant. Intuitively, this makes sense.

In teamwork, left dominants do a project by organizing and structuring facts. Rights rarely plan. If they do, it's by visualizing an outcome. Lefts use directions; rights glance at directions and sense from there. Lefts become impatient with meetings; rights enjoy the personal interaction. Leadership is primarily a right-brain function, being able to deal on emotional and cognitive levels, function in ambiguity, and deal with diversity and conflict. Change is a right-brain activity. Right-brain dominants like change. Left-brain dominants prefer order and stability, and so left-brain people have to work harder at change.

Listening

Listening is essential to problem solving. We can also analyze listening according to which hemisphere of our brain dominates. Both analytical and comprehensive listening rely on left-brain thinking. Empathetic listening uses both left-brain and right-brain thinking. Left-brain dominants tend to use less nonverbal response when listening than right-brain people, but they have more energy and concentrate better. Right-brain dominants show more emotional support but are more easily distracted than left-brain people. Right-brain people are better at reading body language and other nonverbal communication. Being aware of an underlying message is mostly a right-brain activity. Curiously, our right ear (left brain) is better for listening to facts and our left ear for hearing an emotional message. It's said that switching from the right ear, analytical listening, on the telephone to the left ear switches us to empathetic listening.

If we are having difficulty listening, using both sides of our brain will help us concentrate and listen better. Take notes or check off items that have been covered. Make an effort to notice nonverbal communication. Picture what the speaker is saying. If preoccupation or daydreaming is a barrier, allow your right brain to take over and concentrate on your preoccupation for a set amount of time. Then switch to your left brain and focus on listening. If the other thoughts creep in, use your left brain to remind yourself that you will think about it later. If we are trying to listen to and remember names and details on the telephone, we need to use our left brain. Again, the way to switch from right to left is to take notes. Write down customers' names. Think left brain before you answer the phone and focus on the customer.[4]

Problem Solving

Having explained left- and right-brain activity, next we will discuss how it helps with problem solving. Sometimes we are concentrating on a problem very hard and we are stuck. Being able to switch to the opposite mode can help. We can use more of our brainpower by consciously choosing the appropriate brain style. Switching increases energy levels and releases creativity. We can learn to switch back and forth and to integrate both sides. We can think about how we think. When we can identify how we are processing, with the right or left brain, we can consciously switch sides, enhance the style we are using, or move between the two sides. This allows us to adapt or change our job for higher performance. It helps us understand the behavior of others and adapt to it.

One researcher's study showed that people could activate left- or right-brain skills simply by looking to the right or left. Looking to the right stimulates our left brain. Test takers did better at verbal memory problems when looking to the right. Another researcher found that blocking out left vision caused subjects to do better on word analogy tests ("daffodil is to flower as hammer is to ____").

Recent research suggests that we process positive emotion on the left side and negative emotions on the right side. It is interesting to note that when we are thinking pleasant thoughts, our eyes will shift right; with sad thoughts, our eyes look left. Sometimes stress and anxiety excite our right brain, overwhelming our left brain. One situation is the "flight or fight" reaction in a difficult customer situation, created by the right brain. Taking notes and writing down key points will force our left brain into activity and calm our right brain. When we talk to ourselves, our right brain listens, so use positive self-talk.[5]

Skill Development 11.2

Trigger the Opposite Side of Your Brain

Using your dominant hand, write down six words that describe you. Take the pencil out of your hand, and to relax your brain, focus your eyes on any stationary object for 1 minute. Using your opposite hand, write down six different words that describe you. Place them anywhere on the sheet of paper. Just do not put one on top of the other. What similarities and differences do you see between the two sets of words?

STYLES AND THINKING

There are differences in the way people with different styles think, learn, and solve problems. Here is a description based on the Myers-Briggs preferences. Extraverts solve problems by trying solutions out; introverts by thinking problems through. Sensors focus on facts and procedures. They are more practical and detail-oriented. Intuitors focus on meanings and possibilities. They are more concept-oriented and imaginative. Thinkers are skeptical and tend to make decisions based on rules and logic. Feelers are supportive and tend to make decisions based on personal and relationship considerations. Judgers seek closure even with incomplete data. Perceivers resist closure to obtain more data.[6]

Going back to the responsiveness/assertiveness styles, analyticals have a Brain Preference Indicator (BPI) of 1–3 (on the left-brain side), drivers 3–5, amiables 5–7, and expressives 7–9 (right-brain side) (see Figure 11.2). When under stress, drivers and expressives get more active, and analyticals and amiables get more passive. Be aware that this tendency creates problems in resolving conflicts. Drivers and expressives may overwhelm customers, and analyticals and amiables may seem disinterested.[7]

Another way we differ in the way we learn and solve problems is our perceptual style. We vary in how we receive information best. Some people are better visually (seeing), other are better kinesthetically (moving), and others are better aurally (listening). Visual ("I see what you mean") is most common, followed by kinesthetic ("I can handle that"), and then by aural ("I hear you"). If we notice what people are wearing, that's visual. If we noticed their handshake and posture, that's kinesthetic. If we remember what they said, that's aural. If employees cannot learn

FIGURE 11.2   Brain Preference Indicator (BPI)

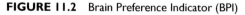
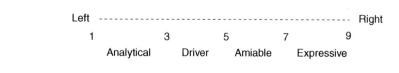

and remember directions, perhaps the information is not delivered in the way they learn best. If it was entirely in writing, the aural employees didn't hear it. If it was delivered by verbal presentation, the visual employees didn't see it. Kinesthetic employees need more hands-on learning, using the information. The best way to present information is using all three styles: visual, verbal, and kinesthetic.[8]

ENVIRONMENT AND THINKING

Our productivity is affected by factors that affect our thinking and concentrating ability. The factors include a preference for formal or informal design, sound, temperature, time of day, and our peers. In this sense, our working conditions will contribute to employee satisfaction.

Do you prefer a warm or cool room? Do you need to move around? Do you need silence or music? Do you need to drink or eat to concentrate? Are you more creative with peers, a partner, or alone?

Most business environments are set up with bright lights, formal design, restricted movement, silence, cool temperature, and limited food and drink. Work begins in the early morning, we receive verbal instruction, and tasks are sequential and analytical. Our productivity will be affected by whether we do well in this type of environment or not.

* Some people think better in a formal, structured atmosphere, and others in an informal situation.
* Right-brain-dominant people prefer low light and informal design. Bright lights overstimulate some people. Switching to a desk lamp and turning off fluorescent lights can help.
* Some people need food or a beverage to work better.
* Others need mobility, and they get their best ideas during a walk.
* Some people work better with sound; others want complete silence.
* Just over half, 55 percent, of all adults are morning people, and 28 percent are night people. Late morning or early afternoon is the peak time for the rest, 17 percent. Scheduling important work during peak time is important for these individuals.
* Some people like to have other people around; others work best alone.[9]

You probably know how you work best. We cannot completely change our environment to enhance our preferences. Still, we can incorporate some factors in order to improve our productivity and communication with others.

CREATIVITY

Our society is very complex and changing rapidly, as we discussed in Chapter 4 concerning the next-generation workforce. Information changes daily. We have new problems. Competition requires constant change. Providing exceptional customer service requires companies and personnel to change. We covered organizational change in Chapter 5. Change requires new solutions. We need new answers and new ideas. Old solutions no longer work. We are overloaded with information but some-times do not know what to do with it. Our problems and challenges require more *creativity*. Since our educational system has been focused on a left-brain world, we are less experienced in being creative. This section discusses what keeps us from being creative and describes ideas for being more creative.

Blocking Creativity

Why aren't we more creative? In order for us to think about how we can be more cre-ative, here are some possible reasons why we are not. Most of the time we don't need to be. It would complicate life. We really don't want to be too creative driving down the road. Routines are valuable. We would never get anything done if we didn't do some of it mindlessly.

We are not more creative partly because we are not taught to be creative. We are educated to find the right answer. Our attitudes and beliefs lock our thinking into more of the same and create mental blocks. We believe that we have to get the right answer, follow the rules, and be practical. We want to avoid ambiguity. We believe that making mistakes is bad. We believe that we should not be foolish and that play is frivolous. Finally, we believe that we are not creative, and so we don't try.

Below is a list of *creativity blocks* with examples and brief explanations.

* Cultural Blocks
  * Taboos—not suggesting really off-the-wall ideas.
  * Tradition is preferred to change—we've always done it that way.
  * Fantasy is a waste of time—it's lazy daydreaming.
  * Playfulness is for children only—we ignore our curiosity and inventiveness.
  * Humor is not helpful—problem solving is serious.
  * Scientific thinking and lots of money can solve any problem.
  * Left-brain thinking is good; right-brain thinking is bad.
* Emotional Blocks
  * Fear of risk—fear of making a mistake or failing.
  * Dislike for chaos and ambiguity—solving a complex problem is a messy process.
  * Judging rather than generating ideas—being overly critical.
  * Inability to incubate—not being able to relax and "sleep on it."
  * Lack of challenge—need for proper motivation.
  * Excessive zeal—trying to go too fast and choosing the first solution.
  * Lack of imagination—not allowing imagination to work fully.
* Intellectual Blocks
  * Using incorrect language—using math language instead of visual language.
  * Lack of flexibility in the use of strategies.
  * Lack of, or incorrect, information.
  * Using inadequate or imprecise language to express an idea.
* Perceptual Blocks
  * Seeing what we expect to see—prevents us from seeing new combinations.
  * Difficulty in isolating the problem—not identifying the problem correctly.
  * Delimiting the problem area too closely—seeing the problem too narrowly.
  * Inability to see the problem from various viewpoints—not using team input.
  * Failure to utilize all sensory inputs—using only one sense to solve a problem.

- Environmental Blocks
  - Lack of cooperation and trust among colleagues.
  - An autocratic boss—has all the answers.
  - Lack of support for implementation—no resources.
  - Distraction of trivial duties, noise—cannot concentrate with phone ringing.
  - Inappropriate environment—as discussed under Environment and Thinking above[10].

Experience Discussion 11.1

Give an example of an experience that illustrates how someone you know blocked creativity.

Promoting Creativity

The best way to get a new idea is to get many ideas. Hard thinking means that there is only one right answer. Hard thinking and logic ignore intuition. Soft thinking means that there are many right answers. There are many shades of gray versus just black and white. Soft thinking is like a floodlight rather than a spotlight. Creative people are curious about everything. They break rules. They risk. They try crazy ideas. They know that eventually ideas will come together to form a new idea.

Breakthrough ideas come from integrating right- and left-brain thinking—imagination and logic. Right-brain, or divergent, thinkers are more creative and have many ideas, but they find it hard to focus to develop and implement a concept. Left-brain, or convergent, thinkers find it difficult to think outside the box. They need more flexibility of thinking and a questioning attitude. To be creative, we need both sides interacting. The left side is used for defining the problem, gathering information, and analyzing information. The right side is used for incubating information, free-associating, and producing intuitive flashes. Then the left side is used for evaluating and implementing solutions. If we want a fresh approach, we should do the opposite from what we are used to. Exercise the nondominant side.

Creativity Tools

This is a "dump" of ideas for generating creativity. Be creative and see where they lead you. It's a good idea to write ideas down immediately so they don't get lost.

- Use *metaphors*, which are words or phrases that symbolize something other than their literal meaning. We use metaphors all the time, such as "horseless carriages," "tables have legs," and "cities have hearts." Sports and war terminology, such as "guerrilla marketing," are used to explain concepts in business. Have you ever noticed that many financial terms are water-related terminology? Examples are "liquid assets," "laundered money," "cash flow," "frozen assets," and "float a loan." To use a metaphor, visualize a company as an animal, car, sports team, or fruit. Ask how improving customer service is like planting a garden.
- Use word association. Start with a related word or any word. Write down the word that that word brings to mind. Then, the next word that comes to mind. Generate as many words as you can.
- Generate a random piece of information. Interpret the information as the answer to your question.

* Search newspapers, magazines, or anything visual for random ideas that might have a bearing on the problem at hand.
* Consider how a problem can be an opportunity. Look for the positive side. Customer complaints are an opportunity to correct problems and satisfy customers.
* Think of practical ideas. For instance, what if highway blacktop came in red-top or bluetop for speed limits? What if you lived your life backwards? Once you have thoughts on these, you can use them as stepping-stones to the problem.
* Ask the six universal questions.
  1. What is it?
  2. Where does it happen?
  3. When does it happen?
  4. How does it happen?
  5. Why does it happen?
  6. To whom does it happen? Who causes it to happen?
* Ask for the second right answer.
* Ask dumb questions.
  * Why have we always done it that way?
  * What's a ____?
  * Why don't we just not do it at all?
  * What do we use the information for?
* Rule 1. Follow the rules. Rule 2. Break the rules. Every rule here can be challenged except Rule 2. The idea behind breaking rules is that we should get rid of sacred cows. Do you know why the letters on the typewriter spell "qwerty"? The typewriter was originally designed to slow typists down because the keys stuck when they went too fast. We still use the same keyboard because so many people have learned to type that way. What if we start right now to teach people to use a new keyboard that has the most often used letters in different places? Eventually everyone will be using it. The problem, of course, is that companies will have to produce and sell two different keyboards, but maybe that's a good idea.
* We are told not to be foolish and that conformity is good. Be a fool. Take risks. Get rid of the idea that to err is wrong. A mistake is a stepping-stone to a new idea. Try to come up with wild options. Think the opposite of what's expected. Take a sacred cow and be foolish.
* Use the power of opposite thinking.
  * Change the question. Turn it upside down. Turn it around. Think about people who live in dry areas of the country. Instead of asking how they can find water, they ask how to get water to come to them.
  * Make the statement negative. Make various parts of the statement negative by adding "no", "not", "non-", "un-", "dis-", or an antonym to the statement.
  * Define what the problem is and then define what it is not.
  * Write down what everyone else is doing. Write down what they are not doing.
  * Deliberately generate ideas to make the problem worse. If you wanted to reduce customer complaints, what could you do to infuriate every customer who walks in the door of a retail store?
* Think ambiguously. A paradox is two different, often contradictory, notions at the same time. What was Tom Peters's paradox in Chapter 5?
* Fill your environment with things that stimulate your brain. Try to arrange your environment to help you be more productive and creative.

* Increase your exposure to ideas. Explore places you've never been. Read outside your area.
* Repeat the problem several times before you go to sleep at night, when you exercise, or when you listen to music—and then let it go. Some time in the next day or so, an idea will come to you.
* Use your dreams. As you are falling asleep, tell yourself you want to remember your dreams. When you wake up, don't open your eyes for at least a minute. Record the dreams you remember, and then look for any metaphors that may represent a solution to a problem.[11]

Experience Discussion 11.2

As a team, think of a customer service problem at a company. Use one or more of the ways to generate creativity to develop solutions.

MIND MAPPING

Mind mapping, introduced by Tony Buzan, is another technique for promoting creativity. It is a whole-brain, visual version of outlining. It is not the left-brain outline version using Roman numerals, ABC, and 1-2-3, but a nonlinear, cluster form. It starts with right-brain thinking. It grew out of Buzan's realization that two of the main factors in recall are association and emphasis. A *mind map* is an external expression of radiant thinking, associating thoughts out from a central point. It is a visual problem-solving technique.

It is applicable to problem solving, project planning, note taking, report writing, to-do lists, brainstorming, or just a brain dump to get a flood of ideas off our mind temporarily. Buzan believes that the traditional method of outlining ideas or taking notes uses less than half of our brain's capacity, our left brain. In fact, it works against our natural inclination to make associations and look for patterns, which is a right-brain specialty.

Process

The process begins with writing the topic or question in the center of a piece of paper. As subtopics or ideas occur to us, key words representing those are written around the box and branch off as additional information and thoughts are introduced (see Figure 1.5 in Chapter 1 for an example). Ideas are allowed to flow freely without judgment. You can draw pictures like a lightbulb to illustrate a good or new idea or a key for a key idea. Use symbols, such as an up arrow meaning more or increasing, a right arrow meaning faster, a question mark for uncertainty, or an asterisk for an important idea. Use whatever makes sense to you. Color can be used to emphasize ideas. By incorporating relationships, symbols, and pictures, you help your brain associate ideas and, thus, remember them more easily. Traditional note taking in a linear form is too structured and monotonous, causing us to lose our concentration. Once the mind map is created, you can switch to left-brain thinking to select ideas or solutions that are feasible.

Take a piece of paper and print the focus of the topic in a box in the center. Select the focus carefully. It should be one or two words that convey the crux of the topic or problem. It's like a trigger word. As thoughts on the topic begin, print a key word on a line connected to the focus. The key word should be a noun or a verb. Put only one or two words on a line. Print. Other words and lines should radiate out from the key words or from the focus. Put a thought or idea down even if it doesn't seem relevant. Perhaps it will turn out to be. Remember, mind mapping is a process, not an end result. There are no wrong mind maps. Add color, symbols, and pictures to highlight and organize information.

Another technique is to do more mind maps. Mind map what the desired future situation would be or what it would be like if the problem were solved. Then, mind map where the problem comes from or its causes. A third mind map is to use the opposite trigger word, a metaphor, or a random trigger word from something like a dictionary, the Yellow Pages, or a newspaper. All these mind maps will help us refine the problem and create more ideas.[12]

BRAINSTORMING

Another way to generate creative ideas is to brainstorm. Before team members can make a decision, they should make sure they have examined as broad a range of options as possible. One of the easiest and most enjoyable ways to generate a list of ideas is to brainstorm. A successful brainstorm lets people be as creative as possible and does not restrict their ideas in any way. This free-form approach can generate excitement in the group, equalize involvement, and often result in original ideas and solutions to problems. Below are the rules and process for *brainstorming*.

Ground Rules

1. Encourage everyone to freewheel. Do not hold back on any ideas, even if they seem silly at the time. The more ideas the better. Invite wild and risky ideas.
2. There is to be no discussion during the brainstorm. That will come later.
3. There should also be no judgments made during the brainstorm. No one is allowed to criticize another's ideas, not even with a groan or a grimace. Quantity, not quality, counts.
4. Let people hitchhike—build upon ideas generated by others in the group.
5. Write all ideas down so everyone can easily see them.

The meeting facilitator should enforce ground rules for the initial idea generation, which are no discussion and no criticism. An alternative called nominal brainstorming is to have all the participants write down their ideas and then go around the group and have team members say one of their ideas until everyone's list is complete. Again, no criticism is allowed, but clarification is.

Process

1. Review the topic, defining the subject of the brainstorm.
2. Give everyone a minute or two of complete silence to think about the question.

3. Invite all team members to call out their ideas.
4. Have one team member write down all ideas on a flipchart.
5. Once there is a complete list of ideas, discuss the pros and cons of each.
6. Eliminate ideas that are unacceptable.
7. Whittle the list down to several choices.
8. Reach a consensus about the final choice.

If ideas aren't flowing, try exaggerating the problem. Make it more difficult than it is. For example, perhaps a team is trying to speed up the process of answering e-mail from customers. Say the turnaround time is now a week and the department wants to reduce it to 24 hours. Try asking what would happen if instead of receiving 20 e-mails a day, the department receives 100 a day. What system could be used to solve this problem?

Another way to spur creative thinking is to think about how we could make a problem worse. Ask the team to brainstorm ways to mistreat customers and make them angry. This is very effective if there are employees with less-than-positive attitudes. During the discussion, they may realize that they actually do some of those things.[13]

Skill Development 11.3

As a team, make a "bug" list, which is a list of things that bug you at your job, your pet peeves. Pick one and see if the team can invent a way to fix the problem. Use one of the methods to promote creativity, mind mapping, or brainstorming.

CONSENSUS DECISION MAKING

There are four types of shared decision making in which more than one individual makes a decision. (There are four other types of decision making, in which the decision is made by an individual, which we will not address in this text.) Two of the types of group decision making are a partial group decision: one in which less than half decides, and the other in which more than half decides. A "less than half" partial group decision is useful when the group defers to a minority group because it has the knowledge and expertise to make a decision that the group can support. An example of the "more than half" partial group decision is majority rule in which six out of ten people vote for an option and the other four vote against it. It is often a compromise decision in which some parties give up something, a win-lose result.

In the other two types, the whole group decides using complete consensus or using unanimity of consent. In these last two types, the decision is a win-win decision. *Consensus* is a decision that all parties agree to, or, at least, agree to support. The ultimate win-win decision-making type is when all group members are unanimous and agree to a given course of action.

Consensus is not the only way or always the best way to make a decision. A consensus decision will be superior to a decision made by even the brightest member of a group. A team can generate and evaluate more options. People will be more committed to a consensus decision than a majority rule decision or one that just one person makes because their contributions have been considered and they believe their decision is the best that could be made. However, consensus decisions do take more time and patience. If a team is cross-functional—that is, made up of team members from different departments, such as sales, customer service, operations, and finance—members will view issues from their own perspective. Each member will have his or her own agenda, goals, and needs. Sales will be concerned about its quotas. Operations will worry about productivity. Finance, of course, will keep its focus on costs. The team may become polarized and hostile and never reach a decision. Reaching consensus will be difficult unless the team members first determine what their common interests are. When the vision, values, and philosophy of the company are customer-oriented and a team focuses on customer loyalty as the common interest, the team can use this to reach agreement on approaches and implementation.

A group using consensus attempts to combine the best insights of all group members to find a solution that incorporates all points of view. All participants should have a full say and should voice even their smallest concerns. They should feel that they have had sufficient opportunity to influence the final outcome. All positions should be clearly understood. Debate and negative comments are discouraged at first so that all the members feel free to state their opinion. Emphasize the positive points of a proposal, those that are good, that might work, and that everyone agrees on. Find out how serious the negatives are. One problem may be more important than others, and if we solve it, the objections go away. By summarizing the negatives, we may realize that they all have to do with one area, like the length of time a project should take, and we can work that out. Keep summing up the areas of agreement. Deal with problems or disagreements, working out obstacles, and eventually consensus may emerge quite suddenly.

Team members should not keep arguing for their own opinions or be confrontational and critical. Nor should team members change their minds just to reach agreement. Consensus is not compromise, splitting the difference and resulting in team members not being committed. A team member should not press for a solution because the time for the meeting is over.

To determine if the group has reached consensus, the way to find out is to go around and ask each person directly, "Do you agree with. . . , or if you do not agree, will you support the proposed course of action?" Members may not agree but will support the decision if they believe they have been heard and their input was considered. Someone who says, "I can live with it," may be ready to support the decision. However, usually this means, "I can live with it, but I am not committed to it." If there are members who do not agree, the leader should find out precisely what their objections are and what they would modify. If everyone agrees with the decision, the team has reached a rare situation of unanimity.[14]

Some tips to arrive at consensus:

* Be careful of quick and easy agreements. Examine the reason for the apparent agreement to be sure that a true consensus has been reached.
* Do listen and pay attention to what others have to say. Encourage all participants to provide input.
* Wait your turn to explain your opinion.
* Try to avoid win-lose statements. Try not to compete. Even if you win, the group may lose in the long run.
* Try to avoid either-or propositions.
* Try to stick with the discussion even if somebody attacks you or your idea. Emphasize the positives.

* Do not attack people. Address issues.
* Do not ignore conflict. Find out why it exists so that it can be dealt with and resolved.
* Do not settle an issue by voting. It will split the team into winners and losers.
* Try to avoid compromise if you feel your position is the most reasonable. Do carefully listen to and answer objections to your point of view.
* Keep summing up the areas of agreement.[15]

CONFLICT RESOLUTION

Conflict management training has been shown to improve employee performance and increase customer satisfaction. The training of customer service representatives for an electricity utility also lowered the length of high-bill complaint calls and reduced employee stress. Customer service providers are one of the fastest-growing segments of the labor force and have one of the ten most stressful jobs in America. People skills, including conflict resolution skills, are essential. Frontline employees need coping and problem-solving skills to handle customers as well as their own personal feelings. When we have to handle conflict, our natural instinct is to fight or flee. Doing the exact opposite is counterintuitive, and so it requires special training.[16]

One definition of a *conflict* is a belief, which is not necessarily a fact, that "if you get what you want, I can't get what I want—a win-lose situation." The most positive way to resolve a conflict is to figure out a win-win solution. We need to understand that helping others get what they want can help us get what we want.

The number one misstep that causes people to argue and not reach a resolution is focusing on positions instead of interests. A *position* is **what** we want. An *interest* is **why** we want it. Positions are often diametrically opposed. For example, a manager needs an employee to work late to finish a project, and the employee has promised her son that she will attend a school event. If the parties learn more about why others want something, often a solution presents itself that gives both parties what they want. To resolve the conflict we also need to separate the people from the problem.

Process

1. Eliminate "false" conflicts or misunderstandings. Make sure everyone understands what the other people want and why. Figure out each person's position, what each person wants or doesn't want. Put yourself in his or her shoes. Then find out each person's interest, his or her reasons for wanting or not wanting something.
2. Analyze everyone's positions and interests. Have the parties communicate what they want and why. Discuss problems, not solutions, at this point. Discuss perceptions and emotions. State what you see and hear and your interpretation. Check to see if you have it right.
3. Find solutions that work for all people.
   a. Brainstorm ideas.
   b. Look for integrative (win-win) solutions. The following are methods for arriving at win-win solutions:
   * When the conflict comes from a shortage of resources, expand the pie. Find new resources or use them in a new way.

* Buy a concession. Give something to the person making the concession, something that is unrelated to the conflict but of high interest.
* Use cost cutting. Reduce the cost to the person making a concession. Offer something related to the conflict and of high interest.
* Do logrolling. Make a concession of low priority to one person but high priority to the other.
* Try bridging. Reformulate the problem by addressing only the key interests of all parties. Both sides have high-priority interests that can be settled simultaneously.

4. Decide. The decision should not be dictated. It should be based on consensus. People should be flexible on solutions and firm on their interests.

In the conflict noted above in which the manager needs a project finished and the employee has another commitment, neither cost cutting—offering extra time off some other time—nor buying a concession—offering some other incentive—is likely to work in this situation because the employee is not going to concede attending the school event. An alternative solution is to expand the pie by having another employee finish the project. Or perhaps the employee could finish the project after the school event at home on a laptop computer. Still another option is to use bridging by clarifying precisely when the project needs to be finished. Perhaps the manager has a deadline because she has another project pending. In this case, the employee could help her finish both projects the next day. Both people win.[17]

TERMS

problem solving	metaphor
hemispheric dominance	mind map
left-brain dominants	brainstorming
right-brain dominants	consensus
lateralization	conflict
creativity	position
creativity blocks	interest

DISCUSSION QUESTIONS

1. What are the differences between right- and left-brain processing?
2. Discuss whether you are more right-brain or left-brain-dominant and how it affects your job performance.
3. Pair up with a classmate with opposite brain dominance and talk through a decision. Note the differences in your approach.
4. How do you block your own creativity? What idea(s) for increasing creativity seem to fit you best?
5. What is a mind map?
6. What are the guidelines for brainstorming?
7. Brainstorm or mind-map a solution to a problem.
8. What is a consensus? How does a team reach a consensus?

EXERCISE—CONFLICT RESOLUTION[*]

Divide the class into teams of eight—seven participants and at least one (or more) observers. Charlie's role can be eliminated if there are not enough students. Allow 15 to 30 minutes for the team to reach a decision.

The Scenario

The sales department of LFC Corporation, a medical equipment manufacturer in Ohio, received a new car to add to the existing group of company cars used by the sales representatives in the field. As has been done in the past, the new car is exchanged for an old car. The company has to decide which of the six sales reps should get the new car.

The Task

1. Each person on the sales rep team assumes a role. Students determine how they play the role. They may elaborate on it, but they should stick to the facts as given.
2. Decide which sales rep should get the new car. The decision must be based on consensus.
3. Ignore issues concerning what was done previously (except those stated).
4. Future issues may be considered.
5. Discuss how the team arrived at the decision.

The Roles

1. *Taylor, Sales Manager.* As the manager, you have the problem of deciding which sales rep should get the new car. Often there are hard feelings because each member of the sales team seems to feel he or she is entitled to the new car, so you have a tough time being fair. In fact, it usually turns out that whatever you decide, most of the team considers it wrong. You now have to face the same issue again because a new car has just been allocated to you for distribution. In order to handle this problem, you have decided to put the decision to the team. You should tell the team that it must reach a consensus decision.
2. *Lee.* You have been with the company 15 years. You received the sales manager's car a year ago when he or she got a new one. Now the car is 2 years old. You feel you deserve the new car because you have been with the company longer than any of the other reps. Your car is in excellent shape, and you want to receive the new car. Seniority is the only way to determine who gets the new car.
3. *Alex.* You have been with the company 10 years and have a 3-year-old car. You feel you deserve the new car, and it is certainly your turn. Since the more senior member of the crew has a fairly new car, you should get the next one. You have taken excellent care of your present car and have kept it looking like new. You believe that a person who treats a company car like his or her own deserves to be rewarded.
4. *Joey.* You have been with the company 9 years and have a 3-year-old car. You have to do more driving than most of the other reps because your territory is larger geographically. You feel you should have the new one because you do so much driving. Besides, Taylor's spouse is your cousin.

5. *Casey.*   You have been with the company 6 years and have a 4-year-old car. Since Andy backed into the door of the car, it has never fit right and lets in cold air. The heater can't keep the car warm. You want to have a warm car since you have a good deal of driving to do. As long as your car has good tires and brakes and is comfortable, you don't care how old it is.

6. *Andy.*   You have been with the company 4 years and have a 4-year-old car. You have the worst car of the sales team. Before you got it, it had been in a bad wreck. It looks like a piece of junk and doesn't handle right. You've put up with it for 3 years. It's about time you got a good car to drive. You have a good accident record. The only accident you had was when you hit the door of Casey's car when Casey opened it as you backed out of the parking lot.

7. *Charlie.*   You are the newest sales rep, having been there only a year. Your car is the oldest at 5 years. It occasionally gives you problems and has been in for repairs four times since you started the job. You are making your sales quotas and keeping customers happy, but feel you could do even better if you had a more reliable car and did not have to worry about it so much.

8. *Observer.*   Your task is to observe the activities of the members of your team and take notes. The questions you should consider are:

   1. What procedure or steps did the team use in deciding who was to get the car? What problem-solving techniques did the team use?
   2. What conflict was the strongest? How was it managed or resolved?
   3. What conflict resolution strategies were used?
   4. Did everyone participate equally?
   5. Was the decision arrived at by consensus?
   6. Did you see any evidence of different styles or left- or right-brain thinking?

*Adapted from Spencer Kagan, *Cooperative Learning* (n.p.: Resources for Teachers, Inc., n.d.).

NOTES

1. Allen D. Bragdon and David Gamon, *Building Left-Brain Power* (Bass River, MA: Brainwaves Books, 1999), 109.
2. Eric Haseltine, "Your Better Half," *Discover* 20, no. 6 (June 1999): 112.
3. Jacquelyn Wonder and Priscilla Donovan, *Whole Brain Thinking: Working from Both Sides of the Brain to Achieve Peak Job Performance* (New York: William Morrow and Company, 1984).
4. Wonder and Donovan, *Whole Brain Thinking*.
5. This section is based on Wonder and Donovan, *Whole Brain Thinking;* Bragdon and Gamon, *Building Left-Brain Power;* Tony Buzan and Barry Buzan, *The Mind Map Book: How to Use Radiant Thinking to Maximize Your Brain's Untapped Potential* (New York: Penguin Books USA, 1993); and Charles Thompson, *What a Great Idea! The Key Steps Creative People Take* (New York: HarperPerennial, 1992).
6. Richard M. Felder, "Matters of Style," available from http://www2.ncsu.edu, accessed on September 2, 1997, originally in *ASEE Prism* 6, no. 4 (December 1996): 18–23.
7. Wonder and Donovan, *Whole Brain Thinking*.
8. Alana Cash, "Productivity Style: A Look at How Your Surroundings Affect Your Work," *Manage* 44, no. 3 (January 1993): 10–13.
9. Cash, "Productivity Style."
10. James L. Adams, *Conceptual Blockbusting: A Guide to Better Ideas,* 3d ed. (Reading, MA: Addison-Wesley, 1986).

11. Roger von Oech, *A Whack on the Side of the Head: How You Can Be More Creative,* rev. ed. (New York: Warner Books, 1990); Thompson, *What a Great Idea!;* and Donna M. Partow, "Great Ideas: How You Can Generate Breakthroughs," *Home Office Computing* 12, no. 6 (June 1994): 85–90.

12. Buzan and Buzan, *The Mind Map Book;* Rebecca Z. Shafir, *The Zen of Listening: Mindful Communication in the Age of Distraction* (Wheaton, IL: Theosophical Publishing House, 2000); and Joyce Wycoff, *Mindmapping, Your Personal Guide to Exploring Creativity and Problem-Solving* (Berkeley, CA: Berkeley Books, 1991).

13. "Brainstorming: A Key to Innovative Ideas," *Mobius,* June 1993, 41–42.

14. Thomas L. Quick, *Successful Team Building* (New York: AMACOM, 1992); and Thomas A. Kayser, *Team Power: How to Unleash the Collaborative Genius of Work Teams* (Carlsbad, CA: CRM Films, 1994): 90–96, 108–115.

15. National Education Association of New York, "Tips for Practicing Consensus Decision Making," handout.

16. Rosanne D'Ausilio, "The Impact of Conflict Management Training on Customer Service Delivery," *Customer Relationship Management,* December 1997, 20–23.

17. CareerTrack, *Conflict Resolution and Confrontation Skills,* developed by Helga Rhode (Boulder, CO: CareerTrack, 1994).

EXCEPTIONAL CUSTOMER SERVICE

OBJECTIVES

1. Explain best practices for providing service to dissatisfied or angry customers.
2. Explain best practices for providing service to mistaken customers.
3. Explain best practices for providing service to problem customers.
4. Outline customer responsibilities.
5. Explain best practices for providing service to diverse customers
6. Explain best practices for providing service to multicultural customers.
7. Explain best practices for providing service to customers with disabilities.
8. Describe how emotional labor affects employees and how the effects can be decreased.

EXCEPTIONAL CUSTOMER SERVICE IN CHALLENGING SITUATIONS

Customers are often dissatisfied with products and services. Customers sometimes become frustrated, upset, even angry. Customers are often wrong or mistaken. Some customers are truly problem customers. Some customers have special needs. This chapter discusses how to provide exceptional customer service in all these challenging situations.

Experience Discussion 12.1

Describe a situation in which you encountered a customer who was:

a. Angry
b. Wrong

c. Overly demanding
d. Dishonest
e. Abusive
f. Non-English speaking

DISSATISFIED OR ANGRY CUSTOMERS

It takes a lot of skill to deal with displeased and angry people when they have a problem with our product or service. Dealing with nice people is easy—anybody can do that. We prove our real value to our company when we can turn dissatisfied or angry customers into loyal customers. Customer service providers need to learn the attitudes, behaviors, and skills that will assist them in handling challenging situations.

Customers can get under our skin. As hard as we try to meet customers' needs and provide good customer service, it is easy to get angry with customers and give them a taste of what they have been giving us. Remember that customers are not angry with us. Our emotions will work against us if we believe that. There is no reason to feel guilty or defensive and get angry back. They are angry at the situation, which we most likely did not cause. Customers' problems are usually transitory rather than permanent and due to circumstances rather than something pervasive.[1]

Customer service providers need to understand that people's communication styles are different based on individual, family, social, and cultural differences. People from large cities and from the North may have more brusque verbal styles. Some of our role models from television and sports demonstrate an insulting, snippy, or belligerent style. Consider television shows like *The Simpsons* and *Roseanne* and certain sports stars.

The pace of our lives seems to be faster and more demanding due to rapid change, and so people experience more stress, which shows in their behavior toward others. Everyone gets cranky occasionally. We also find that customers are often nasty when they do not expect their complaint or situation to be taken seriously. Complaining takes time and effort, and customers are impatient beyond what dissatisfied them in the first place.

Resist putting a label on customers. If you start to think negatively about customers, using negative self-talk, it will carry over into your nonverbal and verbal communication. Providers often call difficult customers "jerks," "losers," "stupid," "pushy," "clueless," and "rude." We've heard them all. As soon as you label someone "clueless," you may treat her that way. Ask instead, "What does this customer need?"

One way to reduce confrontation is to focus on the situation, not on yourself. Have confidence that you can turn an ugly situation into a positive customer experience. Consider it a challenge. The problem won't escalate, and you will have less stress in the end. Remember, about 2 percent of customers will be dissatisfied no matter how you treat them or what you do. With these customers, the best you can do is the best you can do.

Process

The steps you need to take for unhappy, annoyed, or angry customers are as follows:

1. *In a single word, listen. Let customers vent.*   Customers want two things when they have a problem. They want to express their feelings, and then they want you to

solve their problem. It's very natural to want a confrontation over as quickly as possible. It's difficult to listen to angry people. We experience the fight or flight response. We get angry ourselves or feel somehow guilty and become submissive. Service providers just want the facts so they can fix a problem immediately. However, emotional customers are not ready for a reasonable, rational discussion. They must express their emotions first. Customers are not ready at this point for logic and will not hear what we have to say. Accept customers' anger as a normal human emotion that we all feel occasionally. Realize that the anger is not personal.

The key is to make sure customers know you are listening and taking them seriously. Resist the urge to listen defensively. Listen empathetically. Use appropriate nonverbal and verbal signals. Maintain eye contact. Stay at eye level with the customer. If the customer is standing, you stand. Nod your head. Use neutral verbal responses that demonstrate you are listening and are concerned, like "Uh-huh" and "I see." Don't match the anger; do match the intensity. Show you are concerned. Be very respectful and courteous. It is hard to be rude to someone who is being sincerely polite.

Be patient. Do not interrupt. The customers have been rehearsing their speech long before they got to you. If you interrupt, they will have a tendency to just start over again. Never say something like "Please calm down." Because you seem to be discounting their feelings, this is guaranteed to turn annoyed into irate.

If appropriate, take a few notes so you do not have to ask for some fact they already told you. Listen for the basic information—who, what, where, and when. Do not debate the facts at this point. Customers are not being logical and may exaggerate. When they are finished venting, you can "prove" you were listening by verifying a fact.

If customers seem dissatisfied but have not told you directly why they feel that way, it's a good idea to inquire about the reasons. It's better to not let them walk away and spread negative word-of-mouth information. For example, if a group of customers were to say in a restaurant at the cash register as they are leaving, "Our service was terrible!" you should say, "It was? What happened?" Don't ignore it and hope it will go away. Here's a case in which you don't match the emotion, but you should match the intensity so the customers are clear that you are concerned.

2. *Empathize.*   In a couple of minutes, customers will finish venting. When they pause and take a deep breath, you'll know. The next step is to *empathize* with their feelings. Do not go to problem solving yet. Use their name and express that you understand how they feel. Acknowledge them as people with a problem. Be sincere and say something so that customers believe you care about the problem and will do something. Customers want to be understood even when they are wrong. Phrases that you can use are:

"That must have been frustrating."

"I understand why you would feel that way."

"I can imagine you were upset."

"I see what you mean."

Agreeing with a customer is an effective technique. It's hard for customers to be disagreeable when you are agreeing with them. You can agree with a fact, in principle, or with their right to have an opinion. If what the customer is telling us is true, denial is useless. "Yes, we said we would deliver it on Thursday afternoon and we didn't. You have every right to be upset." An example of agreeing in principle with their feelings is "I agree. It would be frustrating to have that happen." In the case of their opinion, they do have a right to it, so say, "I understand you are unhappy with the service you received." If the customer does continue venting after this, listen a little more and provide another empathetic phrase.

3. *Apologize.* Some service providers see apologizing as an admission of guilt. However, saying "I'm sorry" does not imply you or your company did anything wrong. Apologizing does not mean that you are to blame. It lets customers know you are sincerely sorry that they have a problem and that you are going to fix it. Acknowledge customers' viewpoints or inconvenience. Use the "agree" approach mentioned previously. They want you to understand and empathize. Customer complaints have been known to end up in the legal department because no one apologized. Apologize without accepting or placing blame. One thing you should not say is "Sorry about that." It sounds very offhand and is perceived as insincere. Say:

"I am very sorry that this has been so frustrating for you."

Or "I apologize for the inconvenience you experienced."

4. *Take responsibility.* Tell customers you will personally take care of the problem. Do not cite company policy. Don't blame others, shift the responsibility, or make lame excuses. The customer doesn't care whose fault it is.

Customers often want an explanation about why something happened. Customers may not like your explanation, but if they understand it, they will be more likely to give the company a second chance.

5. *Gather the facts.* Verify anything that is not clear. Listen so you don't jump to conclusions and lose your credibility. Ask closed-ended questions to encourage customers to think rationally. Asking "why" questions implies blame and may make customers defensive, for example, "Why didn't you call us when it happened?" Ask for any additional details you need to find a solution. Double-check facts. Paraphrase back what the customer said.

Focus on finding a solution, not rehashing the problem. If customers get off track, wait until they take a breath, quickly jump in with another empathetic phrase, and ask for the information you need. If customers are ineffective communicators, it's up to you to help them tell you the problem.

6. *Solve the problem.* Save the relationship. Take corrective action in a way that is visible to customers. If it's clear at this point how to solve the problem, do so. Do what you would want done. Otherwise, if you can be flexible, ask what they want done, or describe the acceptable alternatives.

"What would be a good solution from your point of view?"

"We can do x, y, or z; which would be best?"

Some customers will order you around, "What do I want to have happen? I'm going to tell you exactly what will happen. . . " If their suggestion has merit, follow it. Say, "That's a great idea. I can do that." If you can't do what they want even if you wanted to, redirect customers back to their real need and offer alternative suggestions that will work.

If the customer is demanding something contrary to company policy and you must say no, explain the reasons behind the policy and offer alternatives. Your company should already be aware that these situations could crop up and have solutions. If necessary, get a supervisor involved.

Then do what is needed to solve the problem. Make sure customers know what you are doing. If the problem cannot be solved on the spot, let them know what you are going to do. Set a time limit on resolving the problem. Keep them informed. Call them back with progress reports if necessary.

Even if you cannot fix the problem in exactly the way the customer wishes, if you do the rest sincerely and consistently, research indicates that customers will still be willing to repurchase and recommend (discussed in Chapter 3).

7. *Follow up.* Make sure customers are satisfied by following up with telephone, letter, or e-mail. Show your appreciation for their business.[2]

Here are 10 things you should *not* do[3]:

1. Blame the customers.
2. Challenge them if they have made a factual error.
3. Imply the problem has happened before.
4. Mismatch your verbal and nonverbal communication. Don't offer help in a resigned voice.
5. Use jargon or technospeak. It will make customers feel insecure and stupid.
6. Use humor unless you are good at saying the right thing. It may backfire.
7. Be sarcastic by words or tone.
8. Use the "poor me" approach, explaining that you are overworked or understaffed.
9. Bad-mouth the company or any employee.
10. Shift the responsibility. Satisfaction decreases when customers have to repeat themselves to another employee.

MISTAKEN CUSTOMERS

Customers are not always right. They know it. You know it. We all know it. We all make mistakes. Companies lose credibility with their employees if they insist customers are always right.

However, customers are always. . . customers. Think about it this way—customers' perceptions are always right. No two people see a situation exactly the same way. In addition, for the company to win, customers must always win. Calculate what the loss of a customer would be to the company. When customers are wrong, it is our job to manage the experience in a manner that neither embarrasses nor blames and the customer remains our customer. Keeping customers happy is what matters.

Assuming customers are always right can put the service provider in a one-down position. We hate that. Service begins to feel like servitude. We feel like we're wrong. It seems like a win-lose situation: Customers win and the company loses. A marketing transaction should be based on a mutually beneficial exchange. Companies and managers must acknowledge that sometimes customers are not right and provide training for coping and problem-solving skills so that employees know how to handle these customers and deal with their personal feelings.

Experience Discussion 12.2

What are some of the things customers do to cause their own dissatisfaction?

As mentioned in Chapter 3, customers cause about one-quarter of their own problems. On the other hand, companies cause the remaining three-quarters. The company's products and policies cause 37 percent, and employees cause 38 percent. When we think about customers causing their own problems, do not forget that our customers are not nearly as familiar with our company and its policies and procedures as we think they are. Whether they are consumers or business-to-business customers, they deal with numerous other companies with different policies and procedures from ours. They will not be able to distinguish and remember. We know our company because we are there 8 hours a day. They don't because they aren't. Customers should read instructions and disclosures; however, maybe there's a reason they don't. For example, perhaps the print is too small to read without a magnifying glass.

The steps you need to take for *mistaken customers* are as follows:

1. *Always assume innocence.* Believe your customers. "Guilty until proved innocent" does not play well with customers. Even if you can prove customers are wrong, you lose and the company loses. Never treat customers like they are stupid. Never act like "I'm right and you're wrong." Customers are not always right, but it does not cost you anything to give them the benefit of the doubt. Never argue with customers. Do not put customers on the defensive. When you rudely or insensitively cut off, put down, or demean customers for having a confused or wrong idea of what exactly they need or what you can do for them, you lose customers.

Sometimes customers are right after all. If you have overruled their request or complaint, you may find yourself embarrassed. Keep your credibility and keep customer relations intact. Do say, "Let's check the advertising flyer to verify that the price you saw is for this model. Sure enough, there it is. Thanks for pointing that out to me. I'll make sure we get the shelf tags corrected so everyone knows which model is on sale." Customers love being right.

2. *Empathize.* Apologize for the customer's inconvenience. Remember that their perception is that they are right. If appropriate, relate a similar type mistake you made.

3. *Solve the problem.* Help customers save face. Avoid using the blaming word "you," as in "You didn't send it in by the deadline."

4. *Provide assistance.* After you have solved the problem, look for teaching opportunities. If we assume customers are right, it puts a stop to problem solving and customer education. We are so familiar with our products that we forget how much there is to know, how much we have to help our customers learn. Train customers to understand their role and appropriate behaviors.

Blame it on an inanimate object, not a person. Do say, "I see what happened. The directions are not very clear; this part goes here."

Avoid pointing out their error, as in "You should have. . . " or "What you have to do in the future is. . . " Say, "In the future, we suggest. . . ," or "We recommend. . . "

A college financial aid representative could say, "I'm glad you brought this to my attention. The information you needed was here in the packet, but I can see that it would be easy to miss, with all the forms you have to fill out. Let's review your packet to make sure you've done everything you need to."

PROBLEM CUSTOMERS

We have all had problem customers. Problem customers range from chronic complainers, to annoying customers, to scammers, to psychotic. Abnormal, criminal, and abusive customers are rare. Nevertheless, they do exist. Customers' calls or presence can be bizarre or threatening. These customers' behaviors cause employees annoyance, anxiety, emotional distress, or, in some cases, even fear. Problems may escalate.

High-Maintenance Customers

High-maintenance customers are those who are overly demanding and critical and, therefore, costly to companies. Sometimes problem customers must be "fired." Otherwise, the honest, polite customers may be penalized. However, the temptation to weed out or blackball merely difficult customers seems to be gaining ground. To label and segment customers based on bad manners or behavior, a subjective judgment, seems unfair at best, discriminatory at worst. There are customers that generate too much organizational stress. Difficult customers can be sent to highly trained, highly tolerant reps. Companies must determine where they stand on the continuum between "refuse to serve" and "satisfy them at all costs." A question for a company to answer is: Does resolving the problem fit with the company's values? Even if a customer is profitable, when the perception is that the company is letting a customer "steal" from the company, it should stop.

One dubious practice in customer relationship management is customer service representatives annotating customers' records with comments like "obnoxious boor," "frequent complainer," or "manipulator." The upside, of course, is that another representative is forewarned and may be better able to manage an interaction with one of these high-maintenance customers. There are, however, questions of ethical behavior. Is the customer always obnoxious, or was he or she provoked? It would be better to annotate the history with "Bill Smith is very detail-oriented so double-check his order" or "Mrs. Smith is always in a hurry, so try to accommodate her."[4]

Sometimes it is appropriate to "fire" a *chronic complainer* as a last resort. Management needs to handle this diplomatically and tactfully. A student once told a story about a woman who drove the customer service personnel at a dry-cleaning store crazy with her continual complaints about her clothing when she picked it up—wrinkles, infinitesimal stains that only she could see, buttons missing that weren't there when she brought the garment in, shrinkage, etc. The owner of the company finally wrote her a letter explaining that the company could not seem to dry-clean her clothing the way she wanted and suggested other convenient stores.

Skill Development 12.1

Is it OK for employees to joke about problem customers?

Scammers

One group of problem customers is repeaters, who make multiple calls with frivolous complaints. Some customers call every 2 or 3 months praising a product in the hopes of getting a coupon. It may be innocent; they call with questions, compliments, or problems about several products over a long period, not realizing the products are produced by the same company. We might think they have too much time on their hands, but they are just being informed, cautious consumers as they should be.

A subgroup of the repeaters is *scammers,* who are persistent and potentially dishonest. This subgroup should not be ignored. Customer service providers need to use the information provided by the database, their intuition, and their good judgment. If they suspect a scammer, they should ask the customer to hold and take time to read the historical information. If confirmed, the employee can say, "Thank you for waiting, Mrs. Jones. My computer tells me the same thing happened last month." Otherwise, proceed as usual. Others make outright requests for coupons. For customers who insist on a coupon, a representative can tell them, "I wish I could send out coupons on every call, but we have just so many to send out so I'll have to pass this time, but I do appreciate your letting us know how much you like our product." Sometimes it becomes a justified, noble crusade for service representatives to "catch" scammers. The problem with this line of thinking is they may be mistaken about customers' motives. In addition, if service representatives approach every customer with the suspicion that the person is a scammer, their body language and voice are affected, and that may affect every customer negatively.[5]

For another solution for customers who are trying to take advantage, try a "three strikes and you're out policy." When the clerk and the customer disagree on whether the video was returned on time—the first time, forget the late fee; the second time, no charge; the third time, sorry.

Bizarre Customers

Abnormal communications from customers can vary from amusing to dangerous. The recommended procedures for handling this type of communication are the following:

1. Do not respond to extremely strange mail or calls. This legitimizes the customer's activity.
2. Respond only to normality. Ignore weird talk and respond only to the normal comments from the customer.
3. Record and save all information on the communication. It can be used to identify the customer and may be needed at some point.
4. Report the communication to management and security.
5. Provide support for staff. Employees may be upset or frightened. Give the customer service agent emotional support and allow the agent to vent.
6. Use the resources of law enforcement and mental health agencies to resolve problems if necessary.[6]

Litigious Customers

Litigious customers threaten a lawsuit at every opportunity. Find out how you should handle it when customers threaten to sue the company or you suspect they might. Some lawsuits seem to have begun when the frontline employees exhibited the attitude, "I'm right, and if you don't like it, you can just leave." Therefore, the customers left angry and sued. Remember the woman who sued McDonald's after she spilled hot coffee on herself? The news reported that the jury awarded her $2.9 million. What you may not have seen is that the award was appealed and reduced by 75 percent and finally settled out of court for an undisclosed sum. It still cost McDonald's, but not $2.9 million. Product injury lawsuits have actually leveled off since 1986.

On the other hand, companies should not let headlines cause them to overreact to problem customers. Beware of anecdotal, misleading, incomplete information and urban legends, especially on web "gripe" sites. There's no doubt that there are greedy, litigious customers, but most customers are not out to get whatever they can out of us. Give customers want they want: an apology, a fair resolution, compensation for injury or inconvenience, and treat them as valued customers.

Abusive Customers

Abusive customers begin with the loud-mouthed, vulgar customer and escalate to the out of control, potentially violent customer.

1. The best thing to do initially is to ignore the language and behavior and follow the same procedures you use with an angry customer. Don't assume some customers deserve help and those that are obnoxious do not. Experts say some of these "customers from hell" are people who have been through hell. It's not personal. Listen. Empathize. Apologize. Solve the problem.[7]

Do say, "Mr. Baker, I don't blame you for being upset. I understand how you feel. Let's see if we can solve this problem and make things right for you."

It is not a good practice to hang up on abusive customers. Ignore the language or behavior, stay calm and polite, and do what you can to help. The customer is not directing the language at you, so consider it "noise." You could say, "I want to correct this problem quickly for you. I can help you better if you do not use that language." If absolutely necessary, when all else fails, have someone else take the call. Say, "This doesn't seem to be working; let me find someone who can help us resolve this." As a very last resort, inform customers you will hang up if the abuse does not stop and follow through. You can say, "Excuse me, I can't help you if you are going to use such strong language. If you continue, I am going to hang up." If the customer continues, do it.

2. For a potentially violent customer, call the manager or someone else if a situation escalates. Managers should be watchful. Employees should have some way to signal for help.

3. For these situations, there should be a company policy and guidelines. Make sure you know it. If there is not, ask for guidelines. The company and employees must decide whether and when to draw a line in the sand. Perhaps the manager should consider "firing" these abusive customers as well. Employees should not be required to endure abusive language, cursing, or frightening behavior.

Experience Discussion 12.3

Does your company have policies and procedures for abusive customers? Do you know what they are?

Criminal Customers

Dishonest and dangerous customer behavior can range from shoplifting, to product tampering, to violence, to terrorism. If the situation is potentially dangerous to employees or other customers, immediately call a manager or the police. Find out what the company's procedures are for these situations.

Effect on Other Customers

One characteristic of service businesses is that since production and consumption are sometimes simultaneous, a customer receiving service may affect the service other customers are receiving. Any time customers share the same public business environment, such as a retail store, a restaurant, or an airline flight, the potential exists. The result may affect a business's relationship-building strategy by lowering customers' level of satisfaction, willingness to return, and willingness to recommend. We discussed the perception that Americans are less civil in an earlier chapter. A study of 774 hotel, restaurant, and airline dissatisfactory incidents, reported by front-line employees, revealed that 22 percent were caused by problem customer behavior. The remainder of the problems, 78 percent, was attributed to system and employee failures. The problem behaviors of customers included breaking laws or company policies; being rude, uncooperative, and unreasonably demanding; becoming verbally and physically abusive to an employee or another customer; and being drunk.[8]

One research study found that satisfaction decreased when fellow customers were inconsiderate, crude (lacking taste, polish, tact), malcontent (chronically dissatisfied), violent (using excessive force or sudden intense behavior), grungy (shabby, dirty condition or demeanor), and leisurely (not overly time-conscious). In particular, perceived violent behavior and unsavory appearance were the most dissatisfying behaviors. The effect varied by the age, gender, situation, and attitudes of customers toward smoking, drinking, loudness, profanity, and noisy children, to name a few. The main differences existed between older and younger customers and between males and females.

Part of the solution is for employees to model the appropriate behaviors and appearance, verbally reinforce positive behaviors, and verbally enforce codes of conduct, such as saying, "I'm sorry, but smoking is not permitted here." Through the physical environment, policies, and signage, a company can discourage some behaviors. Smoking sections and family restaurant designations are two typical ways of doing this. Businesses may need to market to a segment of consumers that are more homogeneous and more compatible. If companies fail to act, dissatisfied customers may resort to government intervention, as they have done concerning smoking, alcohol consumption, and noise levels.[9]

CUSTOMER RESPONSIBILITIES

As noted above, customers can be difficult. As a customer service provider, you might be tempted to "do unto them what customers do unto you," obviously not a good idea. However, customers cause employee anxiety, frustration, confusion, and anger. As customers ourselves, we might want to think about that. What are some of the behaviors that customers should use toward providers? What are customers' responsibilities? The author's web course students listed these:

* Follow the Golden Rule.
* Appreciate and respect the employee and the company.
* Communicate effectively.
* Be courteous, not rude.
* Have patience.
* Be calm.
* Do not be impossible to please.
* Do not have a bad attitude.
* Do not be hostile when a problem occurs.
* Do not make a scene.

* Do not curse.
* Be honest, truthful.
* Do not take advantage.
* Know and understand return and other policies.
* Understand and follow through on warranties.
* Understand that things can go wrong.
* Be clear about what they want to solve a problem.
* Have the facts and information when things go wrong.
* Understand their part in their problem.
* Understand their problem may not be the employee's fault.
* Tell companies about poor service and about good service.

DIVERSE CUSTOMERS

In a broad sense, *diversity* encompasses every individual difference that affects a task or relationship. It includes anything that goes into forming an individual's unique perspective. It includes differences in age, race, gender, income, marital status, physical ability, sexual orientation, religious beliefs, socioeconomic class, education, geographic origin, language, beliefs, values, life experience, lifestyle, food preferences, position in the family, personality, job function, job status, work experience, etc. Customer diversity includes Gen Xers, attorneys, preschoolers, Native Americans, soccer players, North Dakotans, craftspeople, autistic children, vegetarians, Koreans, veterans, single fathers, Mormons, FBI agents. . . everyone.

This broad definition of diversity means that service providers need to understand that a customer's values, perceptions, needs, and expectations may vary. Most of the time, we think of diversity as cultural- and ethnic-based. The following section focuses on cultural diversity because that is the main type that is confronting us in the twenty-first century. But the definition of diversity in this textbook goes beyond that to the realization that diversity is based on many factors. To provide exceptional customer service, providers need to adapt their style and approach to meet the customers' needs and expectations. The best way to do this is to use the basics of exceptional customer service and work on connecting with the individual. We need to be aware that often our assumptions about people may be incorrect. The challenge is identifying expectations with which we may not be immediately familiar. There is little difference between that and customer service when culture was not a consideration. We already know that Americans from different parts of the United States are different from each other and that our customers' and coworkers' reactions are based on diverse values. Any time we change jobs, move, begin college, or start a new hobby, we learn to adjust to the subcultural environment. We already know how it's done.

Business bottom lines depend on companies knowing their customers, designing appropriate marketing strategies, and developing an inclusive customer service strategy. Businesses know that by recruiting, training, and promoting a diverse group of individuals, they become more desirable employers and more successful in reaching customers. Recognizing diversity makes the best use of employee talents and skills and enhances teamwork productivity and creativity. Instead of being detrimental, differences are a great source of strength. Diversity management is not about what is right or wrong but about what works.

Customers vary widely in their needs and expectations, and so providers need to fulfill special requirements. However, all customers should be treated the same. That sounds like a contradiction, but it isn't if each customer is treated as an individual with different needs. Give extra value to every customer and his or her unique needs. The following are a few examples of out-of-the-ordinary circumstances and customers who are different.

* Children and teenagers are becoming very sophisticated shoppers with money to spend. Remember that children are our future customers. They need to be respected and trusted unless and until there's a reason not to. Young customers, teenagers, have found that they are followed around a store as if they will steal. Teenagers have a lot of money to spend.
* Critical customers tend to be overtly critical, but they can be right. For example:
  * "You people never listen to students anyway." You should say, "I apologize. I am listening now. Tell me what happened."
  * "I pay your salary." You should say, "You are exactly right. You do help pay my salary, and I apologize."
  * "Excuse me, are you two going to stop chatting? I'm trying to buy something here." You should say, "I'm sorry I wasn't paying attention. I'll check that out right away."
* Impatient customers just want you to hurry. Change your pace.
* Talkative customers want someone to listen. Listen and make sure they know you are listening. Give them your complete attention if only briefly. Then you can gracefully end the conversation because they know there is another customer in line behind them.
* Indecisive customers probably want information and help. Or they may just want time to think and don't like you hanging over them.

MULTICULTURAL CUSTOMERS

Culture means a way of life for a group of people. It defines what is acceptable. Culture is a set of shared ideas about how to live and how to get along with people. This section borrows a convention that Thiederman uses in her book, *Profiting in America's Multicultural Marketplace,* to refer to people born and raised in America or assimilated into American culture, that of referring to the culture that Americans are used to as *mainstream American culture*. This section is also obviously written from the point of view of a mainstream American.[10]

Importance of Multicultural Understanding

The traditional and historic view of culture in the United States has been the melting pot, in which ethnic and racial differences were blended, assimilated, and homogenized. As Irvine Hockaday, Jr., president and CEO of Hallmark Cards, says, "If ever that metaphor were apt, it isn't today."[11] Others have suggested our society is now more of a mulligan stew or a tossed salad, where minorities are integrated but not assimilated. Assimilation means sameness. Integration recognizes differences.

Learning about diversity is an opportunity to develop new ways of thinking and new perspectives. Employees need to be able to adapt to new or ambiguous situations and learn new standards and practices. Understanding multicultural diversity will help us increase our job satisfaction and increase customer satisfaction by recognizing variations in customer needs, values, and beliefs. Understanding will help us communicate despite accent and language differences. Several studies have shown that the success of international business depends largely on employees' intercultural communication competence. Employees need to adjust communication skills to fit cross-cultural needs.[12]

Hockaday believes that people are businesses' single sustainable competitive advantage. He has said that businesses must develop a culture of inclusiveness to achieve their goals. The building blocks of this culture are empowerment and education to enable employees to reach their potential, corporate flexibility to meet customer and employee needs, and open two-way communication to promote information and opinion sharing.[13] Allstate Insurance Company has been a pioneer in diversity management. The company believes that a diverse workforce translates into diverse customers and vice versa, giving it a competitive advantage. Allstate wants to encourage all employees to bring their talents and perspectives to the table. The company incorporates diversity into its product development, employee recruitment and retention, customer service, and decision making. Allstate employees were surveyed to measure the effectiveness of their leadership and diversity education efforts. The company found that the better that employees perceived their managers' efforts to promote a diverse work environment, the more satisfied they were. In fact, they also found that the higher the leadership and diversity indices, the more likely it was for customers to renew their policies.[14]

Culture shock is confusion, disorientation, and sometimes frustration and anxiety arising from experiences with cultural diversity. Culture shock can come from an unexpected behavior of another person, an unexpected response to our behavior, or the opposite of the behavior or response we expected. It is easier to deny differences than it is to change our beliefs. We may not want to face the fact that our culture does not have a monopoly on truth. If we get confused and impatient because things seem so different, remember that the United States was founded by immigrants. There's never really been a long period in American history when we were culturally homogeneous. Each decade has brought changes. The pioneers, electricity, the Industrial Revolution, automobiles, the Depression, World War II, the Vietnam War, space exploration, television, computers, contemporary music and movies, the Internet, 911, etc., have all contributed to differences.

Some foreign-born people prefer to assimilate into mainstream America. However, for others, assimilation is seen as abandoning their culture and traditions. Maintaining their cultural uniqueness is very important to them. Think about it. If you are mainstream American, could you move to another country and give up speaking English, dressing the way you do, driving on the right side of the road, and celebrating the Fourth of July?

Demographic and Economic Changes

Let's explain how demographics and economics have changed and are changing. Our economy is global. American customer service contact centers are receiving calls and e-mails from around the world. The American population and workforce composition is changing in gender, age, race, national origin, sexual orientation, and physical ability. It has always varied in terms of other sources of diversity. Where does your company's customer and employee diversity come from?

According to the 2000 census, 75 percent of the U.S. population reported that they were "white only," so 25 percent were nonwhite or some combination of white and one or more other races. The 2000 census asked for race information differently from the way it had previously asked for it. In 1990, people could report only one race; in 2000, they could report more than one race. About 13 percent of the population considered themselves Hispanics (they could report that they were white or nonwhite). The proportion of African Americans in the population was 12.3 percent and Asian Americans 3.6 percent. These populations were concentrated in only a few geographic areas, such as California and Texas, but the rest of the United States has changed as well.[15]

The U.S. population grew 13.2 percent from 1990 to 2000. The differences in ethnic populations between 1990 and 2000 are not directly comparable because of the change in reporting. Using race alone, the Asian-American population grew 48.3 percent and the black, or African-American, population grew 15.6 percent. The Hispanic, or Latino, population increased about 57.9 percent. The white population grew about 5.9 percent (see Figure 12.1).[16]

The number of immigrants is increasing due to changes in immigration laws. The growth in the foreign-born population, 27 percent, was nearly four times that of the native population, 7 percent, from 1990 to 1998. The proportion of foreign-born residents, 9.3 percent, in the United States in 1997 is midway between the peak of 14.7 percent in 1890 and the low point of 4.7 percent reported in the 1970 census.[17] In addition, the transitional population, those who come to the United States to work temporarily or go to school, is increasing. Transitionals tend to be highly educated and have considerable buying power and are an important consumer market. English is a second language for about one out of seven American residents.[18]

Workers between 45 and 54 are the fastest-growing segment of the workforce in the 2000s because the Baby Boomers are moving into that age bracket.[19] It was predicted that by 2000, only about 15 percent of new entrants to the workforce

FIGURE 12.1   Increase in Ethnic Populations from 1990 to 2000 Census Based on Race

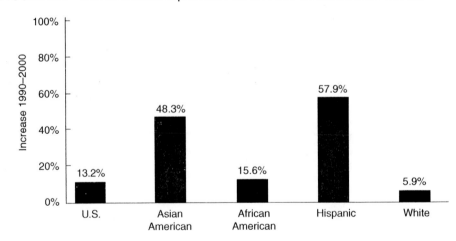

would be white males. According to Department of Labor estimates, nearly 85 percent would be women, minorities, and immigrants.[20] In 1999, it was reported that there were 8 million women-owned businesses in the United States, employing one out of every four workers. Fifty percent of all jobs created in the previous 3 years were started by women. The rate of growth of women-owned businesses was twice as fast as overall business growth. Minority women–owned business growth was three times faster than overall business growth between 1987 and 1996.[21]

Technology and the *Americans with Disabilities Act* of 1990 are enabling more and more people with disabilities to enter the workforce. The move for the rights of the disabled is predicted to continue in the twenty-first century. A 1997 U.S. Bureau of the Census report estimated that about 20 percent of the population, about 50 million people, have a disability. According to the Census Bureau, "A person is considered to have a disability if he or she has difficulty performing certain functions (seeing, hearing, talking, walking, climbing stairs and lifting and carrying), or has difficulty performing activities of daily living, or has difficulty with certain social roles (doing school work for children, working at a job and around the house for adults). A person who is unable to perform one or more activities, or who uses an assistive device to get around, or who needs assistance from another person to perform basic activities is considered to have a severe disability." About three-quarters, 77 percent, of those between the ages of 21 and 64 with a nonsevere disability were employed compared with 82 percent of people without a disability. About one-quarter, 26 percent, of those with a severe disability were employed, an increase from 23 percent in 1991. Specifically, of those with difficulty hearing, 64 percent were employed, and of those with difficulty seeing, 44 percent were employed.[22]

Other changes in the work environment include Generation Xers and retirees as the new entrepreneurs. Their best customers will be the Baby Boomers. Due to need for advanced skills, women are just beginning to break the glass ceiling and move into executive jobs. Jobs will be less separated into men's work and women's work as manufacturing jobs decline and require less physical strength and more computer knowledge. Some companies will hire older job candidates with previous long-term time with one employer to boost employee morale and commitment to companies and take advantage of their knowledge and experience. The workforce hierarchy will be a mishmash of ages.

According to accepted statistics, at least 2 percent of the U.S. population is gay or lesbian although estimates vary widely, to as high as 10 percent. There are now more than 1500 primary religious organizations functioning in the United States. Muslims will soon become the second largest religious group in the United States. Companies may begin to offer flexible holidays rather than the traditional American holidays like Thanksgiving.

Experts predict that flexible hours and access to technology will lead to 24/7 workers, the demise of the weekend, and a fusion of home and work. Employees may become increasingly isolated, with e-mail and voice mail replacing face-to-face exchanges. Telecommuting will increase. Corporate headquarters will be smaller. Companies will use temporary space for employees as needed. The latter three trends suggest lower costs but decreasing control over employee behavior. The number of retail stores will decrease due to the Internet. Those that do survive will focus more on entertainment shopping, which will require a higher degree of employee "acting," similar to the Disney strategy. The customer service skills needed to adapt to these changes can only be guessed at this point.[23]

FIGURE 12.2   The Ethnocentrism Continuum

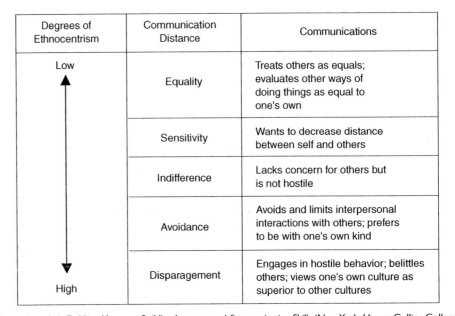

Degrees of Ethnocentrism	Communication Distance	Communications
Low ↑↓ High	Equality	Treats others as equals; evaluates other ways of doing things as equal to one's own
	Sensitivity	Wants to decrease distance between self and others
	Indifference	Lacks concern for others but is not hostile
	Avoidance	Avoids and limits interpersonal interactions with others; prefers to be with one's own kind
	Disparagement	Engages in hostile behavior; belittles others; views one's own culture as superior to other cultures

Source: Joseph A. DeVito, *Messages: Building Interpersonal Communication Skills* (New York: HarperCollins College Publishers, 1996), 253.

Ethnocentrism

Ethnocentrism is the tendency to evaluate the values, beliefs, and behaviors of one's own culture as more positive, superior, logical, and natural than those of other cultures. Ethnocentrism is the belief that our own beliefs and behavior are superior or the only right ones. It has elements of racial superiority, cultural elitism, and the insinuation that other cultures are exactly like ours, or if not, should be. Ethnocentric people think that the behavior of others can be interpreted according to the values and rules of their own culture and that their culture is a way of life toward which everyone else is striving. The catch is that it's not true. Everybody's actions do not have the same meaning and are not derived from the same motives. Not that it's wrong to like and prefer our own culture, but it causes us to misinterpret people from other cultures (see Figure 12.2).

Ethnocentrism is an attitude that is comfortable, and so it is hard to change. The first step in overcoming it is to learn about other cultures. The second step is to become aware that our culturally tinted glasses distort perception and cause us to misinterpret the behavior of others. One way to do that is to become aware of our own specific points of view. What culture and subcultures influence your view? If you are Christian, how does that influence your perception of a non-Christian? What if you are a woman, a man, wealthy, poor, a Texan, or a Tennessean?

As we get older, we may become less ethnocentric. Many parents in the 1960s were aghast at the way teenagers dressed and wore beards and long hair. In the 2000s, the then-teenagers are now parents and grandparents of teenagers, and some may well be aghast at body piercing and tattoos. Those of you who are 20-something, what are your teenagers going to do in the 2020s?

Stereotyping

Stereotyping is believing that all people in a group are alike and leaving no room for individual differences. This is human nature because we have a strong urge to categorize and associate to simplify remembering and thinking. However, stereotyping is generally considered negative because it tends to be inflexible and based on ignorance rather than evidence. Stereotypes are judgments whether someone is good or bad, normal or abnormal, or right or wrong. A judgment based on a stereotype says more about the speaker than the person judged.

Stereotypes are inaccurate because individuals differ according to numerous influences. One is socioeconomic background in terms of education, social status, and financial status. Others are geographic, age, gender, historical experiences, individual personality and style, maturity, time, and assimilation. Do you stereotype?

* Do you categorize whole groups of people without recognizing individuals? "Gen Xers are slackers."
* Do you consider an individual an exception to the rule if he or she does not fit the stereotype, or do you question why the person is acting differently? "You're OK for a woman." "Old people don't act like that."
* Do you expect an individual to be a spokesperson for a group? Rather than ask what Kevin, who is gay, thinks, do you say, "Kevin, what do gay men think about this?"
* Do you describe or picture people in stereotypical terms? A historic example is the way women have been pictured in subordinate roles in television commercials.
* Do you label or judge behavior rather than seek to understand it? Do you think "Brazilians are rude and pushy," rather than realize that their sense of space is just different from that of mainstream Americans?
* Do you think that people who are blind have much better hearing than sighted people?

Stereotyping can result in lost opportunities, can be very offensive, and could be self-fulfilling. Learn to recognize your and others' stereotypes. If they are unconscious, we may act on them without being aware of it. Identify your silent assumptions. Think about the source of information for the assumptions. Check to see if they are true for this individual. Gen Xers are not homogeneous, not all alike. A more minor attitude issue, pet peeves, can be a problem as well. They are hot buttons concerning behavior or language that we have a strong reaction to, and they may affect how we treat our customers.[24]

A student told this story about a salesperson in an automotive parts store. There were four 20-something Hispanic men in the store. The salesperson behind the counter was loudly belittling them, saying, "What are you people doing in here? You don't need anything. You can't speak English. You don't have any money." The young men were embarrassed, laughing, and trying to pretend the man was kidding. The student asked another salesperson if the man knew the young men and was just joking around or serious, and he said, "No, he just doesn't like them." She went up to the counter and told the salesperson that he was being rude and if he wasn't careful, the young men were going to come back with knives. We guess she was stereotyping a little herself.

Cultural Differences

Most non-Western cultures value harmony and balance, and so people avoid direct or negative confrontations and believe in saving face to minimize embarrassment. They believe that maintaining group harmony is more important than expressing personal opinions. In over two-thirds of non-American cultures, the needs of the group, company, or family are more important than the needs of an individual. This is the very opposite of mainstream American culture. Americans think they should express their opinion even if it is in opposition to the beliefs of others in the group.

In general, mainstream Americans believe in planning and controlling the future and bringing about change. We believe new ideas and new ways of doing things are usually beneficial. This is not the case in most other cultures. Other cultures use history as a guide for the present and believe tradition should be maintained.

Values and beliefs determine:

* Right and wrong
* Whether fate or we control our lives
* Who has authority, what their powers are, and how those in authority should be treated
* Whether privacy is desirable or undesirable
* How time is scheduled and used
* Whether old age is valuable
* What are worthwhile goals
* Differences in the roles of men and women and how they should behave in the society
* How decisions are made
* The meaning of competition

How we view time is influenced by culture. According to Thiederman, in the English language, clocks "run," in Spanish, they "walk," and in Native American dialect, they "tick." Time is precious to mainstream Americans. As explained in Chapter 6 on nonverbal communication, we operate on monochronic time. We believe that schedules should be established and maintained rather than that schedules are flexible and less important than people and events. Much of the rest of the world views time as polychronic. However, most immigrants who are in business adjust to Americans' sense of time.

Cultures differ on what is beautiful, ugly, humorous, risqué, and embarrassing. Culture determines what foods are considered edible, what foods are taboo, and what foods taste good. We differ on what is appropriate personal hygiene and clothing. Colors mean different things in different cultures. Culture affects logistical needs in terms of money, transportation, measurements, and sizing. People in many other countries think Americans are backward because we do not use the metric system. Imagine their confusion with our measuring system. They think using feet and inches is rather strange.

There are numerous subcultures in the United States, geographically, within cities, and within states. One of the subcultures is people living in poverty. Poverty has a very real impact on how people conduct transactions and receive information. People living in poverty may lack basic needs of decent housing, good food, and transportation, and so their attitudes and priorities are very different from those of the mainstream culture. They may feel a loss of control over their lives. They often mistrust and fear those in authority, including service providers. Being aware of these differences can help us meet the needs of these customers, offering them the same respect, attention, and dignity that any other customers receive.

ADAPTATION

Given the significant numbers of immigrants and transitional residents, companies that can adapt to these customers will gain a competitive edge. Adaptations include changing marketing strategies, training the workforce, and educating foreign-born customers about goods and services. Companies can adjust systems and service to address needs and accommodate norms if necessary and possible. Companies have begun providing informational materials in multiple languages. Other companies are hiring multilingual customer service providers. Firms should provide internal sources of support for employees with questions. There are no formulas; every situation will be different.

Companies need to increase the cultural literacy and sensitivity of their employees. Education will help them adjust their customer service behavior. We need to familiarize ourselves with the cultures we serve and learn about their values, attitudes, and norms. Their perceptions, how they see the world, are based on their culture. Many people believe that different means wrong. We cannot assume our "common sense" is everyone's common sense. If we make judgments about people and do not make an effort to see beyond stereotypes, we will be unable to provide our customers with exceptional service. Realize that everyone is different in some way. None of us sees the world in exactly the same way. The bottom line is that everyone should receive respectful, fair treatment. We should be polite and conduct ourselves professionally. Character traits to develop are open-mindedness, tolerance, adaptability, a sense of humor, curiosity, empathy, and respect.

Remember that our standards are culturally influenced as well. We queue and consider cutting in line rude. In other countries, they crowd, and first shove, first serve wins. We should not take cultural slights personally. They are a reflection of cultural background and not meant to offend. For example, men from some other cultures are not accustomed to dealing with women as equals or professionals. Therefore, we should not take offense if they treat women differently.

On the other hand, cultural understanding is a two-way street. Ethnocentrism is a two-way street. We are all ethnocentric and we are all human, and so give-and-take is important. We should not assume that in America, the only people who must adjust are mainstream Americans. The understanding and respect goes both ways. It is impossible to meet the cultural expectations of every non-American customer. We need to teach non-American customers about American business practices. Clarify American terminology. Minimize cultural confusions by explaining the "whys" behind certain practices. Education done responsibly and tactfully is a way to help people from different backgrounds adjust to new norms.

Some types of diversity training can make a situation worse because they trivialize individuality and encourage stereotyping. Companies begin treating everyone differently based on race, culture, or sex. Civil rights laws forbid employers from making decisions, no matter how well intentioned, on the basis of any class- or category-based assumptions. In addition, it is too complicated to apply different rules to each person based on his or her ethnic background, culture, or gender. It is not possible to remember all the rules, and it's not possible always to figure out which rule applies when. It is permissible to acknowledge the differences among people and cultures. It is not considered racist. On the contrary, ignoring differences is implying they do not exist and is disrespectful.[25]

Nonverbal Communication

The art of listening and speaking is greatly valued in many Hispanic, black, and Asian cultures. You may have had the experience with someone who fidgets, picks up papers, and turns his back momentarily to look at something while you are talking. How did you feel? You probably felt as if the person was not listening. He would tell you that he heard everything you said. You don't believe it though, because he was not attentive. This may offend in not only some cultural situations but also based on gender and regional origin.[26]

Body language is more important to people from other cultures than it is to mainstream Americans. As discussed in Chapter 6, there are many different meanings in eye contact, facial expressions, hand gestures, body movement, and proxemics. Determine the customers' culture, and learn the critical nonverbal differences.

A smile is understood almost universally as a sign of goodwill. However, whom we smile at, how often we smile, and under what circumstances we smile does vary. We think service providers should smile and make friendly conversation with customers, whereas in other cultures providers should be reserved and respectful toward customers. We consider service providers as equals. Elsewhere they may be seen as a different social class. Cultures differ on whether browsing, touching merchandise, and trying on apparel is acceptable.[27]

If you are not able to understand customers because of a foreign accent, it is okay to tactfully tell them you are having difficulty. Ask if they will slow down a little bit so you can get all the information correct. Do not pretend to understand if you do not. Take the time and listen to the pattern of speech so you will be able to pick up a few key words. There is no need to repeat one word over and over. Be careful how you say you can't understand. An abrupt "I can't understand you" or "What did you say?" is rude. Keep job aids available for translations.[28]

Etiquette and protocol are different among different cultures. Mainstream America is quite informal. We have relatively few rules about proper behavior. We consider formality somewhat cold and distant. However, with other cultures we must maintain more formality in order not to offend. Americans need to take more time developing relationships with those from other cultures, we should be receptive to the use of last names and titles, we should be restrained with compliments, we should respect and observe small rituals of relationships, and we should respect older members of a group.

It is the spirit of etiquette that matters, not the letter. It is all right to ask about etiquette differences. It is okay to observe the other person's actions. If you genuinely make an effort and make a mistake out of ignorance, it is all right to apologize. A mistake is often overlooked out of embarrassment or pride, and people may deny they were offended, but an apology will be heard and appreciated.[29]

Verbal Communication

In terms of verbal behavior, we must be aware of what should be said, what should not be said, and whether communication should be direct or indirect. To be safe, we should not ask intrusive personal questions. Interruptions are often considered rude, and pauses and silence are good. Humor and sarcasm may be misunderstood. We should not refer to employees or customers by ethnic-, disability-, or gender-based nicknames. We should not make disparaging remarks or joke about race, ethnicity, gender, and disabilities.

Learn how your customers prefer to be addressed. Koreans write their last name first, but when they come to the United States, they reverse it to fit in. Some countries do not use last names. Ask, "How would you like me to address you?" Even if you must ask more than once, pronounce names correctly. Do not give someone a nickname just because it's easier. Americans believe that using first names is friendly; in other cultures, first names are disrespectful. Americans assume we can address anyone in a group. Elsewhere, whom it is acceptable to address is based on age and gender. Be formal until you are told differently. Avoid assuming anything.

What is it like to speak English or another language as a second language? People may be anxious about being misunderstood, feel inexperienced, or be passive and not ask questions when they should. When immigrants speak their native language among themselves around people who do not understand it, it is a misconception that they are trying to exclude outsiders. The real reason is that they feel less isolated, it's easier, and it reduces stress. Speaking a new language is a strain.

We may assume someone who cannot speak our language does not understand it. The truth is that it is easier to understand than it is to speak it. Those of us who have learned another language know that pronunciation is the toughest part. In addition, speakers often confuse pronouns, mispronounce words, use incorrect words and endings, and have different voice intonation and inflection stressing inappropriate words or syllables and speaking in a different rhythm. How do you react to an accent? Do you assume the person is uneducated, not assimilated into the culture, and ignorant of grammar?

English as a language is complicated and confusing. For one thing, English uses sounds that other languages lack. Some English sounds do not exist in other languages, like the "sh" and "ch" for Spanish people and the "r" and "l" for Japanese. Foreign speakers may raise their voice at the end of each statement as is customary in their language. Americans perceive that as a question. Did you ever consider that "fat chance" and "slim chance" mean the same thing? Why do we park our car in a driveway and drive on the parkway? "Bad" and "cool" and "hot" are all good. What's the difference between calling your boss a "wise man" or a "wise guy"? American *idioms* (see Table 12.1) confuse people; some of them confuse mainstream Americans.

As English-speaking service providers in America, we can improve communication with those for whom English is a second language by the following:

* Face customers and let them read your lips.
* Organize your thoughts to avoid backtracking and information overload.
* Speak slower than usual. Be patient. Be willing to repeat.
* Speak distinctly. Enunciate each word. Be aware of your accent.
* Do not talk louder.
* Use short sentences. Avoid run-on sentences.
* Emphasize key words.
* Use simple, familiar English. Avoid jargon, slang, and acronyms.
* Say exactly what you mean. Don't use idioms.
* Allow longer pauses between sentences or after questions to allow customers time to translate.

TABLE 12.1   Idioms

Horse of a different color
Pulling my leg
Jump down my throat
Snow job
Spill the beans
Jump the gun
Scratch my back
Go fly a kite
Bite the bullet
Face the music
Bury the hatchet
Let sleeping dogs lie

* Repeat and recap frequently. Check for understanding.
* Provide written materials. Use visual aids.

Speak your customer's language. It pays to speak, or have someone in your organization speak, the language of the community you serve. When asking another person to assist you, it is very rude to say, "So and so doesn't speak English very well." Another good idea is to learn a few appropriate phrases in each language you encounter. Using a few words in someone's language, even if not pronounced correctly, will be appreciated.[30]

Use interpreters if customers prefer. When using an interpreter, speak to the customer, not to the interpreter. Allow more time. Be careful when hiring interpreters. Even if they are independent contractors, they still represent your company. Just being able to speak another language does not make one an interpreter. Interpretation requires facilitating a conversation between two parties. It may involve terminology and knowledge of medical, financial, and other technical fields. Interpreters must have proven qualifications. Assess a candidate for interpreter just as you would any other staff. Check for certification. Check references.[31]

One approach for providing customer service for a contact center with a diverse customer base is Language Line Services, founded in the late 1970s in California and now owned by AT&T. Language Line provides online translation for 140 languages throughout the United States, Canada, and Great Britain. A customer service representative calls Language Line and is connected to an interpreter, usually in less than 45 seconds. A three-way conversation is then conducted. Language Line has 8000 business customers. The company employs hundreds of interpreters, 70 percent of whom work out of their homes. The interpreters must pass stringent tests in native, nonnative, and English languages.[32]

Complaints

Americans believe that it's all right to point out an employee's mistake or complain. In other cultures, it is inappropriate because the service provider would lose face. Asian and Hispanic customers tend to complain in very softened terms. Asians consider it wrong to say anything negative. To save face, an unhappy Asian customer will just disappear even more quietly than a mainstream American customer. If you ask directly if everything is satisfactory, you may not be able to tell if it really is or if it is a vague answer to cover up real dissatisfaction.

1. Learn to recognize the softened complaints.
2. Let customers know that you want and need their complaints and advice in order to run a more successful business.
3. Make certain that your customers know that their suggestions will be listened to and that they will make a real difference.
4. Make certain that your customers understand how, where, and to whom to complain.
5. Make it easy for customers to complain in private, thus minimizing embarrassment.
6. Invite anonymous complaints by using complaint forms and a suggestion box.[33]

CUSTOMERS WITH DISABILITIES

In our business careers, we will encounter customers and coworkers with a disability. The customers have buying power. Coworkers, internal customers, have talent and expertise. Smile and treat anyone with a disability with respect and dignity. Appropriate language when talking about people with disabilities should be positive and straightforward. Address a person with a disability directly rather than addressing someone with the person. Use a title rather than a first name, as we should with all customers. Do not refer to a disability unless it is relevant. Verbal language should not be insensitive or negative. The words should not emphasize the disability over the person, as in "the disabled person," "the blind," or "the handicapped." Say "people with disabilities" or "a woman who is blind" rather than "disabled people" or "a blind woman." Remember that the overwhelming majority of people with disabilities are not ill. Avoid emotional descriptions, such as "confined to a wheelchair" or "afflicted with MS."[34]

When meeting with a person in a wheelchair, do not have the person look up at you all during the conversation. Sit in a chair or kneel so you are at eye level. Avoid bumping the chair; it is an extension of the person. Ask if you may push the wheelchair before you do so. Some people appreciate it; others like maintaining their independence.

Greet a person who is visually impaired face-to-face; introduce yourself, speaking clearly. You may make physical contact on the arm. The worst thing to do is to not look at someone who is visually impaired. Because people who are visually impaired may have acute hearing, they know when you are not facing them or are doing something else while speaking, and they will consider your behavior rude. Introduce anyone who comes in the room. Let them know if you leave the room or area. Again, ask if they need assistance rather than just helping.[35]

When speaking with people who are hearing-impaired, face them, make sure they can see your entire face, and maintain eye contact. Take off dark glasses. Do not look down to write or look away while speaking in case they are reading lips. Don't shout, because it distorts the sound of words and lip movements. Don't assume they can lip-read long or unusual words. Rephrase if they do not understand rather than repeating the same words. Don't be embarrassed to write something down, like technical or difficult words. Provide American Sign Language interpreters. Speak to customers, not to their interpreters.[36]

Give people with a speech impairment time to express themselves; resist the temptation to finish sentences. A person with a speech or mobility impairment does not necessarily have a mental limitation. A developmental challenge may be mental or physical or both. You need to listen and be patient. You may need to repeat yourself, especially if you are explaining or instructing. Be sensitive to the person's needs. Often, independence is very important.

The 1990 Americans with Disabilities Act applies to business accommodation for employees and customers. It covers people with physical, mental, and emotional impairment. Each business must provide reasonable accommodations for employees and customers. The meaning of "reasonable" has been evolving since the legislation was passed. If an "undue hardship," such as excessive cost, is involved, the business may not be required to provide the accommodation. Many of the accommodations involve building and interior structure and access.

In most cases, a retail store is not required to have a sign language interpreter for customers who are hearing-impaired or Braille signs for those who are vision-impaired. However, to provide exceptional service, an individual customer service provider could read labels for a visually impaired customer or write information down for a hearing-impaired customer. Make it easy for customers with disabilities to shop in your store. Service personnel should be on the lookout for ways they can help when they are needed.[37]

Skill Development 12.2

1. How does your company assist multicultural customers?
2. How does your company assist customers with disabilities?

EMOTIONAL LABOR

Frontline customer service jobs—from call centers, to retail, to the hospitality industry—are very stressful due to the need to serve demanding, angry, and abusive customers who are "always right." Frustration is worse if all complaints are treated equally, justified or not. Employees who are criticized for the way they dealt with an unreasonable customer for an unjustified complaint will resent it. Studies have found that *"emotional labor,"* in which employees are faced with managing their emotions on the job, is damaging to the health and morale of employees. Especially interesting is the finding that employees who bury their emotions and fake their feelings were more likely to suffer burnout and emotional exhaustion. They also received lower ratings on their customer service skills from coworkers. Research shows that the stress from bottling up feelings leads to health problems, which cost companies millions of dollars every year.

A research study found that when customers become angry with salespeople, much of the time salespeople respond with hostility. Most of the customer anger was generated by something the salesperson did, for example, being rude, being unhelpful, or having a personal telephone conversation and ignoring a customer. In a few cases, the anger resulted from problems with a legitimate request for a refund or lack of product knowledge. The anger display by customers included a frown and aggressive behavior such as glaring, using bad language, yelling, and saying they would never shop there again. The customers expected the salesperson to apologize and help overcome the problem or compensate them. When the salesperson responded as the customer expected, customer satisfaction was higher. In this study, salespeople displayed anger back or did not respond at all. Psychology research shows that anger consistently threatens and causes anger in others, making it one of the most contagious emotions. The study recommends that salespeople learn to recognize customer emotions and respond according to customer expectations. However, there is evidence that the emotional cost of controlling the natural reaction to anger too often results in lower employee satisfaction and long-term work alienation.

Lack of resources and poor work design and scheduling contribute to this problem. In addition, productivity goals, time limits on helping customers, and requirements to complete daily non-customer service tasks may interfere with employees' abilities to handle challenging customers. Therefore, customers are even more upset and take it out on the employees. If customer service is a priority and customers are number one, then customers should be number one and everything else second.

Employees must be supported in these difficult situations. Companies should find ways to reduce employee stress. Supervisors and managers need to be on the front line to show support and show that they understand what the employees are dealing with. Give an employee who has just handled a tough customer a short break.

Should employees talk about their problem customers and vent to other employees? Sometimes it is helpful to let off steam. However, if an employee is constantly talking about problems, it will eventually seem very negative, which may affect other employees' moods. Perhaps there should be set times to vent. An employee could vent to a supervisor or an experienced coworker. Some employees might benefit just from writing out the story, then throwing it away. Some problem situations are the kind that should be discussed in a staff meeting. A representative can talk about how she solved a problem so others can benefit. A representative can ask how others have solved a problem.

One solution, especially for inexperienced entry-level workers, is to have them turn excessively demanding and abusive customers over to an experienced coworker. Frontline employees learn how to handle most angry customers, but when they cannot, the more experienced employees or management should take over. When the manager has tried the appropriate solutions and has been flexible, but still nothing will satisfy the customer, the problem should be handed over to the corporate office. Another solution is more empowerment of frontline employees and training in problem solving. Employees need to know what they can and cannot do, how much leeway they have in terms of satisfying the customer, and when to get help. Telling them exactly what to do and say increases their confidence and morale.

A recommendation for employees to reduce the effect of emotional labor is to do what works best for them. Each person's style is different. Perhaps an employee is great at eye contact but not so good at remembering names. Maybe an employee is an introvert who is not going to turn into a gregarious, bubbly person overnight. If employees try to change their nature, it will be emotionally draining, and they may not pull it off anyway. Employees should emphasize what comes naturally, what they do well, and what does not require extraordinary effort. Then gradually work on other skills.[38]

Skill Development 12.3

How does your company assist employees with stress and emotional labor?

TERMS

vent
empathize
mistaken customers
high-maintenance customers
chronic complainers
scammers
litigious customers
abusive customers
diversity

mainstream American culture
culture shock
Americans with Disabilities Act
ethnocentrism
stereotyping
idioms
emotional labor

DISCUSSION QUESTIONS

1. What is the difference between a dissatisfied customer and an angry customer?
2. What steps should a customer service provider follow in an angry customer situation?
3. Are customers always right? How should companies approach this concept?
4. Name one type of problem customer. Why is this customer challenging? How do you handle this situation?
5. How do problem customers affect other customers? What can be done?
6. What are customer responsibilities? Describe a situation you experienced in which the customer was not being responsible.
7. What does diversity mean in a customer service context?
8. Why is understanding multicultural diversity important in today's business environment?
9. Name some of the demographic and economic changes in the United States that affect customer service.
10. Define ethnocentrism and stereotyping.
11. How can customer service providers adapt to multicultural customers' needs? To the needs of customers with disabilities?
12. What is emotional labor? What can companies do about this problem?

CASE—NOWHERE YOU WANT TO BE

On a Monday, Erica received a telephone call at her office from her bank credit card company asking if she had paid her bill. She told the company representative that she had mailed the bill that morning. When he asked how much she sent, she said that she paid the entire bill. She explained that the payment was late because it had been misplaced on her desk and had not been mailed. When she arrived home, in the mail was a past due notice stating that, "YOUR [credit card] ACCOUNT IS NOW 07 DAYS PAST DUE IN THE AMOUNT OF $25.00. WE REALIZE THIS IS PROBABLY AN OVERSIGHT BUT IT IS NECESSARY THAT YOU FORWARD THIS DELINQUENT AMOUNT OR CALL US AT THE NUMBER SHOWN. IF PAYMENT HAS BEEN MADE, THANK YOU. IF NOT, PLEASE CALL TODAY." There was also a message on her voice mail from the same person who had called at work asking her to return his call, to a non-800 number.

At this point, Erica was irate, having received two phone calls, one at work no less, and the past due notice, especially since she had never had a late payment before on any credit card. She decided to call the bank's 800 number to express her dissatisfaction. She had to wait 15 minutes for a representative to answer the telephone, with the message "Your call is very important to us" repeated over and over. She told the rep that she was extremely displeased with the past due notice process and that she had been on hold for 15 minutes. The customer service representative was flustered and did not know how to handle the call. She transferred Erica to someone else. The second person was reasonably nice and apologized that this had happened. He offered to deduct the $15 late fee, but Erica said the late fee was not the problem since her payment was indeed late.

To follow up, she wrote a letter to the company on February 3, saying, "The number of, timing of, and attitude expressed by the calls and notice was rude and uncalled for." She outlined the following:

"I think your telephone calls and 7-day past due notice were precipitous. I did not like the language and tone of the past due notice. You recognize it was 'probably an oversight,' but the terminology is rude and in capital letters. I resent being called at work and receiving a message at home to call a long distance number. I resent being asked how much I had sent since the minimum was only $25. I have an excellent credit history, always send the full amount, and have never had a balance due. Furthermore, if you are going to have an 800 number, you need to staff it. The phone rep told me it was 'after hours' and so it took longer to answer. There is nothing on your notice to indicate what your hours are, so I assumed they were 24/7 and staffed accordingly." She also wrote that she was considering moving her and her husband's three bank accounts worth about $200,000 to another bank.

On February 17, she received a letter of apology. The letter was as follows:

"Thank you for taking the time to write us. We agree the 7-day past due notice was precipitous, and effective last month the notice was deleted. It seems that you received the notice just prior to this change being made. Our Customer Service Department is staffed Monday through Friday, 7 a.m. to 7 p.m. The wait time you experienced is inexcusable, and this, along with the manner in which we handled your call, is being addressed. The $15 late charge has been credited to your account. It is our desire to provide excellent customer service, and we appreciate your comments and complaints. We value your business and will strive to provide you the best service possible. Please do not hesitate to contact me should you have any problems in the future."

1. What are the customer service problems in this case?
2. Would you have done what Erica did?
3. How well was this handled?

NOTES

1. Erskine Ausbrooks, "Keys to Handle Customer Complaints and Deal with Nasty Acting People without Becoming One of Them," presentation to customer service class, Pellissippi State Technical Community College, Knoxville, TN, Spring 1994.

2. This information is from Mary Beth Ingram, "How to Handle an Irate Caller," *Modern Office Technology,* reprint, March 1992; Lucy W. Gibson, "Being Nice to Nasty People," presentation to customer service class, Pellissippi State Technical Community College, Knoxville, TN, Spring 1994; Monica Jenks, "Ten Easy Steps to Defusing Anger," *Mobius,* June 1993, 36–39; and Ausbrooks, "Keys to Handle Customer Complaints."

3. Jenks, "Ten Easy Steps to Defusing Anger," 38–39.

4. Michael Schrage, "Honest, I Am Not a Boor: Reader-Relationship Management," *Fortune,* 140, no. 9 (November 8, 1999): 324; and Chris Penttila, "Touch Customers," *Entrepreneur* 29, no. 5 (May 2001): 94.

5. Mary Beth Ingram, "Dealing with Repeaters and Prank Calls," *Mobius,* March 1994, 18–19.

6. Park Elliott Dietz, "Abnormal Consumer Behavior," *Mobius,* Spring 1989, 14–15.

7. Kristin Anderson and Ron Zemke, "Customers from Hell: When Is Enough, Enough?" *Mobius,* September 1995, 4–5.

8. Mary Jo Bitner, Bernard H. Booms, and Lois A. Mohr, "Critical Service Encounters: The Employee's Viewpoint," *Journal of Marketing,* October 1994, 95–106.

9. Charles L. Martin, "Consumer-to-Consumer Relationships: Satisfaction with Other Consumers' Public Behavior," *Journal of Consumer Affairs* 30, no. 1 (Summer 1996): 146–170.

10. Sondra Thiederman, *Profiting in America's Multicultural Marketplace: How to Do Business across Cultural Lines* (New York: Lexington Books, 1991).

11. Irvine O. Hockaday, Jr., "Developing a Culture of Inclusiveness," *Mobius* 10, no. 3 (Summer 1991): 13–15.

12. Jensen J. Zhao and Calvin Parks, "Self-Assessment of Communication Behavior: An Experiential Learning Exercise for Intercultural Business Success," *Business Communication Quarterly* 58, no. 1 (March 1995): 20–27.

13. Hockaday, "Developing a Culture of Inclusiveness."

14. American Management Association, "Diversity: A Competitive Weapon," *Management Review,* July–August 1999, 24.

15. U.S. Bureau of the Census, "Overview of Race and Hispanic Origin," [Census Brief online], March 2001, 2–3, available from http://census.gov, accessed September 14, 2001.

16. U.S. Bureau of the Census, "Population by Race and Hispanic or Latino Origin for the United States: 1990 and 2000," April 2, 2001, available from http://www.census.gov, accessed September 14, 2001.

17. U.S. Bureau of the Census, "Nearly 1 in 10 U.S. Residents Are Foreign-Born, Census Bureau Reports," news release, September 17, 1999, available from http://www.census.gov/Press-Release/www/1999/cb99-171.html, accessed March 12, 2001.

18. Barbara Collins, "Serving the Foreign-Born Consumer," *Mobius,* Winter 1990, 18–22.

19. Raymond L. Hilgert and Edwin C. Leonard, Jr., *Supervision: Concepts and Practices of Management* (Cincinnati: South-Western College Publishing, 2001), 12.

20. Genevieve Capowski, "Managing Diversity," *Management Review* 85, no. 6 (June 1996): 12–20.

21. "Women in Business: An Update for Women's History Month," *Diversity Suppliers & Business Magazine* 7, no. 5 (Spring 1999): 25.

22. U.S. Bureau of the Census, "Disabilities Affect One-Fifth of All Americans," [Census Brief online], December 1997, available from http://www.census.gov, accessed September 13, 2001.

23. John A. Challenger, "24 Trends Reshaping the Workplace," *Futurist,* September/October 2000, 35–41.

24. Joseph A. DeVito, *Messages, Building Interpersonal Communication Skills* (New York: HarperCollins College Publishers, 1996), 67–68; and Thiederman, *Profiting in America's Multicultural Marketplace,* 11–19.

25. Summarized from Thiederman, *Profiting in America's Multicultural Marketplace;* Phyllis Haynes and Elizabeth Miu-Lan Young, "Effective Cross-Cultural Communication," *Mobius* 10, no. 3 (Summer 1991): 23–24; Lee Gardenswartz and Anita Rowe, "Customer Service. The Accent Is on Diversity," *Working World,* May 14, 1990, 50–52; Stephen M. Paskoff, "Ending the Workplace Diversity Wars," *Training* 33, no. 8 (August 1996): 42–48; and Collins, "Serving the Foreign-Born Consumer."

26. Haynes and Young, "Effective Cross-Cultural Communication."

27. Thiederman, *Profiting in America's Multicultural Marketplace.*

28. Nancy Friedman, "How to Deal with a Foreign Accent," *Customer Relationship Management,* September 1997, 35.

29. Dana May Casperson, *Power Etiquette: What You Don't Know Can Kill Your Career* (New York: AMACOM, 1999), 109.

30. Thiederman, *Profiting in America's Multicultural Marketplace.*

31. Jeanan Yasiri, "Building an Interpretive Services Area," *Customer Relationship Management,* December 1997, 11–13.

32. Janet Webb, "Customer Retention: Language on the Line: Translation Helps to Hang On to a Diverse Customer Base." *Financial Services Marketing* 2, no. 1 (January–February 2000): 46.

33. Thiederman, *Profiting in America's Multicultural Marketplace.*

34. Opportunity Development Center, "How (and When) to Discuss Disabilities, a Guide to Descriptive Words and Images," *Brochure* (Nashville, TN: Office of University Publications, Vanderbilt University, 1988).

35. Casperson, *Power Etiquette.*

36. Terry Wildemann, *1–800 Courtesy, Connecting with a Winning Telephone Image* (Newport, RI: Aegis Publishing, 1999).

37. Laurie A. Shuster, "How Should You Comply with the ADA," *Chilton's Hardware Age* 230, no. 6 (June 1993): 53–57.

38. Kalyani Menon and Laurette Dube, "Ensuring Greater Satisfaction by Engineering Salesperson Response to Customer Emotions," *Journal of Retailing* 76, no. 3 (Fall 2000): 285; and Penttila, "Touch Customers."

13

CUSTOMER PROBLEM RESOLUTION AND RECOVERY

OBJECTIVES

1. Describe customer complaint behavior.
2. Explain customer problem resolution and recovery strategies.
3. Describe customer problem resolution and recovery systems.
4. Describe customer problem resolution and recovery procedures.

CUSTOMER COMPLAINT BEHAVIOR

There will always be a certain number of customer problems and complaints. No one and no company are perfect. Mistakes will be made. This chapter covers problem resolution and recovery—what companies should do to solve customers' problems and keep people as customers.

A *complaint* is a formal expression of dissatisfaction with any aspect of a product or service experience.[1] The term "complaint" seems somewhat misleading. The word implies irate customers; however, many complaints are just requests for adjustments or mild expressions of dissatisfaction. One contact center consultant has stated that only about 5 calls per 100 could be classified as irate, and only 1 per 1000 was actually rude.[2] Most customer contacts concern returns, exchanges, errors, and need for information.

Complaining

When customers have a problem, they do one or a combination of the following:

* Do nothing
* Switch companies, unless there are high switching costs, such as finding a new physician and moving their records

* Complain to the company
* Take action through a third party, such as state consumer affairs department, regulatory agency, small claims court, Better Business Bureau, or consumer advocacy group
* Engage in negative word of mouth

Customers complain to recover economic loss and rebuild self-esteem. They are more likely to complain if the problem is severe, if the product is important to them, and if there is financial loss. They are more likely to complain about a technology failure during self-service than they are to complain about a dissatisfactory encounter with a service person. If customers are high income, younger, and more knowledgeable about products and how to complain, they are more likely to complain. They are less likely to complain if they perceive they have "low-power" ability to influence or control transactions, for example with professional service providers, such as doctors and lawyers.

Experience Discussion 13.1

1. Describe a situation in which you complained to a company.
2. What was the outcome?
3. Were you satisfied with the outcome?
4. How were you treated by the service provider?
5. How much did complaining cost you?
6. If you rarely complain to companies, why is that?
7. What problems are you most likely to complain about?

Not Complaining

If a company does not get many complaints, does that mean it is doing a great job? Not necessarily and probably not. Research convincingly shows that only a small proportion of dissatisfied customers complain.

* Only 25 to 30 percent complained about a problem with manufactured consumer products.
* Only 40 percent complained about large-ticket durables.
* Fewer than 5 percent of complaints about large-ticket durable goods or services ever reach corporate headquarters.[3]

Customers do not complain because:

1. They believe that companies don't care and will not be responsive. They believe it won't do any good. In fact, based on experience, some customers know that companies and their employees won't respond effectively. This brings us to the next reason.
2. They don't think it's worth the cost, time, effort, and hassle.
3. They don't know how. Companies do not make it easy to complain. They don't tell customers where or how to file a complaint. Even if customers know how, complaining may involve complicated forms and steps.
4. They are uncertain about their rights and the firm's obligations, especially for services.

5. They do not like confrontation, especially if they know the service provider. Most people want to be viewed as nice. Complaining feels awkward and pushy. If they are angry, their emotions make it difficult to express their complaint effectively.

6. They know that they will get their revenge by not going back. There's enough competition for customers to take their business elsewhere, and so they are silent.

7. They don't feel they should do a company's work for it, correcting its mistakes. They think companies don't deserve their comments and that companies deserve to go out of business.

8. Some fear that there will be negative consequences or retaliation, such as getting lower-quality care in health care.[4]

Many problems and complaints cost customers considerable time, money, and effort without any guarantee of a resolution. Customers consciously or unconsciously consider the costs of complaining compared with the benefits they expect (see Table 13.1). One cost is the time it takes to determine how to complain and then to do it. Time costs increase if customers must use a complex telephone menu or are put on hold. Complaining also involves actual dollars spent on making trips to a store, photocopying, shipping the product back, making telephone calls, and the like. Another cost is the mental effort, often substantial. The perceived cost is higher if customers are uncomfortable in that type of situation and if they perceive themselves powerless relative to the company. It's higher if they have gotten the runaround previously. The mental cost is higher if they are not familiar with the technology or bureaucracy.

TABLE 13.1   Examples of the Benefits and Costs of Complaining
Benefits must be perceived as greater than the costs for customers to complain.

Benefits

Company resolves problem
Company resolves problem quickly
Service representative apologizes
Resolution is hassle-free
Resolution makes up for financial or other loss
Compensation makes up for costs of complaining
Service representative understands dissatisfaction
Service representative is courteous, helpful, and sincere
Company promises to correct situation that led to problem

Costs

Time to figure out how to complain
Time to collect needed information
Time to complain
Money for trip to store, toll telephone calls, return shipping, photocopying, etc.
Mental effort of confrontation
Mental effort of figuring out company's technology
Mental effort of understanding company's procedures
Discomfort from rude and unhelpful service representative
Runaround
Negative consequences or retaliation

The probability of a company responding and the outcome or type and size of resolution are based on experience with complaining and word of mouth from friends with experience with the company. The benefit may be zero if there is no response at all. The resolution may not be what they wanted and not enough to make it worthwhile. The perceived benefits of complaining need to be high and the perceived costs low.[5]

PROBLEM RESOLUTION AND RECOVERY STRATEGIES

Product

First, companies need to make sure their product has quality and value. They should not promise what they can't deliver. Company promotion should not overstate the case. Companies need to set realistic expectations for customers. If companies have a service guarantee, they need to make sure that their systems are capable of fulfilling it and that employees can and will deliver accordingly. To head off complaints, companies can provide comprehensive product information and troubleshooting guidelines to answer questions and solve customer problems.

If companies do not ensure product quality and service delivery, they may create situations from which there is no recovery. This is particularly true for services since quality is variable, since it cannot be assessed until after a service is performed, and since once the service activity occurs, some services cannot be performed again. The following are examples of problems that have no realistic solution.

* Solving the problem is impossible; there's no acceptable solution. One example is a haircut that is too short. Another is an inexperienced employee spraying weed killer on a customer's prize rose bushes. What about a photo shop that loses a month's worth of photos from a family's first vacation to Australia? Perhaps the photo company could pay for a trip back, but it will not be the same the second time. The family won't catch that look of wonder on Susie's face when she sees a kangaroo for the first time.
* The solution is unknown. The company has not been able to figure out how to fix a software bug.
* There is no time to solve the problem. The traveler gets the wrong type of ticket, but there are no first-class seats available.
* It's too costly to solve the problem, like replacing a car, roof, or refrigerator.

Not only should products and services be right the first time; operating systems must be effective, and people must have skills to provide service. Experts point out six roadblocks: unworkable company systems and procedures, inadequate equipment and supplies, work overload, lack of job know-how, lack of support from internal coworkers, and an uncaring corporate culture.[6] These factors complicate problem resolution and recovery.

Although companies can learn about problems from customer complaints, they should, first of all, develop a system for spotting service failures and quality problems before they get complaints. Frontline employees need to understand their responsibility for noticing problems and approaching dissatisfied customers.[7]

Since a small proportion of dissatisfied customers complain, companies need to be proactive and use preventative measures to identify potential defectors early. Two methods that have been shown to work are service guarantees and pulse calls.

A guarantee tells customers what to expect and that the company values their business and satisfaction. Service guarantees that are unconditional, easy to understand, meaningful, easy to invoke, and easy and quick to collect on encourage customers to report their dissatisfaction so companies can intervene before they lose the customer. Pulse calls are random telephone calls to recent customers to provide an early warning system about problems. One catalog company includes a short survey with every order for the same purpose. If there's a problem, the company apologizes and fixes it. If there are additional problems, the company offers compensation. Any customer with a problem is included in the next periodic satisfaction survey to measure ongoing satisfaction and loyalty.[8]

Experience Discussion 13.2

Describe a product or service failure at your company that would be difficult or impossible to recover from.

Complaint Fact and Fiction

Fiction: Complaints are random and unpredictable. No, many complaints are predictable. Some problems are not 100 percent avoidable, such as billing errors, scanner pricing errors, late delivery, and long waits. Companies should develop decision rules to deal with these mistakes when they do happen.

Fiction: The objective should be to eliminate complaints. Since very few customers complain, companies should actually try to increase complaints to learn about problems. On one level, though, this objective is true—when it means eliminating complaints about a fixable problem. The cost of being 100 percent error-free is prohibitive; however, the better the product, the fewer complaints about a given problem.

Fact: It's not always how well a problem is resolved, but how fast it's resolved. This is essentially true. A fast response is perceived as a desire to correct the problem, satisfy the customer, and maintain the relationship. Delay is seen as stonewalling.

Fiction: If companies delegate too much authority to lower-level personnel, they will be too generous to customers. This is not true. In fact, employees frequently err on the side of being undergenerous rather than overgenerous. In addition, it may well cost companies more when complaints escalate to management. Frontline employees learn when they should not give customers the benefit of the doubt. We're told that they can tell even on the telephone. They can and do check with a supervisor if there is any question. The lack of empowerment causes more dissatisfaction and lost customers than overgenerosity. We will discuss empowerment further later in the chapter.

Fiction: All frontline personnel need high levels of training to deal with angry customers. This is false. When companies have reasonable procedures and policies, most customer problems can be quickly resolved without confrontation. The proportion of angry customers is actually quite low, and so if necessary, those can be turned over to qualified representatives to handle. Training everyone may not be a cost-effective investment.

Fact: If customers are asked what they want to resolve the problem, they will quite often ask for less than a representative intended to offer. This is true. If you ask customers, "What do you think would be fair?" their request may be more than reasonable. Customers will accept a decision in which they participated more easily than being forced to accept what the company wants to do.

Fiction: All complaints should be investigated and responsibility established before being resolved. No, these are two separate issues. If there is a no-fault policy, no questions asked below a certain dollar amount, the problem should be resolved immediately. The problem can be investigated later. Those over a certain dollar amount may need to be investigated, but there should be a time limit on these as well.

Fact: It costs more to get new customers than it does to keep current customers. This is true. How much more is unclear because it depends on so many variables, but customer acquisition costs are labor-intensive and inefficient, whereas retention costs are more equipment-intensive and relatively efficient. Personal selling and advertising are expensive.

Fiction: Reviewing a cross-section of complaints is a good way to measure overall customer satisfaction. This is not true. Complaints are usually the most costly problems from the most articulate customers but are not necessarily the most critical problems or from the most important customers.[9]

Experience Discussion 13.3

1. What are some complaints, like a late delivery, that are predictable and unavoidable?
2. What do you do and say to customers when problems like these occur?

Opportunity

See complaints or expressions of dissatisfaction as an opportunity to show that you really mean to take care of customers. See complaints as information, not criticism. Complaints are information for product improvement. Companies spend considerable amounts of money for marketing research to tell them what customers think. Each customer that contacts the company to complain, adjust a problem, or ask a question is providing the information free.

Problems are an opportunity to prevent customers from going to a competitor. Satisfying customers with problems is about customer retention. Research shows that preventing just 5 percent of customers from defecting can increase profits, and customers are more likely to become loyal customers if their problems are resolved and resolved quickly.[10] Complaint handling costs should be charged as a marketing expense, not an operating or a manufacturing expense. It's a legitimate marketing expense and replaces acquisition costs of getting new customers, which are known to be higher than the costs of keeping customers. A customer contact center that handles complaints should be seen as a profit center, not a cost center, due to the potential for a long-term stream of profits from satisfied customers.[11]

Remember that complaints brought to the company by customers are only the tip of the iceberg. For every actual complainant, there are many more who aren't complaining. One expert suggests using a multiplier to understand the impact of complaints. For instance, 200 complaints about a product or service out of 1 million buying households doesn't seem like much. Companies can survey a representative sample of customers to find out the magnitude of the problem. Say a company finds out that 1 percent of the random sample had the problem. Then, 1 percent of 1 million is 10,000 dissatisfied customers. Assume that the company knows that roughly only 5 percent of dissatisfied customers would complain about this type of problem. The 200 complaints could represent 4000 customers. Therefore, the number dissatisfied could be between 4000 and 10,000 out 1 million. Now the number of dissatisfied customers is more apparent. Even if the estimates are off somewhat, it's still quite a few customers who potentially are dissatisfied.[12]

A 1999 study of complaints that escalated to the Better Business Bureau in a major city found that the businesses often saw the complaints as aberrations or illegitimate efforts by "professional complainers." The fact was that the complainants were average people who had a serious problem and had never or only once before reported a complaint to a third party. The research showed that a primary cause of escalation was the lack of communication and responsiveness to their complaints. These was a large gap between what resolution customers wanted and what the businesses offered. In the end, two-thirds said the company did nothing. Initial complaints about poor product and service quality, when ignored, developed into claims of unethical or illegal business practices.[13]

Problem management does pay off. National Car Rental and IBM have reported a 90 percent-plus intention-to-repurchase rate among customers whose problem was resolved to their satisfaction quickly and easily.[14] A classic study conducted by Technical Assistance Research Programs found that the return on investment in complaint handling departments was 20 to 400 percent depending on the company and industry.[15] Remember the benefits of exceptional customer service—loyal customers and positive word of mouth—from Chapter 3. Remember that customers who are satisfied with a company's response to a complaint are actually more likely to buy from that company. Loyal customers cost less than new customers. Exceptional problem resolution also enhances employee loyalty, which, in turn, contributes to customer loyalty. Keep in mind that poor recovery can result in active negative word of mouth. Resolution and recovery are simply good business sense.

Customer Expectations

Some customers just want the company to do something about the problem so it does not happen to anyone else. They may realize they cannot be compensated, but they want the company to fix the problem. They feel as if they are doing the company a favor to bring it to the company's attention. Others want an employee to be corrected, better trained, or reprimanded. Representatives should assure them they will report the situation.

Research shows that 40 to 60 percent of customers who complain are dissatisfied with the outcome.[16] When customers have a serious problem, they want justice or fairness, which includes *outcome fairness, procedural fairness,* and *interactional justice.* A fair outcome is compensation of some kind. Customers expect a refund, repair or replacement, correction or adjustment of charges, or some combination. In a worst case scenario, customers are ignored and their problem is never resolved. Customers often believe that the compensation is inadequate given the costs they incurred to complain, such as making three telephone calls or two trips to the store. If customers think the resolution and treatment are unfair, they are likely to defect and engage in negative word-of-mouth behavior, especially if they believe that the problem is preventable but will continue to occur.[17] Customers have favorable attitudes toward a resolution when there are no-hassle refunds or exchanges, apologies, and some type of compensation for inconvenience. Customers also prefer being given a choice of options to resolve the problem.[18]

The first requirement for procedural fairness is that companies must assume responsibility for a failure. Second, problems should be handled quickly, preferably by the first service person contacted. Customers resent repeating their complaint to several employees, especially if they seem unconcerned or, worse, have the attitude that it's not the company's responsibility. Third, procedures and policies should be flexible so individual circumstances can be considered.

Customer perceptions of interactional justice or interpersonal treatment include courtesy, concern, honesty, and a genuine effort to fix a problem. A recent study found that customers who received a fair outcome, but who were treated rudely, were less likely to return and more likely to make negative comments about the company.[19] Two barriers for employees in this regard are lack of empowerment to resolve problems and lack of training in how to react to unhappy or even angry customers. Customers also want to know why a problem happened. This can be a touchy issue to address without admitting a service failure or laying blame. Be prepared to explain what might have happened or why a policy exists. Customers do not have to like your explanation, but they need to understand it.[20]

A study of restaurant customers outlines a way to evaluate problem recovery strategies. Service failures were rated on the effectiveness of the recovery strategy, with 1 equal to very poor and 10 equal to very good. The research found that it was particularly difficult to recover from facility problems (cleanliness), employee behavior (rudeness and poor attitudes), seating problems (noisy party at the next table), and out-of-stock conditions. There was no resolution or attempt to recover in quite a few circumstances. Not surprisingly, this was considered the worst approach. A simple correction of a failure and an apology were also not considered effective. Recoveries that involved some type of compensation were rated the most favorably. Customers preferred compensation that could be used on the spot rather than not being redeemable until another visit.[21]

PROBLEM RESOLUTION AND RECOVERY SYSTEMS

Service recovery is defined by Tax and Brown as a process that identifies service failures, effectively resolves customer problems, classifies their root causes(s), and yields data that can be integrated with other measures of performance to assess and improve the service system.[22]

Encourage Complaints

A company should let customers know that it respects the right of customers to complain. To create the belief that they want customers to complain, companies should issue explicit guarantees of satisfaction. A recent study found that customers who believe companies will respond positively and customers who have a positive attitude toward complaining were more likely to complain. Even if customers do not like to complain, they will if a company has a reputation for responding positively. Those that did not expect companies to respond positively and did not like to complain were less likely to complain and more likely to engage in negative word-of-mouth behavior. Policies, such as "No refund after 30 days or without a receipt" send a negative signal.[23]

To decrease the costs of complaining, make it easy for customers to complain. Give them a clear process for reporting a complaint. The system should be visible and accessible. Publicize where and how they should do it and what to expect. Companies that want customers to complain put messages on products, product packaging and labeling, sales slips, brochures, and signs in store sales and service areas. They include information in mailings, use and care manuals, advertising, and consumer educational materials.[24]

Customers have traditionally written to companies or called toll-free numbers. Other options are available today through the Internet. Companies provide e-mail addresses and web forms on their website. Web forms, which are delivered to an agent, have fields for customer information and radio buttons to select choices. One disadvantage of web forms is company requirements for personal information, that customers would rather not provide, such as a telephone number that could be used for telemarketing. Some companies make this type of information optional. A second disadvantage is loss of entries due to a lost connection.

Newer options are live web chat and instant messaging, in which a user is informed that someone is online and available to talk with them. It's been reported that a service representative can handle up to six web chat sessions at a time. An even newer option is VoIP, voice over the Internet (IP stands for Internet protocol), which involves talking through the computer with an agent. Customers need a plug-in, microphone, and speakers. The advantages are that it doesn't require two phone lines and the company has no call charges. As of May 2002, the voice quality was considered too poor to be useful. Other new developments for customer information are interactive television, which is used to show customers rather than just tell them the answer to their question; capacity to retrieve video instructions; intelligent agents to help customers find what they need; simultaneous, automatic translation to another language; and, eventually, virtual reality over the Internet.[25]

An indirect option for customers to obtain assistance with a problem is Internet-based professional complaint agencies. They charge a fee to contact companies on behalf of dissatisfied customers who lack the time and patience to do it themselves.[26] Customers also vent their dissatisfaction with companies through online customer complaint sites—word of mouth to thousands rather than the typical eight to ten friends and associates. Some companies have countered these sites by threatening and initiating legal action against the person who set up the site. These actions serve only to generate more bad publicity and public relations nightmares. Even if companies win a court action, mirror complaint sites just appear elsewhere. Other companies have ignored the anticorporate sites and do their best to support and satisfy customers. Experts contend that the best option is to track the sites and deal with the problems rather than fight the sites themselves. The complaint web sites and other forms of customer information sharing are here to stay and should be considered an opportunity.[27]

Customers often do not have well-defined expectations and are not sure their dissatisfaction is warranted, especially for services. If companies set clear standards or guarantees, customers will know what to expect and know when they can legitimately complain. Educate customers about their rights and responsibilities as consumers. Customers should read product literature before purchase. They should read directions and follow use and care manuals. They should make sure they understand contracts, credit terms, refund policies, warranties, and guarantees. Advise them about the consumer protection laws related to the product or service. They will understand more about whether to complain, how to do it, and what to expect.[28]

Skill Development 13.1

1. Describe the problem resolution and recovery systems and procedures at a company with which you are familiar.
2. What would you change if you had a magic wand?

Standards

Establish resolution and recovery guidelines and standards. There should be clear procedures for acknowledging, resolving, compensating, following up, investigating, and preventing complaints. Some complaints are predictable, and so companies can plan how to address the most common ones. Discuss these with staff and decide what to do and say.

No-fault and *goodwill* return *policies* are based on sound economics. The cost of investigating and adjudicating a complaint is higher than using a no-fault–based approach. For example, it is more cost effective to have a no-questions-asked, on-the-spot money-back return policy than spending time asking questions, filling out forms, getting a manager's permission, and risking a dissatisfied customer. A goodwill approach applies when customers bring back merchandise just because they decided they did not like it after all. It's less costly, it's less hassle, and it's more likely to keep customers as well. If a problem is not handled to the customer's satisfaction, the result may be a lost customer.

Designate levels of authority and accountability. If no one is in charge, no one is accountable. Keep track of complaints to make sure they are handled promptly or settled within a reasonable time. One option is to have the person who receives a complaint "own" it and follow it through. Ensure complaints are processed according to company policy. Remind employees and reinforce procedures. Some employees, who are offended by customers' rude attitudes and who have misplaced loyalty to the company, decide to ignore a no-fault policy. So that employees do not assume that the policy doesn't "apply to situations like that," ask them to employ the no-fault policy across the board. The same thing can happen with more restrictive policies. Employees can decide to be flexible for nice customers but not for rude ones. This creates fairness issues and could even trigger legal problems from the Federal Trade Commission on the grounds of favoring some customers over others.

Design follow-up procedures. Follow up with customers to apologize again and make sure they are satisfied. Second, follow up with the company to verify that the problem will not occur again.

Legal Requirements

Products and services are legally covered by an implied warranty (of suitability or fitness) that states the product must be fit for the purpose for which it was sold and must be of merchantable quality. That means a chair must be suitable for sitting (not break), a boat must float, a garment must be wearable, and a pen must write. There does not need to be an express (written) warranty for an implied warranty to be applicable. The implied warranty exists anytime something is sold unless it is sold "as is." A company cannot ignore customers' legal rights, for example, using the time terms of a manufacturer's guarantee to wrongly deny customers' rights to merchandise that is both fit for purpose and of merchantable quality. This is one reason for no-fault and goodwill return policies. There is also a legal requirement that all customers in a given class, such as sales volume, be given equal treatment in the matter of actual service as well as adjustments.[29]

Employee Skills

Communicating the importance of problem resolution and recovery signals its value to employees and contributes to a culture of awareness and helpfulness toward dissatisfied customers. Employees need to understand that complaints are an opportunity for product and company improvement and customer retention. The marketing staff pays thousands of dollars for researchers to do studies to collect customer information. Complaints are "free."

Service representatives should know how to problem-solve and how to deal with the emotions involved in the complaint resolution process. In one research study, customer service representatives were perceived to be less courteous and more detached when handling complaints than they were handling inquiries or compliments. Handling complaints is more difficult emotionally, and so providers need additional insight into how to react.[30] Employees may handle problems badly because they do not know what to do. In fact, what to do is counterintuitive because the natural reaction is fight or flee. One tool is scripted dialogues. This helps untrained, unmotivated, or new employees handle situations better. However, dialogues should be used as a guide rather than hard-and-fast rules. Teach problem-solving skills to your employees so they can deal with complaints better. Teach them how to turn a complaint into a problem statement. Training gives employees confidence, and they can distance themselves from angry customers and focus on solutions.[31]

Research has shown that conflict management training reduces job stress, improves communication and empathetic responsiveness, improves job satisfaction, and increases customer satisfaction. In the study, training included:

* Acknowledgement of frontline employees' critical importance to the company
* Listening/communication skills
* Empathy response
* Problem-solving techniques
* Anger management
* Stress management[32]

One of the most effective ways to improve problem recovery is to empower representatives to resolve the problem on the spot. This affects all three dimensions of unfairness: the outcome, procedures and timeliness, and interpersonal treatment. Empowerment improves employee performance. Resolution is faster and more convenient. Employees can be more flexible with resolution and compensation based on circumstances.

If companies train well, empowerment should not lead to operation and cost problems. In Chapter 4, we covered a system for empowerment based on employee capability and the effect of decisions on the company. Many companies use a variation of this system, providing "safe zones" with prescribed action and dollar limits. Employees will not make unwise decisions as long as they understand how decisions will affect the rest of the company.[33]

One other helpful way to provide guidance is to classify the rules under which employees work as rules that cannot be broken versus rules that are guides. Call them red rules and blue rules. *Red rules* govern the ways things are done. Break those and the employee may not have a job. *Blue rules* may be bent or broken. Deciding when to make exceptions involves three situations: the little favor, the big favor, and the "special" customer. Little favors such as a small discount as compensation, are easy and not costly for the company but can mean a great deal to customers. Just make sure customers understand it's not a normal business practice, just "a little favor." The big favor, say a large discount, may have an impact on the company itself, on coworkers, and on other customers in dollars or time. The cost should be judged by the expected benefit of keeping the customer. If other customers expect the same big favor, then the cost may be too high. It is the nature of business that we will bend a little further for some key, "special," customers. Employees need to know who the key customers are, what has been promised, and how far to bend. Legal requirements in terms of equal treatment must be followed.[34]

Frontline employees receive 65 percent of complaints. However, all employees need to understand procedures. Customers tend to complain to the handiest person, who could be a maintenance employee, so make sure everyone either knows how to handle the complaint or knows to direct the customer to someone who can. In supermarkets and other retail stores, often manufacturer's representatives who are stocking shelves or checking merchandise and who are not supermarket employees are asked questions or get complaints. Many just say, "I don't work for [supermarket company]. I can't help you." Since some customers do not understand a manufacturer's rep's job, they may be offended. It's to the reps' advantage to help customers so customers buy their products. Let the reps know how they can help, perhaps by pointing out an employee who can help the customers.

Tracking Complaints

Maintain customer and product databases to record and track complaints. There should be clear procedures for recording, tracking, and analyzing complaints via mail, e-mail, telephone, and in person. Complaints to any employee, third-party agencies, managers, and subcontractors and intermediaries should also be recorded and tracked. Problems should be recorded by type, frequency, and importance. Complaints should be analyzed to identify patterns, trends, and root causes. The information should systematically be delivered to the functions that can correct problems at their cause. It's essential to use the information to improve products and services and fix what customers perceive as wrong.

Two university researchers found that many companies fail to record and track complaints for four reasons. First, employees treat problems as one-time incidents. Second, employees tend to downplay company responsibility and blame customers for problems. Third, many complaints are never resolved, and so they fall through the cracks. Fourth, there is no way to deliver complaint information to those responsible for the cause of the problem. To change this, make sure employees understand the value of recording this information to improve the company's products and services. Reward problem resolution efforts and celebrate improvements based on problem tracking. Make the system workable and seamless.

Track complaints by customers as well. If customers have another problem, it will undo the good from the first recovery. One catalog company puts these customers on a special list, and their shipment is double-checked to make sure that it's right. Another case is the chronic complainer or someone who is never satisfied. These customers may require more resources than the profit generated or may even behave criminally. Hampton Inn handles customers who take advantage by maintaining a database of customers who have invoked their guarantee. If customers become a problem, the company recommends another hotel.[35]

PROBLEM RESOLUTION AND RECOVERY PROCEDURES

Effective problem management uses a no-fault approach whenever possible and practical. Procedures include appropriate decision rules and scripts. Standards include the quality and the timeliness of the process. Customers want to be heard, understood, and respected. They want to talk to an empowered, knowledgeable representative who offers an apology, a resolution, compensation, and an explanation. The following sections describe the procedures for addressing a problem (see Figure 13.1).[36]

Listen

Listen to customers' request or complaint. Let customers vent. Hear customers out. Listen first. If you cut off what customers want to say, they will feel like you do not want to hear it and will feel cheated. They want you to know how their life has been affected by what the company did. They are emotional and not ready to be reasonable. Goodwin and Ross found that letting customers express their concerns was directly related to the perception of fairness, even more so than offering an apology. Don't argue. Don't let self-talk start a negative filter tape, like "This guy is a jerk" or "He is clueless."[37]

Not listening carefully can cause an employee to miss the real problem. The Better Business Bureau study, noted earlier in the chapter, found that employees became defensive and did not listen carefully, and so the customers' real complaint was never understood.[38]

Empathize

You very likely have upset, frustrated, if not angry, customers, so put yourself in their shoes, and let them know you understand their feelings. They want to be understood. Since we know that customers sometimes cause their own problems, this can be difficult. If you've never made a mistake with a product and caused your own problem, feel free to be cynical. Otherwise, treat them like you would want to be treated. Be empathetic and respectful.

Focus on the customer, not on the company or the mistake. Never blame another person or another department in the company nor disparage the company in general. If the frontline person does not feel loyalty to the company and goes to find the offending party or he or she sympathizes with customers about the poor-quality

FIGURE 13.1 Customer Problem Resolution and Recovery Procedures

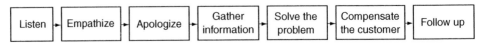

service the company is providing, customers believe the worst. Don't say, "I can't understand how one of our salespeople could have told you that." Customers begin to wonder about the competence or honesty of salespeople. Don't say, "We've had trouble with that before . . . " This makes the company look inept. Customers think, "Well, if they know this is a problem, why don't they fix it?"

Some employees believe that customers try to make things difficult, that customers like to complain, and that customers expect the impossible. This is not true of 98 percent of them. They don't like confrontation any more than you do. They really don't like to complain; it's uncomfortable for them. They don't want to take the time. What they expect is for the company to do what is fair.

Employee attitudes that are barriers to recovery are:

* *"It's not my problem. I didn't cause it."*   Actually, it is the employee's problem since it's a company problem and employees represent the company. It's true that the employee most likely did not cause the problem. Customers do not care; they just want it fixed. They are not mad at you but at the situation.
* *"The customer is unfair."*   Maybe, maybe not. If customers perceive the situation to be unfair, it is. Perception is reality. A few customers try to take advantage, but most customers have legitimate reasons. Remember, assume innocence first. Put yourself in customers' shoes. Know what your company wants you to do if customers are wrong.
* *"It's an uncomfortable situation."*   Without much experience, it is. Our instinct is to fight or flee. Do not take it personally. Again, customers are frustrated with the situation, not you. The more you know about how to handle the situation and possible solutions, the more comfortable you will be.
* *"I don't have to listen to this."*   Actually, if you want your paycheck, you do. Again, it's not directed at you.[39]

Skill Development 13.2

Do you think customer service providers should apologize when customers have complaints?

Apologize

Apologies are a rather controversial issue. In 1990, Zemke and Bell reported that consumer affairs professionals apologized only about 48 percent of the time in service recovery situations. There is evidence that has not changed much today.

Some service representatives believe apologizing is admitting failure and makes the company look bad. Others believe that it means the company is admitting fault. By not apologizing, they are protecting the company. Still others do not think they should apologize when customers are wrong. They assume that if customers cannot follow directions or adhere to policies, the company has no reason to apologize. Another objection is that apologizing seems weak and lowers status and authority. A final argument is that it doesn't change anything; what customers need are solutions.[40]

Experts say apologizing during problem recovery is about rebuilding relationships and restoring trust. Martin and Smart found that callers who received apologies were more satisfied than those who did not.[41] Customers want their problems fixed, but they also want to feel better about the situation. Proponents of apologies believe that an apology acknowledges that the customer's feeling of emotional or material harm is legitimate and meaningful. Not apologizing may cause customers to think you blame them for the problem. An apology shows customers that the company genuinely cares about its customers. Apologizing is an expression of understanding and empathy rather than an admission of guilt or weakness. An apology for inconvenience is clearly not an automatic admission of guilt. You do not have to say, "I apologize that we goofed."

An apology is a way of taking responsibility for a problem. Most customers already believe the company made a mistake, and they expect an apology. Denials are not believed and serve to make customers angrier. Sometimes all that can be offered is an apology. Apologies are particularly important when a mistake cannot be corrected.

Experts recommend that apologies wait until customers are finished venting. If an apology comes too soon, customers believe that the service provider doesn't want to hear what they have to say. Service representatives should say, "I'm sorry," rather than, "We're sorry," because it's more personal and someone in particular is taking responsibility. For example, say, "I'm sorry there is a problem. Let me see what I can do." Employees need to mean it and say it with regret and sincerity. Be careful of saying, "I'm sorry 'if'. . . " The "if" implies some doubt about the customer's credibility.[42]

There are occasions when apologizing could lead to a liability issue. Some customers will leap to believe that you are assuming blame. Companies should train their employees and discuss how to handle these situations. Service representatives need to know when to send customers to the legal department. For example, one company instructs its frontline people to immediately end the conversation and transfer customers to their supervisor if the customer threatens to sue. Sometimes it is just a threat, but considering the potential for lawsuits, there is no sense taking chances. However, headlines and anecdotes should not drive companies to overreact. A company that tries to prove a customer is wrong in a lawsuit always loses even if the company is right. The media reports about people who get huge settlements are often distorted or incomplete, and appeals that reduce awards are buried on a back page.[43]

Gather Information

Gather any additional information you need. Double-check facts. Ask questions if you are not sure about something. Make sure you listen fully so you don't solve the wrong problem. It's easy to assume that you've heard this before.

Beware of agreeing with the complaint. Customers may assume they will get what they want, making a later turndown more difficult. Focus on solving the problem, not on getting all the details. You do not need to investigate a complaint to death before you resolve it. Don't say, "I'm sorry to hear about your problem, and I'm sure we can take care of it. Please tell me exactly what happened again slowly so I can write it down and send it to our technical folks. You know, they plan our improvements based on feedback from customers like you." Do say, "I'll take care of it right away." Remember how many customers will repurchase if the problem is resolved on the spot.

Solve the Problem

Assess the balance between the problem and the solution. A solution should not outweigh the seriousness of the problem, nor should it fall short. It needs to achieve an equal balance between the two, weighing severity, inconvenience, cost versus value, and the customer's wants. You should keep customer expectations, policy, and what is possible in mind. If the solution is outside typical company policy, be sure to indicate that it is an exception and why the specific circumstances dictated the resolution. Otherwise, unreasonable future expectations will be created.

Give customers what they want if you can. Customers often know exactly what will satisfy them. As mentioned earlier in the chapter, it may be less than what you have in mind.

Sometimes you must say no and cannot give the customers what they want. This is the case when laws and regulations are involved. At colleges, government laws require students to follow rules for financial aid. Federal, state, and local health and safety laws forbid certain actions in eating establishments and supermarkets. At other times, company policies may not allow flexibility. If the company has told you that under no circumstances do you bend this rule, then you can't, or you face losing your job. Sometimes, no matter how good your inventory or delivery systems are, you are out of stock or the delivery is late. At the immediate time, you can't give customers what they want. Customers do not have to get everything they want; but the solution must be acceptable.

Companies have to decide under what circumstances they cannot accommodate customers. The following are some of the considerations:

* Policies should never be more restrictive than the competition's.
* A company has to consider how much it needs to depend on repeat customers and word-of-mouth advertising. If it's a one-time customer, the company may be able to be more rigid. Retailers along the interstate sometimes think that they don't have to rely on repeat business from travelers, but some people stop at the same places year after year.
* How much does the company want to depend on the honesty and integrity of its customers? L.L. Bean believes in its customers' integrity. Not all customers fit this standard.
* Target policies to your customers' characteristics. If they are busy people and mistakes are a big problem, you might be more willing to be flexible.
* How sophisticated are the customers? The more sophisticated will aggressively look out for themselves, so perhaps a company can stick to policy.
* Decide whom you want to have as your customers. Loyal customers who buy regularly from you but return 75 percent of what they buy for a refund? High-volume customers who threaten to take their business elsewhere if you don't make an exception to your policy and take back an order?
* You have service standards that were not met and customers are dissatisfied, and so you apologize, fix the problem, and compensate. However, if your service standards were met and customers are dissatisfied, do you point out that their expectations are unrealistic and arbitrary?
* If you establish service standards that are competitive and exceptional, do you exceed them to please a minority of customers?
* Do you provide what customers want even if it is unprofitable?
* Do you provide what customers want even if it inconveniences other customers?
* Is the solution fair to other customers? A legal requirement is that all customers in a given category be given equal treatment in service as well as adjustments. That means you cannot be more generous with one $10,000-per-year customer than another $10,000-per-year customer, even if one is always pleasant and courteous and the other is rude and obnoxious.

If you must say no, do it tactfully. Explain why. Turn your explanation into a positive response. Even if you cannot solve the problem, all the other steps will go a long way toward keeping customers. Do not use negative or rude words. Don't start with the words "no" or "can't." Don't say:

"No, we can't refund your money."

"I'm not allowed to do that."

"It's our policy."

"You'll have to. . . " or "You'll need to. . . "

Saying no isn't necessarily the worst thing that could happen. If you go the extra mile, customers may be just as happy with an alternative. If you can offer anything else reasonable and relevant, offer it. Say:

"What I will do is. . . "

"We aren't able to refund your money, but we can replace the product."

"Here's how I can help you with that."

"I think the fastest way to handle this would be. . . "

If the response is negative, indicate that the issue was given careful consideration and suggest alternatives. Provide an apologetic, firm turndown and a restatement of counteroffers and options, and emphasize closure. Customers will appreciate receiving closure more than false hope. Thank customers for their understanding and patience. Tell them that even though their request could not be granted, they should feel free to contact you in the future.

If the customer is abusive, follow the procedures for an angry customer. Guide the conversation to keep it on track. Sometimes you will just have to let the customer vent. Avoid past and ancillary issues that have nothing to do with the problem at hand. Aggressively work toward an alternative solution. Restate that you wish to help the customer. Provide closure even if it's not a resolution.

Make sure customers know what's going to happen, who will initiate action, and when. If the action does not occur and the customer has to follow up, you will lose a customer.

Managers and supervisors should back up their staff. Have you ever told a customer you could give her a store credit but not give her a refund? Then she asks for your boss. The supervisor overrules you and becomes the good guy. You are the bad guy, and this ruins morale. The supervisor has undermined your empowerment and made you feel useless. As a result, employees will either stretch policies to the limit giving customers whatever they want or immediately refer everything up the line to their boss. The best way to handle a reversal is to talk to the employee off to the side and the two of you decide to stretch the policy. Then the employee tells the customer, and so the employee is the hero. Or if the supervisor decides to overrule an employee, another option is to say, "Marsha's right about the policy and telling you she could not give you a refund. However, since I can see a refund is better for you, I'll make an exception in this case." Marsha should be right there and smile in understanding. This is the little favor. Keep in mind though that if you intend to overrule every time, you might as well allow your front line to do it.

If you must send customers to other personnel, do not make them feel like you are trying to get rid of them and their problem. Don't say, "You'll have to talk with

Bob Green in sales. His number is 000-0000; if you can hold for a moment, I'll transfer you, OK?" This sounds like "that's not my department" or like the call is being downgraded. "You'll have to" will be interpreted as a command. Do say, "Bob Green in operations is the real expert on that, and I know he'll be glad to help you." Make sure you brief Bob so the customer does not have to repeat the whole story.[44]

As more customers become savvy to methods of obtaining their way, the number of *executive complaints* is on the rise. Customers may escalate their complaint to the executive office believing that this will get them the result they want. Resolve these complaints according to the company's decision rules based on accommodating customers discussed previously. Set a standard for turnaround of escalated complaints. Contact the customer if the problem solution will be more time-consuming than usual. These situations can "snowball" into publicity nightmares. If any customer or company information is confidential or requires an enclosure, a response should be sent by mail. However, remember that letter and e-mail responses can be shared with a huge audience on the Internet and that they can be one-sided, and so telephone may be more appropriate. If it is an inflammatory issue, do not use e-mail to avoid negative experiences being shared.[45]

Compensate

Here is a story to illustrate the idea of compensating customers for their problem. Valerie ordered a pair of shoes from a shoe catalog company. She could have ordered the very same pair of shoes from two other companies, but she chose Shoewrights because she had found it to be fair and reputable in the past. She paid $59.95 plus $7.95 for shipping and handling. The shoes arrived, and she inspected the shoes before she tried them on. When she examined the left shoe, she discovered a nail sticking out of the footbed near the ball of the foot. Needless to say, she did not put the shoe on her foot. She called the company to report the problem. Unbelievably, the agent seemed unconcerned about the potential for the nail to cause injury. Valerie expected a return postage-paid label, an immediate refund of $59.95, and reimbursement for the original shipping cost of $7.95. The company said that it would pay the return postage when it received the return and it would refund all her money. Valerie returned the shoes by mail. When she received her next credit card bill, she noticed that the company had credited her for the shoes but had not given her a credit for the original shipping or the return postage. Valerie called again. The customer service representative said the company would reimburse her for the original and return shipping. On the next bill, the company had credited her account for the original shipping but not the return shipping. She called again. This time the company said it would reimburse her for the $3.95 in return postage, which they eventually did.

Valerie now has all her money back. Is she satisfied?

No, she does not have the shoes. Since summer was already half over, she no longer needed the shoes, and so she did not reorder. She is still out the time for packaging and mailing the return and making telephone calls—not to mention the cost of hassle and aggravation.

"Focus on saving the customer, not on saving the sale."[46] The goal is customer retention. To satisfy an unhappy customer, you must *compensate* the customer by adding extra value to make up for the value you promised but failed to provide in the first place. When customers are dissatisfied, it's because they haven't gotten the value they paid for. If all a company does is provide them with what they thought they bought in the first place, it's still behind. The fact that the customers had to take time and effort to complain has diminished the original value of your product or service. It's an unfair outcome. To restore value, you have to provide them with more than they initially bought. It's a way of saying that the mistake was unacceptable, that it won't happen again, and that you care about keeping their business. You can provide them with something that only has value if they deal with you again so you can prove that the dissatisfaction was an isolated event. However, this may not satisfy customers who want immediate value. Remember you are not just giving something away; you are getting customers back. In addition, compensation cannot replace continued unacceptable service and products. If customers come back and the same thing happens, you will lose customers. How would you compensate Valerie for her problem with the shoes?

An example of good compensation is the 25 percent off certificate that a customer received when she wrote expressing dissatisfaction with the indifference she experienced at a department store's jewelry counter. Contrast that with a problem with a $250 watch, given as a Christmas gift, that did not work and took 6 months to resolve. The letter about this situation was fine, but enclosed was a gift certificate for gift wrapping. Which is the fairer of these two examples?

Here's an example of a company that went the extra mile:

Toni phoned the Goody Company to ask about a hairbrush that she could no longer find. The customer service representative was very courteous and helpful. She said she did not think they manufactured that kind any more and asked her to hold while she checked with inventory. She came back to the phone and said she was sorry, but they no longer had any left. Toni thanked her for her help and hung up.

A few days later, Toni received a package with a letter. Inside the package was a brush. The letter said:

> "Thank you very much for calling about the brush you were looking for. We certainly appreciate both your telephone call and efforts, but we do not carry anything in our line that fits your description. If we did carry it at one time, it has now been discontinued and there are none in our leftover inventory.
>
> Enclosed is our popular rubber base brush that we think you can use.
>
> Thanks for calling and we hope that when you do go shopping again, you will look for and choose a Goody's product."

Contrast that response to this one: "Thank you for taking the time to write. We sincerely regret that the product you mentioned has been discontinued."

How much compensation do you provide in cases of customer dissatisfaction? What do you do for an incomplete order at a fast-food restaurant? What about a bad haircut? What if your car isn't ready when they said it would be? It often takes less than you expect. Getting the customers to come back is one consideration. You must fix the problem and provide compensation when there is a service breakdown. If a deadline is missed, if an order is filled incorrectly, if customers are treated rudely or unprofessionally, and if customers are given incorrect information; it is the company's fault.[47]

In offering additional value, offer relevant compensation.[48] Make sure customers see your solution as the solution. Ask the customer. For instance, say a customer buys new tires at a tire store and a few weeks later has a tire that's almost flat. She stops by the same company to have them fix it. When she gets the car back, she realizes that the rear tires are now unbalanced. She takes it in and they rebalance the tires and then offer to rotate them free as compensation. Part of her new tire deal included free rotation. What should they have offered her?

Skill Development 13.3

What does your company do to compensate customers for problems?

Follow Up

If you have resolved the problem, *follow up* with customers to ensure they are satisfied. Call them to make sure a delivery arrives on time. Call to ask if everything is all right. Let them know no issue is too small to be addressed. Send them a card to thank them. If the problem was turned over to someone else, follow up to make sure the person did what was promised.

TERMS

complaint
outcome fairness
procedural fairness
interactional justice
service recovery
no-fault policy

goodwill policy
red and blue rules
apologies
executive complaint
compensate
follow up

DISCUSSION QUESTIONS

1. Why don't customers complain?
2. What are some problems at your company for which there is no good solution?
3. Name several customer complaints that are predictable at your company. What do employees do and say?
4. Why do we consider a customer complaint an opportunity?
5. How can companies encourage customers to complain?
6. Why should a company use no-fault resolution for complaints?
7. Customers expect fairness when they have a complaint? What does that mean?
8. Why should customer complaints be recorded and tracked?
9. What are the considerations concerning apologizing to a customer?
10. Why and how do we compensate a customer for a problem?

CASE—DIFFERENTIAL INDIFFERENCE

Jill Nichols purchased a new car on May 4 with cash that she had been saving for 5 years. Since she had wanted this particular car for years, she was delighted with her new car. The auto dealer had urged her to bring it in to them for its 1000-mile checkup and first oil change. Although normally this was a do-it-yourself job, to make sure all was well, she did. The job took about an hour and cost $19.95, which she figured was a little excessive since normally her husband did it for the cost of oil in about half an hour. Nevertheless, she drove home ready to enjoy driving her convertible over the coming Memorial Day weekend.

The Friday morning of that week she drove to a nearby town on some errands. On the way, she began to hear an awful noise from her car. She pulled off the road, got out, and noticed an awful smell as well. She looked under the car and under the hood and could not see anything that would clearly account for the problem. She called her husband. He drove out to her location, leaned down and looked under the back of the car, and pronounced that all the gear oil had leaked out of the differential and most likely destroyed it. He could see that the plug was missing.

Jill called the dealer and explained the problem. All the service department said was that she should call a tow truck and have the car brought in. The only other instructions were that she had to come to the dealership to sign a paper to have it covered under warranty before the mechanics worked on it. So she called the towing company, and eventually the tow truck showed up and took her car off. Meanwhile, Jill no longer had a car, and so she had lunch with her husband and then borrowed his car to drive to the dealership, which was about 35 miles away. She arrived at the dealer a couple of hours after the tow truck. She saw her car parked in the back, went into the service department, and inquired. The employees said that they had not had time to look at it, but she should sign a form. She was extremely unhappy. They didn't appear to care all that much. They told her they would let her know the next day when it would be ready. She signed the form and left.

By about noon the next day, she had not heard from the service department and so she called them. The person she spoke to said her car would be ready next week because they had to order a new differential. No apology of any kind.

The service department said little else. Jill called her salesperson to find out more. About all he did was assure her it would be fixed as soon as possible.

On Tuesday the following week she had not heard anything from the service department, and so she called. They said the car would probably be ready on Wednesday and they would let her know. Mid-afternoon Wednesday they finally called to say it was ready. She made arrangements to pick it up early Thursday morning since she needed to have her husband take her in, again 35 miles. She suggested to them since they had had it all this time and the problem was not her fault, they might want to make sure it was washed before she picked it up. When she went to get it, they had not had time to wash it and said they could do it within the next half hour. That was an unacceptable wait, and so she just took her car and went home. No one in the service department seemed the least concerned about her car or her satisfaction. The question of what happened to the plug was never answered. Jill wondered if they thought she removed it—she eventually complained to a representative at the company's toll-free number and wrote a 4-page letter of complaint. About all this accomplished was that she got to vent. She has never returned to this dealership.

1. Describe the car dealer's problem resolution and recovery.
2. Was Jill justified? Why do you think the service department personnel reacted the way they did?
3. What else should Jill have done?
4. What should the car dealer have done?

NOTES

1. Christopher Lovelock and Lauren Wright, *Principles of Service Marketing and Management,* 2d ed. (Upper Saddle River, NJ: Prentice Hall, 2002), 120.
2. Rebecca L. Morgan, *Calming Upset Customers,* rev. ed. (Menlo Park, CA: Crisp Publications, 1996), 12.
3. Lovelock and Wright, *Principles of Service Marketing and Management.*
4. Stephen S. Tax and Stephen W. Brown, "Recovering and Learning from Service Failure," *Customer Relationship Management,* March 1999, 22–27; Jack W. Cushman and Linda M. Cushman, "Service Recovery: Implementation Strategies for Operations," *Customer Relationship Management,* September 1998, 22–25; and Shirley Bednarz, "Fine Whine," *Entrepreneur* 27, no. 2 (February 1999): 103.
5. Loren V. Geistfeld, "Getting Consumers to Complain," *Customer Relationship Management,* December 2000, 5.
6. Morgan, *Calming Upset Customers.*
7. Christian Gronroos, *Service Management and Marketing: A Customer Relationship Management Approach,* 2d ed. (Chichester, West Sussex, UK: John Wiley & Sons, 2000), 117.
8. Ron Zemke, "Preventative Recovery," *Customer Service Management,* November/December 1999, 40–41.
9. Warren Blanding, *Customer Service Operations, The Complete Guide* (New York: AMACOM, 1991), 104–108.
10. Frederick F. Reichheld, Robert G. Markey, Jr., and Christopher Hopton, "The Loyalty Effect—The Relationship Between Loyalty and Profits," *European Business Journal* 12, no. 3 (Autumn 2000): 134.
11. Lovelock and Wright, *Principles of Service Marketing and Management,* p. 127.
12. David Glenn, "Find Underlying Reasons for Complaints," *Marketing News,* October 23, 2000, 46.
13. James E. Fisher and Dennis E. Garrett, "Customer Satisfaction and Service: Lessons from Problematic Industries," *Customer Relationship Management,* February 2000, p. 5.
14. Zemke, "Preventative Recovery."
15. U.S. Office of Consumer Affairs, *Increasing Customer Satisfaction through Effective Corporate Complaint Handling,* 1986.
16. Lovelock and Wright, *Principles of Service Marketing and Management,* p. 122.
17. James G. Blodgett, Kirk L. Wakefield, and James H. Barnes, "The Effects of Customer Service on Consumer Complaining Behavior," *Journal of Services Marketing* 9, no. 4 (1995): 31–42.
18. Tax and Brown, "Recovering and Learning from Service Failure."
19. Blodgett, Wakefield, and Barnes, "The Effects of Customer Service on Consumer Complaining Behavior."
20. Tax and Brown, "Recovering and Learning from Service Failure."
21. K. Douglas Hoffman, Scott W. Kelley, and Holly M. Rotalsky, "Tracking Service Failures and Employee Recovery Efforts," *Journal of Services Marketing* 9, no. 2 (1995): 49–61.
22. Tax and Brown, "Recovering and Learning from Service Failure," 22.
23. Blodgett, Wakefield, and Barnes, "The Effects of Customer Service on Consumer Complaining Behavior."
24. Society of Consumer Affairs Professionals, "Making It Easy for Your Customers to Complain," *Checklist 8,* available from http://www.socap.org/chklst/list8.html, accessed January 31, 2000.
25. Simon Beresford, "Customer Communication: Multiple Ways for a Customer to Articulate Their Wrath," available at http://www.crm-forum.com/cgi-bin/library.cgi?action=detail&id=883&dir_publisher_varid=26, accessed May 30, 2002 and Jim Sterne, *Customer Service on the Internet ,* 2d ed. (New York: John Wiley & Sons, 2000) 161–181.
26. "Complaints 'R' Us," *Customer Service Management,* November/December 1999, 8.

27. Jamais Cascio, "Smile: Your Company's under Attack—Smart Businesses Are Turning Their Harshest Critics into Allies," *PC/Computing*, March 2000, 42.

28. Society of Consumer Affairs Professionals, "Making It Easy for Your Customers to Complain."

29. Diane Bailey, "Recovery from Customer Service Shortfalls," *Managing Service Quality* 4, no. 6 (1994): 25–28.

30. Charles L. Martin and Denise T. Smart, "Consumer Experiences Calling Toll-Free Corporate Hotlines," *The Journal of Business Communication* 31, no. 3 (July 1994): 195–213.

31. Perry W. Buffington, "Capitalizing on Complaints," *Sky*, June 1991, n.p.

32. Roseanne D'Ausilio, "The Impact of Conflict Management Training on Customer Service Delivery," *Customer Relationship Management*, December 1997, 22–23.

33. Tax and Brown, "Recovering and Learning from Service Failure," 22–27; and Cushman and Cushman, "Service Recovery: Implementation Strategies for Operations."

34. Kristin Anderson and Ron Zemke, *Knock Your Socks Off Answers* (New York: AMACOM, 1995), 92–95.

35. Tax and Brown, "Recovering and Learning from Service Failure."

36. Monica L. Jenks, "Fix the Customer," *Customer Service Management*, November/December 1999, 46–49.

37. Cushman and Cushman, "Service Recovery."

38. Fisher and Garrett, "Customer Satisfaction and Service: Lessons from Problematic Industries."

39. Clay Carr, *Front-Line Customer Service* (New York: John Wiley & Sons, 1990), 75–79.

40. Saundra Washington, "The Value of an Apology," *Customer Relationship Management*, December 1999, 5–7.

41. Martin and Smart, "Consumer Experiences Calling Toll-Free Corporate Hotlines."

42. Washington, "The Value of an Apology"; and Jeffrey Gitomer, *Customer Satisfaction Is Worthless, Customer Loyalty Is Priceless: How to Make Customers Love You, Keep Them Coming Back and Tell Everyone They Know* (Marietta, GA: Bard Press, 1998).

43. Kristin Anderson and Ron Zemke, "Customers from Hell: When Is Enough, Enough?" *Mobius*, September 1995, 4–5.

44. These guidelines are compiled from Jenks, "Fix the Customer"; Carr, *Front-Line Customer Service*; Anderson and Zemke, "Customers from Hell;" and Bailey, "Recovery from Customer Service Shortfalls."

45. Tom Zapf, "Presidential Complaints: How to Meet These Challenges Head On," *Customer Relationship Management*, June 2000, p. 31.

46. Carr, *Front-Line Customer Service*, 150.

47. Karen Leland and Keith Bailey, *Customer Service for Dummies*, 2d ed. (New York: IDG Books Worldwide, 1999), 135.

48. Carr, *Front-line Customer Service*, 160.

INDEX